DICTIONARY of
American Communal and
Utopian History

DICTIONARY of
American Communal and
Utopian History

Robert S. Fogarty

GREENWOOD PRESS
WESTPORT, CONNECTICUT • LONDON, ENGLAND

Library of Congress Cataloging in Publication Data

Fogarty, Robert S
   Dictionary of American communal and utopian history.

   Bibliography: p.
   Includes index.
   1. Collective settlements—United States.
2. Utopias. 3. Socialists—United States—Biography.
I. Title.
HX653.F65   335'.9'73   79-7476
ISBN 0-313-21347-X lib. bdg.

Library of Congress Catalog Card Number: 79-7476
ISBN: 0-313-21347-X

First published in 1980

Greenwood Press
A division of Congressional Information Service, Inc.
88 Post Road West, Westport, Connecticut 06881

Printed in the United States of America

10 9 8 7 6 5 4 3 2

Contents

Preface

Until five years ago, there were only three major sources of biographical and bibliographical information about the leaders and participants in community ventures: Arthur Bestor Jr., *Backwoods Utopias* (1950), Stow Persons and Donald Egbert, *Socialism and American Life* (1952), and Edward Deming Andrews, *The People Called Shakers* (1953). To be sure, there were occasional studies of individual figures, such as Herbert Wisbey's biography of Jemima Wilkinson, *Pioneer Prophetess* (1964) or studies of particular communities, such as the Alyeas' economic analyses of the Georgeist single tax colony, *Fairhope, 1894-1954* (1956).

During recent years, there has been an explosion of interest—both popular and scholarly—in the subject, but the sources remain unsatisfactory. Where, for example, can one find rudimentary data about the Ferrer Colony or about the leading figure of the Amana Community, Christian Metz? The standard biographical source, *Dictionary of American Biography*, is of little help, as only a handful of the leaders of utopian societies are included. John H. Noyes, Frances Wright, Katherine Tingley, and Thomas Low Nichols all appear, but what of William Hinds of Oneida, Martha McWhirter of the Sanctified Sisters, Richard Pelham of the Shakers, or Warren Chase of the Wisconsin Phalanx? Where can a researcher find basic information about these individuals?

This volume attempts to provide that information through biographical sketches of more than one hundred forty figures who played a prominent role in developing, leading, or inspiring utopian settlements and "biographies" of fifty-nine of the most important or interesting colonies. Bare-boned information on 270 settlements is presented in an annotated chronology of communal and utopian societies established between 1787 and 1919. The chronology was compiled by Professor Otohiko Okugawa and is included here as Appendix A.

For the most part, the writers of utopian fiction have been excluded from among the biographies in this collection. Individuals who had peripheral contact with established colonies were considered for inclusion but ultimately they too were excluded, because their lives were barely touched by their community experiences. Among these was Francis C. Barlow, the famous Civil War general and, later, prosecutor of Boss Tweed, who was schooled at Brook Farm. Both Steele Mackaye, America's leading Shakespearean actor in the 1890s, and Edward Livingston Youmans, the chemist and Darwinist, were passed over because they, like Barlow, were only educated at a colony (the Raritan Bay Union). Felix Greene, the China expert, and Alexander Wolcott, the dramatist, had utopian connections but never lived in a community.

Also omitted were those individuals for whom there was too little information. Andrew Fahnestock, one of the leaders of the Snow Hill Nunnery, is remembered for that fact, though only his life dates are known. William Crowdy, the founder and only prophet of the black Church of God and Saints of Christ Colony, deserves study, but the bare facts of his life are not known. Louis Schlesinger, the founder of the Societas Fraternia at Anaheim, California, may be the same Louis Schlesinger who came to America in 1848 from Liverpool, England, and became a well-known spiritualist medium and publisher of the *Carrier Dove*, the spiritualist magazine. Yet, the facts of his life are too sketchy to allow any firm conclusions about his connections to the vegetarian colony. There are others—Augustus Wattles, Benjamin Fish, Thomas Dorsey, Lyman Wright, William Zeuch, to name a few—for whom future researchers will have to ferret out additional data.

The colonies selected for inclusion suggest the wide range and diverse histories of American utopian settlements. All too often, scholars single out the "important" communities—the Shakers, Oneida, Brook Farm, and Amana—as typical utopian ventures and ignore other important settlements. Hence, in the communal sketches I attempt to highlight a variety of traditions and to amplify the annotations for some of the groups listed in Appendix A.

Information about colonies founded after 1919 is scant. While many different cooperative ventures have been started since the end of World War I, we lack even an elementary list of such colonies. As a result, this work contains few sketches of contemporary groups. A notable representative is the now infamous People's Temple.

The problems of defining a communal settlement have perplexed writers so much that a standard is difficult to obtain. Kenneth Lockridge's study of Dedham, Massachusetts, *A New England Town: The First 100 Years* (1970) states: "It was also a utopian experiment, hardly less so than the famous Amana, Oneida, and Brook Farm experiments of the nineteenth century. The founders of this community set out to construct a unified social organism in which the whole would be more than the sum of the parts." A recent study of Owenite communities, R. G. Garnett's *Co-operation and the Owenite Socialist Communities in Britain, 1824-1845* (1972), suggests that the Fourierist joint-stock companies should not be considered part of the communal tradition, because they are just variants of corporate and capitalist schemes. Rosabeth Kanter's treatment of the problem in *Commitment and Community* (1971) is the most intelligent so far, and I have tried to use a combined historical and sociological approach in deciding the "commonality of a community." I have used a functional definition in this study. If a community organized its economic affairs, its living arrangements, its practical life around cooperative or communal principles I have included it. I have relied heavily on the participants' statements of what they intended to do and have taken those statements at face value. Therefore, if groups or individuals wrote about their intentions to form a communal venture and circumstances later dictated that they abandon cooperation, they have still been included.

The criteria used for including in this study individuals have been much the same. The majority included were the leaders of communal settlements, such as John H. Noyes of Oneida. Yet there were other noteworthy figures associated with communal settlements other than the leaders and I have included some of them. Two cases in point are William Hinds of Oneida, best known as a historian of communal societies, and Olaf Krans, the primitivist painter and member of Bishop Hill. There are sketches of individuals who never lived in colonies, but whose writings or support made particular settlements possible. Figures such as Horace Greeley and Elizabeth Rowell Thompson had colonies named after them and were advocates of cooperation throughout their lives. Other individuals promoted cooperation as a general principle even though they did not specifically endorse communal projects. Such individuals encouraged utopian experiments by their own experimental efforts. Melusina Fay Peirce, the advocate of cooperative kitchens, and Edward Bellamy, the writer of utopian fantasies, in their own ways, suggested an alternative vision in their own times.

This work is both a biographical dictionary of significant figures and a directory of communal settlements. The bulk of both the biographical sketches and the community sketches is from the eighteenth, nineteenth and early twentieth centuries. Individuals who founded groups in the 1920s and 1930s are included, and there is a single sketch of a 1970s community leader, Jim Jones of the People's Temple. The fifty-nine colonies included are broadly representative of the communal tradition and include (as with Ephrata and Snow Hill) colonies begun before Professor Okugawa's listing (1787) and those begun after (1919) his compilation ends (as with Ananda Cooperative Village and Twin Oaks). There are both large and small and long- and short-lived groups represented.

Obviously, more systematic work needs to be done in documenting and analyzing the societies and personalities involved in recent communal history. Likewise, data from the past must be unearthed or reinterpreted. One of my hopes is that this survey will spur additional research.

Each biographical and communal entry contains a number of pertinent sources. For a discussion of the extant literature and for a full list of the works cited, the reader should consult Appendix B.

I am indebted to all those scholars who have written the books, monographs, and papers which I consulted in preparing this work. Particular thanks go to Professors Dolores Hayden, Oto Okugawa, Jayme Sokolow, Samuel Walker, and Donald Whisenhut for their help. Thanks go to Bruce Thomas and Joseph Cali, the Olive Kettering Library, Antioch College and the staff of the Newberry Library, Chicago, where I was able to complete this project. Over the several years it took to compile this material, several students aided in the process, especially Robert Edlavitch, Marilyn Woodman, and Gary Tate. Yet I alone am responsible for the contents of this volume. Released time and research monies were provided for this and a complementary project from the Faculty Development Committee, Antioch College, and the American Philosophical Society.

Oto Okugawa has performed an invaluable service for scholars with his Annotated List of Communal and Utopian Societies (Appendix B). Some of these colonies have substantial histories, while others have been recorded only in passing in obscure reform journals. His listing provides a firm base for other researchers interested in comparative and regional studies, studies of longevity and success, and studies that go beyond the bare facts suggested by his compilation. He extends his survey beyond the Owenite and Fourierist periods and clarifies some inconsistencies in dating and site identification. It is hoped that further work will follow.

Finally, my bibliographical essay, originally published in 1973 and now updated, will help point scholars and students in the direction of critical works necessary for an understanding of the history of American utopianism. Among the major works published in the last few years, those by Laurence Veysey and Dolores Hayden deserve special mention.

This volume seeks to add both detail and depth to a particular facet of our social history. By providing some of the facts (birth, death, college, career) in the singular lives of the utopian leaders, we can place them in a larger perspective. All too often these people are seen only as fragments, as figures who emerged because there was a communal society and then receded when the colony failed. John Collins, the founder of the Skaneateles Community, is a case in point. Collins was active in reform work in the 1830s, then left for California to join the Gold Rush. While in California, he continued his reform interests and worked with the Cooperative Homesteading Society and with California spiritualists. He did not turn his back on reform; he continued to work in constructive areas in the post-Civil War period.

Piecing together the lives of such individuals was often difficult and sometimes impossible. The standard sources give little attention to them, and often there are clues that lead nowhere or, worse, no clues at all. This work of collective biography is intended to suggest new lines of inquiry, provide a basic lode of information and bibliographic material, and, ultimately, enhance our understanding of these "paradise planters," as Amos Bronson Alcott called himself. With the addition of the sketches of the communes and the chronological listing, it is hoped that these individuals also will be viewed in relationship to others and in the context of American communal and utopian history.

Introduction: "Paradise Planters"*

In 1928, the editors of *The Nation* invited several prominent writers to describe the world they would like to live in. Among those who responded was H. L. Mencken who wrote that "Utopia, like virtue, is a concept shot full of relativity." Mencken was satisfied with his own state, Maryland, because the mayor of Baltimore was an "honest Moose" and in the whole of the United States there were only five newspapers that were liberal, wet, sinful, and intelligent. Two of them, he argued, were in Baltimore. He was content to let the status quo thrive in Maryland and to let the utopians hatch their plans elsewhere, since the local American Legion was "polite, modest, soldierly," and "its grand dragon had actually served in the war." Other writers, like Edna Ferber, the novelist, and Charles Lorimer, the famed editor of the *Saturday Evening Post,* believed that improvements could be made in the present state of affairs, and they offered what they thought were practical solutions for the year 1928. Wherever utopia was, it was certainly not around the corner, since within a year the country would be in the depths of economic depression.

The tension between practical needs and utopian solutions is central to our understanding of the communal tradition in America. Some writers, such as Oscar Wilde, asserted that utopias were essential: "A map of the world that does not include Utopia is not even worth glancing at"; others shunned the word and its practitioners, believing that such dreamers were simply impractical or, even worse, would attempt to impose their version of practicality on all of us. Who is to say what is practical and what is utopian? Bronson Alcott, the Connecticut-born founder of Fruitlands, went to see Thomas Carlyle in search of some idealism and came away horrified. According to Alcott, all that Carlyle was interested in was "Work,

---

*Portions of this paper appeared in an essay by the author, "Paradise Planters," published in *Simple Gifts* (Storrs, Connecticut, 1978), a catalog for a special exhibit of Shaker craftsmanship at the William Benton Museum of Art and in "Notes of a Radical Nominalist" in *Alternative Futures* (1979).

Work! his creed and motto: toil of brain, dire draughts of memory, the sacrifice of sentiment to intellect, devotion to thought at the cost of affection.'' Alcott called himself a "Paradise Planter" and participated in one of the most impractical schemes ever hatched. His fellow communist in the "consociate family" was Charles Lane, once editor of the *London Mercantile Price-Current.*

The founders of communal societies usually thought themselves eminently practical, and some had careers as successful entrepreneurs before embarking on colony ventures, Robert Owen being the outstanding example. Others—usually religious leaders—believed that the only practical way for an individual to proceed in the world was to ask the question: what shall I do to be saved? rather than the commensensical one: how can I get ahead? Such religious utopians were intent on achieving spiritual perfection through community living and thereby saving their collective souls. And, of course, some communal groups believed that practical achievements and commercial enterprise enhanced their spiritual success.

Members of the Oneida Community, which originated as a religious colony, attributed their success to their ability to gear into the world's commerce. In 1854, they published an essay entitled "Christ: A Business Character," suggesting a close connection between their business dealings and their religious dedication. "The work which was given Christ required his individual attention and the constant application of all his powers. Indeed so great did he feel the pressure of business upon him that he worked seven days a week." The community members were encouraged to "study Christ as a true model of business character." Oneida, like Amana and several modern communes, let their utopian aspirations develop into million dollar corporations.

Measuring the success or failure of such ventures is more complex than looking at the bottom line. Henry Demarest Lloyd, the 1890s reformer, believed that many communes were successful:

Only within these communities has there been seen, in the wide boundaries of the United States, a social life where hunger and cold, prostitution, intemperance, poverty, slavery, crime, premature old age and unnecessary mortality, panic and industrial terror, have been abolished. If they had done this for only a year, they would have deserved to be called the only successful "society" on this continent, and some of them are generations old. All this has not been done by saints in heaven, but on earth by average men and women.[1]

But does a year's duration warrant calling a collective experiment a success? And what about those communities that had a long life but were marred in one way or another? The House of David at Benton Harbor, Michigan, was founded in 1903 and still exists today as a community. Could one call it a success in the face of indictments handed down against the leader charging fraud and seduction—charges, in fact, that were largely true? Or would one call the Oneida Community successful even though it burned dolls, banned books, and held views of mental illness that were even oppressive? Or what of the Harmony Society which lasted for over a hundred years and accumulated a fortune in the millions? That wealth, however, was put to formidable social uses in its mature years; it supported in 1903 both a tour of the Metropolitan Opera House Orchestra and Carrie Nation on tour in "Ten Nights in a Barroom." The Harmonists also operated a distillery.

The longevity standard fails to deal with an important question: namely, how are we to assess these communities as embodiments of new ideas, even though their life span may have been short? Or, more important, what impact did such colonies have on the lives of their members, even if their stay was brief? The success of Robert Owen's short-lived New Harmony Community, for example, may be seen within the context of educational reform; the impact of Upton Sinclair's Helicon Hall on the publication of *The Industrial Republic* written at the colony; or the meaning of George Inness's stay at the Raritan Bay Union in his "Peace and Plenty."

Such collective efforts tell us a great deal about American life and culture. Though they exist on the periphery of American history and society, they reflect larger and persistent themes in our history. Questions about individualism, about social and sexual rights, about economic arrangements and alternative structures, about the tensions between the practical and the ideal, all emerge directly when we look at these utopian societies. How we respond to those questions may in great measure determine our future.

The impulse to experiment, to start new ventures, to explore new territory, and to challenge orthodox patterns is deeply ingrained in our social history. Equally powerful is the impulse to hold on to what we have, to preserve what is valued, to remain put when others move on, to uphold traditional beliefs, and to counter any reformation simply because it is a reformation. Such impulses have all led to the formation of utopias in America. Our history has been both conservative and liberal, and on occasion even radical, but usually an admixture of the three in varying proportions. Such terms as conservative, liberal, or radical may not be particularly helpful in looking at utopianism in America, because they are so loaded with prior meaning that they obscure the essential meaning implicit in an idea, a movement, or a colony that espouses another way—a contrary path.

The German sociologist Karl Mannheim wrote that the idea of utopia was always defined by ideology, or the given set of historical presumptions at any one time. For Mannheim, the utopian mind moved against what *was* (what he called ideology) in order to produce something new.[2] According to his scheme, there are four types of utopian minds: the orgiastic-chiliastic, the liberal humanitarian, the conservative, and the socialist-communist.

The first—the chiliastic—represents an internal spirit that erupts and demands a new community at once. For the chiliast, the present becomes the breach through which what was once an inward force bursts out suddenly, taking hold of the outer world and transforming it. He had in mind the uprisings of the Anabaptists at Muenster in 1534 and of the Diggers who, in 1649, seized and dug up the common land at St. George's Hill in defiance of local landlords. Gerard Winnstanley's followers promised to make barren land fruitful and to distribute the land to the poor and needy. Winnstanley had preached that "When the Lord doth show me the place and manner, he will have us that are called the common people, to manure and work the common land." Inspirational power, the grace of God, and the promptings of special voices often goaded the chiliasts into action.

The second group—the liberal humanitarian—developed out of Enlightenment assumptions as to man's role in shaping society, the possibilities of progress, and man's capacity to give an ethical tone to his culture and to shape it to his own ends. Robert Owen, the nineteenth-century entrepreneur and planner and founder of New Harmony, is the prototype of this type of utopian mind. His *New View of Society* (1814) was based on a crude environmentalism which presumed that individuals could be shaped and guided toward better ends. In a letter to a London newspaper in August 1817, he wrote:

He [the participant in his planned society] will be trained from earliest infancy to acquire only kind and benevolent dispositions. He will be taught facts only. These will enable him very early in life to understand clearly how his own character and the character of his fellow creatures have been formed and are forming. He will thus be secured from being enveloped by any evil and demoralising atmospheres with which ever man yet has been surrounded.[3]

The contemporary new town developers and much of the planning tradition flow from similar assumptions.

The third group—the conservative—represents a separate force because older ideas, driven by new ones, must continuously transform themselves and accommodate themselves to the level of their most recent opponents. Although Mannheim gives us no real examples of this phenomenon, it is easy to point to present-day examples. Many of our declining inner city areas are in direct competition with suburban shopping malls which appear to have been taken right out of Edward Bellamy's *Looking Backward.* One solution for the downtown developers has been the historic restoration of warehouses, breweries, or abandoned canneries. Such downtown projects hope to attract shoppers, single people with considerable discretionary income, and people who enjoy eating quiche while seated around butcher blocks. Mannheim asserts, and I believe he is right, that there is an ever-shifting and dynamic conservative utopian ideal. Much of the 1960s' counterculture now flourishes in suburban malls, and we have a strong push toward success as a desirable social goal after a decade when the almighty dollar was scorned. There are communal arrangements in California called "Morehouse" where the good life is achieved through economic cooperation, where individualism is prized, and where each member can have a color television set and a water bed if he or she chooses.

The fourth utopian type—the socialist-communist—goes well beyond the liberal humanitarian utopia that had coexisted with the pre-economic structure and simply tried to reform it. The socialist-communist utopia is associated with the breakdown of the capitalist system and the transformations which necessarily flow from that breakdown. The development of the Soviet state after the Revolution of 1917 and the Chinese ideal, under Mao, of the new socialist man are obvious examples of this utopian mind-set in the modern period.

There are yet other categories of the utopian mind-set which I would like to outline before examining some specific facets of the utopian ideal in America. These categories, like the earlier ones, are historically determined. That is, they represent the dominant utopian mood of a period, an epoch. For example, for Mannheim, the chiliastic was characteristic of the medieval period, the liberal humanitarian of the eighteenth and nineteenth centuries, the conservative of the capitalist industrial phase of human development, and the socialist-communist of the post-1917 period.

With regard to these other categories, Frank Manuel describes what he calls utopias of "calm felicity" wherein tranquility is the highest good.[4] These were found in the literary utopias from the fifteenth to the eighteenth century and were passive places, places where conflit was at a minimum. Such utopias were often pastoral in setting and drew upon a strong classical tradition of the pastoral. With the rise of the nation-state, the expansion of individual rights and liberties, and the popularization of the idea of progress, there developed what Manuel calls "open ended utopias" wherein change was an essential element and conflict was resolved by removing to another place. Utopia was ever-changing and malleable to human needs and aspirations. Fourier's phalanxes and the industrial republic of Edward Bellamy fit this pattern wherein individuals grow and make choices and their material needs are met. Broadly conceived, these ideas flourished from the period of the French Revolution to the close of World War II.

With the end of the war, a whole series of ideas—some a half century old—began to emerge. Manuel calls these new utopias "eupsychias," a term taken from the writings of the psychologist Abraham Maslow. In these utopias, individuals have been freed from such notions as sin and from most social restraints, and they find their potential when they go beyond sexual and social oppression. People are increasingly spiritual in their concerns, and new dimensions of humanness based on drugs, Eastern philosophy, and certain neo-Freudian ideas about man's capacity for perfectibility emerge. The writings of such diverse figures as Aldous Huxley and Teilhard de Chardin have influenced this latest phase in utopian idealism. Many of the questions of concern to the eupsychians are psychological and have to do with growth, adaptation to perpetual change, and exploration of new definitions of human potential.

Thus, Mannheim and Manuel present at least seven ways of looking at utopian ideas, movements, individuals, or communal settlements. Other writers have outlined even more elaborate taxonomies for purposes of classification and analyses. Yet, their approach seems too abstract, too remote, to describe the variety of ideas and experiments that America has seen over the past three hundred years. One should be chary of grand theories and broad categories, and with Hobbes believe that "the things named are every one of them singular and individual" (*Leviathan*, chapter 4). There are, of course, resemblances between things and, in fact, such resemblances emerge in this work, but our purposes are better served by studying specific individual lives rather than general types, the communal society and the specifics of colony life rather than the stated aspirations of the group.

In an article in *The Journal of Interdisciplinary History* (1975), Hilda Geertz wrote a critique of Keith Thomas' *Religion and the Decline of Magic* (1971). She argued that Thomas' "extraordinary achievement" had been accomplished by "casting as wide a research net as possible over the life of the period, by studying a broad range of activities, by examining thousands of specific events and statements, by following out the connotational ramifications of every salient cluster of ideas." Geertz asserts that "the cultural answers given at any one moment are highly particular, and this particularity of the 'Thing Itself' must be given its full due before our explanations can make sense."[5]

In accepting her criticisms, Thomas provided a telling statement for students of communal societies:

We are still, I think, very much in the dark, historians and anthropologists alike, as to the precise mechanisms by which collective beliefs change over long periods of time. But no satisfactory future interpretation of the process will be able to ignore the fact that beliefs derive much of their prestige from their social relevance. Their internal structures have their own logic and this logic is not utilitarian. But if we are to understand why the beliefs are held or rejected, we must examine their relationship to the society of which they operate.[6]

Therefore, this book emphasizes specific utopian communities, rather than the idea of utopia, and specific leaders rather than the theory of community. For it is in an examination of the particulars that we may find some appropriate generalizations.

By the most conservative estimates, nearly six hundred communities were organized in the United States from 1663 to 1970. Most were short-lived, many had volatile and explosive histories, and a few were successful by any standard employed. In their membership they varied considerably. For example, in 1870 the Oneida Community had a membership of three hundred in several locations. By that time, they lived in comfortable dwellings, were in touch with the intellectual and social currents of the day, and were operating several prosperous industries. In fact, in 1869 they had been offered $800,000 for their property at Kenwood, New York.

On the other hand, there have been communities (and here I use the word "communities" advisedly) made up of a few individuals who printed pamphlets announcing the birth of their community and detailing the principles of organization. In addition, some individuals hatched schemes for colonies throughout their lives and generated projects wherever they went. Alcander Longley of St. Louis was associated with at least seven colonies in his long life. His last effort in the 1890s (his first was in the 1850s) consisted of "himself and an elderly woman stricken with paralysis and rheumatism, bedridden but enthusiastic."[7]

Some communities owned extensive property, and a few were clearly entrepreneurial in character. The Amana colonies in Iowa covered twenty-four thousand acres of productive farmland, while the Bishop Hill Colony in Illinois occupied what was the tallest building outside of Chicago in the state in the 1850s. The Pacific City scheme at Topolobampo Bay on the west coast of Mexico was part of a vast land and railroad scheme, and much of its appeal was to enterprising socialists who felt the profit motive as strongly as any robber baron. John Humphrey Noyes, the founder of Oneida and the author of the *History of American Socialisms* (1870), wrote that one of the causes for the failure of utopian colonies in the 1840s was what he called their "land mania." Too many communities were carried away with their vision of utopia and saw their domain extending as far as the speculative land market would allow. As a result, many had too much land to cultivate and too few hands to work it. In hindsight, we can see how some groups sought isolation and tried to define themselves vis-à-vis the outside world which they had either rejected, fled from, or attempted to instruct by their pious example. "Boundary maintenance," as the sociologists call it, was an important part of the community building process. But the idea of boundary maintenance raises a central question: how did a community symbolically define itself and its aspirations?

Most took the simplest way open to them: they moved. By the simple act of journeying, they gave their new venture a religious significance. It then became a hegira, usually to what they considered a holy place and one that they invested with special meaning. They did not have to call it Zion, or the New Jerusalem, or New Harmony; yet, it signified new beginnings, a rejection of the past. Even the secular utopians engaged in that process. When Robert Owen's principal followers journeyed to New Harmony, they took a highly publicized boat trip from Pittsburgh to the banks of the Wabash in Indiana. It was called the "Boatland of Knowledge," since aboard were several distinguished European educators and scientists, all of whom were committed to creating a new moral order in the New World. They were pilgrims loaded down with gifts (their new ideas) that would blossom in the New World.

The Shaker journey from Manchester to New York was part of that pattern, as was the settlement of Shaker villages in the West by Elder Richard McNemar. In the mid-nineteenth century, the religious community of Bethel, under the guidance of William Keil, moved its membership from Missouri to Oregon, and they took with them the embalmed body of their founder's daughter for burial in the New Eden. They thought there was no better way to consecrate new ground than with a piece of the old.

There are some resemblances among communal ventures, and for purposes of illustration, I have constructed three categories that may help explain the utopian impulse in America. Most historians have been content with the simple division of communal experiments into the religious and the secular. The Shakers were religious, the Owenites secular. While this division is very neat in theory, it does not hold practically. For example, the Owenites in England had chapels and had many of the characteristics of a religious sect. In the twentieth century, some groups (Synanon, for example) developed a secular creed as potent and compelling as any religious body's.

The first and most prevalent type of colony has been the charismatic perfectionist group. The greatest number of colonies belong to this category, and it is within this group that one finds the colonies which survived for the longest period. Such communities were charismatic in one of two ways: they were based either on the personal sanctity of the membership as a whole and/or on the personal sanctity, special gifts, or power of a forceful leader. They were perfectionist in their promise that the perfected life could be led within the confines of a community and that the community was the way to perfection. Such communities quite often served immediate religious and spiritual goals within a millennialist or spiritualist tradition. Their concern for social questions was secondary to their concern for the personal and religious development of the members within an evolving set of collective goals as outlined by the leadership.

The second type—the cooperative colonizers—consisted of colonists who believed that secular salvation could be attained by establishing groups of people in new settlements and that by collectively assuming financial responsibility for such communities, the colonists would improve their economic and moral condition. The leaders and sponsors of such communities saw them as ordered environments wherein the predator habits developed in the cities could be eliminated; wherein the bonds of family and marriage would be strengthened; and wherein the conditions for moral growth would exist. Such settlements emphasized economic cooperation, showed little interest in political philosophy, and addressed themselves to immediate social and ethical problems.

The third type—the political pragmatists—consisted of political and social radicals who sought an arena in which they could test and publicize their principles in action. Such groups often sought an outlet for their political and social energy, and were impatient with the pace of American democracy. They wanted to show the world and their fellow radicals that socialism could work and that there was a method by which practical socialism could be put to use in direct fashion. They tended to emphasize cooperation in the face of a Marxist emphasis on class warfare and social strife.

American communal history had its origins in the religious upheavals of seventeenth-century Europe, particularly in Germany and Switzerland. For it was in places such as Wurttemberg, Germany, and Berne, Switzerland, that a movement began to restore to the churches (particularly the Lutheran) a religious commitment to a devout and holy life among the believers. In 1675, Philip Jakob Spener attacked the Lutheran church for its lack of spirituality and urged a six point program to revive the churches. He believed there was a need for: reform of theological education, Bible study, a renewal of evangelical preaching, an ethical revival, an end to divisive and polemical writing, and an increase in lay activity within the church. His pietist faith called for a restoration of simplicity to the churches and a restoration of the primacy of religious experience as the true test of faith.

In 1699 Gottfried Arnold, a follower of Spener, argued that heretical opinions and doctrines had often been the source of true values and that orthodoxy did not always produce true Christian virtue. Pietism encouraged both the rise of a sectarian spirit within the established churches, because it challenged current practices, and a simplification of creedal belief. Although Spener had seen his philosophy as reformist rather than separatist, it often became the basis for separation from the church rather than reformation from within. According to E. S. Waterhouse in his essay on "Pietism" in E. B. Hastings, *Encyclopedia of Religion and Ethics* (1951 ed.): "Some Pietists indulged in millennial speculation; many dabbled in mysticism; but in the main, Pietism is justly to be called a movement of revaluation, which tried to attach to regeneration and sanctification as accomplished facts a higher value than to justification by faith as an approved theory."

Regeneration and sanctification are the key terms here. Pietism developed in reaction to orthodoxy and one outcome was the formation of communal groups of believers who thought that such sects were the only vehicles for salvation and regeneration. Persecutions usually followed the establishment of such sects, as with the "Renewed Church of the United Brethren" (the Moravians) who fled Bohemia and Moravia in the eighteenth century and found refuge with Count Nicholas von Zinzendorf before emigrating to the United States in the 1730s. The colonies at Ephrata (1732), Snow Hill (1799), and Harmony (1805) all grew out of the pietist tradition. These groups came to America to practice their faith, to live a common religious life, and to separate themselves from an unregenerate world. Nearly all the groups founded in the United States in the seventeenth and eighteenth centuries were religious in origin.

The Shakers had their origins in an evangelical awakening that swept England in the mid-eighteenth century. Ann Lee, the sect's founder, joined a group of "Shaking Quakers" at Bolton, near Manchester, England, in 1747. This group had embraced the millennialist faith of the Camisard Prophets, who had emigrated to England in 1705 following persecution in France. The prophets, both in England and France, were hostile to all ecclesiastical authority, held services marked by trembling and dancing, and believed that the millennium was imminent. The Bolton sect was led by some dissenting Quakers, and Ann Lee rose to a position of leadership in the group. In 1770, she was jailed for profaning the Sabbath, and while in prison she had a vision that sin had entered the world through sexual intercourse and that celibacy was the preferred state.

Mother Ann Lee migrated to the United States in 1774, and when she died in 1784, her sect had gained a foothold in the New World. Between 1787 and 1825, members established separate "families" from New York and Massachusetts in the East to Indiana and Kentucky on the western frontier. At the height of their influence they had 6,000 members and their colonies were noted for the excellence of their agricultural products, their practical furniture, and their ability to get along with their neighbors. During the post-Civil War period, the number of Shakers declined and, beginning in 1875, several communities were either dissolved or consolidated with other declining families. There are now fewer than a dozen Shakers in two locations, in Maine and New Hampshire. Although the German colonies and the Shakers dominate the early history of communal settlements, there were other groups, such as the followers of Jemima Wilkinson, who simply followed the teachings and preachings of a forceful and charismatic personality.

It was with Robert Owen that the secular utopians received their first significant spokesman in America. After a successful career as a textile manufacturer and social reformer in England, Owen turned his eyes toward America as a possible site for a community. He visited the United States in 1824 and addressed Congress in February and March 1825, with the second speech lasting three hours. But it was not an opportunity to speak that brought him to America, but rather the opportunity to purchase a ready-made utopian village. The Harmonist Society had advertised their land in western Indiana for sale because they wished to return to Pennsylvania, the site of their original settlement. Owen bought the land from the Rappites, issued a call for settlers to come to the colony on the Wabash River, and assembled a distinguished group of European scientists and educators at New Harmony. Though New Harmony was a glorious failure, it did establish the idea that progress might be achieved by planting what the historian Arthur Bestor, Jr., has called "patent office models for the good society." The notion that from small beginnings great things come is central to the patent office theory. Owen, and numerous utopians after him, believed that a small group of individuals could demonstrate both the effectiveness and the superiority of their social theory by putting it into practice. They wanted to prove that their dreams could become real and that such dreams were practical.

During 1825 and 1826, seven Owenite colonies, including New Harmony, were established. None lasted more than two years and, when they are compared with religious colonies founded in the eighteenth century, an obvious fact emerges: The religious groups lasted longer than their secular counterparts. That pattern continued throughout the nineteenth century and continues till this day. Successful utopian colonies are usually religious; however, such a fact has never deterred the secular utopians from starting new projects.

The failure of New Harmony did not influence the next wave of communities—the Fourierist. Their inspiration came from the writings of the eccentric French traveller, Charles Fourier, whose theories about the destructive effect of civilization upon mankind had found a limited audience in Europe in the 1830s. Fourier did find an American publicist and disciple in Albert Brisbane, and it was through Brisbane that Fourier's ideas found an audience in America. Those ideas exalted both individualism and collectivity and constituted a critique of the emerging industrial order which, according to Fourier, systematically denied any outlet for creative passions. Civilization had both shaped and stunted mankind.

Individuals could escape their oppressive conditions by organizing themselves into communities (phalanxes), and by systematically combining the needs, the drives, and the wants of the members (1520 was the desired number) a new social synthesis could be achieved. That synthesis allowed individuals to choose the tasks that fitted them and allowed for a full range of human interests to find its natural channel. What Fourier called "passional attraction" would bring individuals together for constructive work and play. Brisbane was able to popularize Fourier's ideas through a column he wrote for Horace Greeley's *New York Tribune* in 1842. From 1842 to 1858, there were twenty-nine Fourierist societies started in the United States. Brook Farm, the famous literary community, began in 1841 as an educational association, but in 1843 fell under Fourierist influence and became the Brook Farm Phalanx in 1843. The North American Phalanx was started in 1843 and lasted till 1856, by its longevity contradicting the theory that secular groups fail. Most of the Fourierist phalanxes of the forties and fifties did, in fact, have short lives.

The 1840s—the mad forties as one writer has charactrized them—was a decade when utopian colonies flourished. Religious groups, like the Perfectionists at Putney, Vermont, and later Kenwood, New York, and the Society of Inspirations (later the Amana Society) were founded on separatist principles and led by inspirational father figures. Reformers, such as the pacifist Adin Ballou, and the anarchist John Collins, believed that small colonies could be testing grounds for their ideas and could influence the larger society. Between 1841 and 1850, fifty communities were founded. And between 1850 and 1860, another forty-one were organized. Throughout this "Age of Reform" the older religious groups, such as the Shakers and the Harmonists, grew prosperous and were standing models of successful cooperative enterprise.

Though it is often assumed that only a handful of utopian colonies were founded after the Civil War, my own research and that of other scholars dispute that assumption. Between 1861 and 1919, one hundred and forty-two communal groups were founded as compared with one hundred thirty-seven for the period from 1787 to 1860, including twenty-two Shaker settlements. The period after the war saw a marked rise in population and a significant increase in the sizes of towns and cities. Despite such growth, these small, cooperative communities remained attractive to individuals.

During the 1890s, thirty-four colonies were founded. Many were socialist and inspired by Edward Bellamy's *Looking Backward: The Year 2000* (1888) and by the growth of the Social Gospel that emphasized practical Christianity. Talk of the "cooperative commonwealth" was commonplace among socialists and radicals, who were impatient with the pace of American democracy and who were looking for an alternative to capitalism and communism. Figures such as Ralph Albertson and George Howard Gibson cooperated to form the Christian Commonwealth and found the periodical, *Social Gospel.* Laborers sought a buffer against the uncertainties of the economy that swept through long economic cycles and left them with little security. Cooperative colonies seemed to some such a buffer.

After 1900, one sees the emergence of urban communes though the dominant location for communal societies remains rural. Between 1900 and 1919, there were thirty-nine colonies established, but no distinct pattern emerges except that groups founded on principles derived from Eastern philosophies emerge. One literary utopia, Upton Sinclair's Helicon Hall, was founded in this period and several charismatic and perfectionist groups like the House of David at Benton Harbor and the racist Holy City group gain footholds in Michigan and California, respectively. After 1900 there is no dominant pattern or a dominant figure, such as Owen and Fourier for an earlier period, but rather an eclectic array of personalities and groups.

During the 1920s and 1930s, there is a strong movement for decentralist communities based on self-sufficiency and a distrust of the new corporate and centralized political system. And there is evidence that during the Depression there were numerous cooperative housing arrangements begun in urban areas and efforts at collective agriculture in the farm states. And, of course, there were groups that started in one era and survived into the next. The remnants of the Llano del Rio Company, which had started in southern California in 1911, had moved to Louisiana in 1917 and struggled through the Depression years only to die in 1938. But it had, in one form or another, a generational life and radicals, both in the North and the South, knew about the group.

During the late 1960s and early 1970s, there was, according to Rosabeth Kanter, a "search for utopia and community in America—for alternatives, group-oriented ways of life." Communal groups began to appear in the mountains of the Southwest, in the lush valleys of northern California and in the low rent areas of the northeastern cities. Kanter divided them into two groups: those who served and those who retreated. Service-oriented groups such as Synanon had a mission, a clarity of purpose, and demanded a strong commitment from their members. The retreat communities had few rules, made few demands upon the membership and had an open-ended admissions policy. Groups such as Morning Star in California had dramatic and volatile histories, but were short lived.

This brief examination of communal history emphasizes a few facets of utopianism in America:

(1) There has been a long and continuous history of utopian experiments in the United States, including the current crop of communards, or those adherents to the principles of communalism.

(2) They have been varied in their philosophy, size, and purposes.

(3) There has been a remarkable constancy in the founding of such colonies. The urge to start new colonies in a culture as intensely individualistic as ours serves a need for the cooperatively minded. One should keep in mind that the Shaker sect, our most persistent and most long-lived group, was founded in 1774 and continues in the twentieth century as a standing model for the cooperative impulse. The success of the Shakers was often pointed to as a rationale for founding a colony.

(4) By and large, Americans have been more hospitable than hostile to such enterprises. More of them have existed here than in Europe over a comparable period of time and the religious colonies have succeeded where the secular failed.

NOTES

1. James Dombroski, *The Early Days of Christian Socialism in America,* 1936.

2. Karl Mannheim, *Ideology and Utopia*, 1936.

3. "Letter to London Newspapers, August 7, 1817." *A Supplementary Appendix to the First Volume of the Life of Robert Owen, Containing a Series of Reports, Addresses, Memorials and Other Documents,* London, 1967.

4. Frank Manuel (ed.), *Utopias and Utopian Thought,* New York, 1966.

5. Hilda Geertz, "An Anthropology of Religion and Magic," *Journal of Interdisciplinary History*, 6, no. 1 (summer 1975): 71-89.

6. Keith Thomas, "An Anthropology of Religion and Magic," *Journal of Interdisciplinary History*, 6, no. 1 (summer 1975): 91-109.

7. Cited in Hal Sears, "Alcander Longley, Missouri Communist," *Bulletin of the Missouri Historical Society*, 25 (January 1969): 123-37.

BIOGRAPHIES

A

ABBOTT, LEONARD (b. May 20, 1878, Liverpool, England; d. 1953, New York City), leader of the Ferrer Colony* (see also Appendix A, No. 267). Abbott was raised in England and attended English schools. His father represented American firms in Liverpool and young Abbott attended Uppingham, a public school for the wealthy. His intellectual life did not take form until he read Tom Paine's *The Age of Reason.* In 1898, he came to the United States where he joined the staff of *The Literary Digest* (1899) and later (1905) became associate editor of *Current Digest.* In 1902, he was influential in introducing Upton Sinclair* to socialism by giving him a copy of *Wilshire's Magazine* to read.

Abbott's libertarian ideas had their roots in his friendship with J. William Lloyd with whom he co-published the *Free Comrade* (1900-1902, 1910-1912). Abbott was the "front man" in New York for the anarchist Francisco Ferrer Association, and in 1910 he edited *Francisco Ferrer, His Life, Work and Martyrdom.* In 1914, Abbott was one of the leaders in the move to establish the Ferrer Colony as a center for libertarian education and to divorce it from the politically volatile Ferrer Association in 1916. He was an ideal public spokesman for radical causes because of his respectable demeanor and slight British accent. Abbott was a complex figure who, on the one hand, was revolting against his upper-class background and, on the other, maintained his aristocratic manners and dress while working for the anarchist cause. He believed in anarchism as a social philosophy which could liberate individuals from political oppression. The execution of Francisco Ferrer, the Spanish anarchist, in 1908 stirred his sense of injustice. Yet in the dispute that led to the formation of the colony at Stelton, New Jersey, he sided with those who wanted to make education, rather than politics, the focus of activity of the Ferrer Center in New York. During the 1930s, he worked briefly for the Works Progress Administration in Washington, D.C.

*An asterisk denotes the presence of a main entry in this dictionary.

SELECTED WORKS: Ernest H. Crosby (1907); Francisco Ferrer, His Life, Work, Martyrdom (1910); Masterworks of Economics (1946); Masterworks of Government (1947).
SOURCES: Laurence Veysey, The Communal Experience (1973); Who's Who in America (1923).

ADAMS, GEORGE JONES (b. ca. 1810, Boston, Massachusetts; d.?), Shakespearean actor, Adventist preacher, Mormon secessionist, and itinerant prophet. Adams, who worked in the 1830s on the Boston stage and has been characterized by O. W. Riegel as a "strange mixture of buffoon, fanatic, ne'er-do-well, and simpleton," converted to Mormonism in 1840. In 1841, the Mormon leadership asked him to do missionary work in Jerusalem and Russia, but the trips failed to materialize. In 1844, he became a member of the Navoou Theatre Repertory Company, the first Mormon theatrical company. Adams soon gained an unsavory reputation for his drinking and was excommunicated in April 1845 for adultery. After a brief stay in Cincinnati, he became a trusted lieutenant of James Jesse Strang,* the Beaver Island prophet and leader of the Kingdom of St. James Colony. Strang had been excommunicated by Brigham Young in August 1844 for attempting to establish a separate and independent colony at Voree, Wisconsin. Strang had been baptized by Joseph Smith and had suggested a site in Racine County, Wisconsin, for the persecuted Mormon group (see also Appendix A, No. 91). Adams was a member of Strang's inner circle, but he was always torn between his stage work and his religious work. It was Adams who crowned Strang "King James of Beaver Island," but Strang later banished him for attempting to pass off a prostitute as his wife.

In 1862, Adams established the Church of the Messiah at Jonesport, Maine. He published his Sword of Truth and The Harbinger of Peace and urged the return of the Jews to the Holy Land. Adventist sects had flourished in the United States, despite the failure of William Miller's prediction that the millenium would come in 1843-1844. It was believed that the Holy Land would witness great events prior to the day of judgment and it would be in Palestine that the Messiah would gather in the elect and rout the forces of evil. The "Church of the Messiah" was such an Adventist church and Adams ordained two bishops and a number of elders. In 1865, he organized the Palestine Emigration Association and led a group of 156 men, women, and children to Palestine in August 1866. Adams had prophesied that on their arrival his followers would renew their youth. Shortly after they arrived, several members died and Adams became a public drunk. The colony was soon destitute. The original plan had called for communal sharing, but the colonists were forced to fend for themselves. In September 1867, the

group returned to Maine without Adams on the steamer "Quaker City."
One of their co-passengers was Mark Twain, who observed them and used
their plight in his *Innocents Abroad.* Adams left Palestine for England
around May 1868. Nothing is known of him after 1872 when he was reportedly involved in the real estate business in Philadelphia.

SELECTED WORKS: Lecture on the Destiny and Mission of America (1860);
The Sword of Truth (1862-1865).

SOURCES: Harold Davis, "The Jaffa Colonists from Downeast," *American
Quarterly* 3 (1951); O. W. Reigel, *Crown of Glory* (1935).

ALBERTSON, RALPH (b. October 21, 1866, Jamesport, New York;
d. ca. 1926), religious reformer associated with the Willard Co-operative
Colony (see Appendix A, No. 210) and the Christian Commonwealth Colony*
(see also Appendix A, No. 214). Albertson attended Greenport Academy
(1880-1884) and Oberlin College and Theological Seminary (1888-1891), and
was much influenced by the writing of Edward Bellamy,* Henry George,
Leo Tolstoy, and Washington Gladden. Ordained a Congregational minister
in 1890, he was pastor at Penfield, Ohio, during 1889-1891 and at Lagonda
Congregational Church, Springfield, Ohio, during 1891-1895. In 1895,
during a labor dispute he resigned his pastorate in Springfield. A strike had
broken out in the factories surrounding his church, and he was unable to
support the strikers because of his belief in Christian nonresistance. He
then joined a small colony of Christian Socialists at Andrews, North Carolina, headed by William C. Damon, a classics professor from California
who wanted a better environment in which to educate his children. In 1895,
this group started a temperance colony and named it the Willard Co-operative
Colony after the temperance leader Frances Willard. In addition, the group
hoped to start "The People's University," whose prospectus stated "that
the political economy taught and lived by Jesus Christ is practicable, that
the love and brotherhood of the Kingdom of Heaven may be realized on
earth." They publicized their efforts in the reform periodical, *The Kingdom.*

Correspondence with George Howard Gibson* led to the establishment
of another colony, the Christian Commonwealth* at Commonwealth,
Georgia, in 1896. Albertson became editor of the colony magazine, *The
Social Gospel* (1897-1900) which gave its name to a wider social movement.
The colony at Commonwealth attracted widespread interest with "Golden
Rule" Jones, Jane Addams, and Luther Burbank supporting it financially.
According to Albertson, the colony had more in common with St. Francis
than with Karl Marx, but that inspirational source was insufficient to avoid
a failure. Improper management practices and crop failures forced the
colony into bankruptcy in 1899.

Albertson edited *The American Cooperator* (1902-1904) at Lewiston, Maine, and spent the rest of his career in the publishing and mercantile business. He was on the editorial staff of the *Arena* in 1904. In 1906, he was president of the Twentieth Century Company (the publisher of *Twentieth Century Magazine*) and the Cooperative Publishing Company (the publisher of *The Boston Common*).

SELECTED WORKS: *Little Jeremiads* (1902); *Little Preachments* (1903); *Fighting Without a War* (1920); *The Mental Agility Book* (1925).
SOURCES: James Dombrowski, *The Early Days of Christian Socialism in America* (1936); Howard Quint, *The Forging of American Socialism* (1953).

ALCOTT, AMOS BRONSON (b. November 29, 1799, Wolcott, Connecticut; d. March 4, 1888, Concord, Massachusetts), transcendental author and co-founder of the Fruitlands Colony* (see also Appendix A, No. 71). Emerson said of Alcott, one of the most ephemeral of community organizers and practitioners: "It must be conceded it is speculation that he loves and not action." Alcott's formal education was limited, but his early travels and reading brought him into contact with the mysticism of the Quakers. After an early career as a peddler, he turned to teaching and ran a series of progressive schools in Connecticut, Massachusetts, and Pennsylvania (1823-1833). His most advanced experiment in schooling began in 1834 in Boston, where he tried to develop a rational and integrated system of instruction based on the Socratic method. The school was criticized because of its irreligiosity, and when it admitted a Negro girl in 1839, parents withdrew their children and the school failed.

In 1840, Alcott moved to Concord, and in 1842, he traveled to England to meet with some disciples who had organized a school (Alcott House) using his philosophy. In 1843, he returned to Concord with Henry Wright and Charles Lane* and together, in June 1843, they began a communal experiment called Fruitlands on a one hundred-acre tract near Harvard, Massachusetts. Alcott had participated in the original discussions for founding Brook Farm* (see also Appendix A, No. 53), but found that community project insufficient in idealism. The ideal at Fruitlands was a spiritual one, with Alcott, Lane, and Wright striving to develop higher qualities through vegetarianism, spiritual reading, and reform work. While the men meditated, Abigail Alcott and her daughters worked at sustaining the colony farm and serving the eclectic needs of the men. The colony disintegrated because of friction between Lane and the Alcotts. After the colony's failure in 1845, Alcott returned to Concord where he continued to write, lecture, teach, and live in genteel poverty until his death.

Among the reformers of his day, Alcott was considered gentle and sublime, but impractical, with Emerson coming to his aid on several occasions by loaning money. His daughter, Louisa May Alcott, made good use of her bitter experiences at Fruitlands in *Transcendental Wild Oats* (1876); her success as a writer enabled the family to escape poverty. She had watched her mother act as a servant to the philosophers Alcott and Lane and had no sympathy for what she considered their self-indulgent communal experiment. Alcott's influence was widespread, with Emerson, Thoreau, Hawthorne, and the English reformer James Pierrepont Greaves all deeply affected by his philosophy of simple harmonious living.

SELECTED WORKS: *Observations on the Principles and Methods of Infant Instruction* (1830); *Conversations with Children on the Gospels* (1836); *The Doctrine and Discipline of Human Culture* (1836); *Concord Days* (1872).
SOURCES: *An Historical and Biographical Introduction to Accompany The Dial* (1961); George Willis Cooke (ed.), *Appleton's Cyclopedia of American Biography* (1886); Clara Endicott Sears, *Bronson Alcott's Fruitlands* (1915).

ANDREWS, STEPHEN PEARL (b. March 22, 1812, Templeton, Massachusetts; d. May 21, 1886, New York City), founder of the Modern Times community (see also Appendix A, No. 116). Andrews's family moved to Hinsdale, Vermont, from Massachusetts in 1816 after his father, the Reverend Elisha Andrews, had opposed the War of 1812 and had lost his parish. In 1829, Andrews graduated from the Amherst Academy and in 1830 journeyed to Louisiana to teach at the Jackson Female Seminary, then taught at the College of Louisiana, and later at Centenary College before abandoning teaching for the study of the law in 1831. He was admitted to the Louisiana bar in 1833 and married in 1835. In 1839 he moved from New Orleans to Houston where, in the early 1840s, he became involved in abolitionism, the cause that took him to London with the reformer and editor, Lewis Tappan, for the Second World's Anti-Slavery Convention. In 1845, he turned away from the law profession and opened a Phonetic Institute to promote phonography (short hand). He promoted his varied reform interests in the journal, *The Propagandist* (1850) and in 1851 fell under the influence of the utopian reformer, Josiah Warren,* and the economic theories Warren had put into practice at his Equity Colony (see also Appendix A, No. 46).

Andrews and Warren established the Modern Times Colony at Islip, Suffolk County, New York, in 1851. Over a hundred individuals eventually joined this anarchist group including Thomas Low,* Mary Gove Nichols, and the American Positivist, Henry Edger. Free love was practiced at Modern Times and the publicity surrounding Andrews' espousal of free love wrecked the society. By 1854 Modern Times was in decline and Andrews moved to New York City where in 1859 he established a cooperative house, Unitary Home, which attracted various reformers including Marie Howland.* During 1860 Andrews declared himself the Pantarch and head of a new spiritual order. He outlined his spiritualist views in his *Constitution or Organic Basis of the Pantarchy* whose publication was subsidized by the cooperative colony supporter, Elizabeth Rowell Thompson.*

In 1877, he published *The Basic Outlines of Universology,* a volume of esoteric philosophy. During the 1880s, he was prominent in radical groups in New York, particularly in the Manhattan Club.

SELECTED WORKS: The Comprehensive Phonographic Class Book (1845); *The Science of Society,* I, II (1851-1853); *Love, Marriage and Divorce, and the Sovereignty of the Individual* (1853); *The Basic Outline of Universology* (1872).
SOURCES: DAB, 1: Madeline Stern, *The Pantarch* (1968).

ARMSTRONG, PETER (b. ca. 1800, Philadelphia; d. 1892), founder of the Celesta Colony (see Appendix A, No. 140) in Sullivan County, Pennsylvania, in 1863. Armstrong was a rag peddler and tinware salesman until 1852 when he purchased 2,400 acres in the Allegheny Mountains to prepare a place for the elect 144,000 mentioned in the Book of Revelations as those who will be "gathered-in" prior to the millenium. Armstrong was a Millerite Second Adventist who kept his faith alive after the failure of William Miller's prophecy about Christ's Second Coming in 1843-1844. He published a paper, *The Day Star of Zion and the Banner of Life of Philadelphia and Celesta,* in the 1860s to spread the Adventist gospel, and he maintained a combined general store, printing office, and auditorium for church services. He had a large family and some of his followers (about twenty) settled at Celesta in 1863. Armstrong had worked for about eleven years to clear a thousand acres and worked out an elaborate plan for the "town of Celesta" with straight avenues and level squares to accommodate the 144,000 in this hilly country. In 1864, he deeded the land to "Almighty God, who inhabiteth eternity" and not to his children. The Armstrong children nonetheless prospered and the Armstrong Paper Company was founded by his son. According to one settler: ". . . his [Armstrong's] fanaticism so forced itself upon us that we were compelled to abandon the place . . . ; and finally Mr. Armstrong had to abandon the place and with his family went to Philadelphia." (William Hinds, *American Communities and Cooperative Colonies,* 1908 ed.) The last issue of *The Day Star of Zion* was published in 1880.

SOURCES: William Hinds, *American Communities and Co-operative Colonies* (1908 ed.); Kenneth Wood, *"Celesta" Now and Then,* V, 17-27; Ernest Wooster, *Communities of the Past and Present* (1971 reprint).

AVERY, GILES (b. November 3, 1815, Saybrook, Connecticut; d. December 27, 1890, Watervliet, New York), member of the Lebanon, New York, Shaker Colony (see Appendix A, No. 1). Avery came to the Lebanon Shaker

Colony with his parents in 1819 (three of his aunts also became Shakers). When he was twenty-five, he was appointed to the order of elders, and in 1859, he became a co-elder at New Lebanon. During the period of intense religious revitalization and excitement known as Mother Ann's Work (1837-1843), Avery took an active role. He was a singing and speaking medium, and according to his *Autobiography*, he saw the spirit of Joseph Meachem* and received instructions from him.

After the awakening had subsided, he was asked to write an inspirational account of the revivals, but the task of recording the events of that period finally fell to another Shaker. For thirty years (1859-1889), Avery led the central ministry of the Shakers at New Lebanon. Before assuming his position as elder in the leading Shaker community at New Lebanon in 1859 Avery worked as a joiner, cooper, wagonmaker, plumber, mason, and carpenter.

SELECTED WORKS: *A Juvenile Guide* (1844); *Autobiography* (1891); *Sketches of Shakers and Shakerism* (1884).
SOURCES: Edward D. Andrews, *The People Called Shakers* (1963 reprint).

B

BAKER, ROMELIUS (b. November 1, 1793; d. January 11, Economy, Pennsylvania), co-director of the Harmony Society* (see also Appendix A, No. 17). Baker's father joined the Harmony Society at Economy, Pennsylvania, in 1805, and soon the Baker family became prominent in the colony. It was a family of seven, all of whom were well educated and members of the society since its beginning. While the Harmonists were in Indiana, young Baker was sent to Germany on colony business and was a trusted member from the earliest days of the Society. Romelius Baker became the principal elder and principal trustee, and with Jacob Henrici* he directed the external affairs of the society after George Rapp's* death in 1847. Baker and Henrici worked well together and successfully guided the affairs of the society from 1836 to 1868. The Harmonists believed in a literal reading of the Bible in the inspired leadership of George Rapp and from 1807 to 1817 celibacy was the rule. They were industrious and frugal and developed some large industries, including cotton and textiles. Baker was a deeply religious man who turned to mystical texts for guidance in business and practical affairs. Much admired within the society, he was a dedicated leader during a period of economic growth and religious stabilization.

SOURCES: Karl Arndt, *George Rapp's Successors and Material Heirs, 1847-1916* (1972).

BALLOU, ADIN (b. April 23, 1803, Cumberland, Rhode Island; d. August 5, 1890, Hopedale, Massachusetts), Universalist clergyman and founder of the Hopedale Community* (see Appendix A, No. 56). Ballou was a leading Universalist clergyman in Milford, Massachusetts, during the 1820s. In 1831, he withdrew from the Universalist association over a dispute about the doctrine of punishment after death, an idea he opposed, and formed the Massachusetts Association of Universal Restoration, which stressed the practical side of Christianity.

As an experiment in "practical Christianity," Ballou founded the Hopedale Community on 250 acres at Milford, Massachusetts, in 1842; there he edited *The Practical Christian*, a reform journal. Hopedale was a joint-stock company that stressed the brotherhood of man and the benevolent teachings of Jesus Christ. Colony members were active in numerous reform causes in the 1840s, especially peace, antislavery, and temperance. Ballou was a pacifist and promoted Christian nonresistance throughout his career, even during the Civil War when radicals like William Lloyd Garrison supported violent means. Throughout his life Ballou was a defender of Spiritualism against its critics. According to his *Autobiography*: "I attended and took part in conventions held in its behalf, wrote for papers devoted to its extension, and consented for a time to be accounted an agent of the Spiritualist Association."

From an original membership of thirty-one and a capital investment of $4,000, by 1852, the membership had grown to one hundred and ten with property valued at $40,000. With the ascendancy of Ebenezer Draper, an abolitionist and financial backer of the group, to community leadership, the colony underwent a transformation from a joint-stock operation (the Hopedale Association) to the Hopedale Manufacturing Company. As the colony became more business oriented, Ballou felt that it lost its moral character. In 1862, he withdrew from community affairs and continued his reform career as director of the Hopedale Home School.

SELECTED WORKS: An Exposition (1853); *Hopedale Community* (1853); *Practical Christian Socialism* (1854); *Primitive Christianity and its Corruptions* (1870); *History of the Town of Milford* (1882).

SOURCES: William Heywood (ed.), *The Autobiography of Adin Ballou; DAB;* Lewis Perry, *Radical Abolitionism* (1973).

BATES, ISSACHAR (b. January 29, 1758, Hingham, Massachusetts; d. March 17, 1837, New Lebanon, New York), prominent Shaker leader. Bates was a farmer prior to the Revolutionary War in which he served as a fifer. After the war, he married, had eleven children, and worked as a Baptist minister and preacher. He joined the Shakers in 1801. Bates was an accomplished preacher and along with Benjamin Young* led the Shaker campaign to "win" the West for Shakerism in 1805. In addition to his preaching, he was one of the twenty-three who established the South Union

Society (see Appendix A, No. 20) in Kentucky. Throughout the formative years of the Shakers in the West, Bates was an indefatigable preacher who promoted this new religion against all comers. In 1835, he returned to New Lebanon where he died two years later.

SELECTED WORKS: Sketch of the Life and Experiences of Issachar Bates (n.d.).
SOURCES: Edward D. Andrews, *The People Called Shakers* (1963 reprint).

BEILHART, JACOB (b. March 4, 1867, Columbiana County, Ohio; d. November 24, 1908, Waukegon, Illinois), leader and founder of the Spirit Fruit Society (see Appendix A, no. 229). He was born into a religious farm family with his father attending the German Lutheran church and his mother the Mennonite church. He left the farm when he was seventeen to work in a harness shop, then a year later moved to Kansas with a relative and worked for a time as a sheepherder. While in Kansas (1887), he became a Seventh Day Adventist and traveled for the church in Kansas and Colorado distributing devotional literature.

He attended an Adventist college at Healdsburg, California, in 1888, then traveled to Ohio as an Adventist preacher. A desire to help the sick led him to enroll in a nursing program at the Seventh Day Adventist Sanitarium in Battle Creek, Michigan, in 1890. While there, he turned to Christian Science, studied theosophy and spiritualism and became acquainted with C. W. Post, the food manufacturer. Beilhart was a stockholder in Post's health sanitarium, La Vita Inn. During 1893, Beilhart married and supported himself by working at odd jobs in the Battle Creek area.

In 1899 he decided to launch a communal organization and located it on a farm in Lisbon, Ohio. A dozen or so members joined him at the Spirit Fruit Society, many coming from the Chicago area. Two years later, in 1901, rumors began to circulate about the group. Local newspapers called it a "free love nest" and a Chicago man charged that his wife had been abducted into the colony. In 1904 there was another scandal involving a young Chicago woman who joined. In October, 1905, Beilhart relocated the group (thirteen members) after a mob had come to the farm and threatened him. Their new home was on a 90-acre site at Ingleside, Lake County, Illinois, about forty-five miles northwest of Chicago. At Ingleside the group peacefully co-existed with their neighbors.

Beilhart's philosophy was a mixture of faith healing, positive thinking, and free love of the "varietism" kind wherein individuals might have more than one mate and platonic friendships were encouraged. Among his admirers were Elbert Hubbard of the Roycrofters and C. W. Post. In late 1908, he was stricken with appendicitis and never recovered from the attack.

SELECTED WORKS: Jacob Beilhart; Life and Teachings (1925).
SOURCES: William Hinds, *American Communities and Cooperative Colonies* (1908 ed.); Nettie L. Major, *C. W. Post, the Man and the Hour* (1963).

BEISSEL, JOHANN CONRAD (b. March 1, 1690, Eberbach, Germany; d. July 6, 1768, Ephrata, Pennsylvania), hymn writer and founder of the Solitary Brethren of the Community of the Seventh Day Baptists, or the Ephrata Colony.* Born into a poverty-stricken, fatherless family, Beissel was orphaned at age seven and received little education. He learned to play the violin and later distinguished himself as a hymnist. He was deeply influenced by the Anabaptist and pietist traditions and the writings of Jacob Boehme, the 16th century mystic and philosopher. He left the Palatinate area in 1720, migrating to the United States and settling in western Pennsylvania, a seat of Anabaptist dissenters. There he came under the tutelage of Peter Becker, a weaver and leader of the German Baptist congregation at Germantown.

Toward the end of 1728, Beissel decided to separate himself from the Germantown Baptists, and in 1732, he established a hermitage at Ephrata, near Lancaster City, where followers soon gathered. They followed a monastic regime, with celibacy, community of goods, and common worship central to their belief. Members of the congregation initially lived in isolated huts, but in 1735 they all moved to a central building. They then began wearing a monastic habit, writing spiritual confessions, observing Judaic customs, and adhering to Beissel's rule. That rule was often autocratic, but his spiritual leadership was profound and long lasting. He often compared himself to Christ and taught that his followers had to conquer their flesh and lead purified lives. The membership at Ephrata eventually reached three hundred, though there were often disputes between Beissel and others who sought to assert their spiritual rule. During the 1750s, the number of monks and sisters declined, and during Beissel's late years the colony deteriorated. During his declining years, Beissel drank heavily. In 1770, a land transfer agreement enabled individuals to hold land in their own right with some trustee supervision.

SELECTED WORKS: *Beissel's Dissertation on Harmony* (1747); *A Dissertation on Man's Fall* (1765).
SOURCES: James E. Ernst, *Ephrata: A History* (1963); Walter C. Klein, *Johann Conrad Beissel: Mystic and Martinet* (1972 reprint); *DAB* 2.

BELLAMY, EDWARD (b. March 26, 1850, Chicopee Falls, Massachusetts; d. May 22, 1898, Chicopee Falls, Massachusetts), writer and social visionary. Bellamy was responsible for the upsurge in utopian thinking and planning in the late nineteenth century. He was educated at local schools and attended Union College briefly in 1868 before studying for the law. In 1880, he founded the *Springfield News* and in that same year published *Dr. Heidenhoff's Process*, a science fiction work. With the publication in 1888 of *Looking Backward*, Bellamy became a celebrity and the book an enormous success, both in the United States and abroad. This utopian romance expressed the hope that cooperation was possible and that national socialism could be achieved by peaceful means. The work also suggested that rational planning and a humane social order could be found and a new religion of humanity developed. Bellamy Clubs were formed to study the work, and Nationalist Clubs started to implement the social philosophy expressed in the novel. Out of these Nationalist Clubs several colony ventures developed Kaweah* (see also Appendix A, No. 189), and Altruria* (see Appendix A, No. 203), and figures like Cyrus Willard* emerged as colony leaders at later dates.

In 1891, Bellamy founded *The New Nation,* a journal devoted to the philosophy of social improvement and progress; it lasted until 1894. When the Nationalist movement failed to gain any political power, many of its members drifted into the Populist party. In 1894, Bellamy published *Equality,* a powerful novel that contained a strong critique of industrial capitalism. Bellamy never believed that individual utopian colonies were the key to societal change. Rather, he thought that a national network of organizations committed to cooperation and peaceful change could press for social change through moral suasion and the ballot box. Bellamy spent most of his life at Chicopee Falls and died there.

SELECTED WORKS: Dr. Heidenhoff's Process (1880); *Looking Backward 2000-1887.* (1888); *Equality* (1898); *The Duke of Stockbridge* (1900).

SOURCES: Sylvia Bowman, *Edward Bellamy Abroad* (1962); Arthur Morgan, *Edward Bellamy* (1975 reprint); Kenneth Roemer, *The Obsolete Necessity* (1976).

BELLANGEE, JAMES (b. ca. 1844; d. August 7, 1915, Fairhope, Alabama), leader of Fairhope* (see also Appendix A, No. 211). After graduating from the University of Michigan with a M.S. in 1868, Bellangee taught at the University of Illinois from 1869 to 1873. Later he became a professor of mathematics at the State Normal School of Nebraska and then a school principal in several midwestern states. He was the editor of the journal *Opinion and Outlook,* a single tax journal, published in Des Moines in 1890. In 1892, he was temporary chairman of the Peoples party meeting held at Omaha and was their candidate for state auditor that year. He was a member of the Des Moines Single Tax Club in 1893 and during that period taught classes in science and mathematics at the Des Moines Collegiate Institute. During the 1892 presidential campaign, Belangee worked behind the scenes to unite the Populists with the Democrats. After that effort failed, his interests again turned to the single tax, and in 1894 he became one of the leaders in the Fairhope Single Tax Corporation in Alabama. During this period, he wrote for the *Arena* and the *Progressive Economist.*

Fairhope was founded by socialists who wanted to establish according to their constitution a "model community or colony, free from all forms of private monopoly" and followers of Henry George who wanted to put his single-tax principles to work. George had urged that the government tax the full annual use value of land and should levy no other taxes. From this land tax all community services would be provided. It was both a plan for fiscal reform and a system that would enhance individual freedom by eliminating injurious taxes. Bellangee was the spokesman for a group within the colony who believed that all capital expenditures for public services should be financed from ground rents. This "pay as you go" policy was opposed by a group who wanted to provide services even if some deficits were incurred. In 1904, Bellangee traveled about the country lecturing for the single tax and the colony. In 1905, he was defeated in a colony election for treasurer after some colonists objected to higher rentals. He remained an influential member till his death, but did not hold office after his treasurer election defeat.

SOURCES: Paul and Blanche Alyea, *Fairhope, 1894-1954* (1956); Frederick Haynes, *Third Party Movements* (1966).

BIMELER, JOSEPH (b. 1778, Wurttemberg, Germany; d. August 27, 1853, Zoar, Ohio), founder of the Society of Separatists of Zoar (see Appendix A, No. 25) in Tuscarawas County, Ohio. Bimeler was born into a poor family and had several physical disabilities, including a lame leg and a large protruding eye. He was self-educated and served as a teacher among the persecuted Separatists at Wurttemberg for ten years before joining some three hundred followers of the mystic Barbara Gruberman on their journey to America in 1817. During the journey, Bimeler nursed the sick and gave religious instructions.

When the group moved westward to Ohio after landing in America, Bimeler emerged as a leader. The Separatists were one of the many German sects that migrated to the United States in the seventeenth and eighteenth centuries. In their revolt against what they considered the decadent practices of the Lutheran church, they embraced a simple belief system based on the Sermon on the Mount. They were opposed to war and refused to bear arms; they refused to take oaths and to acknoweldge their temporal rulers; they rejected baptism, confirmation, and other established practices. For this they were persecuted. As a member of the first large party on the 5,500 acres which the group purchased, Bimeler helped clear the land and plan the first settlement. The group decided to lead celibate lives until the land was paid for, and in a brief period they were operating successful industries, including a brewery and woolen and linen mills. Under Bimeler's autocratic but benign leadership the colony prospered. Marriage was reinstated after Bimeler fell in love with one of his maidservants. It was a model Christian community with well-landscaped gardens and a firm commercial foundation. Much of the colony's growth and prosperity was due to Bimeler's business acumen. There were suits brought against the group in 1851 and

1861 by former members seeking property, but these were decided in the colony's favor. During the post-Civil War period, there was a slow economic decline at Zoar and in 1898 the 222 colony members agreed to divide the property on an equitable basis. In 1875, the colony's worth had been estimated at $1 million.

SELECTED WORKS: Die Wahre Separation (1858-1860); *Etwas furs herz!* (1860-1861).
SOURCE: E. Randall, *History of the Zoar Society* (1904).

BLINN, HENRY CLAY (b. July 16, 1824, Providence, Rhode Island; d. April 1, 1905, East Canterbury, New Hampshire), associated with Shaker Community at Canterbury (see Appendix A, No. 8). Blinn attended Providence public schools and at age thirteen was apprenticed to a jeweler. In 1838, he visited the Shaker colony at Canterbury, New Hampshire, and gained admittance to the First, or Church, family. He attended school at the colony and in 1842 was placed in charge of the Canterbury school. Blinn was to make his mark as a printer and publicist, and in 1849 he became the colony printer. He was appointed to the ministry in 1852 and became senior elder in 1859. By 1859, there were fifty-seven men and seventy-three women at Canterbury. In 1863, Blinn received a draft notice for service in the Union Army but was placed on permanent furlough by the local official.

During the 1870s and 1880s, Blinn frequently traveled to various Shaker societies. His *The Manifestations of Spiritualism Among the Shakers* (1899) and *The Life and Gospel Experience of Mother Ann Lee* (1883) helped to explain the Shaker society to the outside world during the colony's declining years. On his death, he was memorialized by the *Concord Evening Monitor* as "the embodiment of most of the traditions of old time Shakerism, though it was due to him in large measure, also, that Shakerism adapted itself to modern life and maintained itself in the face of adverse social conditions."

SELECTED WORKS: A Sacred Repository of Anthems and Hymns (1852); *The Life and Gospel Experience of Mother Ann Lee* (1883); *Advent of the Christ in Man and Woman* (1896); *The Manifestations of Spiritualism Among the Shakers, 1837-1847* (1899).
SOURCES: Edward D. Andrews, *The People Called Shakers* (1965 reprint); H. C. Blinn, *In Memoriam* (1905).

BOOKWALTER, JOHN WESLEY (b. June 30, 1839, Rob Roy, Indiana; d. September 25, 1915, Springfield, Ohio), founder of the model town Bookwalter, Nebraska. In 1860, Bookwalter moved to Springfield, Ohio, where he married the daughter of a prominent manufacturer, James Leffel, and took a leading position with his father-in-law's company. During the presidential campaign of 1872, he became a Democrat. He won the Democratic nomination for governor in 1881, only to lose the election by a narrow margin. Earlier, during the 1870s, he purchased large tracts of land in Nebraska; two decades later, he used the land as the basis for a utopian experiment in village life based on the French system where farmers lived in villages and went out to till the surrounding lands. He was a free silver advocate, publishing *If Not Silver, What?* in 1896, and was an opponent of urbanization, which he attacked in *Rural vs. Urban* (1896).

By 1891, Bookwalter had accumulated a considerable fortune, had traveled widely, and had both the means and experience to attempt an experiment in rural utopianism on a fifteen thousand acre tract in Shawnee County, Nebraska. He hoped to make farm life attractive by constructing a town at the center of an agricultural district and having the tenants live in the town rather than out on the land. He hoped that Bookwalter, Nebraska, would be a model town with a free library and a town hall for meetings and the theater. Although it was not socialistic or communal, one newspaper believed that "it . . . may be said to lean in that direction." By 1897, the village population had reached one hundred, but there is no evidence that a cooperative village based on French village life ever developed. Bookwalter believed that farmers needed "to come together, to organize for their mutual good and here they will have an opportunity to do so." Much of his wealth was spent to benefit his neighbors in Springfield, Ohio, where he endowed a chair in philosophy at Wittenberg College.

SELECTED WORKS: If Not Silver, What (1896); *Rural vs. Urban* (1896).

SOURCES: Musetta Gilman, "Bookwalter, Agricultural Commune in Nebraska," *Nebraska History* (Spring 1975); *Biographical Cyclopedia and Portrait Gallery* (1883), I.

BORLAND, WILFRED (b. 1860; d.?), a founder of Cooperative Brotherhood or Burley Colony* (see Appendix A, No. 218). Borland was a railway fireman until a train accident in 1889 crippled him. He then turned to journalism, writing for labor periodicals such as the *Fireman's Magazine* and the *Railway Times*. In 1897, he became editor of the *Social Democrat,* the organ of the Social Democracy of America group. He was one of the commission members selected to serve on the party's colonization committee, along with Cyrus Willard,* a journalist, and Richard Hinton,* an English-born socialist. After the 1898 Social Democracy convention split over the colonization issue, Borland joined the Burley, Washington, Cooperative Brotherhood Colony where he edited the colony journal, *The Cooperator.* The colony was based on the collective ownership, distribution, and manufacture of goods. It was essentially a corporation run by twelve directors chosen by legal stockholders. The colony, located on 294 acres in Kitsap County, was originally settled by sixteen persons.

Borland left the colony in 1900 and worked in government service during the remainder of his years. According to Charles LeWarne, Borland gambled away colony funds in California and that may have precipitated his departure.

SOURCE: Charles LeWarne, *Utopias on Puget Sound* (1975).

BORSODI, RALPH (b. December 20, 1886, New York City; d. October 28, 1977, Exeter, New Hampshire), decentralist philosopher and community organizer. Although Borsodi attended private school for a few years, much of his early education came from his own reading. He was influenced by Locke, Paine, Schopenhauer, Nietzsche, and, in particular, Zola's *Emile*. American writers such as Henry George, Bolton Hall, and Fiske Warren also shaped his thinking. He was active in the Single Tax party and editor of the *Single Taxer*. After working for his father's publishing firm, he started his own marketing and advertising service.

In 1919, Borsodi moved his family to Suffern, New York, where they established a decentralist homestead. They yearned for self-sufficiency and independence from the limitations of city life and their dependence on others for their survival. He experimented with labor- and money-saving mechanical devices (the pressure cooker, sewing machine) in order to maximize the family's self-sufficiency. The Borsodis farmed, canned foods, and made some of their own clothing. In the next fourteen years, he published a number of critiques of modern economy: *National Advertising and Prosperity* (1923), which was an analysis of the economics of advertising and the adverse effect it had on the producer and consumer; *The Distribution Age* (1926) where he looked at the question of why distribution costs were more than production costs; *This Ugly Civilization* (1928), which examined the factory system and its consequences for American democracy; *Flight from the City* (1933), which is an account of his homesteading experience at Suffern. In 1933, Borsodi was involved in planning for the first subsistence homestead unit formed under local sponsorship to receive federal support from the Farm Resettlement Agency. The goal of the plan was to settle families in units around Dayton, Ohio, where, on an acre and a third, families could grow their own food, raise some animals, and supplement their farm income with cash-paying jobs in the immediate area. It operated from May 1933 to December 1935.

After the Dayton project failed, Borsodi established the School of Living at Suffern to test his decentralist ideas. At the School of Living (their home), they tested products and kept careful records of all home experiments in domestic production. They published a series of bulletins on sewing, weaving, knitting, and home canning. In 1935, he helped start the Bayard Lane Community, a decentralist homestead town, and other projects at Nyack and Stillwater, New York, and Ringwood, New Jersey, with the aid of the Independence Foundation, established in 1935 to promote self-sufficient agricultural colonies. Those projects in community ownership failed to grow, and Borsodi was forced to resign as director of the School of Living in 1941.

In 1940, Borsodi wrote *Prosperity and Security* and in 1943, *Inflation Is Coming* in which he turned his attention from community projects to commodity-based currency. In 1966, he moved to Melbourne Homestead Village in Florida and was associated with Melbourne University. He spent four years in India during the 1960s and lived out his last years in Exeter, New Hampshire, working on his monetary theories. He had little success as an organizer of community projects, but his writings on home economy, his insistence on quality living, and his critique of industrialism helped sustain the anarchist tradition.

SELECTED WORKS: National Advertising and Prosperity (1923); *The Distribution Age* (1926); *This Ugly Civilization* (1928); *Flight from the City* (1933); *Inflation Is Coming* (1943).

SOURCES: Robert S. Fogarty, "Ralph Borsodi: Decentralist and Community Builder," Introduction to *This Ugly Civilization* (1975 reprint); *The Green Revolution* (December 1977).

BRAY, R. E. (b. 1862, New York State; d. ?), leader of the Llano del Rio Company of Nevada (see Appendix A, No. 268). Bray homesteaded in Oklahoma in 1889, but shortly thereafter he moved to Kansas to work for several newspapers, among them the *Wellington People's Voice* and the *Hutcheson Gazette*. He was involved in Populist politics for a time, and in 1892 he led a delegation in the state convention to nominate "Sockless" Jerry Simpson for the Congress. After 1892, he returned to Oklahoma where he founded *Coming Events* at Enid and worked for papers in Oklahoma City. Between 1900 and 1913, he moved around the country working for numerous papers in Illinois and New York.

In 1915, Bray joined the Llano Colony and in 1917 he became a director of Llano del Rio of Nevada Colony (see Appendix A, No. 268), the spinoff from the original group in southern California. He was the colony's chief publicist and promoter, and the printer of the colony paper *The Cooperative Colonist*. In his effort to promote the Nevada Colony, Bray bombarded socialist and cooperative papers throughout the country with material. During 1917, he ran the community and was the driving force behind its reorganization. When he attempted to consolidate his control of the society, a group of dissident socialists organized to oust him through legal action. In October 1918, he sold his interest in the colony and, just prior to its collapse, in 1918 moved to Washington, D.C. There is no record of his later life.

SOURCE: Wilbur Shepperson, *Retreat to Nevada: A Socialist Colony of World War I* (1966).

BRISBANE, ALBERT (b. Batavia, New York, August 22, 1809; d. May 1, 1890, Richmond, Virginia), social reformer and Fourierist propagandist. Brisbane was born in the Holland Purchase section of western New York into an entrepreneurial family. After a private education at a boarding school, he moved to New York where he embraced the theories of John Monesca who had devised a new system for the teaching of living languages. Brisbane studied French under Monesca, and in 1828 he went to Europe. In Paris, he associated with the eclectic philosopher Victor Cousin and the historian François Guizot, and then he journeyed to Berlin to study and to hear Hegel. Beginning in 1830, Brisbane embarked on a course of independent travel throughout southern Europe, observing a wide range of social conditions, an experience unique for an American in that period. As a result of his travels, he became convinced that social misery could be alleviated only by a fundamental reconstruction of society.

After a brief involvement with Saint-Simonism in 1831, Brisbane turned toward the theories of Charles Fourier whom he met in 1832. Fourier agreed to tutor Brisbane in his philosophy, and when Brisbane returned to New York in 1834, he began to promote his mentor's ideas. By 1839, little had been accomplished to spread those ideas beyond the existence of a Fourierist society and the publication of Fourier's essay, *The Social System of Charles Fourier.* In 1840, Brisbane published his *Social Destiny of Man; or, Association and Reorganization of Industry,* which was a complete exposition of Fourierism for an American audience. In addition, he launched *The Phalanx* (1843-1845), a short-lived periodical for the movement, and traveled widely explaining Fourier's system. In March 1842, he purchased space in Horace Greeley's* *Tribune* for a weekly column on Fourierism. Through the *Tribune*, Brisbane reached a wide audience and popularized the system by defining it in relation to other reforms of the day. Throughout the 1840s, he wrote and lectured about Fourierism. He remained convinced of its practicality even after the colonies had failed.

During the late 1860s, Brisbane was associated with Charles Sears, Elijah Grant* and Ernest Valeton de Boissiere* in the Silkville,* Kansas, venture (see also Appendix A, No. 148). During the same period he was associated with the American Social Science Association in its efforts to promote rational and scientific planning.

After 1877, he moved to France where he continued to write and to work on his inventions. He invented a system of transportation by means of hollow spheres in pneumatic tubes; a system of underground fertilization; a compressed wood pavement; and an oven designed to cook in a vacuum. In fall 1889, he returned to America and during his travels in the South died at Richmond, Virginia.

SELECTED WORKS: A Concise Exposition of the Doctrine of Association (1843);

The Social Destiny of Man (1857); *Philosophy of Money* (1863); *General Introduction to the Social Sciences* (1876).

SOURCES: Arthur Bestor, Jr., "Albert Brisbane—Propagandist for Socialism in the 1840s," *New York History* (April 1947); Redelia Brisbane, *Albert Brisbane* (1893).

BULLARD, ISAAC (b. ?; d. ?), prophet to the Pilgrims (see Appendix A, No. 26). Little is known about Bullard's life prior to the time he led the "Mummyjums" from Canada to the Southwest in search of the New Jerusalem. The "Mummyjums" were so called because of the chant they employed: "My God, My God, What wouldst thou have me do?— Mummyjum, Mummyjum." They began their pilgrimage under Bullard's leadership in 1816. Their religious beliefs were governed by Bullard's inspirations and his dislike for formal organized religions. Sect members fasted, prayed, and never bathed or changed their garments. During 1817 Bullard converted a Methodist minister, John Ball, in Woodstock, Vermont, and the group settled in that area for a brief time. They lived a communal life (there were about ten members) and shared a common purse of about $10,000. In July 1817, Bullard received a celestial message to strike out for the Southwest and seek the Promised Land. By that time, the group numbered about fifty-five, but by March 1818 the group had dwindled because of sickness and Bullard's erratic revelations. For example, he commanded them to eat standing up and to suck their food through straws. The pilgrimage ended in Arkansas on a desolate island with the prophet, his wife, his child (named Christ), and another small family living in squalor. It is estimated that half the members perished during the journey, with ten of the members joining the Shaker Community at Union Village, Ohio (see Appendix A, No. 18), during the trip.

SOURCES: Timothy Flint, *Recollections of the Last Ten Years* (1826); F. Gerald Ham, "The Prophet and the Mummyjums, Isaac Bullard and the Vermont Pilgrims of 1817," *Wisconsin Magazine of History* (Summer 1973).

BYERS, ABRAHAMS S. (b. ?; d. ca. 1935), founder of the Hiawatha Village Association (see Appendix A, No. 201) at Manistique, Michigan. In 1882, Byers moved from Bangor, Michigan, to the Upper Peninsula where he began homesteading. After reading Walter Thomas Mills' *The Product Sharing Village* (1894), Byers wrote to Mills offering his farm as the site for a cooperative experiment. Under Mills' guidance, the Hiawatha Village Association was formed in 1893 from several farms in the surrounding area with the main objective of providing "equalization for everybody." A $100 membership fee was required, and a time-credit labor system was used for work and community exchange. The colony assets consisted of 1,080 acres of land, 125 head of cattle, and 25 horses. Those who gave $1,000 in cash or property were exempt from labor and awarded time credits like the workers received. One-time credit was granted for each hour's labor and the time credits could be exchanged for supplies at the association store. The colony paper, *The Industrial Christian,* stated in 1895, "Let every man, woman and child use his or her strongest energy in defending, in spreading and in perpetuating the ideas of the product-sharing village begun here." This community of socialists farmed, operated a sawmill, and erected several dwellings for the families involved. They recruited their membership from laboring circles. The colony began to disintegrate in late 1895 after Mills resigned as president. In 1896, the land reverted back to family ownership.

It was Byers who provided the initial impetus behind the colony's founding. The core of the Hiawatha Colony consisted of the Byers settlement and six other farms. Byers had deeded 240 acres to the new association, and after the split up in 1896, he received 120 back. Nothing is known of his later life.

SOURCES: David C. Byers and Willis F. Dunbar, "Utopia in Upper Michigan," *Quarterly Review* (1955).

C

CABET, ETIENNE (b. January 1, 1788, Dijon, France; d. November 8, 1858, St. Louis, Illinois), born into the family of a master cooper and educated at local schools. He attended the Dijon School of Law and received his law degree in 1812. Between 1812 and 1820, he defended several liberal politicians and officials and acquired a reputation in the area for his opposition to Bourbon rule. During the same period he associated with Lafayette and the Charbonnerie, the radical group opposed to the government. From 1824 to 1827, he was a limited partner in a bank financed by liberal lawyers and bankers. In 1827, he published a political pamphlet *Une Expose d'une revolution necessaire dans le gouvernement de France*, which was a defense of republican government. After the Revolution of 1830 he was appointed the chief judicial officer of Corsica, but the appointment was revoked when Cabet decided to run for the Chamber of Deputies. He was elected. In 1833, he published *La Revolution de 1830*, which supported the role of the working class and condemned the monarchy. In that same year he published a journal, *Le Populaire* aimed at and for the working class. His philosophy in 1833 has been described by Christopher Johnson as "non-Jacobin republicanism adorned with a humanitarian desire to better the conditions of the working classes."

In 1834, *Le Populaire* was indicted on two counts for publishing articles against Louis Philippe. In order to avoid jail Cabet chose to take another punishment, a five-year exile. From 1834 to 1839, he lived in London where he met and was influenced by Robert Owen.* By late 1838, he had completed his *History of the French Revolution* and *Voyage en Icarie*, a utopian fantasy. Both were published in 1839. In *Voyage en Icarie* Cabet described a centrally planned, but egalitarian state where neither property, money, courts, or police existed. The book had an enormous appeal to the French working class because his utopia promised a world of both political freedom and material abundance.

He returned to Paris in 1839 and for the next ten years directed the Icarian movement. He was a major spokesman for communism, and he preached pacificism, fraternity, equality and adherence to the legal system. In 1841, he began publication once again of *Le Populaire.* During the 1840s Cabet toyed with the idea of establishing an experimental community, but it was not until an article appeared in the May 1847 issue of *Le Populaire* that he urged "Workers, let us go to Icaria." Between 1848 and 1858, three Icarian communities were established in America. In December 1848, he sailed for New York in an effort to salvage the abortive first colony established in Texas in March 1948. That group relocated in Nauvoo, Illinois, in 1849. Cabet returned in Paris in 1850 and remained involved in revolutionary activity against Louis Napoleon.

In 1854, Cabet became an American citizen. He held the presidency of the society at Nauvoo until 1855 when some dissidents ousted him. Cabet, with 150 supporters, left and established a colony in St. Louis. He died there shortly after the move.

SELECTED WORKS: *Le Revolution de 1830* (1833); *Histoire populaire de la Revolution francais* (1839-40); *Voyage en Icarie* (1839).

SOURCES: Christopher Johnson, *Utopian Communism in France: Cabet and the Icarian, 1839-1851* (1974); Albert Shaw, *Icaria, A Chapter in the History of Communism* (1884); *DAB*, 3.

CHASE, WARREN B. (b. January 3, 1813, Pittsfield, New Hampshire; d. 1891, Cobden, Illinois), social reformer and political radical. Chase was born out of wedlock, and his mother died when he was five. He had a difficult childhood, for, upon his mother's death, he was bound out as a farmhand to a brutal taskmaster. As a young man, he headed west to find work in the Michigan Territory, marrying there in 1838 and then moving to Southport (now Kenosha), Wisconsin.

Chase was attracted to the writings of Emmanuel Swedenborg and Charles Fourier. He wrote and lectured on scientific rationalism, social science, and Fourierism. In 1844, a discussion group in which he participated decided to put into practice an American version of Fourier's philosophy. They obtained land at Ripon, Wisconsin, and started the Wisconsin Phalanx (see Appendix A, No. 87) which they named Ceresco after the Roman goddess of grain. Chase drew up the initial charter and steered its passage through the territorial legislature. In 1847, he was elected to the state constitutional convention as a delegate from Fond du Lac County. In this role, he was active in arguing for prohibition of capital punishment, for removal of discrimination based on race and sex in voting qualifications, and for the abolition of private ownership of land not occupied by the owner. He argued against an organized militia and against laws for the collection of debts. In 1848, when Wisconsin became a state, he was elected to the State Senate and continued to agitate for reforms. In 1850, the Ceresco Community broke up. Chase planned and executed the settlement and distribution of the group's assets. It was a credit to his integrity that there were no lawsuits over the dissolution—a rare situation in communal history. Its dissolution resulted from several factors: a lack of working capital, a slow erosion of communal practices (the common eating table was abandoned), and the development of towns nearby which attracted the colonists.

In 1872, Chase was a presidential elector on the Greeley* ticket as a St. Louis, Missouri, resident. Later he moved to San Bernardino, California, where he was a newspaper editor and a member of the California State Senate. His moving autobiography, *The Life Line of the Lone One* (1855), recounts his early reform career, but little is known of his later life.

SELECTED WORKS: *The Life Line of the Lone One* (1855); *The Fugitive Wife* (1861); *The American Crisis* (1865); *Essence and Substance* (1866); *Forty Years on the Spiritual Rostrum* (1888).
SOURCES: "Warren Chase—Activist Pioneer on the Frontiers of Thought," *Wisconsin Then and Now* (October 1973).

COHEN, JOSEPH B. (b. 1881, Russia; d. September 28, 1953, New York City), founder of the Sunrise Community.* Cohen was born into an artisan Jewish family and studied to be a rabbi at the seminary in Mir. However, his studies moved into radical and revolutionary literature, and at one point he was arrested by the Czarist police. In 1898, he served in the Czarist army at Grodono and developed a libertarian philosophy while in the service. In 1903, he emigrated to Philadelphia where he worked as a cigarmaker and associated with anarchists. During his ten years in Philadelphia, he helped found the Radical Library, a center for libertarian education. In 1913, he came to New York and became involved with the Ferrer Center, and in 1916 he moved with it to Stelton, New Jersey. He remained in the Ferrer Colony* until 1925 when he began to turn his full attention to editing the *Freie Arbeiter Stimme*, the Jewish libertarian paper which he edited until 1932. In that year, he founded the Sunrise Community at Saginaw, Michigan. Many of the members were Jewish anarchists from New York. The colony lasted until 1939. Cohen left it in 1938 because litigation by former members had placed the colony in jeopardy and lived for a while at the Home Colony, near Seattle. In 1946, he traveled to Mexico and then to France where he edited the Yiddish anarchist magazine, *Der Freier Gedank.* He returned to the United States in 1952 and died in New York in 1953. His autobiographical memoir, *In Quest of Heaven* (1935), details his early career and cooperative experiences at Sunrise.

SELECTED WORKS: *In Quest of Heaven* (1935); *Anarchism and Anarchists* (1945); *The House Stood Forlorn* (1954).
SOURCE: Laurence Veysey, *The Communal Experience* (1973).

COLLINS, JOHN ANDERSON (b. ca. 1810, Vermont; d. April 3, 1890), abolitionist, perfectionist, and founder of the Skaneateles Community* (see also Appendix A, No. 72). Collins attended Middlebury College and graduated from Andover Theological Seminary. During the 1830s, he worked with William Lloyd Garrison in the Massachusetts Anti-Slavery Society, and in 1840 he journeyed to England to raise funds for the society. While in England, he attended Chartist lectures, talked with Robert Owen,* and read French and English socialist tracts. On his return to America, he turned from Garrisonian perfectionism to a communal solution for human misery.

As general agent for the American Anti-Slavery Society, Collins organized the One Hundred Convention in 1843 at Syracuse where the abolitionists hoped to increase their membership in the "western states." Although he was paid to promote the abolitionist cause, his first interest was in other reforms, and he used the slavery issue to promote them. During the spring of 1843, discussions were held by individuals interested in founding a colony at Skaneateles* (see Appendix A, No. 72) in Syracuse, New York, and the rough outlines of a joint-stock society emerged. In October 1843, a convention was held on the site, with Collins and other reformers like John Wattles, Ernestine Rose, and Nathaniel Peabody Rogers in attendance. Out of this convention the Skaneateles Community emerged, with Collins the leading figure. Practical operation on a full scale began in January 1844, but Collins alienated some of the ninety residents with his radical views on property, religion, and marriage. Some called him "No God, No Government, No Money, No Meat, No Salt and Pepper" Collins. Yet, reports by visitors to the community indicated a prosperous one by the end of 1845, and the group's paper, *The Communitist,* carried a range of reform notes. Robert Owen visited in May, 1845. In May 1846, Collins resigned his position, even though its economic future was bright. In the public press, Collins announced he had abandoned his plans for radical renovation, and it was sardonically noted that he was returning to the "decencies and respectability of Whiggery." In June 1849, he moved to California to prospect for gold.

While in California, Collins organized a National Cooperative Homestead Society which was directed at reforming the industrial system by organizing production and distributive cooperatives. In addition, he was an active spiritualist and served as president of the Society of Progressive Spiritualists just prior to his death.

SOURCES: *The Carrier Dove* (April 1890); John L. Thomas, "Anti-Slavery and Utopia," in Martin Duberman (ed.), *The Anti-Slavery Vanguard* (1965); Lester G. Wells, "The Skaneateles Communal Experiment, 1843-1846," Onandaga Historical Association, Syracuse, New York, 1953.

CONSIDERANT, VICTOR PROSPER (b. October 12, 1808, Salina, Jura, France; d. December 27, 1893, Paris, France), leader of the Reunion Colony* (see Appendix A, No. 127). Considerant was educated at the Ecole Polytechnique and became a captain in the engineering division of the French army. In 1830, he gave up his military career to publicize the theories of Charles Fourier, helped establish the journal *Le Phalanstere*, and published a series of pamphlets detailing and explicating Fourier's ideas. His three-volume work, *Destinee Sociale* (1835-1844), was his most important. According to Rondel Davidson, Considerant worked out his basic social theory in *Destinee Sociale:* "He [Considerant] assumed the basic goodness and perfectability of mankind and argued that man was intellectually and morally capable of controlling his own destiny. What was needed was a total reorganization of man's social and economic institutions and in his mind."

After Fourier's death in 1837, Considerant became the acknowledged leader of the French cooperative movement and established a Fourierist daily, *La Democratic Pacifique* (1843). After the Revolution of 1848, he was elected to represent Loire in the Constitutional Assembly but, with Louis Napoleon's ascendancy, had to flee France in 1849.

In 1852, Considerant visited America and met with Albert Brisbane,* the American popularizer of Fourier, and traveled as far west as Texas. On his return to Europe, he published *Au Texas* (1854) and promoted a colonization scheme for Texas. A company was formed with a capitalization of $300,000, and in April 1855, the first contingent of colonists settled at Reunion, within the limits of the city of Dallas. Reunion was a Fourierist society where Considerant believed he could provide the proper structure to realign man's social and economic drives. At Reunion man's passions would be directed into their proper social spheres and away from the destructive attraction of civilization.

After two successive droughts, however, the colony began to disintegrate. In addition, the colony was attacked by Know Nothings in the state; Considerant responded with his pamphlet *European Colonization in Texas, An Address to the American People* (1857). With the finances of the colony shaky, he moved to San Antonio. He eventually took out American citizenship and remained in America until 1859 when he returned to Paris. He died there in poverty.

SELECTED WORKS: *Au Texas* (1845); *Destinee Sociale*, 3 vols. (1835-1844); *European Colonization in Texas, An Address to the American People* (1857).

SOURCES: Rondel Davidson, "Victor Considerant and the Failure of La Reunion," *Southwestern Historical Quarterly* (January 1973); *DAB* 4.

COPELAND, WILBUR F. (b. 1869; d. ?), founder of the Straight Edge Industrial Settlement* (see also Appendix A, No. 224). This son of a Methodist minister was educated at Ohio Wesleyan and graduated in 1889. After graduation, he worked with the university president and then with Funk and Wagnall's Publishing House before going to New York City to work in rescue houses.

While working for the board of education of the Methodist church in New York, Copeland called a meeting in 1898 to launch a practical experiment in Christianity. Among those who attended the meeting were the reformer and philanthropist Ernest H. Crosby, who later contributed support to Copeland's venture. In May 1899, the Straight Edge Society was formed. It called itself a "School of Methods for the Application of the Teaching of Jesus to Business and Society." Copeland was a Christian Socialist who had been influenced by religious revivals while a student at Ohio Wesleyan and by the writings of Edward Bellamy,* Laurence Gronlund,* and Leo Tolstoy. His colony was, in effect, a settlement house in lower Manhattan run on cooperative principles. He did not believe that the group should separate from the rest of society; he considered his mission an urban one. He had wide-ranging support, including that of Edward Everett Hale, the utopian author and reformer, and M. R. Heber Newton, the Unitarian minister.

Copeland was a life-long advocate of cooperation rather than of communalism, and during the 1930s he attempted to get a Farm Resettlement Loan to start a subsistence homesteading colony in New Jersey. That project never materialized. Copeland's later activities are unknown.

SELECTED WORKS: *The Straight Edge* (1899-1921).

SOURCE: William Hinds, *American Communities and Co-operative Colonies* (1908 ed.), 548-555.

CURTIS, GEORGE WILLIAM (b. February 24, 1824, Providence, Rhode Island; d. August 31, 1892, Staten Island, New York), editor and social reformer. Curtis was born into an old New England family. In 1839, his family moved to New York City where young Curtis held a clerkship. In 1842, he and his brother Burris went to Brook Farm* (see also Appendix A, No. 53) to study. He had read Emerson since 1832 and had become his follower. At Brook Farm he was a boarder, having made a half-work, half-pay arrangement with the community. During his brief period at the colony, he tried the varied fads that swept the colony but left in the autumn of 1843 to return to New York. His arcadian adventure increased his desire for the simple life, for he and his brother rented a single room in a farmer's house and "lived like Essenes."

Although Curtis wrote for both *The Dial* and *The Harbinger*, he supported an individualist rather than a communal society. In 1846, he left New York and traveled in the Near East, an experience which resulted in the publication of *Nile Notes of Howadji* (1851) and *The Howadji at Syria* (1852). In 1856, he became an associate editor of *Putnam's Monthly*. In addition to his writing, he was well known for his oratorical abilities, particularly on patriotic themes. As editor of *Harper's Weekly*, he wrote in favor of the enfranchisement of women, the need for the reconciliation of capital and labor, and civil service reform.

Grant appointed him to the Civil Service Commission in 1871, and he championed liberal Republican issues in the 1870s. In 1884, he bolted the party and formed a group of Independent Republicans, or Mugwumps. In the 1880s, he gained a national reputation as an orator and was often called on to make lofty statements at public ceremonies. Curtis epitomized the "genteel tradition" in the period after the war. His essays were always positive, his faith in the individual secure, and his belief in American morality and democracy deep.

SELECTED WORKS: *Nile Notes of Howadji* (1851); *The Duty of the American Scholar to Politics and the Times* (1856); *Trumps* (1856); *Literary and Social Essays* (1894).
SOURCES: George Willis Cooke, *An Historical and Biographical Introduction to Accompany the Dial* (1961); *DAB* 4.

D

DANA, CHARLES ANDERSON (b. August 8, 1819, Hinsdale, New Hampshire; d. October 17, 1897, New York City), newspaper editor, reformer, and novelist. Dana came from a poor family. His father was an unsuccessful storekeeper, and his mother died when he was five. He was reared by an uncle until the Panic of 1837 forced him out on his own. In 1839, he matriculated at Harvard, but left in 1841 because of failing eyesight. His leaving Harvard coincided with George Ripley's* organization of the Brook Farm* (see also Appendix A, No. 53) experiment. Dana became a member and stayed for five years. While at Brook Farm, he taught school, sang in the choir, and wrote and lectured extensively. His essays and poems were published in *The Harbinger* and *The Dial.*

After leaving Brook Farm, Dana traveled extensively in the United States and Europe, an experience which modified some of his earlier idealism. Dana had visited during the revolutionary years of 1848-1849, and he had been in Paris and Berlin when the revolutions had taken place. This experience chastened his idealism, and he developed a cynical attitude toward politicians.

During the 1850s, he held major editorial positions with Horace Greeley's* *New York Tribune*, often acting as editor while Greeley traveled or lectured. In 1862, a dispute arose with Greeley over the *Tribune*'s policy on the war. Greeley objected to Dana's bellicose support of the war and forced his resignation. In 1867, Dana acquired the *New York Sun* and under his leadership the paper supported the worst of Tammany Hall and opposed the reformers. By this period he had fully abandoned his early reform interests at Brook Farm. Dana opposed labor unions and was often capricious in his political stands. He opposed Cleveland because he had refused to appoint a friend to public office and in 1884 supported the Greenback party rather than back Blaine. Yet his newspaper the *Sun* set a high standard for reporting and it attracted distinguished writers in the 1890s like Jacob Riis and Richard H. Davis.

SELECTED WORKS: *A Lecture on Association* (1844); *Recollections on the Civil War* (1898).
SOURCE: *DAB* 5.

DANCKAERTS, JASPER (b. May 7, 1639, Flushing, Zeeland; d. ca. 1702, Middleburgh, Netherlands), a founder of the Labadist Colony in Cecil County, Maryland. Danckaerts was a cooper in the service of the East India Company and a member of the Labadist sect at Middleburgh, Netherlands, founded by Jean de Labadie, a former Jesuit and Calvinist reformer who had established a successful communal settlement at Wieward in the 1670s. In 1679, Danckaerts and Peter Sluyter* were sent to America to investigate the possibility of establishing a colony. After considering several sites for the colony, they met Augustine Hermann whose father owned some twenty-four thousand acres of prime land in Maryland and Delaware. In 1683, a number of the colonists arrived in Maryland, settling at Bohemia Manor where they began a society and sustained themselves by cultivating tobacco and other crops. In 1684, Danckaerts became a naturalized Maryland citizen. Shortly thereafter he returned to Wieward and died at Middleburgh between 1702 and 1704.

SELECTED WORK: Henry C. Murphy (ed.), *Journal of a Voyage to New York* (1867).

SOURCES: Bartlett James and J. Franklin Jameson (eds.), *Journal of Jasper Danckaerts* (1913).

DAVIES, WILLIAM W. (b. 1833, Denbigh, Wales; d. 1906, Walla Walla, Washington), leader of the Kingdom of Heaven Colony (see Appendix A, No. 144). When Davies was sixteen, he converted to Mormonism and at age eighteen he became a preacher. In 1855, he and his wife came to the United States and settled at Willard, Utah, about fifty miles north of Salt Lake City. Davies became a follower of Joseph Morris, a Mormon schismatic who had split from the organized church in 1861 and had organized a sect at Weber County, Utah. The Morrisites believed in reincarnation and the imminent coming of Christ. Morris claimed that he was Joseph Smith's spiritual successor, but he granted that Brigham Young was his temporal heir. After Morris was murdered in a battle with Utah officials in 1862, Davies fled to Idaho and then to Montana.

In 1865 Davies had a vision which directed him to found the "Kingdom of Heaven." In 1867, he and about forty followers arrived in Walla Walla, Washington, and established a colony on 480 acres. All property was held in common, goods and provisions were kept in a common stock, and proceeds from their labor went into a common pool. The sect accepted Davies as the spirit of God and one of his sons, born in 1869, as the spirit of God made manifest in the world. The child was known locally as the "Walla Walla Jesus." The group proselytized among the Mormons. Their devotion to the Davies was a strong factor in maintaining the colony. With the death of the young "Jesus" in 1880, the colony began to disintegrate. There was a lawsuit that year by a member, and as the result of the court judgment, the property had to be sold. In 1881, Davies left the area for California. He later returned to Walla Walla where he died.

SOURCES: Russell Blankenship, *And There Were Men* (1942); Andrew Jenson, *Encyclopedic History of the Church of Latter-Day Saints* (1941); *Walla Walla Union Bulletin* (November 12, 1972).

DE BOISSIERE, ERNEST VALETON (b. June 9, 1810, Chateau de Certes, Bordeaux, France; d. January 12, 1894, Bordeaux, France), leader of the Silkville Colony* (see also Appendix A, No. 148). De Boissiere was born on the baronial estate of his family located southwest of Bordeaux. He graduated with high honors from the Polytechnique School of Paris and then was granted a commission in the French Army Corps of Engineers. After serving in the army for several years, he resigned his commission to take charge of the family estate. In 1848, de Boissiere allied himself with the radical wing of the Republican party in opposition to Louis Napoleon's policies. After the failure of the Revolution of 1848, he visited the United States and during the 1850s he returned regularly on business. In 1868, he attracted public attention and censure for his $10,000 gift to the Freedmen's Aid Society of the Methodist Episcopal church for their project to establish a home and school for orphaned Negro children.

In 1856, de Boissiere met Charles Sears, former president of the North American Phalanx* (see also Appendix A, No. 66), just two years after the experiment at Red Bank, New Jersey, had failed. At this time, de Boissiere expressed a desire to devote part of his income to a cooperative venture. Horace Greeley* and John H. Noyes* may have further influenced him, but it was the direct influence of some old Fourierists that led to the Silkville Colony in Kansas. Albert Brisbane,* E. P. Grant,* and Charles Sears all met with de Boissiere in 1868 to plan a Fourierist colony. Early in 1869, Brisbane, Grant, and de Boissiere completed the purchase of thirty-five hundred acres of prairie land in Franklin County, Kansas, near Williamsburg. In 1869, over forty French immigrants came to the experiment. Most were experts in the production and manufacture of silk which was begun in 1869. From 1869 to 1873, de Boissiere planted mulberry trees and put two hundred and fifty acres under cultivation. In 1873, E. P. Grant issued a prospectus, *The Prairie Home Association and Corporation Based on Attractive Industry*, inviting socialists into this communal endeavor. Although the Panic of 1873 destroyed this Fourierist plan, a three-story phalanstery was completed in 1874. The colony continued to produce silk, exhibiting at the Centennial Exposition in Philadelphia in 1876 and winning great praise. Silk production was abandoned in 1882 because it was unprofitable. De Boissiere returned to France in 1884 because the cooperative features of the colony were never fully developed, even though the colony lasted until 1886. In 1892, de Boissiere bequeathed the property to the Odd Fellows Lodge for use as an orphanage. He died at his home in France on January 12, 1894.

SOURCES: Garrett R. Carpenter, *Silkville* (1952); E. P. Grant, *Co-operation* (1870); George A. Huron, "Ernest Valeton Boissiere," *Transactions of the Kansas State Historical Society, 1901-02* (1902).

DIETSCH, ANDREAS ANTON (b. 1807, Alsac, Switzerland; d. 1845, St. Louis, Missouri), founder of the abortive New Helvetia Colony (see also Appendix A, No. 107). In 1843, this brushmaker, alarmed by the social and political changes caused by industrialization, published a millennialist pamphlet that advocated communal living. He was influenced by Charles Fourier and urged that an agricultural community be established where men could live by the Golden Rule. In March 1844, he published a pamphlet containing the constitution of his "Society of New Helvetia." In June, he led a party of forty to Missouri where they purchased a 363-acre tract of land on the Osage River, north of Westphalia. The majority of his followers preferred to live in St. Louis, and so the Dietsch party was reduced to six other adults and eleven children, including two of his own. The colony had a brief life and faltered just after Dietsch's death in the winter of 1845.

SOURCES: H. Roger Grant, "Missouri's Utopian Communities," *Missouri Historical Review* (October 1971).

DIVINE, FATHER (b. George Baker ca. 1877, Hutchinson Island, Georgia; d. September 10, 1965, New York City), head of the Peace Mission Movement in several Eastern cities, 1919-1965. The most important early influence on Baker was an itinerant preacher at Baltimore in 1899 who called himself "Father Eternal." From 1899 until 1912, Baker remained in Baltimore preaching and then he moved to Valdosta, Georgia, where he gathered a small sect around him. By the time he came to New York with his followers in 1915, he had been asserting for several years that he was God.

In New York, Baker began his practice of hosting lavish banquets for his followers and giving aid to all who asked. In 1919, he moved to a large home in Sayville, New York, where he operated his church and an employment agency. Between 1919 and 1927, his membership increased only slightly (from twenty to forty) but after 1927, when he began to publicize his religious beliefs and his free dinners, he attracted massive numbers. During the 1930s, his first white converts joined, and he took the name Father Divine. In 1932, he was charged with being a public nuisance in Sayville because so many people flocked to his home in this middle-class suburban community. He was found guilty and jailed for thirty-three days but was released when the superior court reversed the decision. The judge who passed the original sentence died shortly after Father Divine's release, as a result of which many of Divine's followers believed their leader's wrath had been the cause.

During 1933, Divine opened a center in Harlem and ordered his followers to form groups and set up businesses as "Divine Peace Mission Movement Cooperatives." All profits went back into the sect, and the members lived collectively in boarding houses. There were twenty-five restaurants, two groceries, ten barber shops, and other establishments throughout Harlem. During the 1930s, Father Divine acquired property in other large cities and abroad. By 1935, he had a half million followers and he had Houses of Prayer in every major Eastern city.

Divine's society was interracial, and he urged celibacy on his believers. Converts rejected their old families when they entered the society where they found a haven against economic dislocation and racism. In 1943, a curious coalition was effected between Divine and the Communist party, but he later repudiated the party. In 1942, he moved his headquarters to

Philadelphia rather than pay a court judgment against him resulting from a suit by a former member. During the 1940s and 1950s, he continued to give lavish banquets, but ill health in the 1960s kept him out of the public eye.

SOURCES: Henry Bowden, *Dictionary of American Religious Biography* (1977); Sara Harris, *The Incredible Father Divine* (1954); *The New York Times* (September 11, 1965).

DOWIE, JOHN ALEXANDER (b. May 25, 1847, Edinburgh, Scotland; d. March 9, 1907, Zion City, Illinois), founder of the Christian Catholic church at Zion, Illinois. Dowie attended Edinburgh University briefly during 1869-1871 after having gone with his parents to South Australia in 1860. He returned to Australia in 1872 and became pastor of a Congregational church at Newton, a Sydney suburb. In the 1870s, he was an active reformer, pressing for temperance and free educational programs. In 1876, he gained notoriety for his powers as a healer, and in 1882, he built a healing tabernacle at Melbourne.

In May 1893, Dowie opened Zion's Tabernacle in Chicago, and early in 1896 he organized his Christian Catholic church with headquarters at Zion, Illinois, just north of Chicago. Zion City was planned, and Dowie gained control over sixty-five hundred acres. He had a worldwide following (between twenty-five thousand and fifty thousand), but the center of his activities was in Zion, Illinois, where his followers pursued a strict regime laid down by the church. Alcohol and tobacco were prohibited and celibacy encouraged. Dowie hoped Zion City would be a model city, and it was, in fact, an interracial city where nearly two hundred blacks lived in 1906.

Unable to establish any successful industries at Zion, Dowie was forced to travel abroad to seek other business opportunities. While in Mexico exploring the site for a new colony, there was a revolt against his leadership. Wilbur G. Voliva, a trusted overseer, took control, charging that Dowie not only had squandered funds, but also had advocated polygamy for the group. Later revelations indicated that Dowie had indeed used colony money for personal reasons and had lost over $1 million in the 1903-1904 stock market. He never regained his leadership position.

SELECTED WORKS: Leaves of Healing (periodical) (1893); *The Personal Letters of John Alexander Dowie* (1912); *The Times of the Restoration of All Things* (1918).
SOURCES: Philip L. Cook, "Zion City, Illinois, The Kingdom of Heaven and Race," *Illinois Quarterly* (Winter 1975); DAB 1 (2d supplement).

DUSS, JOHN (b. John Rutz, February 22, 1860, Cincinnati, Ohio; d. December 14, 1951, Florida), trustee of the Economy Colony (see Appendix A, No. 28). Duss's mother came to the Economy Colony in 1862 as a nurse after her husband's death in the Civil War. Young Duss subsequently attended Mount Union College (1879) in Ohio and taught German in the Economy, Pennsylvania, public schools. As a junior trustee of the society, Duss became involved in a factional fight within the colony in 1891 over his dealings with Cyrus Teed* of the Koreshan Unity whose teachings he was allegedly preaching (see Appendix A, No. 196). Although he brought suit against other elders for mismanagement of funds, it was clearly Duss who misspent the colony's fortune.

During the 1890s, after Duss became a full member and trustee, he embarked on an extravagant career as a band director. The Economy band traveled widely and in 1897 gave a concert at the Metropolitan Opera House. Duss was lavish in support of his own musical career and hired press agents to promote himself. During the summer of 1902, he spent over $100,000 to advertise the band since he had ambitions to become musical director of the Metropolitan Opera House Orchestra. He even underwrote the costs of a national tour for that orchestra under his baton. In 1903, he resigned as a colony trustee, but continued to enjoy enormous financial benefits from the colony and, in fact, received $500,000 from the society when he left. After leaving the colony Duss pursued his musical interests and lived in Florida.

SELECTED WORKS: *George Rapp and His Associates* (1914); *The Harmonists, A Personal History* (1943).

SOURCES: Karl Arndt, *George Rapp's Successors and Material Heirs, 1847-1916* (1972).

DWIGHT, JOHN SULLIVAN (b. May 13, 1813, Boston, Massachusetts; d. September 5, 1893, Boston, Massachusetts), music editor and member of Brook Farm* (see also Appendix A, No. 53). Dwight was educated at the Boston Latin School, Harvard College (1832), and the Divinity School (1836). He developed an interest in German literature and music prior to his pastorate at the Unitarian church at Northampton.

After a year Dwight resigned his pastorate and in November 1841, he joined Brook Farm. He had been a member of the Transcendental Club since its inception in 1836, and George Ripley* was a close friend. At Brook Farm, Dwight taught music and Latin, and was responsible for stimulating interest in choral singing and an appreciation of Beethoven, Mozart, and Bach. He was an associate editor of *The Harbinger*, writing extensively on cultural questions and gaining a reputation at the colony for dilettantism. Younger members called him the "Poet." His work schedule fitted his aesthetic interests rather than community needs. After the fire at the Phalanstery in 1847, Dwight sought to raise funds for the colony in New York.

Dwight's later career centered around music and reform; he wrote essays and reviews for numerous journals and directed the choir of the Religious

Association of Unionists at Boston. After his marriage in 1851, he became musical editor of the *Boston Commonwealth* and then of his journal, *Dwight's Journal of Music* (1852). For the next thirty years, his journal was a significant factor in the development of American musical taste. He translated works on music from the German, completed *The History of the Handel and Haydn Society of Boston* (1883), and helped revise musical definitions for *Websters International Dictionary* (1885-1890).

SELECTED WORKS: *A Lecture on Association* (1844); *The History of Music in Boston* (1881); (ed.), *Dwight's Journal of Music* (1852-1881).
SOURCES: Lindsay Swift, *Brook Farm* (1971 reprint); *DAB* 5.

E

ECKERLIN, ISRAEL (b. 1706, Schwarzenau, Germany; d. 1758 ?, Quebec, Canada), leader of the Ephrata Colony.* Eckerlin was born into a radical pietist family. His father had been expelled from Strausbourg because of his association with the Philadelphian Society, a mystical sect that followed the writings of Jacob Boehme. The family joined a Dunker group in southern Germany, and in 1725, the widowed Anna Eckerlin arrived in Pennsylvania with her four sons. In 1727, they moved from Germantown to Conestoga, Pennsylvania, where they fell under Johann Beissel's* influence. In 1728, Beissel baptized Israel Eckerlin. The Eckerlin brothers all joined Ephrata and all assumed prominent positions within the group.

Israel was appointed prior at the men's convent in 1740. He took charge of the colony's practical affairs and improved its economic situation. He laid out a main street, planted trees, set out vineyards, built a paper and flour mill, and organized the religious community into a viable economic unit to guarantee its survival. However, many chaffed under the new system and talked of returning to the hermetic life rather than living in community. In 1745, there was an open dispute between Beissel and Eckerlin, and Eckerlin was stripped of his authority. In October 1745, he left Ephrata with his brother Samuel and another colonist to found another colony. They surveyed a site at New River, Virginia, and called it Mahanaim. They erected temporary shelters, tilled a portion of a 900-acre tract, and tried to attract Dunkers into the area.

They managed to eke out a marginal existence during 1747-1748. Early in 1750 he returned to Ephrata and was received warmly. However, he stayed only seven months, saying as he left "that he would rather be burned at the stake seven times than return to live again in the community." He left in October 1750 and with his brothers resettled at Dunkard Bottom, Preston County, West Virginia. For the next seven years they lived on the Pennsylvania and Virginia borders amidst the hostilities of the French and Indian Wars. In 1757, Eckerlin was captured by the Ottawas and held as a spy. He was sent to Quebec where he probably died in jail in 1758, although a letter from Samuel Eckerlin to Benjamin Franklin states that he believed Israel died in a hospital in France after 1757.

SOURCES: Julius F. Sachse, *The German Sectavians of Pennsylvania, 1708-1800: A Critical and Legendary History of the Ephrata Cloister and Dunkers,* 2 vols. (1970 reprint); Klaus Wust, *The Saint Adventurers of the Virginia Frontier* (1977).

EGGLESTON, C. V. (b. ca. 1855, Oklahoma; d. ?), chief organizer of the Newllano Co-operative Colony (see Appendix A, No. 269). According to Shepperson, Eggleston spent much of his early and middle life in California and in 1914 was president of the Eggleston-King Pigeon Company, a breeder of fancy poultry. Beginning in April 1915, Eggleston began to promote Job Harriman's* Llano del Rio Colony* (see Appendix A, No. 264) in the Antelope Valley, north of Los Angeles. As fiscal agent for the colony, he promoted the community through the pages of *The Western Comrade*, a radical Los Angeles monthly. In 1916, he revealed that a similar colony was to be established near Fallon, in Churchill County, Nevada, to demonstrate the "possibilities of practical cooperation." The Nevada Colony Corporation (incorporated in 1915) issued stock and traded on the prestige of the California Llano del Rio group in socialist circles. In March 1916, Eggleston published *The Cooperative Colonist* which became the major publicity vehicle for the Nevada group. The first members joined in the summer of 1916, and by January 1918 the number had grown to two hundred.

In June 1917, after internal disputes and opposition to Eggleston's leadership surfaced, he resigned from the controlling board. He regained some control of the association in 1919 and was elected vice-president of the Nevada Colony Corporation, later reorganized as the United Development Company. At that point, this experiment in socialist self-reliance became a capitalist land company.

SOURCE: Wilbur Shepperson, *Retreat to Nevada: A Socialist Colony of World War I* (1966).

EVANS, FREDERICK WILLIAMS (b. June 9, 1808, Leominster, Worcestershire, England; d. March 6, 1893, Mount Lebanon, New York), reformer and Shaker elder. Evans migrated from England to the United States in 1820 with his father and brother, settling first at Binghamton and later at Ithaca, New York. In 1820, Evans became an Owenite follower and in his enthusiasm walked eight hundred miles to join a community at Massillon, Ohio. Shortly after the colony's failure, he went back to England, but in

January 1830 he returned to New York where he joined a group of free-thinkers led by Frances Wright* and Robert Dale Owen,* both fresh from their failures at New Harmony* (see also Appendix A, No. 30) and Nashoba* (see also Appendix A, No. 40).

Evans and his brother, George Henry, were by now ardent radical reformers, with their emphasis on labor, educational, and land reform. Evans wrote for the *Working Man's Advocate, Daily Sentinel,* and *Young America.*

In 1830, Evans visited the United Society of Believers (Shakers), underwent a religious conversion, and became a prominent Shaker leader. He served as an elder for fifty-seven years. Evans found in the Shakers what he had sought in the Owenites. His insightful *Autobiography of a Shaker* (1869) chronicles his conversion. Among his many other works are doctrinal and historical works such as *Celibacy from the Shaker Point of View* (1866) and *The Shakers: Compendium of the Origin, History, Principles of the United Society of Believers* (1859). In his role as a Shaker missionary Evans visited England in 1871 and Scotland in 1877. His wide-ranging interests in political and social issues were atypical of the Shaker leader, and his public pronouncements were often in contradiction to general Shaker sentiment. For example, other Shaker elders disapproved both his active support of Henry George and his public correspondence with Leo Tolstoy.

SELECTED WORKS: *Brief and Useful Moral Instruction for the Young* (1858); *Celibacy from the Shaker Standpoint* (1866); *Autobiography of a Shaker and Revelation of the Apocalypse* (1869); *Capitol and Labor* (1890); *The Conditions of Peace* (1890).

SOURCES: Edward D. Andrews, *The People Called Shakers* (1963 reprint); Henri Desroche, *The American Shakers* (1971).

F

FERM, ELIZABETH BYRNE (b. 1857, Galva, Illinois; d. April 12, 1944, New York City), educator associated with the Ferrer Colony* (see also Appendix A, No. 267). Elizabeth Byrne was educated at private schools in Montreal. She married at twenty and moved with her husband, Martin Battle, to New York to establish a bookstore. After leaving her husband in the early 1880s because he abused her, she studied piano at the New York Conservatory of Music in 1885 and was an active supporter of both the suffrage and single tax causes. While caring for her deceased sister's two children, she became interested in education and enrolled in the Training School for Kindergarteners associated with All Souls Episcopal Church. She graduated in 1899, and a year later she took charge of a kindergarten in Brooklyn.

In 1898, Byrne married Alexis Ferm. Together, they embarked on a life-long career in education that took them to the Ferrer Colony in the 1920s. From 1906 until 1913, the Ferms ran a "free school" in a working-class district of Manhattan. Beginning in 1913, they lived at Hampton, Connecticut. In 1920, they took charge of the educational program at the anarchist colony in New Jersey, an offshoot of the Ferrer movement in New York City. The Modern School, as the school at Stelton was called, has been hailed as one of the most radical experiments in the history of American education. Children were encouraged to develop their individual abilities. The qualities the Ferms most wanted to instill in children's minds were "initiative, tenacity and the ability to endure hardship," according to Laurence Veysey. They drew their inspiration from the Swiss educational philosopher, Frederick Froebel, and the Russian anarchist, Leo Tolstoy. Much of the curriculum centered around manual activities: printing, basket making, carpentry, and weaving. Children worked at their own pace and more often than not learned what they were interested in. Self-development was prized at the Modern School. Dissension reached a high point in the colony in 1931 between communists and anarchists, but the Ferms remained as directors at the school. Since its earliest days the Ferror Colony had been racked by disputes between political and cultural anarchists, who prized individualism, and the doctrinaire socialists and communists, who wanted the colony to confront the outside world. The Ferms were anarchists and single-taxers all their lives and believed in inner development and self-reliance. Their educational philosophy often put them in conflict with immigrant parents who wanted their children to gain practical skills.

SELECTED WORKS: The Spirit of Freedom in Education (1919); *Freedom in Education* (1949).

SOURCE: Laurence Veysey, *The Communal Experience* (1973); *The New York Times* (April 13, 1944).

FREY, WILLIAM (b. Vladimir Konstantinovich Geins, October 16, 1839 (O.S.), Odessa, Russia; d. November 5, 1888, London), founder of the Progressive Community (see Appendix A, No. 149). Frey was born into a gentry family. He attended military college and received a commission in the Guards, but rejected it in favor of a career in science by attending the Academy of the General Staff where he specialized in geodesy. The ideas of Fourier, St. Simon, and Cabet attracted him, and he may have been a member of the short-lived underground organization "Land and Liberty" in the 1860s devoted to radical and anarchist issues such as emancipation for the serfs and land rights.

In 1866, Frey suffered an emotional breakdown which led, in 1867, to his plan to start a Russian colony in America, a plan that was spurred by his reading of an account of the Oneida Community* (see also Appendix A,

No. 108) in William H. Dixon's *New America.* Early in 1868, he and his new bride sailed to America; upon arrival, they gave their names as William and Mary Frey. He wrote to Oneida seeking admission, but instead joined Alcander Longley's* Reunion Colony* (see also Appendix A, No. 145) at Jasper County, Missouri, in 1870. During this period, he kept in contact with the Russian Section of the International Workingmen's Association, but his primary interest lay with small practical communal experiments. In 1871, he started the Progressive Community at Cedar Vale, Kansas, with a few families. This socialist colony lasted until 1875 when disputes between the spiritualists and the political faction forced Frey to form the Investigating Community on adjacent land. During the summer of 1870, the colony broke up, with Frey remaining at Cedar Vale through 1879. At that point, he joined the Positivist movement and established a "complex family" (Oneida's practice of voluntary sexual relations rather than marriage) at Clermont, Iowa, in 1880. In 1881, he became involved with the Am Oylom movement of Jewish emigrants to the United States, and in 1883, he joined the New Odessa* (see also Appendix A, No. 184) group at Glendale, Douglas County, Oregon. He left that group in 1885 and journeyed to London where he spent his remaining years as a publicist for the Positivist and Ethical Culture churches. During this period, he corresponded with Tolstoy and may have served as the prototype for a character in Tolstoy's *Resurrection.* Tolstoy in a memorial statement described him as "a person who, from his moral qualities, was one of the most remarkable men of our own, and not only our own, age."

SELECTED WORKS: *The Religion of Humanity* (1886); *Vegetarianism in Connection with the Religion of Humanity* (1887); *Under What Conditions, Positivism Can Successfully Compete with Socialism* (1888); *The Testament of William Frey* (1889).
SOURCE: Avrahm Yarmolinsky, *A Russian's American Dream* (1965).

G

GALLATIN, E. L. (b. 1828, St. Louis, Missouri; d. ?), a founder of the Colorado Cooperative Company* (see also Appendix A, No. 205). After his parents moved to Monroe County, Illinois, Gallatin was apprenticed to a saddler and worked in that business for several years before heading to California in 1860 after hearing about the gold strike. However, he only got as far as Colorado where he continued his work as a saddler. He moved to Montana in 1864 and to Cheyenne, Wyoming, in 1881.

In 1895, Gallatin joined the Colorado Cooperative Company which had been founded in 1894 to cultivate farmland by building an irrigation ditch with common labor. There had been early debate in the colony over whether or not land should be held in common, and it was decided that there would be individual holdings but a common commitment to the irrigation project. G. E. Smith, a former colony member at Topolobampo, argued against common land ownership based on his experience at that colony. In 1894, the colony had about twenty members and little money. In an effort to gain new members, it published a periodical, *The Altrurian.* There was an active group in Denver, and an effort was made to start clubs in other parts of the West. Between April 1896 and May 1897, no work was completed on the irrigation ditch because of internal disputes in the colony. Gallatin stood with the colonists at Pinon since he feared that those away from the site had little understanding of the problems the project faced. He outlined the altruistic purposes of the colony in his autobiography: "The only hope is to unite in bettering the condition of all who come within its gates, and to show the world the advantages that may be derived from a system of co-operation in preference to competition." In 1898, there were fifty-six new members, but another dispute over voting rights held by members outside Pinon, particularly by supporters in Denver, erupted that year. Gallatin became disillusioned: "The colony is drawing its strength from the middle class . . . ; yet one finds this narrow selfishness embedded so firmly in many of them that harmony has a rough road to travel." A suit in 1899 further distracted colony efforts. Gallatin left the colony in 1900. There is no record of his life after this date.

SELECTED WORKS: E. L. Gallatin, *What Life Has Taught Me* (Denver, 1900).
SOURCES: Duane Mercer, "The Colorado Cooperative Company, 1894-1904," *Colorado Magazine* (Spring 1967).

GIBSON, GEORGE HOWARD (b. ?; d. ?), reformer, editor and founder of the Christian Corporation and co-founder of the Christian Common-wealth* (see also Appendix A, Nos. 212, 214 respectively). Little is known about his early years except that he began his reform career as a journalist in the later 1880s by becoming owner/editor of the Omaha temperance publication, the *Rising Tide.* In 1893, he became editor of the *Nebraska Alliance Independent*, a Populist paper he used as a base for his Christian Socialist beliefs.

In January 1896, he sold his interest in the *Wealth Makers* (the old *Alliance Independent*) and organized a group that would form the Christian Com-monwealth. Influenced by the writings of the Christian Socialist George Herron, Gibson wanted to put his Christianity into practice. He had man-aged the *Wealth Makers* as a cooperative and believed that cooperative enter-prises served as an antidote to the rampant individualism of his day. Earlier, in November 1894, he had announced his intention to form a cooperative group, ". . . a farming, stock-raising, fruit-growing, manufacturing and love-educating paradise." He formed the Christian Corporation, a chartered association of twenty-three families with assets of $30,000. It owned 1,360 acres of farmland, most of it brought in by the member families. Gibson characterized the society as a "democratic, industrial, equality, communal organization and an association of Christian Communes to equalize conditions and allow none to lack." It is unclear whether or not they ever lived a communal life in Lincoln, Lancaster County, Nebraska, but when they experienced some financial difficulties in late 1895, Gibson convinced some families to associate with the Christian Commonwealth.

The Christian Commonwealth was founded in 1896 by Ralph Albertson,* Gibson, William C. Damon, a classics professor from California, and a portion of the membership from the Christian Corporation. Twenty-six persons journeyed from Nebraska to Muskogee County, Georgia, in the summer of 1897 to join with another group of colonists who had come from the Willard Cooperative Colony (see Appendix A, No. 210). The Christian Commonwealth lasted only four years because it failed to develop a viable economic system. Its distinguishing feature was its monthly journal, *The Social Gospel*, edited by Gibson and Albertson. Gibson left the colony in 1900 and reportedly joined an "industrial community" in Illinois. Nothing else is known about his later life.

SELECTED WORKS: *The People's Hour* (1909).
SOURCES: James Dombrowski, *The Early Days of Christian Socialism in America* (1937); Samuel Walker, "George Howard Gibson, Christian Socialist Among Populists," *Nebraska History* (Winter 1974).

GODWIN, PARKE (b. February 25, 1816, Paterson, New Jersey; d. January 7, 1904, New York City), newspaper editor. After graduating from Princeton, Godwin read law and practiced in Kentucky and New York. In 1836, William Cullen Bryant offered him a position on the *New York Evening Post* and he began a long journalistic career.

Godwin was an ardent supporter of Fourierism and published *A Popular View of the Doctrine of Fourier* in 1844. In 1845, he became the editor of *The Harbinger,* the major Fourierist journal in the United States and one devoted to reform causes. He supported the development of Brook Farm* (see also Appendix A, No. 53), and even though he never joined, he took an active interest in its welfare. After its breakup, he still maintained his interest in communal societies.

Godwin worked for *Putnam's Monthly Magazine* in 1853, published a volume on the history of France (1860), and edited the works of William Cullen Bryant (1883-1884). In 1878, he became editor of the *New York Post*, remaining with it until 1881. Much of his later career was devoted to editing.

SELECTED WORKS: *Democracy, Constructive and Pacific* (1844); *Out of Our Past* (1870); *A Popular View of the Doctrine of Fourier* (1884); *Little Journeys to the Homes of American Authors* (1896).
SOURCES: *DAB* 7.

GOOD, PETER PEYTON (b. 1833; d. February 21, 1886, Seattle, Washington), colony supporter. Good was a Harvard graduate, practiced law in New York, and served as a judge in Plainfield, New Jersey, before becoming interested in cooperation. A visit to the Familisterie of J. B. Godin at Guise, France, inspired him to seek out an American equivalent. Godin was influenced by the writings of St. Simon, Robert Owen,* and Etienne Cabet* during the 1840s, and in 1859, he built the first wing of his "Familisterie" for his iron workers. There was a collection of united buildings, a group of cooperative shops, and a school that included a nursery and apartments for 350 workers. In November 1885, Good organized a cooperative colony scheme based on Godin's plans, the Topolobampo scheme of Albert K. Owen,* and the Fourierist phalanxes. Good's vision inspired George Venable Smith* to found the Puget Sound Cooperative Colony (see Appendix A, No. 193) in 1887. Good never saw the colony plan come into existence since he died in February 1886 after being imprisoned for calling for revolution at an anti-Chinese meeting. Such anti-Chinese meetings had begun in 1885 when white laborers began to fear that wages would be cut and jobs lost because of the presence of cheap Chinese laborers.

SOURCES: Charles LeWarne, *Utopias on Puget Sound* (1975).

GRANT, ELIJAH (b. 1808, Norfolk, Connecticut; d. December 2, 1874, Canton, Ohio), founder of the Ohio Phalanx (see Appendix A, No. 80). Grant graduated from Yale College in 1830 and received his Master's degree from Yale in 1833. He practiced law first at Winsted, Connecticut, and later, in 1835, at Canton, Ohio. A disciple of Albert Brisbane,* Grant was among the early, regular contributors to *The Phalanx* (1843) along with Horace Greeley* and Mary Gove Nichols.*

In October 1843, announcements concerning the formation of the Ohio Phalanx appeared in reform journals. Grant, now identified as the leading Fourierist in the West, began the colony in February 1844 on thirty thousand acres at Westfield, Ohio, on the Ohio River south of Wheeling, West Virginia. The colony had a brief history and disbanded in December of that same year as a result of internal disputes and inadequate financing. Efforts to reorganize the group proceeded through the early part of 1845, but by August 1845 the colony had closed. While Grant was its principal organizer and driving spirit, he was concerned more with the theoretical aspects of colony life than with its practical side. After its failure, he returned to Canton and engaged in agricultural speculation and the banking business. In 1868, he became involved with Ernest de Boissiere* and the Silkville experiment* (see also Appendix A, No. 148).

Early in 1896 Albert Brisbane,* Grant, and de Boissiere purchased 3,500 acres in Franklin County, Kansas. They drew up the *Articles of Association of the Kansas Cooperative Farm* (1869) and pledged $29,000 to the venture. By June 1869, both Grant and Brisbane left the project because it was not promising enough. In 1870, under Horace Greeley's auspices, Grant published *Co-operation, or, Sketch of the Conditions of Attractive Industry; and Outline of a Plan for the Organization of Labor. With a Notice of the Kansas Cooperative Farm of M. Ernest V. de Boissiere.* Grant continued to support Silkville and in 1873 published the *Prarie Home Association and Corporation Based on Attractive Industry* from Canton, Ohio. One historian, Carlton Smith, reports that he may have been involved with a third group, the Order of the Adelphi, but nothing is known about that group except its name.

SELECTED WORKS: *Co-operation* (1870); *Prairie Home Association and Corporation Based on Attractive Industry* (1874).

SOURCES: *The Phalanx* (1843-1844); Carlton Smith, "Elijah Grant and the Ohio Phalanx," Master's thesis, University of Chicago, 1950.

GREELEY, HORACE (b. February 3, 1811, Amherst, New Hampshire; d. November 29, 1872, New York City), educator, editor, and social reformer. Greeley was irregularly schooled and at the age of fourteen was apprenticed to an editor of a Vermont paper. In March 1834, Greeley and Jonas Winchester founded a weekly literary paper, *The New Yorker*. Six years later, at the urging of Whig leaders, he started a campaign weekly in support of William Henry Harrison, entitled the "Log Cabin." It included what he considered the major issues of the day: sound and uniform currency, tariff protection, a single presidential term, limitations on executive power, and distribution of the proceeds from the sale of public land. The publication ceased after the election but was revived in late 1840, becoming the *New York Tribune* in 1841. As editor of the *Tribune* Greeley set a new standard in American journalism. Sensational articles about crime and sex were dropped, advertisements for bogus medical devices were refused, and the paper began to run serious articles on political and literary subjects. In addition, the paper was open to news about reform movements.

In 1840, Greeley read Albert Brisbane's* *Social Destiny of Man: or Association and Reorganization of Industry.* After meeting Brisbane, he arranged for the American Fourierist to write a regular column on the front page of the paper in 1842 describing Fourierism. Brisbane's column gave this new philosophy both wide exposure and respectability.

Throughout his career, Greeley supported cooperation and employed a host of reformers on the *Tribune*. Charles Dana* and George Ripley* held full-time editorial posts on the paper, while Margaret Fuller published regular essays for a time. He was the most influential supporter of Fourierism. He served as treasurer of the North American Phalanx* (see also Appendix A, No. 66) at Red Bank, New Jersey, though he never lived in that joint-stock colony. He continued to support colonization schemes after the Civil War. His agricultural editor, Nathaniel Meeker,* was the prime organizer of the Union Colony* (see also Appendix A, No. 146) at what became Greeley, Colorado.

In 1872, Greeley ran for the presidency on the Liberal Republican ticket. His loss of the election, combined with his wife's death that same year, brought on nervous collapse. He died that same year.

SELECTED WORKS: *American Conflict* (1866); *Recollections of a Busy Life* (1868); *What I Know of Farming* (1870).
SOURCES: Glyndon G. Van Dusen, *Horace Greeley, Nineteenth Century Crusader; DAB* 7.

GRONLUND, LAURENCE (b. July 13, 1846, Copenhagen, Denmark; d. October 15, 1899, New York City), socialist reformer. Gronlund was educated in Danish schools, served in the Danish-German War, and received his M.A. from the University of Copenhagen in 1865 after the war. He began his law studies there, but emigrated to the United States in 1867. He taught German in the Milwaukee public schools, studied law in his spare time, and was admitted to the Chicago bar in 1869. His first work, published in 1879, was *The Coming Revolution: Its Principles*, which emphasized the exploitative nature of American capitalism. His second and most important book, *The Cooperative Commonwealth* (1884), emphasized the inevitability of class conflict and criticized reforms that strengthened the corporate status quo. It was the first book to explain Marxism to an English-reading audience in such a way that the average reader could understand the complex economic arguments and social alternatives laid out by Marx. It was through Gronlund's *The Cooperative Commonwealth* that the utopian novelist Edward Bellamy* received his socialism.

Gronlund lectured widely on socialism and cooperation though he was opposed to the establishment of separate colonies in the early 1890s. With the publication of Edward Bellamy's *Looking Backward*, Gronlund identified with and supported the nationalist cause even though he had been elected to the executive committee of the Socialist Labor party in 1888. During the 1890s, he became more reformist in his positions as in *Our Destiny, The Influence of Nationalism on Morals and Religion* (1891), where he argued that religious ideas had a place in national socialist development. In 1895, he wrote an article in *The Arena* about the "Social Palace" at Guise, France, built by the French Fourierist, Charles Godin. In the article he expressed continued reservations about the colony idea: "I am sure that American workingmen with their liking for privacy and independent ways of living would give such a 'unitary home' a wide berth."

Yet, when approached by the backers of the colonization scheme at the 1898 Social Democracy convention, he gave his support to the plan to colonize a single state by establishing a series of socialist colonies. He supported the idea because "of its repudiation of the class struggle thesis and partly because he thought the experiment well worth trying," according to Howard Quint. In the *New Economy: A Peaceable Solution to Social Problems* (1898) and in *Socializing the State* (1898), he argued for the need to gain control of the political machinery in order to effectuate societal change. Even though he was lukewarm in his support of communal groups, it was his writing that inspired many socialists in the 1890s to start colony programs. The title of his major work, *The Cooperative Commonwealth*, served as an inspiration for the Maine-based association, the Brotherhood of the Cooperative Commonwealth, which sponsored cooperative colonies in several states.

At the time of his death, Gronlund was a labor reporter for the *New York Journal*.

SELECTED WORKS: *The Coming Revolution* (1878); *The Cooperative Commonwealth* (1884); *Our Destiny, The Influence of Nationalism on Morals and Religion* (1891); "Godin's Social Palace," *The Arena* (1895); *The New Economy* (1898); *Socializing the State* (1898).

SOURCES: Solomon Gemorah, "Laurence Gronlund—Utopian Reformer," *Science and Society*, 33 (1969); Howard Quint, *The Forging of American Socialism* (1953).

H

HAPGOOD, WILLIAM POWERS (b. 1872, Alton, Illinois; d. 1960, Indianapolis, Indiana), founder of an industrial cooperative. Hapgood was born into a prosperous family, graduated from Harvard University in 1894, and then worked briefly in Chicago for a wholesale grocer. In 1903, with his father's help, he organized the Columbia Conserve Company, a canning company that began to show a modest profit by 1916. Between 1917 and 1930, the company became a workers' cooperative, although Hapgood reserved to himself certain veto powers throughout the period. A workers' council was established and other experiments in industrial democracy, including profit-sharing, were begun in this factory of one hundred employees. Workers shared in the decision-making process, received an equal share in the company profits, and were both owners and operators of the enterprise. The workers' council discussed wages, hours, and conditions of labor. Though there have been numerous cooperatives in United States history, most have been distribution cooperatives. Hapgood wanted to make it a utopian example of the workers' capacity to manage and control their own futures. For liberal reformers the Columbia Conserve Company represented a standing model of industrial enterprise, and for Hapgood it was an example of cooperative enterprise. By 1932, however, the company began to decline as profits shrank and legal difficulties developed. The company was further weakened by a power struggle between Hapgood and his son Powers, who was aided by the labor leader John Brophy. In 1943, the company was broken up by a court order.

SELECTED WORKS: The Columbia Conserve Company (1934).
SOURCES: Louis Filler, "William Powers Hapgood and American Options," Introduction to Wiliam P. Hapgood, *The Columbia Conserve Company* (1975 reprint); Kim McQuaid, "Industry and the Cooperative Commonwealth, 1917-1943," *Labor History* (Fall, 1976).

HARRIMAN, JOB (b. January 1861, Clinton County, Indiana; d. October 26, 1925, Sierra Madre, California), founder of the Llano Colony (see Appendix A, No. 264). Harriman was educated for the ministry at North-western Christian University (now Butler University) in Indianapolis, Indiana, but left that vocation for the law, gaining admittance to the Indiana bar in 1885. In 1886, he moved to California where he joined one of the first Nationalist Clubs in San Francisco. During the 1890s, he worked for the Socialist Labor party and associated himself with the Altrurians in their cooperative schemes. In 1898, he became the Socialist party nominee for governor of California and in 1899, the state organizer for the Socialist Labor party. With the merger of the Socialist Labor party and the Social Democrats, Harriman emerged as the vice-presidential candidate on the new ticket headed by Eugene V. Debs in 1900. During this period, he practiced criminal law in Los Angeles and was the Socialist and labor candidate for the mayoralty in 1911.

After the McNamara bombing and subsequent confession destroyed his chances for election in that campaign, Harriman turned to cooperative socialism once again. In 1914, he became president of the Llano del Rio Company at Antelope, California, whose members were drawn from socialist and labor ranks. Harriman's defeat in the 1911 election intensified his belief that there was a "need for an economic rather than a political base for spreading the socialist word," according to Robert Hine in his *California's Utopian Colonies* (1953).

The colony was a viable community until 1918 when internal disputes and the lack of water at the colony in California forced a move to Louisiana. Harriman led the move to Newllano (near Leesville) in 1918. In 1920, he left the community and returned to California where he spent the remaining years of his life. He had long suffered from tuberculosis, and the damp Louisiana climate strained his health.

SELECTED WORKS: *Class War in Idaho* (1900).
SOURCES: Paul Conkin, *Two Paths to Utopia* (1964); Robert Hine, *California's Utopian Colonies* (1953).

HARRIS, THOMAS LAKE (b. May 15, 1823, Fenny Stratford, England; d. March 23, 1906, New York City), founder of Mountain Cove (see Appendix A, No. 117), the Brotherhood of the New Life* (see also Appendix A, No. 141), Brocton Community (see Appendix A, No. 143), and Fountain Grove (see Appendix A, No. 163). Harris's parents emigrated to Utica, New York, when he was four, and he was raised by his stepmother. Harris studied for the Baptist ministry, but converted to Universalism in 1843. During the late 1840s, he fell under the influence of the spiritualist Andrew Jackson Davis, and he organized the Independent Christian Congregation in 1848 through which he became acquainted with Horace Greeley.* In 1851, Harris led a group of followers to Mountain Cove, Fayette County, Virginia, to await the millennium.

The Mountain Cove community was an agricultural cooperative where Harris and James Scott, a spiritualist from New York, acted as mediums through whom the divine direction of the colony operated. There were about one hundred members, the property was held in both Harris' and Scott's names, and they published a journal, *Mountain Cove Journal* (1852). Little else is known about the society other than it "proved to be a fiasco," according to Schneider and Lawton. In 1854-1855, he began to publish spiritualist poetry, including *The Epic of Starry Heaven* and *A Lyric of the Morning Land*; in 1857, he published a Swedenborgian journal, *The Herald of Light.*

Following a trip to England, Harris founded a spiritualist colony at Wassaic, New York, in 1861 called the Brotherhood of the New Life. In 1867, the group moved to a sixteen hundred-acre tract near Brocton, New York. Harris was the spiritual center of this celibate colony. The Colony was based on spiritual marriages, the utilization of special breathing techniques, and Harris's communication with the spirit world. Among his followers at Brocton were the journalist Laurence Oliphant* and his mother, Lady Maria Oliphant.

A split with the Oliphants came in 1875, with the Harris supporters moving to Santa Rosa, California, where they established the Fountain Grove Community on a 700-acre site. It was a financially successful venture, with extensive vineyards and productive farms, and by 1884 they had 1700 acres under cultivation. While at Fountain Grove, Harris grew more ethereal in his beliefs until, in 1894, he believed he had achieved immortality. Stories about free love at the colony forced its dissolution in 1896. Earlier, in February 1892, he married his secretary, Jane Lee Waring; he lived in England with her until his death.

SELECTED WORKS: *A Lyric of the Golden Age* (1856); *Arcana of Christianity* (1858); *Battle Bells* (1891).
SOURCES: Herbert W. Schneider and George Lawton, *A Prophet and a Pilgrim* (1942).

HASKELL, BURNETTE (b. 1857, Sierra County, California; d. November 1907, California), anarchist, labor organizer, and co-founder of the Kaweah Co-operative Commonwealth* (see also Appendix A, No. 189). Haskell attended Oberlin College, the University of Illinois, and the University of California before being admitted to the California bar in 1879. He worked for a time with the California Republican State Committee before devoting his energies to the labor movement and *The Truth*, the official organ of the San Francisco Trade Assembly. A reading of Laurence Gronlund's* *Cooperative Commonwealth* (1884) led him to organize, with James Martin, the Cooperative Land Purchase and Colonization Association of California in 1885. There was a close affinity between this group and the International Workingmen's Association in San Francisco, which was a mixture of unionists, socialists, and anarchists.

Haskell's contemporaries in the labor movement viewed him as brilliant, but erratic because of his habit of moving from cause to cause. Haskell's philosophy was described by Robert Hine in *California's Utopian Colonies* as "the evolutionary political action of Bellamy's Nationalism, the vitalistic mumbo jumbo of a civic organization called the Invisible Republic, and later by Populism."

In 1885, Haskell and Martin led fifty-three colonists to file land claims in the recently opened Sierra Forests in Tulare County, California. The Kaweah Co-operative Commonwealth was founded in 1885 and run on cooperative principles. It supported itself by cutting timber in the area. Nonresident colony members, like the socialist Gerald Geraldson and Laurence Gronlund,* provided outside financial aid to the one hundred and fifty members. Factional disputes, Haskell's prickly personality, and a government land suit against the colony forced its dissolution in January 1892. After the federal government evicted the colonists, Sequoia Park was founded on their territory. Later, Haskell wrote: "We were not fit to survive and we died."

SELECTED WORKS: Burnette Haskell, "A Plan For Action," *Nationalist* (December 1889).
SOURCES: Robert Hine, *California's Utopian Colonies* (1953).

HEARD, HENRY FITZGERALD (b. 1890, London, England; d. August 18, 1971, Los Angeles, California), founder of Trabuco College and mystery writer. Heard was educated at Sherborne and Cambridge. During World War I, he was an aide to a government legal officer. He worked with Sir Horace Plunkett in promoting agricultural cooperatives, but the venture ended when Plunkett's home was blown up by Irish nationalists opposed to any English schemes. During the 1920s, he published *Narcissus: An Anatomy of Clothes* (1925), an attempt to link architecture and costume historically, and *The Agent of Humanity* (1928), a positive view of human evolution. His most popular books were his detective stories, especially, *A Taste for Honey* (1941).

Heard, a pacifist, moved to southern California in 1938. Shortly after his arrival, he and Aldous Huxley fell under the influence of Swami Prabhawananda of the Vedanta Center in Hollywood where individuals received instruction in Eastern philosophy and religion. His contact with the Vedanta group intensified his belief in the necessity of creating a community which would train a new race of spiritual leaders. In 1942, he established Trabuco College in the hills behind Laguna Beach, fifty miles southeast of Los Angeles. Trabuco College was a pacifist meditation community where Heard hoped to train a new race of "spiritual leaders, neo-Brahmins as he called them, to lead mankind away from the destruction threatened by the oncoming Second World War," according to Laurence Veysey. Heard believed that meditation and spiritual training could counteract fascism. Felix Greene, later known for his political radicalism, supervised the construction, and Aldous Huxley wrote the prospectus for the group, although he never joined. An ascetic and celibate community was thus begun, but was unable to develop any true sense of common purpose under Heard's leadership. The community lasted until 1947 when Heard closed it and returned to Los Angeles. In 1946, he won the Ellery Queen prize award for his story, "The President of the United States, Detective, 1977." In 1951, he published a religious fantasy, *The Black Fox,* about an Anglican Canon.

SELECTED WORKS: Narcissus: An Anatomy of Clothes (1925); *The Agent of Humanity* (1928); *The Third Morality* (1937); *Pain, Sex and Time* (1939); *A Taste for Honey* (1941).

SOURCES: Laurence Veysey, *The Communal Experience* (1973); *The New York Times* (August 19, 1971).

HECKER, ISAAC (b. December 18, 1819, New York City; d. December 22, 1888, New York City), reformer, Roman Catholic missionary, and participant in Brook Farm* (see also Appendix A, No. 53) and Fruitlands* (see also Appendix A, No. 71). Forced to leave school at an early age, Hecker was self-educated. Under Orestes Brownson's tutelage, he joined the Workingmen's party in New York and became active in political issues. In January 1843, he entered Brook Farm as a partial boarder at $4 a week and gave his services as a baker in exchange for instruction in German philosophy, French, and music. One member, Georgiana Kirby, spoke of him as "a baker by profession and a mystic by inclination." In July 1843, he left Brook Farm for Fruitlands in search of "a deeper life," and stayed only long enough for Bronson Alcott* to observe that "Hecker has flunked out. he hadn't the courage to persevere. He's a coward."

From Fruitlands Hecker returned to his family business in New York, and in April 1844 he lodged with Henry Thoreau's mother at Cambridge. In June 1844, he joined a larger spiritual community when he became a Roman Catholic. He was ordained a priest in London in 1849 and returned to the United States in 1851 as a Redemptorist missionary to German immigrants. Under Hecker's leadership, the Redemptorists expanded their missionary work among non-Catholics and promoted Catholic publications in the United States. In 1858 he founded a new order, the Missionary Priests of St. Paul the Apostle, more commonly known as the Paulists. He started the *Catholic World* in 1865 and the *Young Catholic* in 1870.

SELECTED WORKS: Aspirations of Nature (1857); *The Catholic Church in the United States* (1879); *The Church and the Age* (1896).
SOURCES: Lindsay Swift, *Brook Farm* (1971 reprint); *DAB* 8.

HEILPRIN, MICHAEL (b. 1823, Piotkrow, Poland; d. May 10, 1888, Summit, New Jersey), member of the New Odessa Community* (see also Appendix A, No. 184). Heilprin was born into a family of Polish patriots who emigrated to Hungary in 1842. He became involved in the 1848 Revolution and fled to France after its failure. In 1856, he moved to the United States and worked with reform causes. He met George Ripley* and Charles Dana* who asked him to work on their *New American Cyclopedia* (1872-1876) as an associate editor. During the 1870s, he worked as an editor and teacher and published his two-volume *The Historical Poetry of the Ancient Hebrews* (1879-1880). Throughout this period, he contributed articles to *The Nation* and became an editor in 1865.

The European pogroms of 1881 affected Heilprin deeply, and he helped develop a program of colonization for the refugees. In 1882, he organized the Montefiore Agricultural Aid Society to help settle refugees in agricultural areas. He was instrumental in aiding Russian refugees settle at the communal colony of New Odessa in Oregon under William Frey's* leadership. He also worked with emigrants who had come to the United States through the Am Olam movement. Beginning in 1882 he worked tirelessly with the Alliance Israel Universelle, helping to settle several colonies in southern New Jersey, the only colonies of the agricultural scheme which had any real success. His work with these varied projects weakened his health, and he died in 1888.

SELECTED WORKS: The Historical Poetry of the Ancient Hebrews (1879-1880). *SOURCES: DAB* 8.

HENRICI, JACOB (b. January 15, 1804, Grosskarlbach, Bavaria; d. December 25, 1892, Economy, Pennsylvania), co-director of the Harmony Society* (see also Appendix A, No. 17). Henrici attended a teacher's seminary at Kaiserlauten in 1822 and then worked as an assistant at a school for boys at Speier. In 1824, he came to the United States and became a member of the Harmony Society in 1827. On the death of Frederick Rapp, the adopted son of the colony leader, George Rapp,* in 1832, he was appointed to influential positions in the colony—the first nonpioneer so chosen— and led its external affairs. When George Rapp died in 1847, he believed the leadership would fall to him, but it did not. Nonetheless, he remained an active trustee working to promote the colony's oil and railroad interests. Henrici represented both sides of the Harmonist tradition: he was a strict millennialist and ardent believer in Rapp's mission, yet he had an acute business sense.

SOURCES: Karl Arndt, *George Rapp's Successors and Material Heirs, 1847-1916* (1972).

HENSON, JOSIAH (b. June 15, 1789, Charles County, Maryland; d. May 5, 1883, Dresden, Ontario, Canada), leader of the British-American Institute, or the Dawn Colony. This prototype for the title figure in Harriet Beecher Stowe's *Uncle Tom* married another slave in 1811 and fathered twelve children. In 1828, he became a preacher of the Methodist Episcopal church. He escaped to Canada in 1830 and headed a small Negro settlement at Colchester in 1840.

Henson was poorly educated and untrained for a leadership position at the Dawn Colony (1842) for freed Negroes. The idea of a settlement for former American slaves in Canada was Henson's idea but he settled in Western Ontario where blacks found themselves shut out from white society and isolated. The central feature of Dawn was its manual labor school, the British-American Institute. In addition, there were farms run by the inhabitants, a sawmill, and fifteen hundred acres under cultivation. But the vocational British-American Institute was the core and its aim was to train blacks for freedom. Controversy surrounding Henson's leadership emerged in 1847 as debts mounted and mismanagement charges were made. The same charges were repeated throughout the 1850s, but Boston philanthropists came to the Institute's rescue on several occasions. In 1868, after two decades of dispute, the colony's land was sold with Henson still at Dawn. On his third visit to England in 1876, he was received by Queen Victoria.

SELECTED WORKS: *The Life of Josiah Henson* (1849); *Truth Is Stranger Than Fiction* (1879).
SOURCE: William and Jane Pease, *Black Utopia* (1963).

HINDS, WILLIAM ALFRED B. (b. February 2, 1833, Belchertown, Massachusetts; d. May, 1910, Sherrill, New York), member of the Oneida Community* (see also Appendix A, No. 108). Hinds spent his early years on a farm and attended public school. At the age of fourteen, he was apprenticed to a storekeeper at Putney, Vermont, where the original group of the Oneida Community had formed. When the group moved to central New York, Hinds moved with them and remained a colony member throughout his life. He was an editor of the colony paper, *The Circular,* and served on central community committees.

In 1867, Hinds entered the Sheffield Scientific School at Yale, graduating with honors in the class of 1870. He had a life-long interest in botany and conducted an international correspondence with experts in the field. In 1876, he published the first edition of his *American Communities and Co-operative Colonies* based on extensive correspondence and visits to communal societies. The work was revised and updated in 1902 and 1908.

When the Oneida Community was reorganized as a joint-stock corporation in 1881, Hinds was chosen a member of the first board of directors. In 1903, he was elected president of that board, a position he held until his death.

SELECTED WORKS: *American Communities and Co-operative Colonies* (1908 ed.).
SOURCES: Robert A. Parker, *A Yankee Saint* (New York, 1975 reprint); *The Quandrangle* (June 1910).

HINTON, RICHARD J. (b. 1830, London; d. December 20, 1901, London), promoter of the Cooperative Brotherhood* (see also Appendix A, No. 220). Hinton was the son of a trade unionist. Around 1851, he emigrated to the United States where he worked as a topographical engineer and journalist. A Boston newspaper sent him to Kansas in the mid-1850s with rifles said to be donated by abolitionists Theodore Parker and W. H. Channing. In Kansas he met John Brown. He served in the Union Army and worked as a reporter for several newspapers after the war. While working as a reporter, he became a socialist. During the 1880s, he was corresponding secretary of the Washington, D.C., section of the International Workingmen's Association and later joined the Socialist Labor party.

In 1897, Hinton, Cyrus Willard,* and Wilfred P. Borland* were selected to head the Social Democracy of America colonization committee. The colonization group examined sites in several western locations, even visiting the Ruskin Colony* (see Appendix A, No. 204) in Tennessee with Mother Jones, the labor agitator. After the defeat of the colonization plan at the Social Democracy of America Chicago conference in 1898, he continued to support the idea by promoting the Cooperative Brotherhood at Burley, Washington. He was never a member of that organization, however.

SELECTED WORKS: *English Radical Leaders* (1875); *The Handbook to Arizona* (1878); *The Newer West* (1890); *John Brown and His Men* (1894).
SOURCE: Charles LeWarne, *Utopias on Puget Sound* (1975).

HOFFMAN, CHRISTIAN BALZAC (b. November 30, 1851, Azmoss, Switzerland; d. September 5, 1914, Kansas City, Kansas), promoter and financial backer of the Topolobampo Bay Colony,* Mochis, Mexico. His parents emigrated to the United States in 1855 from Switzerland and first settled in Wisconsin, then moved to Louden, Dickerson County, Kansas. Hoffman graduated from Central Wesleyan College in 1872 and entered his father's milling business that same year. The family was active in several area businesses, including a land company organized to promote the town of Enterprise, Kansas. In 1882, Christian Hoffman co-authored a pamphlet, *The Kansan: A Few Facts For Those Seeking Homes in Kansas,* which described the state and told about "land bargains" available. By 1883 he was president of the bank of Enterprise and vice-president of the First National Bank of Abilene. In 1884, he organized the Kansas Harvester Company and found time to co-edit and publish *The Anti-Monopolist*, a weekly journal that decried the growth of powerful corporations.

His politics became increasingly radical as his wealth increased. In 1881, he joined the Greenback Party, in 1882 he was elected to the Kansas House of Representatives as a Republican, in 1884 he ran as a Democrat for a state senate seat (he lost), and by 1890 he was supporting the People's Party. In 1887, Hoffman met Albert Kimsey Owen,* the promoter of the cooperative colony and railroad scheme at Topolobampo Bay, Mexico, and he was impressed by his ideas. Hoffman organized the Kansas-Sinoloa Investment Company in 1889 to promote the colonization idea, and he organized a contingent of settlers from Kansas and Colorado to go to Mexico.

In November 1890, about 250 colonists went to Mexico and Hoffman accompanied them. They had come to build an irrigation ditch and establish a model colony, but Owen was interested in having them work on his railroad project. For the next four years Hoffman devoted most of his energies toward the settlement and also had an affair with Marie Howland,* the Fourierist reformer. He lived at Topolobampo in 1889, but his contribuiton was primarily financial. During 1892-1893, a dispute developed within the colony over its management and land policies. Hoffman withdrew his support in 1893.

From 1894 to 1901 he served as a member of the board of regents of the Kansas State Agricultural College at Manhattan, was elected mayor of Enterprise in 1903, and by 1907 began to withdraw from business life. In 1910, he was divorced and remarried that same year. In September 1910, he became an editor at the *Chicago Daily Socialist* and lectured on Socialist subjects throughout the country under their auspices. In 1914, he received the Socialist party nomination for the U.S. Senate from Kansas, and his wife Anna was the party nominee for lieutenant governor. During 1914 he was named chancellor of the People's College, Fort Scott, Kansas, a college dedicated to producing the "best working class lawyers in America," according to their advertisement.

SELECTED WORKS: The Anti-Monopolist (1884).

SOURCES: Patricia Michaelis, "C. B. Hoffman, Kansas Socialist," *Kansas Historical Quarterly* (Summer 1975); Ray Reynolds, *Cat's Paw Utopia* (1973).

HORR, ALEXANDER (b. 1871, Hungary; d. 1947, San Francisco, California), organizer of the Freeland Colony (see Appendix A, No. 232). Raised as an Orthodox Jew, Horr emigrated to the United States in the 1880s. He was an admirer of Marx and Spenser, a friend of Emma Goldman, and in the 1890s joined the Freeland Central Association, a group organized to promote the ideas of Theodor Hertzka, an Austrian economist. Hertzka had published a utopian romance *Freeland* in 1891, and its impact in Europe was similar to the impact of Edward Bellamy's* *Looking Backward* in the United States. Freeland societies were formed to promote his ideas and several colonies were planned. By the late 1890s the movement had come to the United States and Horr became a publicist for the Freeland colony idea.

He wrote an introduction to the American edition of *Freeland* (1904) and then led a group of anarchists to invigorate the fading Equality Colony (see Appendix A, No. 216). Shortly after their arrival they changed the colony name to Freeland, with Horr becoming the colony's secretary and major organizer; however, their arrival split the group. The ideal at Equality had been cooperation; the ideal at Freeland was competition among small groups of individuals to achieve a greater unity and solidarity. The socialists battled with the anarchists and on one occasion, in 1905, Horr was physically assaulted.

During 1906-1907, the colony's fate was in the hands of the local courts. An arbitrator from the Cooperative Brotherhood* at Burley was brought in at one point, but the factions could agree on only one point: dissolution. That occurred in February 1907. Horr moved to San Francisco in 1907 where he continued to publicize the Freeland plan. By 1922, he had abandoned his anarchist beliefs enough to run for governor on the Socialist party ticket. He died in poverty.

SELECTED WORKS: Fabian Anarchism (1911).
SOURCE: Charles LeWarne, *Utopias on Puget Sound* (1975).

HOUSTON, GEORGE (b. between 1770 and 1778, England; d. ca. 1840), North Carolina), freethinker and member of the Franklin Community (see Appendix A, No. 34). Houston was imprisoned at Newgate for two years in 1813 for publishing a translation of D'Holbach's *Histoire de Jesus Christ* under the title *Ecce Homo*. He printed two editions, one in Edinburgh in 1799 and the other in London in 1813, and for the latter he was prosecuted and sentenced. Paul Henri, Baron d'Holbach, believed that history was the best guide to truth and his *Ecce Homo* demythologized the figure of Christ into an historic one. After serving his term, he came to New York City and published *Minerva* (1822-1825), a literary journal. He frequented Robert Owen's* gatherings in that city in 1824-1825 and joined the Franklin Community in May 1826 at Haverstraw, New York, in the Hudson Valley. The colony consisted of eighty members who were mainly artisans, farmers, and intellectuals. Other prominent figures at Franklin were Abner Kneeland, the radical publicist, and Henry A. Fay, the radical New York lawyer. This Owenite colony lasted only five months, and upon its dissolution some members joined the Forestville, New York, Community* (see Appendix A, No. 35).

In early 1827, Houston published *The Correspondent*, an infidel paper which printed defenses of atheism and reprinted the writings of Diderot and Voltaire. In 1828, Houston organized the first infidel tract society, the National Tract Society, and served as its sales agent. *The Correspondent* failed in 1829. During the 1830s, Houston lectured on free thought as a member of the radical Tammany Hall Moral Philanthropist group.

SOURCES: Arthur Bestor, *Backwoods Utopia* (1950); Frank Luther Mott, *History of American Magazines* (1938); Albert Post, *Popular Free Thought in America* (1943).

HOWLAND, EDWARD (b. September 15, 1832, Charlestown, South Carolina; d. March 25, 1890, Topolobampo, Mexico), member of the Topolobampo Bay Colony.* Howland was born into a wealthy cotton merchant family. He was privately educated as a youth, and he graduated from Harvard College in 1853. In October 1858, with Henry Clapp Jr., the writer and Fourierist, he co-founded the *New York Saturday Press*, a literary journal which published William Dean Howells and Thomas Bailey Aldrich. The review lasted until 1869, and by that time Howland was a committed Fourierist. During the 1860s, he traveled to Europe as a bookbuyer for Philes and Company, a New York firm.

In 1865, Howland married Marie Stevens Case,* and they settled at Hammonton, New Jersey. He continued his reform interests and worked as a freelance writer producing a life of Grant and articles about railroads and about travel in North America. He helped organize the first Grange in southern New Jersey and was elected state master in 1873. In 1875, the Howlands became acquainted with Alfred K. Owen,* the founder of the Topolobampo Bay Colony. Owen had read Marie Howland's novel *Papa's Own Girl* and was interested in her ideas about industrial reorganization. During the 1880s, the Howlands were publicists for Owen's scheme, and they edited the journal *Integral Cooperation* from their New Jersey home.

From 1885 onward, Howland suffered from locomotor ataxia and his health deteriorated progressively. The Howlands went to Topolobampo in 1885 as colonists both because they supported Owen's scheme and because they hoped that the climate would help him recover his health. Edward Howland believed that cooperation was the religion of the future and once wrote in an essay on cooperation "the salvation of the soul is eminently a cooperative work." He died at the colony.

SELECTED WORKS: Grant As a Soldier and Statesman (1868); *Annals of North America* (1877).
SOURCE: Ray Reynolds, *Cat's Paw Utopia* (1972).

HOWLAND, MARIE STEVENS (b. 1835, New Hampshire; d. 1921, Fairhope, Alabama), member of the Topolobampo Bay Colony* and Fairhope* (see also Appendix A, No. 211). Marie was twelve when her father died, and it was then that she left home to work in the Lowell textile mills. In the early 1850s, she moved to New York City where she taught school, completed her education at New York Normal College, and married the radical lawyer Lyman Case. During the late 1850s, she lived at Stephen Pearl Andrews's* cooperative boarding house, Unitary House, and moved in a radical circle which included Jane McElheney (the famous actress Ada Clare), and Edward Howland,* the publicist, who became her second husband in 1864.

According to Ray Reynolds, the Howlands lived in Europe during the Civil War and at J. B. Godin's Familisterie during one of those years— probably 1864. In 1866, they returned to the United States, with Edward Howland working as a freelance writer (he was to write a biography of U. S. Grant) and she as a secretary. During 1868, they moved to Hammonton, New Jersey, where they maintained a lively radical household which

Albert Brisbane* visited. The Hammonton house may have been the site of the Progressive Colony mentioned in some sources.

In 1874, Marie Howland published *Papa's Own Girl,* a utopian romance that may have served as the prototype for Edward Bellamy's* *Looking Backward.* The novel went through three editions, two under the title *The Familisterie.*

In 1874, Albert K. Owen,* the railroad entrepreneur, visited the Howlands at Hammonton, after which it became the center of publicity for his railroad and colony venture at Topolobampo Bay,* Mexico, under the name Pacific City. The Howlands edited a variety of publications for Owen and in 1888 joined the colony. She lived there until 1894, by which time Edward was an invalid in a wheelchair and Marie was having an affair with Christian B. Hoffman,* a millionaire socialist and colony backer. When the Topolobampo Colony failed, she moved to another colony, this one the Georgeist single tax settlement at Fairhope,* Alabama (see also Appendix A, No. 211), where she was colony librarian and wrote a regular column for the *Fairhope Courier.* During her later years, she was supported by Fiske Warren, a wealthy Henry George supporter.

SELECTED WORKS: Papa's Own Girl (1874); *Credit Foncier* (1885).
SOURCES: Robert S. Fogarty, "The Familisterie: Radical Reform Through Cooperative Enterprise," Introduction to *The Familisterie* (1975 reprint); Ray Reynolds, *Cat's Paw Utopia* (1972).

HUGHES, THOMAS (b. October 22, 1822, Farringdon, Berkshire, England; d. March 22, 1896, Brighton, England), writer, reformer, cooperator, and founder of the Rugby Colony* (see also Appendix A, No. 173). Hughes is best known for his Tom Brown stories. Educated at Rugby under Thomas Arnold and later at Oxford, he read for the bar and was admitted in 1845. During his residence at Lincoln's Inn, he came under the influence of F. D. Maurice, the Christian Socialist, and his attention was drawn to the cooperative movement. In 1853, he and some friends shared a communal household at Wimbledon where he wrote his famous and enormously successful *Tom Brown's School Days* in 1857. In 1854, he had helped organize the Workingmen's College in London and later was its principal from 1872 to 1883. He was elected to the House of Commons in 1865 and supported reform causes, particularly trade union issues. In 1869, he was chairman of the first Cooperative Congress, and in 1870 he made his first trip to the United States.

In 1879, Hughes gave his support to the establishment of a landed colony in eastern Tennessee run on cooperative principles. The colony was designed specifically for the second and third sons of the English gentry in an attempt to develop their economic skills. When Hughes visited Rugby in 1880, he found a hotel, a store, and some tennis courts. In August 1881, a typhoid epidemic broke out, forcing members to leave and depressing land values. The magnificent Tabard Inn burned down in 1886 and Hughes sold his own community plot in 1892. His mother had been a colony member for a brief time. He ended his life as a county court judge at Uffington.

SELECTED WORKS: Tom Brown's School Days (1857); Alfred the Great (1869); Gone to Texas (1878); Rugby, Tennessee (1881).
SOURCES: W. H. G. Armytage and E. C. Mack, Thomas Hughes: The Life of the Author of Tom Brown's School Days (1952).

HUNTSMAN, MASON T. (b. ?, Stroudsburg, Pennsylvania; d. ?), founder of the Lord's Farm* (see also Appendix A, No. 195). Huntsman's parents died when he was eight, and he lived with a farm family until he was eighteen. At age thirty-one, he underwent a religious conversion and took the name Paul Blandin Mnason, after Mnason of Cyrus. He appears to have lived in Newark for a period. In 1887, he began to attack the village of Park Ridge, New Jersey, as an immoral and corrupt place. As a result, residents attacked his home and cut off his prophet's beard and long hair. In 1889, he was jailed for blasphemy, "impersonating the Saviour," and abducting two young girls. The last charge was made after he convinced the girls to follow his quietist religious beliefs. On his release from prison, he started a religious commune called the Lord's Farm at Woodcliff, New Jersey, which the local residents called the home of the Angel Dancers because they reportedly danced in the nude. The group, consisting of about ten individuals, operated a furniture moving business and hired themselves out to local farmers. Between 1890 and 1893, members of the group were brought before local magistrates on charges ranging from violation of Sunday blue laws to accusations that they conspired to defraud one colony member of his farm. In 1903, Mnason was convicted of running a disorderly house and was imprisoned for one year.

Mnason remained in the area until 1910 and was last encountered at a service at a Negro church called the Church of the Living God in New York City. According to David Cohen, Mnason was influenced by the writings of George Fox, Madame Guyon, and the Bible. His philosophy was a simple one: that men should be guided by an inner light and should follow their impulses since they alone can lead one to a higher and perfected inner life. There is no record of his death.

SOURCES: David Stephen Cohen, "The Angel Dancers: The Folklore of Religious Communitarianism," New Jersey History (Spring 1977); Ernest Wooster, Communities of the Past and Present (1971 reprint).

IJ

JANSSON, ERIK (b. December 19, 1808, Landsberga, Uppland, Sweden; d. May 13, 1850, Springfield, Illinois), leader and founder of the Bishop Hill Colony* (see also Appendix A, No. 102). Jansson was born into a peasant family. He had a religious conversion when he was twenty-two and in subsequent years led religious revivals near his home. He married in 1835. Originally on good terms with the Church of Sweden, Jansson drew its wrath when in 1840 he began to preach a perfectionist doctrine of sinlessness. He preached his doctrine in the Halsingland region, which had long been known for religious enthusiasm. Charges of immorality followed him. In 1844, he moved to the Halsingland area after several years of itinerant preaching. A congregation formed around this first preacher, some considering him a second St. Paul. The Janssonists engaged in public book burning to emphasize the central place of the Bible; Jansson was jailed in 1844 for encouraging such activities.

In October 1845, Jansson was facing another jail term when his followers forced his release and he fled to New York. Between 1846 and 1849, twelve hundred Janssonists left Sweden to establish a pietist community at Bishop Hill in Henry County, Illinois, where they laid out an impressive townsite and farmed the fertile countryside. Jansson was both the temporal and spiritual ruler of the colony.

The strictness of his rule resulted in Jansson's death. In 1850, he stopped the marriage of an apostate to a woman who was his cousin by demanding her return to the colony. The apostate, John Root, sought him out at a courthouse in Cambridge, Illinois, and shot him to death.

SOURCES: Paul Elmen, *Wheat Flour Messiah* (1976); Olov Isaksson, *Bishop Hill, Illinois* (1969); Michael Mikkelsen, *The Bishop Hill Colony* (1974 reprint).

JONES, JAMES WARREN (b. May 13, 1931, Lynn, Indiana; d. November 18, 1978, Jonestown, Guyana), founder and leader of the People's Temple.* Jones was born in a small Indiana town into a large farm family. After attending local schools, he married Marceline Baldwin in 1949, and raised eight children, one natural and seven by adoption. In 1950, he enrolled at Indiana University for a brief time before transferring to Butler University in 1951. During this period he served as a pastor to an Indianapolis church, the Christian Assembly of God Church, which he founded in 1953. Ten years later he changed its name to the People's Temple Full Gospel Church. In 1961, he received a degree in secondary education from Butler University and worked for a missionary project, Belo Horizonte, in Brazil, where he organized orphanages and a mission, and he made a visit to Guyana during the 1962-1963 period.

He was ordained a minister of the Christian Church (Disciples of Christ) in 1964. In 1965, he announced to his Indianapolis congregation that the world was going to be engulfed in a thermonuclear war in 1967 and that it was necessary for the congregation to relocate. In 1966, seventy families moved with him to Ukiah, California, about one hundred miles north of San Francisco, where they purchased a church and other properties. During 1970 Jones began preaching in the poor and black neighborhoods of San Francisco, and in 1971 he moved the People's Temple to that city.

Jones's message was initially Christian, evangelical, and fundamentalist. He had served as chairman of the Indianapolis Human Relations Commission in 1961 and gained a reputation for his interracial work. However, his message became increasingly political and explicitly Marxist beginning in the early 1970s. His philosophy was an eclectic one and combined elements of Marxism, millennialism, faith healing, social protest, and evangelism. He was also known to have admired the work of Father Divine,* who ministered to the poor and oppressed in urban centers from 1930 to 1960. By 1976, Jones had become a powerful political force in San Francisco because he was able to use his People's Temple congregation as a pressure group and a voting bloc. After supporting George Moscone for mayor in 1976, Jones was appointed to the City Housing Authority, later becoming its chairman. In 1977, he made plans to establish a model community at Guyana, South America, a country he had visited twice and where in 1974 he had taken a lease on 27,000 acres of land in an area the socialist government wanted developed and colonized. Jones feared that there were forces in the United States trying to destroy his work, and he wanted a site to escape to. At this time rumors were heard of brutalization of the members and sexual irregularities within the church; nevertheless, a large contingent of his followers went to Guyana to begin this rural utopia that they named Jonestown.

Jones had the endorsement of numerous public officials in his social crusade, including Mrs. Rosalind Carter, the president's wife, Vice-President Walter Mondale, and California Governor Jerry Brown. But complaints by relatives of colony members caused California Congressman Leo Ryan to visit the site. Just prior to his departure from Guyana after talks with Jones and cult members, Ryan and several members of his party were murdered. On November 18, 1978, over nine hundred members of the temple, including Jones, committed suicide. This mass suicide occurred because the colony members had been instructed by Jones to give up their lives, because they were isolated and being attacked by outsiders, and because they believed they were going to a better life.

SOURCES: *Chicago Tribune* (November 21, 1978); Charles A. Krause, *Guyana Massacre* (1978); *The New York Times* (November 26, 1978); *New West* (August, 1978).

JORDAN, CLARENCE (b. July 29, 1912, Talbotton, Georgia; d. October 29, 1969, Americus, Georgia), pacifist and founder of the Koinonia Farm. Jordan, one of ten children, was born into a wealthy Southern family. He entered the University of Georgia at Athens in 1929, intent on becoming a scientific farmer. After his graduation in 1933, he entered the United States Cavalry, but during a training session resigned his commission and decided to become a Baptist minister. He then entered Southern Baptist Theological Seminary at Louisville, Kentucky, receiving his degree in 1936 and marrying the same year. In 1938, he accepted a teaching position at Simmons University in Louisville and became increasingly involved with Negro Baptists. During this period, he took his doctorate in divinity.

In 1942, under the influence of philosopher Martin England, Jordan started an interracial colony at Americus, Georgia, called Koinonia Farm (from the Greek word meaning communion or fellowship) to combine religious training with actual experience in community service. They secured a 440-acre farm and hoped to train Negro ministers and provide a training ground for Christian missionaries, black and white. During the late 1940s, a series of college-educated ministers joined the Jordans at their farm, and by 1950 there were fourteen adults at the farm. At this time, the residents at Koinonia established close contact with the Hutterian Brethren. In 1956-1957, violence was directed against the colony and they received visits from the Ku Klux Klan. Yet, they survived a local boycott begun in 1957 and sustained their community by selling pecan products to Northern markets.

In addition to occasional pamphlets, Jordan wrote *The Cotton Patch Version of the New Testament* as a statement of his faith. In 1968, the group became known as Koinonia Partners with a large outreach program and some low-cost housing on the site at Americus. Jordan died during this new phase of his experiment in Christian fellowship.

SELECTED WORKS: The Cotton Patch Version of the New Testament (1968). *SOURCES:* Dallas Lee, *The Cotton Patch Evidence* (1971).

K

KEIL, WILLIAM (b. March 6, 1812, Nordhausen, Austria; d. December 30, 1877, Aurora, Oregon), founder of the Bethel-Aurora colonies* (see also Appendix A, Nos. 90 and 131). Keil arrived in the United States in 1831 on the same ship as John A. Roebling, the builder of the Brooklyn Bridge. For some time Keil followed his trade as a tailor, but according to Charles Nordhoff he worked as a physician and showed some knowledge of the botanical tradition. He left the Methodist church to form a sect of his own based on his belief that he was one of the witnesses mentioned in the Book of Revelation.

In 1844, Keil and his followers went to Missouri to establish a Christian community. Some of the early members were dissidents from the Rappite settlement (see Appendix A, No. 28) at Economy, Pennsylvania, which had followed Count Leon (Bernard Muller*) for a brief period. The sixty-one colonists settled in Bethel, Shelby County, Missouri. Keil has been variously called a benevolent autocrat and a dictator, but under his rule the colony grew to a thousand members on four thousand acres by the early 1850s, though some two hundred and fifty members left during 1847 because of Keil. In 1853, a small group left Bethel to explore the Oregon country and to select a location for a new home. They chose a tract of land on the Willapa River at Aurora, Oregon.

In 1855, Keil moved to Oregon, and in 1856, the charter of the Aurora Colony (see Appendix A, No. 131), named in honor of his daughter, was signed. A hotel built in 1863 became the source of the colony's financial prosperity, and during the 1870s and 1880s substantial dwelling houses were constructed. By 1872, they owned twenty-three thousand acres of good land and had a thousand members. Keil remained the dominant force and leading spiritual healer in the community until 1872 when colony pressure forced him to deed over colony lands to individual owners.

SOURCES: Robert J. Hendricks, *Bethel and Aurora* (1971 reprint); Charles Nordhoff, *The Communistic Societies of the United States* (1961 reprint).

KELLY, HARRY (b. ca. 1871, St. Charles, Missouri; d. 1953, New Rochelle, New York), founder of the Mohegan and Mt. Airy colonies. A printer by trade and a wanderer by inclination, Kelly was an organizer for the International Typographical Union when he was 19. When he was twenty, he began riding the rails, living with hoboes and rarely staying in one city for more than two years. The Depression of 1893 radicalized him, and in 1894, while living in Boston, he became an anarchist. He wrote regularly for Emma Goldman's magazine *Mother Earth* after its founding in 1906 and was the Ferrer Association's first organizer. Along with Leonard Abbott,* Kelly was influential in moving the anarchists to the Ferrer Colony* (see Appendix A, No. 267) in New Jersey in 1916. Kelly remained with the colony until 1923 when he moved to New York with the idea of establishing a colony at Lake Mohegan. In 1925, he succeeded in starting the Mohegan Colony and a second one, called Mt. Airy, at Harmon, New York. Although Kelly saw Mohegan as an outgrowth of the Ferrer Colony at Stelton, New Jersey, it developed more out his disillusionment with sectarian politics at the colony. He was able to buy a site about thirty miles north of New York City from the Baron de Hirsch organization, which had used the land as part of its rural settlement program for Jewish immigrants. Mohegan attracted intellectuals from New York City and it had—like Ferrer—its own school. Kelly wanted to reanimate the political and social spirit of an earlier radicalism: "In spite of myself I must admit that as far as the eye can see there is an absence of that idealism that was prevalent before the war. Meetings were held and papers published with enthusiasm and sacrifice. Life had color and adventure whereas now it seems a round of quarrels and futilities." (Quoted in Laurence Veysey, *The Communal Experience,* 1973.) He co-edited in 1925 (with Hippolyte Havel) the *Road to Freedom*, an anarchist magazine. During the Great Depression, Kelly had difficulty getting a job and was turned down by the Tennessee Valley Authority for a position because of his radical background.

SELECTED WORKS: *Mother Earth* (1906-1917); *Road to Freedom* (1923-1930).
SOURCES: Laurence Veysey, *The Communal Experience* (1973).

KELPIUS, JOHANN (b. 1673, Halwegen, Germany; d. February, 1708, Coxsackie, Pennsylvania), founder of the Society of the Woman in the Wilderness. Kelpius was orphaned at an early age and received his education in Tubingen and at the University at Altdorf, near Nuremberg, graduating in 1689 as a doctor of philosophy and liberal arts. In the following years, he published several philosophical works and came to know Johann Zimmerman, a noted astronomer and mathematician from Wurttemberg. Zimmerman had hoped to lead sixteen families to Pennsylvania to found a colony in order to be separated from the "Babilonish Coasts" of Germany. However, he died just prior to the voyage to America in 1694, and the leadership of the group fell to his second in command, young Kelpius. Kelpius had been influenced by Jacob Boehme, the mystic, and the group brought a complete set of Boehme's works to America. The members were attracted to the pietistical movement and the symbolism of the Rosicrucian movement.

Upon their arrival in America, they established a colony, The Society of the Woman in the Wilderness, at Coxsackie, Pennsylvania, on 175 acres on the Wissahickon Creek, near Germantown. They constructed a central building for religious services and a schoolroom, and lived in separate cell-like rooms. This mystic fraternity—forty in all—maintained a crude observatory. Kelpius lived in a small cave where he read and contemplated. He hoped to unite all the various sects that existed among the Germans in Pennsylvania into one universal Christian church. To this end, public services stressing Christian love and unity were held every morning to which all were invited. They called upon their neighbors to repent in anticipation of the millennium and urged that individuals seek communion with God in the wilderness as they had done.

The sect was called the Woman in the Wilderness after the figure in Revelations who was to announce the millennium. By 1704, the community had prospered sufficiently to attract new converts, start a school, and conduct its esoteric research, but marriages and defections in the sect weakened it. The community declined after Kelpius's death.

SELECTED WORKS: The Diarium of Magister Johannes Kelpius (1917).
SOURCES: Julius F. Sachse, *The German Pietists of Provincial Pennsylvania* (1970 reprint); Julius F. Sachse, *Proceedings and Addresses*, Pennsylvania-German Association 25 (1917); *DAB* 10.

KING, WILLIAM (b. November 11, 1812, Ireland; d. ?), leader of the Elgin Association. After attending the University of Glasgow, King came to America in 1830. In 1834, he became rector of a select academy in Louisiana, but returned to Edinburgh in 1843 to begin theological studies. After the death of his wife and child in 1844, he completed his training and then went to Canada as a missionary for the Free Presbyterian Church of Scotland.

In 1848, King decided to free his slaves—some of whom he had purchased and others of whom he had gained by inheritance—move them to Canada, and establish a colony. He planned and then led Elgin, the most successful black colonization scheme in the ante-bellum period. In October 1849, the Elgin Association was incorporated with holdings of forty-three hundred acres. At its height, it had two hundred families and one thousand persons, and farmed fifteen hundred acres. The goal of the colony was to make Canadian Negroes self-sufficient and, eventually, landowners. Prospective members were carefully screened and King enforced a high moral code. Despite opposition to the colony from those who opposed the very existence of Negroes in Canada, it lasted until 1873. Of the seventy who returned to the United States, one became a congressman and another a senator.

SOURCES: William and Jane Pease, *Black Utopia* (1963).

KIRBY, GEORGIANA BRUCE (b. December 1818, Bristol, England; d. January 28, 1887, California), member of Brook Farm* (see also Appendix A, No. 53). Kirby attended boarding school at Enfield, near London, and in 1835 came to Canada as a governess for a family. In 1837, she worked as a domestic in New York and shortly thereafter for a minister's family in Boston. Her employer introduced her to the Brook Farm Association, whereupon both she and her brother joined. He was a pupil/worker and she was a domestic working for her board and instruction. She hoped that Brook Farm could prepare her within a year for work as a public school teacher. She attended classes taught by the recent Harvard graduate Charles Dana* and heard lectures by Emerson.

In April 1844, Kirby left Brook Farm and became involved with female prison reform work at Ossining, New York. She then took a job at Monticello Seminary in 1845 at Alton, Illinois, and in 1847 ran a school in Bonne Femme, Missouri. She left Missouri because she found the atmosphere in this slave-holding region too stifling. Her next teaching position was in West Chester, Pennsylvania, in 1848-1849 where she worked with a Quaker anti-slavery group. In 1850, she left New York for California "so that I might become a sharer in the general prosperity," according to her autobiography. Horace Greeley had loaned her money to make her trip westward, and she settled in Santa Cruz where she lived with co-reformer Eliza Farnham. Kirby and Farnham shocked their Santa Cruz neighbors by wearing the Bloomer costume. In 1852 Kirby married a wealthy tanner, raised five children and became, according to one source, "Santa Cruz's most formidable matriarch." Her account of her stay at Brook Farm, *Years of Experience* (1887), is one of the richer accounts of daily life at that colony. Her anecdotal comments about her famous teachers are insightful, as are her comments about the enthusiasm all the members felt in 1843.

SELECTED WORKS: Years of Experience (1887).
SOURCES: The Carrier Dove (February 1887).

KOSTER, HENRY BERNHARD (b. November 1662, Blumberg, Westphalia, Germany; d. 1749, Hanover, Germany), founder and leading spiritual figure in the Irenia, or True Church of Philadelphia or Brotherly Love. Koster's father was a prosperous merchant and leading figure in Westphalia. At age fifteen, Koster went to the gymnasium at Bremen, after which he attended the University at Frankfort, graduating in 1684. In 1685, he became a tutor to the children of Baron Orten von Schwerin with whom he collaborated on a German translation of the Old Testament.

While in Berlin, Koster became interested in the pietistical movement and met the leader of a theosophical movement which was then preparing to emigrate to America and form a colony. This group, called the Woman in the Wilderness, was led by Johann Kelpius* and arrived in the United States in 1694. Koster, the group's spiritual instructor and leading intellectual figure, tried to keep them within the Lutheran church, despite the mystical leanings of the membership. He drew the ire of the Pennsylvania Quakers when he led the establishment of Christ Church in 1695 in Philadelphia which attracted dissenting Quakers. Koster championed the cause of the followers of the schismatic George Keith against the orthodox Quakers. Koster had sided with the dissenting Quakers and Kelpius, always a peacemaker, disapproved of Koster's actions.

After a disagreement with Kelpius, Koster and a few others from the original colony formed a new religious community of evangelists and called themselves the Brethren in America. The community was located at Plymouth just north of Germantown, Pennsylvania, where their tabernacle, or community house, was called Irenia or the House of Peace. In 1697, Kelpius wrote *De Rusurrectione Imperii Aeternitatis,* a theosophical treatise. The community was a failure. Julius F. Sachse attributes the failure to the fact that Koster's evangelical and mystical philosophy was divisive whereas Kelpius' creed was conducive to community life. In 1699, Koster left America for Germany where he remained until his death. During that period he published numerous works in theosophy and continued his varied pamphlets on religious matters, including an attack on the Quakers in 1700.

SELECTED WORKS: History of Protestation (1696); *De Resurrectione Imperii Aeternitatus* (1702); *Harmonie* (1724).
SOURCES: Julius F. Sachse, *The German Pietists of Provincial Pennsylvania* (1970 reprint).

KRANS, OLAF (b. November 2, 1838, Solja, Westmorland, Sweden; d. January 4, 1916, Altoona, Illinois), primitive painter and member of the Bishop Hill Colony* (see also Appendix A, No. 102). Krans' family emigrated to the United States in 1850 as part of a group that departed to join the Bishop Hill, Illinois, colony founded by Erik Jansson* in 1846. Krans became an artist whose paintings of colony life earned him a place among American primitivists in the nineteenth century. His paintings constitute a singular record of colony life. Although he was primarily a portrait painter, he also did scenes depicting the work patterns in the colony. His "Building a Bridge," "Women in Row," and "Helbron and the Indian" are powerful primitive works which Krans completed many years after he left Bishop Hill. Krans left the colony when he was twenty-three in order to join the Union Army in 1861, but served only briefly. When he returned, the colony was in the midst of dissolution.

In 1865, Krans moved to Galesburg and then to Galva, Illinois, where he worked as a sign and house painter. All of his painting was done in his spare time. His later work focused on rural scenes, local events, and portraiture in the limner tradition.

SOURCES: George Swank, *Painter Krans* (1976).

L

LANE, CHARLES (b. 1800; d. January 5, 1870, Hackney, Middlesex, England), co-founder of Fruitlands* (see also Appendix A, No. 71). Little is known of Lane's early life except that for several years he was the editor of a business journal, *The London Merchant Current,* before becoming involved with reform causes in the 1840s. Lane met Bronson Alcott* at James Pierrepont Greaves' colony, Alcott House, at Ham Common, Surrey, in 1842. Lane was then editing the *Healthian, A Journal of Human Physiology, Diet and Regimen* for the group. When the celebrated Alcott visited, the two, along with Henry Wright, began plans for a colony in America where individuals could develop their higher spiritual natures. It was Lane who provided the capital necessary to purchase the land at Harvard, Massachusetts.

Lane believed in the "consociate family"—a term he used to describe a group of like-minded individuals who had a certain intellectual rapport and who needed each other's support to lead a spiritual life. Lane's spirituality was of an aesthetic kind. He refused to use animal products, wool, cotton, tobacco, or spirituous liquors, and urged the hydropathic water cure on his friends. Some found him cold and humorless, but Alcott hung on his every word and followed his advice.

Fruitlands was begun in June 1843 and lasted only until the end of the year. Financial problems and Abigail Alcott's refusal to continue in the consociate household were the primary reasons for its failure. After leaving Fruitlands, Lane joined the Shakers in 1844 at Harvard for only a brief period. In addition, he corresponded with the radical Joseph Palmer about the Leominster Association. He returned to England in September 1846 and subsequently married Hannah Bond who had been a member of Robert Owen's* Harmony Hall Colony. Nothing is known of Lane's later life.

In *Transcendental Wild Oats* (1874), Louisa May Alcott described Lane (or Timon Lion, as she called him): ". . . a bland, bearded Englishman, who expected to be saved by eating uncooked food and going without clothes. He had not yet adopted the primitive costume, however; but contented himself with meditatively chewing dry beans out of a basket." Lane had high standards of morality and personal behavior and he expected others to follow. Some, like Louisa May Alcott, considered him a Puritan and a despot while her father considered him a latter-day saint. Yet his interest in reform measures was wide and he was respected by the Transcendentalists, particularly Emerson, who spoke of Lane as being "so skillful, instant, witty," in an 1843 letter.

SELECTED WORKS: The Healthian (1843-1845).
SOURCES: F. B. Sanborn and W. T. Harris, *A. Bronson Alcott* (1893); Odell Shepard, *Pedlars Progress* (1937).

LEE, ANN (b. February 29, 1736, Manchester, England; d. September 8, 1784, Niskeyuna, New York), founder of the Shakers, or the Society of Believers in Christ's Second Appearing (see also Appendix A, Nos. 1, 2, 4,

5, 6, 7, 8, 9, 10, 11, 12, 13, 18, 19, 20, 21, 22, 24, 27, 29, 202, 220). She was born into a large family of a Manchester blacksmith and received little education. She worked in a textile mill as a young girl and in 1752 as a cook in a public infirmary. In 1758, she joined a religious society at Bolton, north of Manchester, led by two dissenting Quakers, Jane and James Wardley. The group was called derisively by others the "Shaking Quakers" because of their worship service wherein they sang, danced, and spoke in tongues. In 1762, she married. During the next few years she bore four children and all the births were difficult. All of the children died in infancy and she was tormented by their deaths. She believed that their deaths were a punishment for her sins, particularly her sins of the flesh. Her chief sin, and the chief cause of human suffering in the world, was sexual. Sin had entered the world when Adam and Eve lusted for one another. After the death of her last child in 1766, she took a more active role within the sect and in 1770 assumed a leadership role. The Shakers began to preach in the streets of Manchester and attracted considerable notoriety. They condemned sexual intercourse, the worldliness of the churches, and refused to take oaths or observe the Sabbath. They were persecuted for their beliefs, and in 1772 and 1773 she was jailed for violating the Sabbath.

Her imprisonment established her as a martyr to the sect, and while in prison, she claimed that Christ had appeared to her and that she was Jesus Christ in the female form. In 1774, after her release from prison, she became the leader of the group. In that year, eight members of the Bolton sect, including Ann Lee, sailed for the United States because she had repeated visions that a chosen people waited for her there. They arrived in New York City in August 1774, and according to Shaker history, Ann Lee made an announcement: "I am commissioned of the Almighty God to preach the everlasting Gospel to America, and an Angel commanded me to come to this house, and to make a home for me and my people." After a short stay in New York City, she moved in 1776 to Albany, New York, where she and her followers lived quietly on a small farm.

In May 1780, they began to hold public meetings, and converts, many from the revivalistic churches, sought the security of the Shaker faith. She offered them a clear and simple theology and a simple way—celibacy—to atone for their past sins. New converts were always impressed by her calm and deliberate manner, by her startling religious conviction that she was Jesus Christ in female form ("a woman clothed with the sun," according to the Book of Revelations) and by her simple manner. In 1780, she was imprisoned briefly because authorities feared she might be a British spy and because of the sect's refusal to bear arms.

From 1781 until her death, she engaged in vigorous missionary activity throughout New England. During this period incipient Shaker colonies were formed at several sites, but Ann Lee had no clear plan for organizing the society and it was not until 1782 that any thought was given to community planning. Lee was a prophetess and her role was to spread the gospel of celibacy and renunciation of the flesh, to encourage converts to separate from the world, and to give them spiritual guidance. Her missionary work was arduous and weakened her health. In 1784 she died.

SOURCES: Edward D. Andrews, *The People Called Shakers* (1953); Henri Desroche, *The American Shakers* (1971); *DAB* 11; *Dictionary of Notable American Women*, 2.

LEHMAN, PETER (b. May 24, 1757, Glades, Somerset County, Pennsylvania; d. January 4, 1823, Snow Hill, Pennsylvania), leader of the Snow Hill Nunnery* (see also Appendix A, No. 15). Lehman was born into an Amish family. A religious young man, he became a member of the Ephrata Colony* in the 1770s and, in 1798, the leader of the Snow Hill Nunnery. Snow Hill was formed by three German congregations which were seeking a simpler and a communal life to perpetuate the mysticism taught and practiced at Ephrata. Lehman, a lay preacher to one of the congregations, became their spiritual guide and teacher. His role was to organize and direct the spiritual affairs of the congregation in its quest for a purer religious life through community.

The Seventh Day Baptist Church at Snow Hill, or the Snow Hill Nunnery as it was called, was located at Franklin County, Pennsylvania. Begun around 1800, it was organized along the lines of Ephrata with separate brother- and sisterhoods. The first community house was not built until 1814, however. The community never grew beyond forty members at its peak period, 1820-1840. The regimen at Snow Hill copied that established earlier at Ephrata (founded in 1732 under the guidance of Conrad Beissel*). At Snow Hill, prayer and meditation were the focal points of the community's spiritual life, while printing and agricultural labor were the major material interests. Between 1814 and 1843, several houses (intended to serve as chapels and celibate dwelling houses) were constructed. However, the colony barely survived the Civil War.

SOURCE: Julius F. Sachse, *The German Sectarians of Pennsylvania* (1971 reprint).

LERMOND, NORMAN WALLACE (b. ca. 1862, Warren, Maine; d. April 4, 1944, Portland, Maine), early Populist promoter of Equality or Brotherhood of the Cooperative Commonwealth (see Appendix A, No. 216). He was born into a pioneer Maine family, and before becoming involved with socialism and the cooperative, he had worked as a bookstore employee, an accountant, a reporter, and a farmer. Several New England reformers had proposed in 1894 that a chain of socialist colonies be started along the eastern seaboard. F. G. R. Gordon, the New Hampshire reformer, modified the proposal by suggesting that a single state be colonized. Lermond was taken by the idea and began to publicize and promote the idea. He issued a call to found a socialist colony in the pages of the *New York Commonwealth* in 1895. During 1895-1896, he promoted the idea that socialists could colonize a single state. In September 1896, a constitution was written and a group of officers elected, including Myron W. Reed, a reform minister from Denver, and Frank Parsons, an economics instructor at Boston University. In 1897, Eugene V. Debs joined them as organizer. Washington State was settled on as the probable site of the colony, and in August 1897 a tract of land was purchased near Edison. On November 1, 1897, the first Brotherhood of the Cooperative Commonwealth Colony was named "Equality" after the Edward Bellamy* novel of that name. Lermond moved his family and the Brotherhood's offices to Equality in March 1898. He stayed only five months, after a dispute over the formation of a second colony.

Back in Maine, Lermond edited a new publication, *Harmony,* and worked on a variety of reform projects; he ran for governor in 1900. He developed an interest in natural science. Later, a Boston newspaper called him the "John Burroughs of Maine" because he had converted his home into a park and arboretum where he hosted socialist rallies.

SOURCE: Charles LeWarne, *Utopias on Puget Sound* (1975).

LONGLEY, ALCANDER (b. March 31, 1832, Oxford, Ohio; d. April 1918, Chicago, Illinois), a colony organizer and promoter. Longley's career serves as a microcosm of nineteenth-century secular community activity. His father helped establish the Clermont (Ohio) Phalanx (see Appendix A, No. 85), and at age eighteen, young Longley proposed a phalanx of his own but contented himself with joining the North American Phalanx* (see also Appendix A, No. 66) at Red Bank, New Jersey, when he was twenty-one. In 1854, he moved to Cincinnati where he married the first of his three wives. At Cincinnati, Longley and his four brothers established a printing firm for reform literature. In 1857, he began *The Philansterian Record* and attempted to establish a phalanx at Moores Hill, Indiana, with further efforts at Black Lake, Michigan, in 1864 and at Foster's Crossing, Ohio, in 1865. During 1867, he became an Icarian follower and moved to their settlement near Corning, Iowa (see Appendix A, No. 137). After a brief stay, he moved to St. Louis where he began publishing *The Communist* in January 1868.

Longley's first successful effort at forming his own colony came in September 1869 when he established the Reunion Colony* at Carthage, Missouri (see Appendix A, No. 145). During 1871, that settlement faltered and Longley proposed the Friendship Community (see Appendix A, No. 153), to be located near St. Louis. For Longley, the ideal community consisted of a community of goods, equality, brotherhood, and the use of democratic means to control politics and economics. None of his efforts ever had any long-term success, but he continued to try. Between 1877 and 1883, he tried, unsuccessfully, to establish a group in Polk County, Missouri, called Principia. During 1883, he did establish the Mutual Aid Community (see Appendix A, No. 185) at Glen Allen, Bollinger County, Missouri, but it failed to attract either members or financial support. Another unsuccessful effort, this time between 1895 and 1897, was made at Randolph County, Missouri. His last venture was at Sulphur Springs, twenty-two miles south of St. Louis, where the seventy-seven-year-old utopian established the Altruist Community. A newspaper reporter described the community as consisting of "himself [Longley] and an elderly woman stricken with paralysis and rheumatism, bedridden but enthusiastic. (Cited in Hal Sears, "Alcander Longley, Missouri Communist," *Missouri Historical Review* [January 1969].) He continued to publish the *Altruist* until 1917. His best known pamphlet, *Communism: The Right Way, and the Best Way, for All to Live* (1880), outlines his philosophy.

SOURCES: H. Roger Grant, "Missouri's Utopian Communities," *Missouri Historical Review* 66 (October 1971): 20-48; Hal Sears, "Alcander Longley, Missouri Communist," *Missouri Historical Review* (January 1969).

M

MACLURE, WILLIAM (b. October 27, 1763, Ayr, Scotland; d. March 23, 1840, San Angel, Mexico), pioneer geologist and scientist and member of the New Harmony Community* (see also Appendix A, No. 30). Maclure attended elementary school at Ayr. At age nineteen, he entered a mercantile house, becoming a successful partner in the London firm of Miller, Hart and Company, and then retired in 1799 to devote his life to science and philanthropy. Although he had visited New York City briefly in 1782, it was during his second visit in 1796 when "he is reported to have declared legally his intention of becoming an American citizen." In 1803, he became a naturalized citizen of the United States. In that same year, he was appointed to a commission to investigate and settle spoliation claims between the United States and France. He traveled extensively throughout the states, studying natural history and geology and collecting specimens. He made the first substantial geological map of the United States.

In 1824, Maclure visited the site of Robert Owen's* projected colony at New Harmony, became enthusiastic about the project, and purchased an extensive tract of land in the vicinity. He wanted to establish an agricultural school in conjunction with the New Harmony settlement and persuaded other eminent scientists to join him. An admirer of the Pestalozzian method of education, he hoped to see it implemented at New Harmony. Maclure, a social and economic radical, saw utilitarian education as the driving force behind social change. When New Harmony began to disintegrate, one of the splinter groups called their new settlement Macluria in honor of him. Ironically, these religious-motivated dissenters were unaware of Maclure's unfavorable views on religion.

Because of failing health, Maclure moved to Mexico in 1827 where he hoped his plans for an educational school would prosper; they did not. In 1839, he had a serious health failure and decided to return to the United States. He died en route.

SELECTED WORKS: *Observations on the Geology of the United States of America* (1817); *Essay on the Formation of Rocks* (1818); *Opinions on Various Subjects,* 3 vols. (1831-1838).
SOURCES: Arthur Bestor, Jr., *Backwoods Utopias* (1950); J. Percy Moore, "William Maclure—Scientist and Humanitarian," *Proceedings of the American Philosophical Society* (Philadelphia, 1947).

MCCOWEN, HENRY (b. March 23, 1890, Las Cruces, New Mexico; d. March 7, 1970, Elida, New Mexico), newspaper editor and cooperative colony advocate. McCowen received a B.A. in agriculture from the New Mexico College of Agriculture and Mechanic Arts in 1911 and lived at Elida, New Mexico, from that year until his death. An anticapitalist, McCowen advocated the development of cooperative villages based on rational planning, efficiency, and production, ideas which he outlined in his work *Moneyless Government or Why and Why Not*? (1933). Although an original thinker, he derived some of his ideas from Howard Scott, the founder of the technocracy movement, Ralph Borsodi's* decentralist plan for Dayton, Ohio, and some reading of Inca history. McCowen proposed that the United States be reorganized into one hundred thousand communities of two thousand people each. These units would have centralized and efficient services, thereby freeing labor for truly productive work. He said his scheme was "socialism only in part. It is fascism, military discipline, democracy, school life, corporation organization, communism, but above all common sense godliness."

In 1932, McCowen ran for a seat in the New Mexico legislature and was overwhelmingly defeated. In 1934, in the pages of the newspaper *Roosevelt County Record*, he proposed that farmers and ranchers form a cooperative colony. While the scheme never got off the ground, McCowen continued to urge its adoption in the paper. The "Old Moneyless" plan was akin to the more publicized plan offered by successful Depression prophets like John

Coughlin, Charles Townshend, and Huey Long, all of whom offered fiscal and social panaceas in the 1930s. In 1966, McCowen published his *Old Moneyless and Prescription.*

SELECTED WORKS: Moneyless Government (1933); *Old Moneyless and Prescription* (1966).
SOURCES: "Henry C. McCowen, Prairie Radical," *Liberal Arts Review* (Summer 1975); Donald Whisenhut, "Old Moneyless, His Search For Utopia," *Southwest Review* (Autumn 1969).

MCNEMAR, RICHARD (b. November 20, 1770, Tuscarawa Valley, Cumberland County, Pennsylvania; d. September 15, 1839, New Lebanon, New York), the "great apostle to the Shaker West" and founder of the second largest Shaker community. McNemar was born on the Indian frontier and became a school teacher in a pioneer settlement. In 1792, he went to live at Cane Ridge, Kentucky, and married in 1793 while he was studying for the Presbyterian ministry. Ordained a minister in 1798, he became caught up in the 1801 "Kentucky Revival." In 1802, he became the head of the Turtle Creek Church (see Appendix A, No. 18) at New Lebanon, Ohio, and in 1805 was converted by some traveling Shaker missionaries, including John Meachem, a leader from New Lebanon, New York.

After his conversion, McNemar became an active Shaker missionary, organizing several Shaker societies in the West. In addition, he was a prolific writer and the chief publicist for the Shakers against their detractors. His *Kentucky Revival* (1807), the first bound book published by the Shakers, went through several editions. In 1811, Eldress Lucy Wright* singled McNemar out for special missionary work in the West where the Shakers hoped to win new converts. During the spiritualist craze of 1838, he and some other prominent elders were dismissed from Union Village, Ohio (see Appendix A, No. 18), but were restored after a Shaker medium was consulted at New Lebanon, New York (see Appendix A, No. 1). As a result of his long journeys to and from New Lebanon during this period, he became ill and died.

SELECTED WORKS: The Kentucky Revival (1807).
SOURCE: Hazel Spencer Phillips, *Richard the Shaker* (1972).

MCWHIRTER, MARTHA (b. May 18, 1827, Jackson County, Tennessee; d. April 20, 1904, Washington, D.C.), founder and leader of the Women's Commonwealth* (see also Appendix A, No. 157). McWhirter joined the Methodist church at age sixteen and for the next twenty-five years was active in church work. She married in 1845 and went with her family to

Belton, Texas, in 1855. After the death of a brother and two of her children in 1866, she became convinced that God was punishing her. Shortly thereafter, she received a pentecostal baptism (or the Wesleyan second blessing) and believed she was sanctified in the perfectionist tradition.

McWhirter began to hold weekly prayer meetings for the women in the town, many of whom then separated from their husbands or were forced to leave the households of their unsanctified husbands. Communal quarters were established in 1876, with the women living on inheritances and monies earned from domestic labor. Their basic tenets were a belief in dream interpretation, visions, personal holiness, and community of property. In 1882, they established a laundry, and in 1886, they opened a hotel in Belton which catered to travelers going through central Texas. In 1891, they obtained a charter for the Central Hotel Company. The "Sanctificationists," as they were called locally, operated the hotel on a profitable basis with their membership of thirty, but in 1899 they sold the hotel and moved to a comfortable house in Washington, D.C. By 1900, the group membership stood at twenty-three. There were a few men in the group at one point and always several children, but by the time of their move to Washington, there were no men among them. Throughout the history of the group, Martha McWhirter was the acknowledged leader and spiritual guide. When she died in 1904, the colony began to disintegrate.

SOURCES: Llenena Friend, "Texas Communism or Socialism-Early Style," *Library Chronicle of University of Texas* (Summer 1962); George P. Garrison, "A Women's Community in Texas," *Charities Review* (November 1893); Eleanor P. James, "The Sanctificationists of Belton," *American West* (Summer 1945); Alexander Kent, "The Women's Commonwealth," *U.S. Labor Bulletin* No. 35 (July 1901).

MATTHEWS, ROBERT (b. 1787, Cambridge, Washington County, New York; d. ?, New York City), leader of Zion Hill Community. Matthews was a member of the Presbyterian church. He was first a farmer and then turned to carpentry before marrying in 1813 and moving to Cambridge, Massachusetts. In 1816, he was caught up in the religious revivals of the period and subsequently became both a temperance and vegetarian advocate. His prophetic career dates from 1830 when he prophesied that Albany would be destroyed, and shortly thereafter when he had a vision that the only true Christians were the unshaven. He wandered the streets of Albany with his message, calling himself Matthais. He denied ever having been a Christian and now asserted he was a Jew. He traveled throughout New York State and Pennsylvania, and then to New York City where he gathered some disciples, including the abolitionist and suffragette Sojourner Truth.* Matthews had a handful of followers, but a wealthy New York merchant, Benjamin Folger, and his wife were prominent supporters. For his followers he was both the Messiah and God. He wore gorgeous robes and went about town in a handsome livery.

After some disputes in New York, Matthews relocated his community at Zion Hill near Sing Sing, New York, where he lived a communal life with his followers. According to William Stone, it soon evolved into a free love colony with spiritual marriages taking place. Matthews was arrested in 1835 on a charge of having murdered, by poisoning, his chief disciple, Elijah Pierson, in 1834. Matthews was declared not guilty on the murder charge, but was imprisoned on an assault charge brought against him by his married daughter. Sojourner Truth, known as Isabella at that time, helped defend Matthews. She entered a slander suit against his detractors in 1835. Mathews' later career is unknown.

SELECTED WORKS: *The False Prophet* (1835).
SOURCES: Arthur Huff Fausett, *Sojourner Truth* (1938); William L. Stone, *Matthias and his Impostures* (1835).

MEACHEM, JOSEPH (b. February 22, 1741, Enfield, Connecticut; d. August 16, 1796, Enfield, Connecticut), leader of the Shaker community at New Lebanon, New York (see Appendix A, No. 1). Meachem was raised in a religious family (his father had been converted by Jonathan Edwards) and he was a lay preacher at the Baptist church at New Lebanon, New York, in the 1770s. As a lay preacher, he led a revival among the New Light Baptists in the area west of Albany, New York, in 1779. The Shakers lived nearby at the time, and he was converted to their doctrine in March, 1779. Ann Lee* spoke of him as "the wisest man that has been born of a woman for six hundred years" and he became a leader of the society in 1787, after Lee's death.

It was under Meachem's guidance that the society was organized and rules set forth for governing it, for guiding Shakers in their relations with the outside world and for conduct between the sexes. These rules were later codified into laws and distributed to the various societies in 1821 as the *Millennial Laws*. It was Meachem who appointed Lucy Wright* to head the Shaker sisterhood and establish a separate order. He also issued a call to all those Shakers converted under Ann Lee to leave the world and come to New Lebanon, New York, in 1788. Industries were begun, buildings erected, and believers flocked to New Lebanon. He gave the society a commercial foundation and a corporate ethic that enabled it to succeed in the world. Edward D. Andrews wrote: "Eliminate the influence of Joseph Meachem and the church would probably not have survived the death of its founder, or merited more than a footnote in the social, economic, or religious history of America." Under Meachem the Shakers grew in numbers, expanded the number of communities, and established New Lebanon as the leading church within the Shaker hierarchy. Ministers were trained and covenants signed and agreed to by the various families. The Shakers were brought into increasing commercial contact with the world at just the moment they were conscious of their separation from it.

SOURCE: Edward D. Andrews, *The People Called Shakers* (1953).

MEEKER, NATHANIEL C. (b. July 12, 1817, Euclid, Ohio; d. September 29, 1879, White River Reservation, Wyoming), newspaper writer, founder of the Union Colony* (see also Appendix A, No. 146) of Colorado, and Indian agent. Little is known of Meeker's early life except that he held several different positions as a young man before marrying Arvilla Smith at Euclid, Ohio. In the early 1840s, he became interested in Fourier and began to lecture on his philosophy. He lived at the Trumbull Phalanx (see Appendix A, No. 86), Braceville, Ohio, from 1846 to 1849, after which he returned to business at Euclid. In 1865, he joined the staff of the *New York Tribune* as agricultural editor.

In December 1869, Meeker launched the Union Colony with the support of Horace Greeley* and the *Tribune.* A site near the Platte River and on the Denver Pacific Line was found for the colony. Meeker hoped to attract individuals interested in moral and intellectual development through co-operation. The cooperative colony recognized private ownership of land but shared community responsibilites. It had no saloons or billboards, but constructed a school, library, and lyceum in its existence. As president of the colony, Meeker made enemies by his tactless manner; yet his newspaper, the *Greeley Tribune*, urged benevolent reform and was moderate in tone. The Union Colony became like other Colorado towns and its thousand residents developed the town as a commercial center. By 1871 the colonists voted to replace the colony's officers with an elected town government.

In 1878, Meeker once again became restless, and he was being pressed by his creditors, so he accepted a position as a government Indian agent on the White River Reservation. He set out at once to civilize his charges, urging they build log cabins and plow the surrounding fields. His lack of tact and understanding made the Utes hostile. Meeker and two others were killed in an uprising. He published two books, one of which, *The Adventures of Captain Armstrong* (1849), parallels the last phase of his own life. The tale deals with a captain shipwrecked in the South Seas who tries to educate the "savages."

SELECTED WORKS: *The Adventures of Captain Armstrong* (1849); *Life in the West* (1868).
SOURCES: DAB 12.

METZ, CHRISTIAN (b. December 30, 1793, Neuwied, Germany; d. July 25, 1867, Amana, Iowa), leader of the Amana Society* (see also Appendix A, Nos. 68, 128). Little is known abut Metz's childhood except that he was raised in a pietist sect, the Inspirationists, and at age fifteen was apprenticed to a cabinetmaker. In 1817, he participated in a religious revival with other youths in the area, and during this period he experienced revelations. During the early 1840s, Metz became a leader in the Inspirationists, who then were being persecuted by local authorities. Throughout the period, he claimed that he received inspirations from God concerning the sect, and he traveled to Switzerland and Saxony spreading the Inspirationists' simple gospel. In 1842, he received an inspiration indicating that the group should emigrate to a land where there was greater religious toleration.

In September 1842, Metz and a small group left for the United States as an advance party to find a colony site. They looked at land in the Buffalo, New York, area and purchased a five thousand-acre parcel at Ebenezer. Soon there were eight hundred families living at the colony, which became known as the Society of True Inspirationists. Metz then wrote a constitution for the group, which mandated community ownership of property, except personal and household equipment. Community kitchens, gardens, and households would be provided. Communism was considered only a temporary measure to finance the land purchase. Metz visited the Separatists of Zoar in Ohio and was unimpressed by their community, even though he found their religious sentiments acceptable. In 1843, a group of fifty settlers arrived at Buffalo, and by 1855 there were a thousand in the area, clustered around a village they called Ebenezer. In 1854, Metz received a revelation that the colony should move once again, because the membership had become indifferent to spiritual things. After looking at land in Kansas, they purchased several thousand acres in Iowa in 1855. Between 1856 and 1864, settlers began to move from Ebenezer to their new colony site at Amana, Iowa. Metz directed the colony affairs from Ebenezer during this period.

SELECTED WORKS: A Revelation of Jesus Christ Through the True Inspiration to the President of the United States (1860); *Historische Beeschreibung de wagren Inspirations-Gemeinschaft* (1863); *Inspirations-Historie oder Auszuge aus den Tagebuchern von Br. Christian Metz* (1875); *Inspirations* (1875).
SOURCES: Francis Alan DuVal, "Christian Metz, German American Religious Leader and Pioneer," Ph.D. dissertation, State University of Iowa (1948); Bertha Shambaugh, *Amana That Was and Amana That Is* (1932).

MILLER, PETER (b. 1710, Alsenborn, Germany; d. September 25, 1796, Ephrata, Pennsylvania), superintendent of Ephrata Colony.* Miller, the son of a Reformed minister, studied at Heidelberg University and graduated in 1725. In 1730, Miller, then a young deacon, volunteered to go to Pennsylvania as a clergyman. Upon arrival, he applied for ordination with the First Presbyterian church of Philadelphia. After his ordination, his first pastorate was with Lutheran and Reformed congregations living in the Cocalico and Bucherthal valleys.

The Ephrata Colony, under the direction of Conrad Beissel,* was within the bounds of one of the parishes. Miller converted to the Sabbatarian doctrines of the group, quit his ministry, and in 1735 became a member of Ephrata, taking ten families, Reformed and Lutheran, with him. After their baptism, the converts burned all the devotional literature from their old faiths. Miller retired to a hermitage before joining the newly organized (1732) monastic community at Ephrata. Miller was called Brother Jabez in the colony and, with Beissel, was a leading member. On Beissel's death in 1768, he succeeded him as prior, or superintendent, of Ephrata. What had begun as an interest in Sabbatarianism and Separatism developed into a celibate and monastic colony of forty. Some members, however, had been attracted by the mystical and Rosicrucian aspects of the society. Under the name Brother Agrippa, Miller was co-author of the *Chronichon Ephratense,* the history of Ephrata, published in 1786.

SELECTED WORKS: *Chronicon Ephratense* (1786).
SOURCES: Julius F. Sachse, *The German Sectarians of Pennsylvania* 1, 2 (1970 reprint).

MODJESKA, HELENA (b. October 12, 1840, Cracow, Poland; d. April 8, 1909, Bay Island, East Newport, California), actress and founder of Modjeska Colony (see Appendix A, No. 164). Modjeska made her first stage appearance in 1861 and by 1868 was a star on the Polish stage. In 1876, she and a group of fellow actors decided to emigrate to the United States in order to avoid oppressive censorship in the theater, to find a healthful site, since she had been in poor health, and to establish a colony similar to Brook Farm* (see also Appendix A, No. 53). Henry Sienkiewicz had visited southern California earlier that year and had returned with glowing reports about the area. Hence, when they arrived in New York, an advance party was sent to Anaheim, California.

There is dispute over whether or not a utopian colony—variously called Polish Brook Farm, or Modjeska's Colony—was ever established since there was no mention of such a colony in local papers, but Modjeska described a colony in her *Memories and Impressions* (1910). The group moved to the site in 1877 and consisted of Modjeska, her husband Count Chiliapowski, Rudolphe, her son by her first marriage, and three other individuals, including Sienkiewicz who later wrote the novel *Quo Vadis* (1896). Modjeska's knowledge of the Fourierist Reunion Colony* at Dallas may have influenced her thinking about colony plans. They lived on a 1,165-acre site near Irvine, California, and left after about six months when they used up their available savings.

At that point Madame Modjeska resumed her stage career. She created memorable roles in *Camille, Mary Stuart,* and *Adrienne Lecouvier,* and made a national tour with the noted Shakespearean actor Edwin Booth. She remained a staunch Polish nationalist throughout her career and publicly deplored the oppression of Polish women in a speech at the Columbian Exposition in 1893. She died in 1909 and was buried in Cracow, Poland.

SELECTED WORKS: *Memories and Impressions of Helena Modjeska* (1910).
SOURCES: Robert Hine, *California's Utopian Colonies* (1953); *Dictionary of Notable American Women,* 3.

MORTON, JAMES FERDINAND (b. October 18, 1870, Littleton, Massachusetts; d. October 7, 1941, Patterson, New Jersey), editor and member of the Home Colony* (see also Appendix A, No. 218). Morton was the son of a Baptist minister and grandson of Samuel Francis Smith, the author of "America." He attended Harvard for his A.B. and A.M. degrees (1892) and was the originator of intercollegiate debates. While a student, he developed an interest in social questions. After graduation, he moved to San Francisco to work on the libertarian magazine *Free Society.*

In 1900, Morton visited the anarchist colony Home, becoming editor of its paper *Discontent: Mother of Progress* in 1901. During his stay at the community, he served as its chief publicist and public apologist, often defending the colony on lecture tour. Morton left the colony in 1905 and joined the staff of the *Truth Seeker*, an anarchist journal. In 1906, he published *The Curse of Race Prejudice.* He was an active member of the NAACP, and worked as a field secretary for the New York Single Tax League. From 1825 to 1941, he was the curator of the Patterson, New Jersey, Museum.

SELECTED WORKS: *The Curse of Race Prejudice* (1906).
SOURCES: Charles Le Warne, *Utopias on Puget Sound* (1975); Laurence Veysey, *The Communal Experience* (1973); *Who Was Who In America,* I.

MULLER, BERNARD (b. 1787, Aschaffenburg, Germany; d. August 29, 1834, Grand Ecore, Louisiana), religious mystic and entrepreneur. Muller, known as Count Leon, was probably the illegitimate son of a distinguished German nobleman, Karl von Dalberg. He received a religious education and in 1810 published a jeremiad against Napoleon predicting his early downfall. Muller considered himself a prophet. In 1813, he founded a secret order, the Duchy of Jerusalem, while living in Ireland, at which time he changed his name to Proli, which means Son of God. He lived for a while in London and then in several German towns during which he developed a religious following.

In 1831, after a legal dispute, he sold an estate which some wealthy followers had given him and he sailed for the United States. During passage, he announced his new title: Prince Leon. After a triumphal tour of several American cities as a visiting German prince, he came to the Harmonist settlement (see Appendix A, No. 28) at Economy, Pennsylvania, announcing himself as Archduke Maximillian of the Stem of David and the Root of David. The Rappites had expected a spiritual leader to gather in the elect, but the count was too mystical and apocalyptic for them. In 1832, a dispute between George Rapp* and the count over colony leadership resulted in a secessionist split. In April 1832, Muller's followers established the New Philadelphia Society (see Appendix A, No. 44) at Phillipsburg, Pennsylvania, on eight hundred acres. In 1833, the group was dissolved in order to locate the New Jerusalem at another site, this time on the exact same latitude as the original Jerusalem. In 1834, they settled at Grand Ecore, Louisiana, near the correct latitude (see Appendix A, No. 48). But the climate and the land were too harsh for the wandering settlers and Count Leon. He died there at a place the colonists renamed Gethsemane.

SOURCES: Karl Arndt, *George Rapp's Harmony Society, 1785-1847* (1965).

N

NELSON, NELSON O. (b. 1844, Lillisand, Norway; d. October 1922, Los Angeles, California), social reformer and supporter of communal settlements. Nelson, a member of a rural Norwegian family who migrated to Missouri, served in the Union Army during the Civil War. In the late 1870s, he began a plumbing fixture business in St. Louis, becoming a millionaire within a decade. It was not until the Depression of 1886 that he launched into a reform career that would include a major cooperative industrial enterprise and support for communal settlements as a solution to industrial and social problems.

Guided by the careers of two European cooperators and factory owners, J. B. Godin and Edmund Leclaire, Nelson introduced profit-sharing into his business and began to investigate the possibilities of establishing an industrial colony along the lines of Godin's Familisterie at Guise, France. In 1890, he relocated his factory on a 250-acre site near Edwardsville, Illinois. During this period, he generously supported Bellamy's* magazine, *The New Nation,* and attended the First International Cooperative Congress held in London in 1895. During the next five years, he followed the fortunes of the Ruskin Cooperative Association* (see also Appendix A, No. 204) in Tennessee and contributed articles to their paper, *The Coming Nation.*

At the turn of the century, Nelson diverted his support to the garden cities movement inspired by Ebenezer Howard's work and, in 1908, to the development of rural cooperatives in the South. In 1911-1912, he was instrumental in starting a chain of cooperative grocery stores in New Orleans with over three hundred employees, but by 1918 the company was bankrupt and Nelson suffered a nervous breakdown. At the end of his life, he was befriended by Upton Sinclair,* in whose home he lived.

SELECTED WORKS: "Introduction" to Samuel M. Jones, *The New Right* (1899).

SOURCES: Kim McQuaid, "Businessman As Reformer" and "Businessman As Social Innovator," *American Journal of Economics and Sociology* (October 1974-October 1975).

NEWBROUGH, JOHN BALLOU (b. June 5, 1828, Mohicanville, Ohio; d. April 22, 1891, Las Cruces, New Mexico), founder of the Shalam Colony (see Appendix A, No. 188). Newbrough attended Cleveland Medical College for dentistry and traveled to California and Australia before settling in Dayton and Cincinnati during 1853-1857. In 1855, he published a travel romance, *The Lady of the West,* or *The Gold Seekers,* for, as he wrote in his introduction, the "purpose of social reform" and attacked nativism, suffragettes, and abolitionists in the novel. He married Rachel Turnbull in 1857, after which he moved first to Philadelphia and then to New York (in the early 1860s) where he served on the board of the New York Spiritualist Society and, for a short time, joined the Domain* (see Appendix A, No. 119), a spiritualist community at Jamestown, New York.

In 1882 with Elizabeth Rowell Thompson's* help, Newbrough published *Oashpe,* a book written "automatically" under spirit influence. Written in a language all its own, Paneric, it traced the history of man on earth back seventy-three thousand years and through twenty-four "arcs," or cycles of history. The book created a band of followers and eventually two communal societies based on two principles: the care of orphaned children and Newbrough's mystical inspiration. The first community, located at Pearl River, New York, was a gathering-in place for both believers and children; it was established in 1884 after a New York convention of the Faithist Lodge of Oashpe. A second community, Shalam, was founded in New Mexico, near Las Cruces, in 1884. Newbrough and Andrew M. Howland gathered up children from foundling homes and from indigent mothers. About thirty children were taken into the community, placed on special diets, and instructed in the spiritual path laid down by the *Oashpe.* Just prior to his death, Newbrough wrote another inspirational tract, "The Book of Gratyius," in which he urged the starting of another colony, Levitica. That task was left to his wife and co-worker Howland, who married after Newbrough's death and carried on the community until 1901.

SELECTED WORKS: *The Lady of the West* (1855); *Catechism on Human Teeth* (1865); *Oashpe* (1881).
SOURCES: Julia Keleher, "The Land of Shalam," *New Mexico Historical Review* (April 1944); Daniel Simundson, "Strangers in the Valley," *New Mexico Historical Review* (July 1970); K. D. Stoes, "The Land of Shalam," *New Mexico Historical Review* (January and April 1958).

NICHOLS, MARY GOVE (b. August 10, 1810, Goffstown, New Hampshire; d. May 30, 1884, London), social reformer and co-founder of the Memnonia Institute* (see also Appendix A, No. 129). This writer, water cure physician, and reformer was an enthusiastic and energetic figure known in reform circles for her advocacy of mesmerism, spiritualism, Fourierism, temperance, and dress reform. In 1831, she married Hiram Gove. After the birth of their first daughter, she turned her attention to writing about the anatomy and physiology of women. She lectured on the subject throughout New England and published her addresses in 1846 under the title *Lectures to Women on Anatomy and Physiology.* In 1840, she separated from Gove and worked for a time as editor of the *Health Journal and Advocate of Physiological Reform,* a vegetarian publication. In 1842, she met Henry G. Wright, who introduced her to the water cure system, and by 1845 she was a water cure physician in New York City. She held evening gatherings in her home and attracted notable artists, reformers, and writers, including Edgar Allan Poe. She continued to write and publish articles in the *New York Water Cure Journal* and published *Experiences in Water Cure* (1849) as well as several short novels during this period.

In 1848, she married Thomas Low Nichols,* whom she had met at a Fourierist meeting. In 1855, they collaborated on *Nichols Monthly,* a magazine based in Cincinnati. During 1856-1857, they ran the Memnonia Institute, a colony at Yellow Springs, Ohio, devoted to the water cure, free love, and personal advancement. Horace Mann opposed the colony and helped drive it from Yellow Springs. They converted to Catholicism in March 1857 and remained Catholics the rest of their lives. In 1861, the Nicholses left the United States for England because of their opposition to the war; they continued their reform efforts in London.

SELECTED WORKS: *Lectures to Women on Anatomy and Physiology* (1846); *Experiences in Water Cure* (1849); *Mary Lyndon* (1855).
SOURCES: Philip Gleason, "From Free Love to Catholicism," *Ohio Historical Quarterly* (October 1961); *Dictionary of Notable American Women,* 2.

NICHOLS, THOMAS LOW (b. 1815, Orford, New Hampshire; d. 1901, Chaumont-en-Venzin, France), pioneer dietician, hydrotherapist, author, editor, and co-founder of the Memnonia Institute* (see also Appendix A, No. 129). Nichols had a conventional childhood. After beginning a medical program at Dartmouth, he abandoned it for a journalistic career, serving apprenticeships on papers at Lowell, Massachusetts, and New York City. After editing a political paper called *Buffalonian* in 1837, he published his first book, *Journal in Jail,* the result of a brief imprisonment on libel charges. For the next fifteen years, Nichols advocated the major reforms of his day, including Fourierism, Grahamism, and free love.

In 1848, Nichols married Mary Gove,* a water cure physician, and in 1851, after he had completed his medical training in New York, the couple founded a school for the training of hydrotherapists. In 1853, Nichols published *Esoteric Anthropology,* and in 1854 he co-authored, with Mary Nichols, *Marriage: Its History, Character and Results.* He wrote extensively for reform journals, including the *American Vegetarian and Health Journal* and the *Water Cure Journal.* In 1855, the Nicholses moved to Cincinnati where they published *Nichols Monthly,* a magazine devoted to spiritualism, health reform, and individual liberty. Between 1856 and 1857, they conducted a water cure and School for Life, the nucleus of their communal settlement, called the Memnonia Institute at Yellow Springs, Ohio, the site of the newly formed Antioch College. Conflicts with local residents and Horace Mann's active opposition forced these believers in spiritual affinity to abandon their colony. Soon afterwards, the Nicholses converted to Catholicism, and when the Civil War broke out they went to England. There Nichols published an incisive social history, *Forty Years of American Life* (1864), and continued hydropathic and spiritualist endeavors. From 1867 to 1875, they operated an institute at Malvern, and from 1875 to 1886 he co-edited the *London Herald of Health.* His other works include *Eating to Live Well* (1881), *Dyspepsia* (1884), and *Nichols' Health Manual* (1887).

SELECTED WORKS: Journal in Jail (1840); *Marriage: Its History, Character and Results* (1854); *Woman in All Ages & Nations* (1854); *Forty Years of American Life* (1864).
SOURCES: Philip Gleason, "From Free Love to Catholicism: Dr. and Mrs. Thomas L. Nichols A and Yellow Springs"; *The Ohio Historical Quarterly* (October 1961); *DAB* 13.

NOAH, MORDECAI MANUEL (b. July 19, 1785, Philadelphia, Pennsylvania; d. March 22, 1851, New York City, editor and advocate of co-operative settlements. Noah's parents were merchants. Noah became a journalist after reporting the sessions of the legislature at Harrisburg. In 1813, he was appointed consul to Tunis, with the special charge of negotiating the release of Americans held by Algerian pirates; he successfully effected their release. Noah believed he was relieved of that post because he was a Jew. In 1817, he became editor of the *National Advocate,* a daily paper founded by Tammany supporters.

In 1820, he first petitioned the New York State Legislature to make Grand Island a refuge for the Jews, but the bill never passed. However, he was able to convince a friend to purchase 2,555 acres on the island and hoped then to turn it into both a Jewish settlement and a center for commerce. A contemporary of his, Lewis Allen, described him: "He was a Jew, thorough and accomplished" who had many Gentile friends "who adopted him into their political associations."

In 1825, Noah urged the establishment of a colony, "Ararat, a City of Refuge," in America for oppressed Jews. Noah proposed to levy taxes on Jews throughout the world to support the colony. He invited all Jews, Samaritans, black Jews and even Indians, whom he accepted as the ten lost tribes of Israel, to join. The colony was to be located at Grand Island in the Niagara River.

While the proposal was widely discussed, it was never implemented. His pretensions to leadership of the colony were the subject of ridicule. Jews in America and abroad denounced the idea that a marshland on the Niagara frontier was the spot for the scattered remnants of Israel. In fact, Noah had never set foot on the island and the colony was only memorialized in a cornerstone laid at the church where he announced the colony's formation, St. Paul's Episcopal Church, Buffalo. After this disappointing experience, he turned his efforts to the establishment of Palestine. The best known American Jew of his time, he had a varied career as a playwright and editor. A collection of his newspaper essays, *Gleanings from a Gathered Harvest,* was published in 1845.

SELECTED WORKS: Discourse on the Evidence of the American Indians Being the Descendants of the Lost Tribes of Israel (1837); *Gleanings from a Gathered Harvest* (1845).
SOURCES: Selig Adler and Thomas E. Connolly, *From Ararat to Suburbia* (1960); G. H. Cone, "Ararat," *American Jewish Historical Society Proceedings* 21 (1913); *DAB* 13.

NOYES, JOHN HUMPHREY (b. September 11, 1811, Brattleboro, Vermont; d. April 13, 1886, Niagara Falls, Canada), founder of the Oneida Community* (see also Appendix A, No. 108). Noyes was born into a respectable New England family whose forebears had emigrated from England in 1634. His father was a merchant and a member of the U.S. House of Representatives for one term (1816-1817). In 1822, the Noyes family moved to Putney, Vermont, and in 1826, Noyes entered Dartmouth, graduating in

1830. In 1831, he entered the Andover Theological Seminary as the result of a revival meeting at Putney, but in 1832, he transferred to Yale where he fell under the influence of Nathaniel Taylor, a liberal theologian. While at Yale, he became involved in founding the New Haven Anti-Slavery Society and the New Haven Free church. During 1833, he received his license to preach, but it was revoked in 1834 after a controversy with a North Salem, New York, church when he professed his personal holiness and espoused the doctrines of the radical perfectionists. Between 1834 and 1837, he worked with free church groups and helped edit *The Perfectionist.*

In 1837, Noyes began an informal Bible study group at Putney and became increasingly identified with certain free love doctrines. In 1841, the Putney Society (see Appendix A, No. 69) was organized on semi-communal grounds; in 1846, this small group began to practice "complex marriage" wherein the "partition of the sexes" was taken away. Late in 1847, Noyes was charged with adultery and fled Putney for central New York, a perfectionist center. In 1848, he founded the Oneida Community at Oneida Creek, New York, on the principles of Bible Communism, a religous faith grounded in Noyes' desire to return to the teachings of the primitive church, his belief in man's ability to achieve religious security from sin and his commitment to economic communism. From 1848 until 1880, the colony prospered through its manufacture of traps and agricultural products. During this period, the members practiced "complex marriage," their unique system of sexual relations wherein individuals were able to choose their partners, and where they employed male continence, or coitus reservatus, to control family size and to promote spirituality among the members.

There is little doubt that Noyes was a remarkable figure. His willingness to experiment with an unusual sexual theory, his capacity to lead the colony into successful economic projects, and his personal charm all made him the prototype of the charismatic leader. That leadership he exercised through a group of elders who were responsible for the major industries and departments in the society. But it was Noyes who organized and inspired the colony. Some contemporaries, like William Lloyd Garrison, were influenced by his writings; others derided him as a licentious free-lover. To the members at Oneida he was "Father John." Noyes was the undisputed leader of Oneida. It was at his instigation that an experiment in eugenics—called stirpiculture—was inaugurated in 1869. He was not always in residence at Oneida, but spent extended periods at associated communes in Brooklyn, New York, in the early years and at Wallingford, Connecticut, during the 1860s and 1870s. When internal disputes and external forces threatened the colony in the late 1870s, he fled to Canada. He was absent when the colony was reorganized in 1880 as a joint-stock corporation, Oneida Company, Ltd.

SELECTED WORKS: The Berean (1847); *Bible Communism* (1848); *History of American Socialism* (1870); *Essay on Scientific Propagation* (1875).

SOURCES: Robert S. Fogarty, "Oneida: A Utopian Search for Religious Security," *Labor History* (1973); Maren Lockwood, *The Oneida Community* (1969); Robert A. Parker, *A Yankee Saint* (1935).

OLERICH, HENRY (b. December 14, 1851, Hazel Green, Wisconsin; d. May 10, 1927, Omaha, Nebraska), utopian writer and colony supporter. Olerich was born into a large German farm family and worked briefly as a school principal at Arcadia, Iowa, in 1888 before making his career as a utopian writer. That year he published a collection of reform essays entitled *Various Essays.* In 1893, he wrote his famous *A Cityless and Countryless World,* a utopian novel which projected a world of small communities, centralized housing facilities, and progressive reforms concerning sexual relations, child rearing, and dress. Educational reform played a large part in his scheme. Olerich's own adopted daughter, Viola, was reared on experimental principles and toured the United States as a child prodigy.

Olerich was in touch with A. K. Owen* about the Topolobampo Bay Colony* and became involved in an experiment in Colorado in 1895, but he never joined any colony. In 1902, he quit teaching and took a job with the Union Pacific Railroad in Omaha. Shortly before World War I, he proposed the establishment of a communal colony on the Nebraska plains, but the plan never materialized into an actual community. According to Roger Grant, he died a suicide, clutching a copy of his latest work, "The New Life and Future Mating," to his breast.

SELECTED WORKS: Viola Olerich (1900); *Causes and Cure of the High Cost of Living* (1919); *A Cityless and Countryless World* (1971 reprint).
SOURCES: H. Roger Grant, "Henry Olerich and Utopia," *Annals of Iowa* (Summer 1976).

OLIPHANT, LAURENCE (b. 1829, Capetown, South Africa; d. December 23, 1888, London), member of the Brocton Community (see Appendix A, No. 143). Oliphant was born into a distinguished English family (his father was chief justice of Ceylon and was knighted in 1839). In 1828, his father was attorney general of the Cape of Good Hope, living in Capetown, where he met and married Marcia Campbell. In 1837, she returned to England for health reasons and took her nine-year-old son with her. Young Oliphant attended school at Durnford Manor, near Salisbury, and, rather than attending Cambridge, to complete his education, he traveled about Europe with his mother and father, who had returned from Ceylon in 1846. He often traveled with his mother and there was strong bond between them. Oliphant was widely traveled as a young man. After becoming a practicing attorney in Ceylon, he took terms at Lincoln's Inn in 1851 and then studied at Edinburgh in 1852. His real interest was journalism, however. After publishing a series of distinguished travel accounts from Europe, he visited the United States in 1854 with Lord Elgin. Between 1854 and 1863, he covered wars and revolutions from Japan to Poland for several newspapers. In 1860, the Oliphants (mother and son) met Thomas Lake Harris* in London through a mutual friend who was interested in spiritualism, but Laurence Oliphant continued with his journalistic career and in 1865 was elected to Parliament.

Oliphant's life was transformed in 1867 when he decided to resign his parliamentary seat in disgust with politics and join Harris's spiritual community. His mother joined the colony earlier in 1865, bringing with her considerable wealth to support the venture. Harris admitted Oliphant on a temporary status until he had proven he could give up everything he had previously lived for. Harris wanted Oliphant to make a clean break with the past and he wanted to punish him to symbolize his atonement and purification. At the colony, Oliphant was forced to live in a degraded, isolated shack and followed all of Harris's commands. In 1870, Oliphant—acting on Harris's orders—returned to England and covered the Franco-Prussian War for the *Times*. He married in 1872 and, with his wife Alice le Strange, and mother, returned to Brocton. In 1876, when Harris moved his colony to Santa Rosa, California, the Oliphants were separated by Harris as a disciplinary measure since Harris thought there was too much earthly love in this celibate marriage. Early in 1879, Oliphant led an expedition to Palestine in support of a scheme to colonize the land with Jews. He eventually established a colony at Haifa. After his wife's death in 1887, he drifted between England and America, finally marrying Rosamond Owen, the daughter of Robert Dale Owen,* in 1888. He died shortly after the marriage.

SELECTED WORKS: *Patriots and Filibusters* (1860); *Episodes in the Life of Adventure* (1887?); *Scientific Religion* (1888).

SOURCES: Herbert W. Schnieder and George Lawton, *A Prophet and a Pilgrim* (1942); *DAB* 14.

ORVIS, JOHN (b. 1816, Ferrisburgh, Vermont; d. April 1897, Boston, Massachusetts), labor agitator and member of Brook Farm* (see also Appendix A, No. 53). Orvis was born into a Hicksite Quaker family, attended Oberlin College (though he never finished his course of study), and in the 1830s journeyed to Boston where he became involved with antislavery groups. In 1844, he joined Brook Farm where he worked with the "Farming Group" and wrote for *The Harbinger*. Orvis toured New England as a lecturer for Brook Farm and Fourierism, and was active in promoting the cause of association. Shortly after the phalanstery at Brook Farm burned down, he married Marianne Dwight, with William H. Channing officiating at the ceremony.

After leaving the colony, Orvis sold insurance and sewing machines. His interest in cooperation was not dead, however, for in 1862, he journeyed to England to study the subject. After his return, he worked with the Sovereigns of Industry and was elected president in 1873. He was one of their national lecturers and edited the *Sovereigns of Industry Bulletin.* Orvis was a labor agitator who defended the trade unions even while a member of the Knights of Labor. In the 1890s, he joined the Nationalist movement and continued his interest in cooperation.

SOURCES: David Montgomery, *Beyond Equality* (1967); Lindsay Swift, *Brook Farm* (1961 reprint).

OSCHWALD, AMBROSE (b. March 14, 1801, Mundelfingen, Baden, Germany; d. February 27, 1873, St. Nazianz, Wisconsin), founder of the St. Nazianz Community* (see also Appendix A, No. 125). Oschwald attended the University of Freiburg during 1833-1834 and was ordained a priest in 1833. During 1848, he published *Mystischen Schriften,* a work quickly condemned by the archbishop of Baden because it contained wild and imaginative predictions, and even errors that the church had condemned long ago. In the same year he published a chiliastic work, *Revelations of St. Methodius,* which predicted that a New Jerusalem would appear before 1900. Because of his writings, he was relieved of his parish in 1849. Thereupon he proceeded to organize his followers into the Spiritual Magnetic Association under the patronage of St. Gregory Nazianzen. Between 1852 and 1854, he studied medicine and botany at Munich, and in 1854 he prepared his followers to carry through on some spiritual advice: "In imitation of Gregory the members were to flee the corrupt world, enter into themselves and observe the evangelical counsels."

On May 18, 1854, Oschwald and 113 followers migrated to America, establishing the St. Nazianz Colony at Manitowoc County, Wisconsin. At the colony, all things were held in common and both married and celibate orders existed. Oschwald was both their spiritual and temporal ruler, acting as priest, physician, and ruler. Little is known about his life at the colony except that his leadership was the binding force that held this experiment in Catholic communalism together nearly twenty years. After his death, the members drifted away from their communal practices, and the colony dissolved before the advent of the New Jerusalem.

SOURCES: Frank Beck, "Christian Communists in America: A History of the Colony of Saint Naziaz, Wisconsin," M.A. thesis, St. Paul Seminary (1959).

OWEN, ALBERT KIMSEY (b. May 17, 1847, Chester, Pennsylvania; d. July 12, 1916, New York City), cooperative supporter and colony developer. Owen, the son of a Quaker physician, was born into a substantial Pennsylvania family. Owen studied civil engineering at Jefferson College, graduating in 1867. He then worked briefly as Chester's city manager before beginning his career as a railroad engineer and town promoter.

In 1871, Owen went to Colorado to work for General William J. Palmer who was then developing the Clear Creek Canyon Railroad and the growing town of Colorado Springs. During a visit to the west coast of Mexico in 1872 to survey land for a railroad, Owen explored Topolobampo Bay. He spent the next twenty years promoting a railroad scheme that would link the emerging West with the Orient via the harbor at Topolobampo. In search of financing for the road, he urged the adoption of a plan which called for the issuance of special purpose greenbacks supported by the United States and Mexican governments. Earlier, in 1800, Owen had organized the first Greenback Club in Pennsylvania.

After Mexican President Porforio Diaz became interested in the rail link in 1879, a concession to build was granted in 1881. In 1885, Owen organized the Credit Foncier Company for the purpose of establishing colonies along the route and one large city, Pacific City, at the terminal point on Topolobampo Bay. His planned city drew on a number of sources and attracted an interesting collection of reformers, including Marie Howland,* John Lovell, and Christian B. Hoffman.* Owen's newspaper, *Integral Cooperation,* attracted two hundred colonists to Topolobampo Bay Colony* in late 1886 to undertake what would become a frustrating and contentious experience. Between 1886 and 1893, 1,245 men, women, and children came to the colony, with nearly 500 residence in 1892. The colony was doomed to failure from the start, for not only did the members have to contend with tropical conditions and internal disputes, but also Owen was an absentee founder.

After 1893, Owen continued his entrepreneurial and reform career, elaborating his vision of *Integral Cooperation,* originally published in 1885, in pamphlets. He next turned his inventive mind to transportation problems, and at one point he advanced plans for a complex rapid transit system.

SELECTED WORKS: Integral Cooperation at Work (1885); *A Dream of an Ideal City* (1897); *The Problems of the Hour* (1897); *Roads, Their Importance in Nation Building* (1913).
SOURCES: Robert S. Fogarty, "Cooperation and New City Planning," Introduction to *Integral Cooperation* (1975 reprint); Ray Reynolds, *Cat's Paw Utopia* (1972).

OWEN, ROBERT (b. May 14, 1771, Newton, Montgomeryshire, Wales; d. November 17, 1858, London), founder of New Harmony* (see also Appendix A, No. 30). At the age of ten, Owen journeyed to London from Wales to join his brother and was apprenticed to a clothier. By 1790, he was in the textile business. By 1800, when he took control of the New Lanark, Scotland, mills, he had amassed a considerable fortune. At that time, he began an impressive project of reform, seeking to improve working conditions, limit child labor, and institute educational innovations such as infant centers. In 1813, Owens published his famous pamphlet "A New View of Society," wherein he argued that "the character of man, is, without a single exception formed for him." In 1817, he issued a public call through the London papers for individuals to discuss his proposals for the amelioration of social conditions. Thousands of visitors flocked to Lanark to see his model industrial works based on his environmental principles. Owen lost many supporters when he spoke out against organized religion and advocated radical political views which offended men of his own class. Even so, a colony based on Owenite principles was established at Orbiston, England, in 1826 by Abram Combe.

In 1824, Owen visited the United States, spoke before the Congress, and traveled westward. He purchased two thousand acres from the German Harmonists who were at New Harmony, Indiana,* and he made plans to settle a colony on the banks of the Wabash River. Nearly nine hundred settlers came to the site. In April 1825, he addressed his followers and gave them a constitution. Six constitutions later, in June 1827, he met them again to bid them farewell. The colony failed for a number of reasons. Owen was rarely in residence at New Harmony and exercised little leadership over the colony. Potential members were not screened, and Owen's views on religion angered some who believed in his plan for social reform.

After the failure of New Harmony, Owen played a major role in the cooperative and labor movements. During 1830, he worked with working-class and middle-class reformers to support cooperative stores, exchanges, and unions. By this time, there were a large Owenite press, Owenite missionaries, and chapels. In addition, several Owenite colonies were founded: one at Ralahine in Ireland (1831); one at Queenswood in Hampshire (1847); and another at Yorkshire (1847). In the early 1850s, Owen turned to spiritualism, reporting that he had spoken to Thomas Jefferson and Benjamin Franklin. While his colonial ventures had little impact, Owen's views on education and social inequity stirred many. Owen's failure at New Harmony did not dissuade other utopians from starting projects and, in fact, as late as 1843 there were Owenite colonies established. However, the ultimate impart of the New Harmony experience on the history of communal settlements was a negative one.

SELECTED WORKS: *A New View of Society* (1813); *The Book of the New Moral World* (1836); *Life of Robert Owen, Written By Himself* (1857).

SOURCES: Arthur Bestor, Jr., *Backwoods Utopias* (1950); Ronald Garnett, *Cooperation and the Owenite Socialist Communities in Britain* (1972); John F. C. Harrison, *Quest for the New Moral World* (1969); George B. Lockwood, *The New Harmony Movement* (1905).

P

PARAMANANDA, SWAMI (b. 1833, East Bengal, India; d. June 21, 1940, Cohasset, Massachusetts), founder of the Vedanta Society. Paramananda was born into a propertied and Westernized family in East Bengal. As a youth, he entered a Ramakrishna monastery at Behu to become a swami, and when he was twenty-one, he emigrated to the United States to be an assistant to a New York swami. While in New York, he established a band of disciples; in 1908, he moved to Boston where he opened an ashram (a religious retreat for a colony of disciples) at Cohasset. Even though his monastic community at Boston was prosperous, he moved to California in 1923 where he established a center at La Crescenta, north of Los Angeles.

The word *Vedanta* comes from two Sanskrit words: *veda* meaning wisdom and *anta* meaning end; taken together, they mean the end of wisdom. Followers of the Vedanta movement placed themselves under the tutelage of a swami, lived a communal life in ashrams, and tried to purify their lives by simple work and meditation. They hoped to perfect their inner spirit and to lose their "self" through self-realization and good works. Paramananda's Ananda Ashram at La Crescenta was never larger than twenty, most of them being upper-middle-class American women. The ashram consisted of a community house, residential homes for lay brothers and nuns, and a temple. Members submitted themselves to Paramananda's discipline and instruction, and they followed a highly regulated pattern of living. It was a monastery devoted to meditation, prayer, and the sacrifice of individualism to community goals. According to Laurence Veysey, it may have been the "stablest, most long-lived communitarian venture founded during the twentieth century in the United States." Paramananda moved between California and Massachusetts and promoted the Vedanta movement throughout the United States. He wrote numerous pamphlets and edited a periodical, *Message of the East,* for twenty-seven years. During the 1930s, because of competition from other swamis, his ashram faltered. He died of a heart attack at the Cohasset ashram.

SELECTED WORKS: *The True Spirit of Religion Is Universal* (1908); *Christ and Oriental Ideals* (1923); *Reincarnation and Immortality* (1923).
SOURCES: Laurence Veysey, *The Communal Experience* (1973); *The New York Times* (June 23, 1940).

PAYNE, EDWARD BIRON (b. 1845, Vermont; d. 1923, California), founder of Altruria* (see also Appendix A, No. 203). Educated at public schools in Connecticut and Illinois, Payne attended Iowa College and

Oberlin College, graduating from the latter in 1874. He moved to Berkeley, California, in 1875, and served as minister at the university there until 1880, when he became so dissatisfied with Congregationalism that he resigned his pastorate and became a Unitarian. He had parishes in Massachusetts and New Hampshire and as part of his ministry worked with labor groups. Tuberculosis forced him back to the milder Berkeley climate, where in 1890 he headed the first Unitarian congregation. The ethics of the Social Gospel attracted him, and he soon became the leading Christian Socialist in the area.

In 1895, Payne was a member of the charter group that drafted a constitution for the Altruria Community, begun in 1894 on 185 acres at Fountain Grove, California, only a short distance from Thomas Lake Harris's* colony. Although Payne was never a full-time resident of the colony, he served as its president and chief publicist. He was editor of the colony weekly, *The Altrurian* (1894-1896), which carried reform and colony news. Despite help from a network of Altrurian clubs in California, the colony dispersed in January 1895, because it could not maintain itself economically. Payne later edited the *Coming Light* (1898-1899) before it became the *Arena* and he became a spiritualist. His manuscript on Jack London, including accounts of conversations with London's spirit, was published posthumously by Payne's widow, the medium Ninetta Eames, under the title *The Soul of Jack London.*

SELECTED WORKS: Ninetta Eames, *The Soul of Jack London* (1926).
SOURCE: Robert Hine, *California's Utopian Colonies* (1953).

PEERSON, CLENG (b. Kleng Pedersen Hesthammer, 1783, Stavanger Amt, Norway; d. December 16, 1865, Bosque, Illinois), colony supporter. This "Peer Gynt on the Prairies" came to America in 1821 as a Quaker agent and returned to Norway in 1824 to promote a Norwegian colony at Orleans County, New York, near Rochester. The voyage of fifty-two Norwegians in 1825 under Peerson's direction marked the real beginning of Norwegian emigration to America. Between 1821 and 1824, Peerson was active raising money to organize a community. From 1826 to 1834, over a hundred families came to the Orleans County settlement, which was probably managed along cooperative lines, though there is some dispute about that fact.

Peerson's intent was to start a secular utopian colony. He dreamed of Illinois as an Eden for Norwegian settlers after he accompanied his New York group westward in 1834 to establish a settlement in Illinois. Much speculation surrounds the details of his wandering career. It is believed that he may have visited with the Harmonists and that his Norwegian followers joined the Mormons. A freethinker, Peerson briefly joined the religious Swedish colony at Bishop Hill* (see also Appendix A, No. 102) in 1847.

SOURCES: DAB 14; Mario S. De Pillis, ed., "Still More Light on the Kendall Colony," *Norwegian-American Studies and Records* (1959).

PEIRCE, MELUSINA FAY (b. February 24, 1836, Burlington, Vermont; d. 1923, Watertown, Massachusetts), reformer, critic, and leader of the cooperative housekeeping movement. This descendant of Anne Hutchinson attended Louis Agassiz Young Ladies School at Cambridge, Massachusetts. She attended schools in Georgia, Louisiana, and Vermont where her parents taught. In 1862, she married the philosopher Charles Sanders Peirce, whom she later divorced. In 1869, together with the wives of other Harvard professors, she organized the Cambridge Cooperative Housekeeping Society. The group urged the adoption of kitchenless apartments and the centralization of certain domestic chores, such as cooking and laundry, in separate buildings. Her articles on cooperative housekeeping appeared in the *Atlantic Monthly* beginning in November 1868. In 1870, the society established a cooperative store, laundry, and bakery for forty households, but "did not provide child care since the scheme was intended to give women the opportunity to spend more time with children," according to Dolores Hayden. The association had a short life, but Peirce continued to promote the idea; she published her *Cooperative Housekeeping: How Not to Do It and How to Do It* in 1884. During this period, she wrote for the *Atlantic Monthly* (1868-1877) and was music critic for the *Boston Post* (1877-1878) and the Chicago *Evening Journal* (1881-1884).

Peirce was active in women's associations and reform activities in New York where she proposed and started the Women's World's Fair Committee (1876), the Ladies Health Protective Association (1887-1888), and the movement to provide cheap summer concerts for the poor. In addition to her civic reform work, she was concerned with the maintenance of historic buildings. She led efforts to save Poe Cottage and Fraunces Tavern in New York City, and she organized the Women's Auxiliary to the American Scenic and Historic Preservation Society (1900). In 1903, she took out a patent for her "Gallery Block" plan for apartments and tenements. Her best known work was her *Music Study in Germany,* which went through twenty-four editions between 1881 and 1913. In 1918, she published a novel, *New York: A Symphonic Study, in Three Parts,* which she had been working on since 1902.

SELECTED WORKS: Cooperative Housekeeping: How Not to Do It and How to Do It (1884); Amy Fay, *Music Study in Germany* (1882); *New York: A Symphonic Study in Three Parts* (1918).

SOURCES: Dolores Hayden, "Redesigning the Domestic Workplace," *Chrysalis* (1977); *Lamb's Biographical Dictionary of the United States* (Boston, 1903); *Who's Who in America* (1920-1921).

PELHAM, RICHARD (b. May 8, 1797, Indiana; d. January 10, 1873, Union Village, Ohio), member of Union Village (see Appendix A, No. 18) and founder of other Shaker colonies. Pelham, the youngest of eight children, was reared by a physician uncle at Talbot County, Maryland, because his mother had died shortly after his birth. In 1808, his uncle and young Pelham moved to Lyons, New York, where, in 1810, Pelham joined the Methodist church during a religious revival. By the time Pelham was twenty he had grown dissatisfied with the church and sought a purified religious life elsewhere.

According to his autobiography, Pelham set out on a spiritual journey and arrived at the door of Union Village, the Shaker colony in southern Ohio in 1810. He was accepted into the order and became a prominent missionary in the area in 1822, moving between Union Village and North Union, near Cleveland, over twenty times as an itinerant preacher. His fellow Shakers admired his keen intellect, especially his mastery of Greek and Hebrew and his translation of the Bible from Hebrew into English. He was a prominent apologist for the Shakers and authored the widely read pamphlet "A Shaker Answer to the Oft Repeated Question: What Would Become of the World If All Should Become Shakers," originally published in 1868. The pamphlet stated the Shaker position, which was not a total condemnation of marriage or procreation but held that abstinence served a higher purpose. Pelham also argued the Malthusian position that abstinence was in the best interests of the race. The question answered in the pamphlet was one the Shakers often had to respond to when they traveled. He was one of the first founders of Shaker settlements at North Union, Ohio (1822); Groveland, New York (1826); and Whitewater, Ohio (1824).

SELECTED WORKS: Shakers (1868); *The Shakers Answer to a Letter, from an Inquirer* (1868).
SOURCES: J. P. MacLean, *Shakers of Ohio* (1974 reprint); J. P. MacLean, *Bibliography of Shaker Literature* (1971 reprint).

PIO, LOUIS ALBERT FRANÇOIS (b. 1841, Copenhagen, Denmark; d. June 27, 1894, Chicago, Illinois), founder of the Hays Colony (see Appendix A, No. 166). Pio attended the university and engineering college in Copenhagen, served briefly in the Danish-Russian War of 1864, and then worked for the postal system. During 1871-1872, he was active in the socialist movement. In 1872, he was charged with crimes against public authority when he called for a mass meeting to support strikers, was convicted and was ordered to serve three years of a five-year sentence. While in jail, he learned many European languages (eventually, he could read and write eleven). After his release, he became the editor of the socialist newspaper, *Social-Demokraten.* During 1876, he conceived the idea of establishing a colony for unemployed Danish workers, and the following year the *Social-Demokraten* invited workers to participate in the founding of a colony in North America. Pio publicized the scheme by writing articles about Kansas—the proposed colony site—in his paper and by publishing an illustrated booklet called *Kansas According to Various Travel Accounts.*

In March 1877, under pressure from Danish authorities to emigrate, Pio left for America; in fact, the authorities secretly gave Pio the funds necessary for his journey. Eighteen socialists (some Danish and others German) came with him. A small colony was established at Hays, Kansas, in May 1877, but as a result of political and social disputes the experiment ended quickly. Pio moved to Chicago where he worked as a printer and publisher for railroad and land developers, even promoting a "colony" venture in Florida in 1893. Thus, Pio's venture with socialism ended in speculation in the new land.

SOURCES: Kenneth E. Miller, "Danish Socialism and the Kansas Prairie," *Kansas Historical Quarterly* (Summer 1972).

PRESCOTT, JAMES SULLIVAN (b. January 26, 1803, Lancaster, Worcester County, Massachusetts; d. April 3, 1888, North Union, Ohio), member of the North Union Shaker Community (see Appendix A, No. 27). Prescott was born into a strict Congregational family. He lived with an uncle at West Boylston in 1813 and with a family in Springfield in 1819 to learn the mason's trade. From 1820 until 1824, he worked in that trade in Hartford, Connecticut. During this period, he attended the local Literary School and Female Academy, and in 1824, he entered Westfield Academy to complete his education. In 1825, he was employed by the Baptist Missionary Convention of New York to teach a missionary school at Oneida, consisting of about forty Indians of both sexes.

In July 1826, Prescott migrated to Cleveland and was hired by the North Union Shakers to lay the foundation of a dwelling house. At that time, the community was living in log cabins and did its own construction, though some skilled tradesmen were needed. Prescott began a study of Shaker theology and in the fall of 1826 he entered the society. In 1827, he was appointed second elder in the "Cabin Family," so called because of their dwellings. He continued in that position for four years until 1830 when he was released to take charge of the district school. For the next fifty years, he taught school, served as elder in different families, and for forty years was a legal trustee at North Union. In addition, he was an early advocate of eugenics, believing that since the Shakers produced the best spiritual men and women, it was then possible to produce perfected physical beings through scientific selection and combination.

SELECTED WORKS: The Social Evil (1870).
SOURCE: J. P. MacLean, *Shakers of Ohio* (1974 reprint).

PRIBER, CHRISTIAN GOTTLIEB (b. March 21, 1697, Zittau, Germany; d. ca. 1744, Frederica, Georgia), founder of the Kingdom of Paradise Colony. Priber graduated from Erfurt University in 1722 with a dissertation on "The Use and Study of Roman Law and the Ignorance of that Law in the Public Life of Germany" and a doctorate in jurisprudence, after which he returned to Zittau to practice law. He married in 1722 and by 1732 had five children. The details of Priber's life in Germany are sketchy.

Unable to start a utopian colony in Germany, Priber came to America to start one, arriving at Charlestown, South Carolina, in 1735. In the following year, he traveled to eastern Tennessee where he settled at Great Tellico, the chief town of the Cherokees. Priber's utopia, which he called the Kingdom of Paradise, admitted Creeks and Catabaws, French and English, men and women on an equal footing. It would be a refuge for all "criminals, debtors and slaves." He gained the confidence of the Cherokees by adopting their habits and living among them. According to Ludovich Grant, an Indian trader from South Carolina, Priber "trimmed his hair in the Indian manner and painted as they did, going generally naked except for a shirt and a flap." Priber urged them to hold onto their lands, be wary of English traders, and make peace with the French.

In 1739, the Common House of the Assembly of South Carolina appropriated funds for an expedition to capture Priber because they feared that his influence would weaken their trade monopoly with the Cherokees, but the Cherokees protected him and requested that the English live in friendship as "free men and equals." The English believed Priber was a French spy; some later historians, on the other hand, believed he was a Jesuit missionary. The present consensus is that he was an enlightened eighteenth-century idealist who wished to establish a model republic based on liberty and equality.

While on a journey to Alabama in 1743, Priber was captured by Creek Indians who returned him to James Oglethorpe, the English general who feared Priber as a French troublemaker. Oglethorpe described him as a "very extraordinary kind of creature" with a knowledge of several languages, including Cherokee. Priber may have compiled the first dictionary of the Cherokee language, which James Mooney, the anthropologist, called "the first, and even yet, perhaps the most important study of the language ever made." The dictionary, however, is now lost. Priber was imprisoned by Oglethorpe and carefully questioned about his plans and projects. Priber had hoped to bring about a confederation among the southern Indians and to encourage them to throw off their European oppressors. Such plans were sufficient to keep him in jail. He died after 1744 while imprisoned at Frederica, Georgia.

SOURCES: Verner Crane, "A Lost Utopia on the First American Frontier," *Sewanee Review* (January 1919); Knox Mellon, Jr., "Christian Priber's Cherokee Kingdom of Paradise," *Georgia Historical Quarterly* (Fall 1973).

PURNELL, BENJAMIN (b. March 27, 1861, Greenup City, Kentucky; d. December 7, 1927, Benton Harbor, Michigan), founder of the House of David (see Appendix A, No. 24). Little is known of Purnell's early life except that he had a meagre education and married a local girl in August 1877. After their marriage, he began "traveling around," probably preaching. During the 1880s, he lived in Ohio and Indiana, and in 1880, he married for a second time without divorcing his first wife. In 1892, Purnell joined an Anglo-Israelite sect, the New House of Israel, led by one "Prince" Michael Mills. With the breakup of the Mills colony in 1895, Purnell announced that he was Mills' successor and the Shiloh who had come to lead the group. Although rejected by the the the sect, he maintained his messianic mission by publishing a tract called the *Star of Bethlehem* from a small Ohio village.

In 1903, Purnell moved to Benton Harbor, Michigan, where he founded the House of David. This celibate colony was to be the "gathering-in" place for the elect 144,000, and Purnell predicted the millennium for the year 1905. He attracted a large contingent of believers from Australia where there was an Israelite congregation, and by 1910 the colony had grown to three hundred. They operated farms in the Benton Harbor area and ran an amusement park and several other businesses. After World War I, they began their famous baseball team which barnstormed throughout the Midwest, creating a sensation because of their long beards. Purnell and his wife Mary, the undisputed king and queen of the colony, ruled it autocratically.

Throughout the colony's history, there were rumors about sexual irregularities in this celibate community. Federal and state investigations failed to unearth any illegal activity until 1921 when some former members brought suit against Purnell. He went into hiding and a national manhunt was begun for him; however, he never left the colony headquarters, having been sheltered by a faithful membership. The state of Michigan began lengthy court action against Purnell in 1923, charging that he had seduced young women, defrauded members of their money, and was perpetrating a religious fraud. Purnell had, in fact, had sexual relations with many of the young women in the colony over the years, but the membership condoned this, believing in his divine mission and supporting him until the end. He died during the court proceedings against him. Mary Purnell turned against him during his long trial and in 1930 founded the City of David Community, a rival faction to the House of David.

SELECTED WORKS: Benjamins Last Writing (n.d.); *The Key to the House of David* (1910); *The Rolling Ball of Fire* (1915-1925).
SOURCE: Milo Quaife, *Lake Michigan* (1944).

QR

RAPP, GEORGE (b. November 1, 1757, Wurttemberg, Germany; d. August 7, 1847, Economy, Pennsylvania), founder of the Harmony Society* (see also Appendix A, No. 17). Rapp attended elementary school at Wurttemberg, became a weaver, and traveled abroad before marrying in 1783. Repelled by the formalism of the Lutheran church, he sought closer communion with God through prayer and meditation. In 1787, a group of Separatists at Wurttemberg gathered under Rapp's leadership, and in 1791 he announced: "I am a prophet and am called to be one," after the local authorities had imprisoned him for two days because of his religious beliefs. By 1798, Rapp was the head of an organization of primitive Christians who were opposed to military service, believed in baptism by faith, held antistate views, and opposed the established church. In 1803, he left for the United States in search of a site for his followers. He found one in Butler County, Pennsylvania, and in 1804, three hundred believers came to the United States.

The colony was dedicated to a simple Christian life. They expected the millennium within their lifetime. In 1814, the Harmonists moved to Indiana where they established the town of the Harmony. It prospered, and Rapp became an influential figure in the early years of the Indiana territorial government. The Harmonists remained in Indiana for ten years and accumulated real estate and property in excess of $150,000. In 1824, they sold their holdings to Robert Owen* who began his New Harmony Colony* (see also Appendix A, No. 30) on the same site and in Rappite buildings. Throughout this period, Rapp ruled the colony with an iron hand. He urged celibacy on his followers since he believed it was the spiritual way, but his advocacy of the practice created tension between Rapp and some of the younger members. However, the majority followed his lead, as a result of which there was a distinct decline in the society's birth rate.

By the early 1830s, blind faith in his leadership wavered, and a large group followed Bernard Muller,* called Count Leon, into secession and removal to another site (see Appendix A, Nos. 44, 48). The last decade of Rapp's life was a calm one since the society had achieved economic stability and was patiently awaiting the millennium. Rapp had established a gathering-in place for the elect 144,000 and believed that the Harmonists were carrying out the prophecies found in the Book of Revelation. At the time of his death, the society numbered twelve hundred.

SOURCES: Karl Arndt, *George Rapp's Harmony Society, 1785-1847* (1972, 2d ed.); Aaron Williams, *The Harmony Society at Economy, Pennsylvania, Founded by George Rapp, A.D. 1805* (1970 reprint).

RIGDON, SIDNEY (b. February 19, 1793, St. Clair Township, Allegheny County, Pennsylvania; d. July 14, 1876, Friendship, New York), founder of the Kirtland Community* (see also Appendix A, No. 42). Rigdon was born into a Baptist family. He had an intense interest in education and was self-educated. In 1817, he received a license to preach and had congregations in Warren, Ohio, in 1819-1820 and then in Pittsburgh in 1820-1824 after his ordination in 1821. Because of his association with Alexander Campbell, the founder of the Disciples of Christ Church, he lost his pastorate in Pittsburgh in 1824. After working as a tanner between 1824 and 1826, he accepted a pastorate at Mentor, Ohio, near Cleveland. He led great revivals in Ohio during 1828-1829. In 1830, he broke with the Campbellites over doctrinal questions and his desire to organize a community where all property was held in common, as in the early Christian church.

In February 1830, Rigdon organized a communal group at Kirtland, Ohio, with about a hundred members. In the fall of 1830, he was visited by Mormon missionaries, and he accepted the Book of Mormon and Joseph Smith's prophecy. Smith moved to the colony in 1831. Kirtland became the headquarters of the early Mormon church. Community of property was practiced there, a notion that is disputed by some Mormon historians. Smith had a revelation in February 1831 which ended the practice of community property and in March 1831, a second revelation which instructed Rigdon to do missionary work among the Shakers. Rigdon became a trusted friend of Smith and a major preacher for the Mormons. But by 1842 Smith became convinced that Rigdon was aiding his enemies and that his opposition to plural marriages was a sign of apostasy. After his excommunication from the church, Rigdon organized the Church of Christ but the group never grew. In 1865, he returned to Friendship, New York, convinced that the Book of Mormon was a fraud.

SOURCES: Hamilton Gardner, "Communism Among the Mormons," reprinted in William McNiff, *Heaven on Earth* (1972 reprint); F. Mark McKiernan, *The Voice of One Crying in the Wilderness: Sidney Rigdon, Religious Reformer* (1971); *DAB* 15.

RIKER, WILLIAM E. (b. 1873, Oakdale, California; d. December 3, 1969, San Jose, California), founder of the Perfect Christian Divine Way. Riker attended public schools in Oroville, California, until the fourth grade when he began work as a mechanic; he moved to San Francisco when he was nineteen. Interested in magic and spiritualism, Riker claimed in 1918 he received messages from God through his nerves and that his religious doctrines were developed without the aid of what he called book learning.

Riker was a racist, a politician, and a self-proclaimed priest. Although his sect's origins were in San Francisco, the community he founded was located in the Santa Cruz Mountains of central California. "Holy City" was Riker's version of the New Jerusalem which he also called "The World's Most Perfect Government."

Central to most of Riker's ideas was an extreme form of racism. He described the sun as the white race and the other races as planets in orbit around the central force in the universe. During a thirty-year career, Riker was brought to court on charges of fraud, sedition, reckless driving, tax evasion, breech of promise, and murder. Yet, his cooperative religious sect survived all. "Mother Lucille" was his companion and wife throughout the years at "Holy City," although living quarters for members were segregated by sex and only single members could join.

In 1918, he established his sect, the Perfect Christian Divine Way, in San Francisco and in 1919 moved with thirty followers to a few acres in the Santa Cruz Mountains, between Santa Cruz and San Jose. The colony was perched near the summit of a mountain road, and they profited from the considerable automobile traffic past their garage service station, grocery store, and restaurant. Members received no wages and were housed in primitive cabins. They relied on Riker for everything, and he promised to provide for them. Riker constantly promoted the colony, and with San Francisco Bay Area newspapers running numerous articles about the sect, visitors flocked to the site. Riker ran for governor in 1937, was tried on sedition charges in 1942 because he advocated seeking peace with Hitler, and was acquitted because of the defense plea by Melvin Belli, his attorney. By 1952, the community was down to twelve members from a high of forty in the mid-1930s. Riker converted to Roman Catholicism at the age of ninety-four. He died in San Jose in 1969 after spending time in several mental hospitals.

SOURCES: Robert Hine, *California's Utopian Colonies* (1966 reprint); Paul Kagan, *New World Utopias* (1974).

RIPLEY, GEORGE (b. October 3, 1802, Greenfield, Massachusetts; d. July 4, 1880, Brooklyn, New York), reformer, literary critic, and driving force behind the establishment of Brook Farm* (see also Appendix A, No. 53). Ripley graduated from Harvard University (1823) and Harvard Divinity School (1826) and then became minister to the Unitarian Purchase Street

Church in Boston. His attacks on the conservatism of the churches, together with his editing, with F. H. Hedge, of *Specimens of Foreign Standard Literature* (1838) greatly influenced the development of transcendental thought. In September 1836, the first meeting of the Transcendental Club was held in his home and led to the formation of *The Dial* and the founding of Brook Farm. Ripley was the first president of the Brook Farm Institute of Agriculture and Education.

Ripley failed to lead the colony; in fact, he allowed it to move into Fourier-ism, a philosophy he little understood or sympathized with. He edited *The Dial* and acted as a force for optimism within the colony. When the phalanstery burned down, that optimism dimmed, and his own library was sold to Theodore Parker to pay community debts. On the sale of the library he commented: "I can now understand how a man would feel if he could attend his own funeral."

After the Brook Farm property was transferred to a board of trustees, the Ripleys moved to Flatbush in Brooklyn. Ripley continued to edit *The Harbinger* until it closed in 1849 and then began to write for Greeley's* *Tribune* on a regular basis. In 1857, he assumed, with Charles Dana,* the editorship of the multivolumed *American Cyclopedia.* His critical reputation grew in later years through his writings in the *Tribune.*

SELECTED WORKS: *Specimens of Foreign Standard Literature* (1838); *Philo-sophical Miscellanies* (1838); *Handbook of Literature and Fine Arts* (1852).
SOURCES: Lindsay Swift, *Brook Farm* (1961 reprint); *DAB* 15.

RIPLEY, SOPHIA WILLARD DANA (b. July 6, 1803, Cambridge, Massachusetts; d. February 4, 1861, New York City), member of Brook Farm* (see also Appendix A, No. 53). She was from a distinguished New England family. One grandfather, Joseph Willard, was a president of Harvard and the other, Francis Dana, the first American minister to Russia. Washington Allston, the painter, and Richard Henry Dana, the poet, were her uncles. Her father, however, abandoned his young family and her mother. Sophia opened a school in Cambridge to support the family. She taught briefly before marrying George Ripley* in 1827. During the early 1840s, she was drawn into transcendentalism and wrote for *The Dial.* The Ripleys were among the first members at Brook Farm, and while there she managed the "wash group" (the laundry room) and taught. One acquaint-ance at Brook Farm, Isaac Hecker,* said she possessed "superior mental talent and training . . . was vivacious . . . and a good conversationalist." According to her own account, Brook Farm was an "entire separation from worldly care and rest to the spirit which I knew was waiting for me some-where." After the decline of Brook Farm in 1847 she converted to Catholi-cism and worked for benevolent and reform causes, particularly with prostitutes. She died of cancer in New York City in February 1861. Isaac Hecker, a former member of Brook Farm, performed the last rites.

SOURCES: Edith Reolker Curtis, *A Season in Utopia* (1961); *Dictionary of Notable American Women,* 3.

ROOT, JOHN P. (b. June 28, 1799, Pittsfield, Berkshire County, Massachusetts; d. August, 1881, North Union, Ohio), a founder of the North Union Shaker Community (see Appendix A, No. 27). Root moved from Massachusetts to Grafton, Lorain County, Ohio. A member of the Methodist church, he was admitted to the North Union, Ohio, community in 1825 and in that year was appointed farm deacon. When the society was organized in 1822, he became a legal trustee and in 1833 he became the first elder of the middle family. In 1858, he became minister in that family and remained so until 1876. Within the community, he was known for his carpentry work and his espousal of women's rights, with his favorite sermon titled "A Mother as Well as a Father in the Deity." He was one of the early founders of the North Union community and his biography is symbolic of many other elders who rose slowly through the ranks of the Shaker hierarchy. During the early years of their history, the Shakers had to rely on spontaneous leaders because they were so few and their means so limited. Yet during the period from 1837 to 1870 (the years of Root's ascendancy), the society was prosperous, well ordered, and growing. Men and women, like Root, could be given tasks commensurate with their abilities and experience and prepared for higher office. That process was a slow one and one that gave the Shakers stable and competent leaders.

SOURCE: J. P. MacLean, *Shakers of Ohio* (1974 reprint).

ROSENTHAL, HERMAN (b. October 6, 1843, Friedrichsstadt, Russia; d. January 27, 1917, New York City), a founder of Sicily Island* (see also Appendix A, No. 176) and member of the Woodbine Colony. As a young man he learned three languages (German, Russian, and Hebrew) and at sixteen was doing translations of Russian poems into German. In 1870, he published a collection of his own poems, *Gedichte,* while working as a printer in the Ukraine. In 1876, he helped establish a daily paper *Zarya* in Kiev. After the 1881 pogroms, he organized a group of Russian Jews and emigrated with them to Sicily Island, near New Orleans, Louisiana, where they hoped to start an agricultural colony. The group was supported in their emigration by funds from the Alliance Israelite Universelle, a Paris-based philanthropy devoted to aiding Jews. After a brief period on the island, torrential rainstorms, malaria, yellow fever, floods, and oppressive heat forced them to move. Some of the group relocated at Cremieux, South

Dakota, in a colony named after the president of the Alliance (see also Appendix A, No. 179).

In the late 1880s, Rosenthal published *Der Yidisher Farmer.* In 1891, he became a member of Woodbine, an industrial-agricultural colony for Jewish immigrants at Cape May, New Jersey, organized by the Baron de Hirsch Fund. At the request of James Hill, the railroad magnate, he journeyed to Japan, China, and Korea to investigate economic conditions for Hill's Great Northern Railroad. In 1894, he worked with the Immigration Bureau at Ellis Island. After 1898, he headed the Slavonic Department at the New York Public Library and was the editor of the department of Russian Jewry for the *Jewish Encyclopedia.*

SELECTED WORKS: Worte des Sammlers (1885); Poems (1906); *Spätherbstnebel, Report on Japan, China and Korea* (1893).

SOURCES: Joseph Brandes, *Jewish Colonies in New Jersey* (1971 reprint); *DAB* 16.

S

SANDFORD, FRANK (b. October 2, 1862, Bowdoinham, Maine; d. March 4, 1948, Hobart, New York), leader of the Shiloh Colony. Sandford attended Bates College where he was known more for his athletic than his academic prowess. Upon graduation in 1888, he attended the Cobb Divinity School at Utica, New York. Subsequently, he held pastorates in Free Baptist churches at Topsham, Maine, and at Great Falls, New Hampshire. In 1893, he had a revelation while he was attending a religious revival at Ocean Beach, Maine. He proclaimed himself another Elijah and announced his intention to build a prayer temple at Beulah Hill.

Prayer was a central feature of the society and the cooperative colony he established. Prayer meetings were conducted at the community center on a daily basis and a prayer tower was manned night and day by Sandford's followers. In addition, Sandford was a faith healer, and this may account for the appeal of the "Church of the Living God," as he called his group. Between 1893 and 1900, he supervised the construction of a magnificent temple and colony center. The colony had three hundred members. Beginning in 1900, Sandford became embroiled in one controversy after another. He was indicted for manslaughter in 1900 after some other religious groups in the area charged that he was mistreating children when a child died at the colony but the charges were dropped. In 1905, he set out for the Holy Land on a pilgrimage which resulted in the deaths of passengers on the voyage from Boston to Palestine, and he was charged with negligence in the matter. He was jailed in 1912 as a result of the incident and in 1918, after completing his prison term, he returned to Shiloh. At that time, he resumed control of the colony, but it was legally disbanded in 1920.

SELECTED WORKS: Tongues of Fire (1895-1900); *The Everlasting Gospel* (1901-1902); *The Golden Trumpet* (1912-1916).
SOURCES: Victor P. Abraham, *The Restoration of All Things* (1962); Arnold L. White, "The Tragic Voyage of the Shiloh Schooner Coronet," *Down East* (May 1974).

SINCLAIR, UPTON (b. September 20, 1878, Baltimore, Maryland; d. September 26, 1968, Los Angeles, California), novelist and leader of Helicon Hall* (see also Appendix A, No. 246). Sinclair was born into a distinguished Southern family and was raised in New York City. He graduated from City College where he worked for Travers Jerome, an anti-Tammany reformer. He published his first novel in 1901, was introduced to socialism by Leonard Abbott,* and wrote for *Wilshires Weekly* and *The Appeal to Reason.*

In 1904, Sinclair published *The Jungle* and with his royalties from that muckraking novel started a cooperative colony, Helicon Hall, named after the legendary home of the Greek muses. The colony was located on the Palisades near Fort Lee, New Jersey, and lasted from November 1906 to March 1907 when a fire destroyed the main house. The colony attracted distinguished visitors from New York and included among its members Sinclair Lewis, Edwin Bjorkman, Michael Williams, the Strindberg critic and translator and later editor of *Commonweal.* It was less a communal colony than a bohemian experiment since they had servants and lived an expansive rather than spartan life. After the fire, Sinclair hoped to take the idea of Helicon Hall on the road and preach its virtues, but interest in that scheme was short-lived. He became a follower of Bernard McFadden's health regime and sustained his interest in pure foods throughout his career.

Sinclair ran for governor of California in 1934 on the EPIC (End Poverty in California) ticket and polled 436,000 votes. Among his other reform interests were temperance, the American Civil Liberties Union, and cooperative societies. His novel *Co-op* (1935) focuses on the problems and promise of cooperative organization.

SELECTED WORKS: The Autobiography of Upton Sinclair (1962).
SOURCES: The New York Times, November 28, 1968.

SLUYTER, PETER (b. 1645, Wesel, Netherlands; d. 1722, Cecil County, Maryland), leader of the Labadist Colony at Bohemia Manar, Maryland. Sluyter studied theology at Leyden in 1666. In 1683, he journeyed with Jasper Danckaerts* to establish the Labadist Colony in Cecil County,

Maryland. The Labadists were the followers of Jean de Labadie (1610-1674), the French reformer who attacked both the Catholic and Protestant churches for their lack of spirituality, and who in 1650 established a communal society in Amsterdam. After Labadie's death in 1674, Weiward, Netherlands, became the center of their activity. According to Bartlett James, "Labadism was essentially a mystical form of faith, teaching supreme reliance upon the inward illumination of the Spirit. . . . The Church was to be a community of the elect kept separate from the world by its pure teachings." Those teachings included a communal way of life, adult baptism, reenactment of the Lord's Supper, study of the Scriptures, and reliance on the spirit of love as a guide to action.

Sluyter was the nominal head of the group that consisted of one hundred individuals, some of whom were from the Netherlands, others of whom had settled in New York prior to 1683. All those who joined the colony turned over all their possessions, followed a strict regimen (so strict that a register was kept of the number of pieces of bread and butter eaten at a meal), and mortified their flesh by penance. According to James, Sluyter had "morbid religious tendencies . . . yet [was] a man of strong mercenary instincts." His mercenary characteristic gained ascendance in his dealings with the colony, for he reserved a choice piece of land for himself and made a considerable fortune while leading the group.

In 1698, a division of the 3750 acre "Labadist Tract" was effected, with the greater part of the land falling to Sluyter and the other leaders. With the division of the land the community disintegrated and by 1727 they ceased to exist as a colony.

SOURCE: Bartlett James, *The Labadist Colony in Maryland* (1899).

SMITH, GEORGE VENABLE (b. 1843, Kentucky; d. October 1, 1919, Port Angeles, Washington), founder of the Puget Sound Co-operative Colony (see Appendix A, No. 193). Smith came to the California gold fields with his father as a small child and was schooled in Sacramento. Admitted to the bar at twenty-one, he first practiced in Portland, Oregon. As a delegate to the 1879 California State Constitutional Convention, he helped draft the judicial system. He became district attorney for Kern County and in 1883, he moved to Seattle where he was appointed acting city attorney.

Two years later, Smith became involved with an anti-Chinese labor group that was interested in founding a cooperative colony. After the death of the group's leader, Peter Good,* organizational meetings were held in Smith's office. In February 1886, a formal announcement outlined the Puget Sound Co-operative Colony. At a convention in May 1887, Smith was chosen president of the community, which was soon to be located at Port

Angeles. Most of the early members were laborers, and many had belonged to the Knights of Labor. At its height, the colony had four hundred members. Factionalism soon split the colony, with Smith leaving in mid-1888 and opening a law practice at Port Angeles. In 1893, he issued a pamphlet calling for another collective plan, *A Co-operative Plan for Securing Home and Occupations at Port Angeles, Washington.* Thereafter, he became a probate judge, a prosecuting attorney, and finally city attorney for Port Angeles before his death.

SELECTED WORKS: A Co-operative Plan for Securing Home and Occupations at Port Angeles, Washington (1893).
SOURCE: Charles LeWarne, *Utopias on Puget Sound* (1975).

SMOLNIKAR, ANDREAS BERNARDUS (b. November 29, 1795, Austria; d. ?), member of the Grand Prairie Harmonial Community (see Appendix A, No. 97). According to his own biographical sketch, Smolnikar was ordained a priest and then became a Benedictine monk in 1825. He also served as imperial professor of biblical literature at Clagenfurt and in 1826 took a new middle name, Bernardus, after St. Bernard. In January 1837, he had a vision that Christ had appointed him a messenger to prepare people for the millennium and to form a universal republic. He arrived in the United States to carry out that vision in November 1837 and published his views between 1838 and 1842 in five volumes, all in German. He was influenced by the writings of J. A. Etzler, whose *The Paradise Within the Reach of All Men Without Labor* (1833) and *The New World, or the Mechanical System* (1843) had been published in the United States. Etzler, in *The Paradise Within Reach of All Men,* had argued that four phases existed in the utopian transformation of man. The first was collecting funds to sponsor a pilot community, the second was operating a community, the third was forming a hundred communities of 1,000 people, and the fourth was linking these communities by roads.

In April 1844, Smolnikar was one of six vice-presidents, along with Charles Dana,* Albert Brisbane,* and Horace Greeley,* of the National Convention of Associationists held at New York City. In 1844, he tried to form a colony of Germans on ten thousand acres in Warren County, Pennsylvania, that he called the Peace Union Settlement. It apparently failed. He was also involved with the Grand Prairie Community in 1846 in Indiana.

During the 1850s, he attended numerous reform conventions and urged those present to adopt his millennialist schemes. He voted against all resolutions, however, but his own. In 1859, he obtained a five hundred-acre site in Perry County, Pennsylvania, still trying to found the Peace Union Settlement (with a co-worker, Robert Eldridge). In that same year, he published a tract entitled *Secret Enemies of True Republicanism,* which attacked

Catholicism and President James Buchanan and talked about the commencement of a "New Era." There is no record of him after that date.

Smolnikar is an elusive figure whose name crops up in several sources, especially in the writings of other reformers because he was in attendance at many reform conventions in the 1840s and 1850s. He may have been like the English prophet Richard Brothers—whose prophetic career drew notice, but whose sanity was always in question.

SELECTED WORKS: *Redemption of Oppressed Humanity* (1856); *Secret Enemies of True Republicanism* (1859); *The Great Encyclic Epistle* (1865).

SOURCE: John H. Noyes, *History of American Socialisms* (1870).

SMYTHE, WILLIAM ELLSWORTH (b. 1861, Worcester, Massachusetts; d. October 6, 1922, New York City), newspaper writer and editor and organizer of Little Landers Colony* (see also Appendix A, No. 249) in California. In 1891, while he was the editor of *Irrigation Age,* Smythe organized a series of conferences on irrigation in Nebraska and helped arrange a national congress in Los Angeles in 1893 to focus on the water problem. He lectured widely on irrigation and published several books, including *The Conquest of Arid America, Constructive Democracy,* and the *History of San Diego.* Smythe promoted the use of irrigation and the development of conservation and was a spokesman for the rational use of western lands. He promoted Little Lander Colonies in southern California based on his belief that it was possible for a family to live on an acre of irrigated land when large sections were purchased and irrigated cooperatively. An acre was sufficient for a family, particularly if the crops raised were marketed through a cooperative.

In 1909, Smythe launched the Little Lander Colony at San Ysidro, fourteen miles south of San Diego, based on the assumption that families could live on an acre of arid land if the land was properly irrigated and cultivated. Between 1909 and 1916, four other colonies were established in separate locations, but none was able to develop or sustain any cooperative pattern of land use. The first settlement was destroyed by a flood in 1915. In 1917, Smythe worked with the American Homesteaders organization which aided workmen who wished to buy and build their own homes.

SELECTED WORKS: *The Conquest of Arid America* (1900); *Constructive Democracy* (1905); *City Homes on Country Lanes* (1921); *Homelanders of America* (1921).

SOURCES: Robert Hine, *California's Utopian Colonies* (1953); *The New York Times* (October 8, 1922).

SPAFFORD, HORATIO E. (b. ?, New York; d. September 25, 1888, Jerusalem), founder of the American Colony. All that is known about

Spafford's early years is that he was a prominent lawyer in Chicago and that he was listed as a member of a Presbyterian church there in 1867. He and his wife had four children all of whom died in a ship accident. The tragedy intensified the Spaffords' already strong evangelical beliefs. They were convinced that the churches were too worldly.

During the 1870s, the Spaffords began to hold prayer meetings in their home at Lincoln Park and in 1882 led a group of nineteen to Jerusalem to prepare for the Second Coming. The community, known as the American Colony, was supported out of a common purse but made some effort to establish industries. Among those established were a photographic department that produced postcards, a bakery, a weaving school, and a shop where they sold their varied wares. But the principal source of funds came from the members themselves. According to *The Westminster Gazette*, "they have no priests, these theocratic communists, no method of government save the promptings of brotherly love." They read the Bible, ministered to the poor and needy, and lived a common life. Although there were some married couples in the original group, their rule in Jerusalem required that they live a separated celibate life. Anna Spafford, who played a prominent role in the colony, was called Mother Anna. She claimed to be the Bride of Christ and to be in direct communication with him. After Spafford's death in 1888, she presided over the colony, whose membership reached 175 in the 1890s. She returned to Chicago for a year in 1895 to recruit members and had considerable success among Scandanavian evangelicals. In 1907 the colony was still in existence.

SELECTED WORKS: Our Rest and Signs of the Times (July 1883).

SOURCES: Chicago Daily News (December 18, 1897); *The Westminster Gazette* (September 16, 1907).

SPEAR, JOHN MURRAY (b. September 16, 1804; d. ca. 1877), founder of Harmonia, or the Domain* (see also Appendix A, No. 119). Little is known about the early career of this Universalist minister. During the 1840s, he and his brother Charles were active in antislavery and prison reform work, publishing a weekly, *The Prisoner's Friend*. In 1852, he began receiving a series of spirit messages from John Murray, the founder of Universalism, and others, including Benjamin Franklin and Thomas Jefferson, instructing him to make radical changes in society and to inaugurate a model community. A year later, he received a series of spirit messages which indicated where and in what manner he was to begin this colony of universal harmony. Designs for houses, the areas of reform activity, and other instructions all came from a "heavenly directorate" that used Spear as the medium. The colony—called Harmonia, the Association of Beneficents, or the Domain— was located near the village of Kiantone, Chautauqua County, New York, and it consisted of ten oval and octagonal houses. There was probably some common holding of property (Spear himself professed to be a socialist), though many members spent the winter months in their own homes in other areas.

When Spear came in 1853 he brought with him a perpetual motion machine; however, a mob broke into the barn where he had stored it and demolished it. The National Spiritualist Convention was held at the site in 1855 and added to local rumors that it was a free-love colony since spiritualism and free love were synonymous for some Americans in the 1850s. There was some truth to the rumors because of Spear's open liaison with one member, Caroline Hinckley, and her pregnancy (he later divorced his wife and married Hinckley in 1863).

During the autumn of 1859, many members stayed at Kiantone because Spear had received a spirit message urging him to organize a group called the Sacred Order of Unionists to promote world government. In December, a small group set out on the steamer "Cleopatra" to spread the word and journey to New Orleans. On the way, they established a colony at Patriot, Indiana. By 1861, they had spent all their money, and the Sacred Order entered the sewing machine business in cooperation with John Orvis.* The scheme failed, and by February 1863 Orvis dissolved the Order. Spear then moved to London where he came into contact with the leading spiritualists of the day, including François-Jean Cantagrel, a former Fourierist and associate of Victor Considerant.* Spear returned to the United States in 1877 and died shortly thereafter.

SELECTED WORKS: Twenty Years on the Wing (1873).
SOURCES: Russel Duino, "Utopian Theme with Variations: John Murray Spear and His Kiantone Domain," *Pennsylvania History* (April 1962); Frank Podmore, *Modern Spiritualism* (1902).

SPRING, MARCUS (b. 1810, Northbridge, Massachusetts; d. 1874, Perth Amboy, New Jersey), Quaker abolitionist and philanthropist and a founder of the Raritan Bay Union* (see also Appendix A, No. 120). He came from a Congregationalist-Unitarian background and attended Uxbridge Academy as a youth, but became a Quaker as an adult. In 1831, he moved to New York where he became a successful cotton merchant and was interested in reform movements. He and his wife, Rebecca Buffum Spring, were friends of Margaret Fuller and supported her financially. It was the Springs whom Margaret Fuller and her husband, Giovanni Ossoli, were coming to America to visit when their ship was wrecked near Fire Island.

The Springs were frequent travelers and lent their support to numerous cooperative projects. They were stockholders in Brook Farm* (see also Appendix A, No. 53), participants in William Ellery Channing's Religious Union of Associationists in Boston, and directors of the North American

Phalanx* (see also Appendix A, No. 66). In 1853, they purchased 270 acres at Perth Amboy, New Jersey, for the Raritan Bay Union, a joint stock company founded for dissidents from the North American Phalanx. Among the mainstays of the colony were several of their relatives, including Rebecca's parents, who lived in one of the phalanstery suites. The Springs encouraged George Inness, the landscape painter, to come to the colony. The house they built for him was paid in part by his painting "Peace and Plenty." In 1856, the Springs bought back the colony land from the stockholders and continued to live on the site until Marcus Spring's death in 1874.

SOURCES: Jayme Sokolow, "Culture and Utopia, The Raritan Bay Union," *New Jersey History* (Summer/Fall 1976); Dale Warren, "Uncle Marcus," *New England Galaxy* (Summer 1967).

STRANG, JAMES JESSE (b. March 21, 1813, Scipio, New York; d. June 15, 1856, Beaver Island, Michigan), founder of the Kingdom of St. James (Beaver Island Colony) (see Appendix A, No. 109). In 1836, Strang married and became postmaster and editor of the *Randolph Herald* in western New York. In 1843, he moved to Wisconsin where he became interested in Mormonism, converting in 1844.

After Joseph Smith's murder in 1845, Strang announced that he was the new prophet. He gathered around him a group of elders, including William Smith, the prophet's brother, and established the Voree,* Wisconsin, colony (see Appendix A, No. 91). The community lasted until 1847 when Strang decided to move his followers to Beaver Island in Lake Michigan. While at Voree, he issued pronouncements, including one to found a communal society. Strang sought to establish a benevolent theocracy which would temper man's acquisitive instincts and develop his spiritual powers. Christian communism was supposed to rule at Voree, with the church holding title to all the land and acting as trustee for its members in all things financial. A communistic "Order of Enoch" was his ultimate goal, but his dream outran his resources. Members had to tithe in order to sustain Voree and private property, rather than communism, was the true order. He approved of plural marriages but no man should take more wives than his income allowed.

In January 1847, the settlement moved to Beaver Island (called by Strang the Great Corner Stake of Zion), and by the following winter fifty were living on the island. Friction soon developed between the new settlers and the native fishermen over land use and politics. The Beaver Island Mormons became aggressive about their new-found Eden and threatened to go to war to protect their interests. On July 8, 1850, Strang had himself crowned "King" of the island. Armed conflict between the Mormons and the Gentiles erupted and continued for several years, finally resulting in a raid on the island in July 1853 which the Mormons repelled. However, his rule was short lived as he was murdered in 1856 by some Mormons who believed his rule too autocratic.

SOURCES: Milo Quaife, *The Kingdom of St. James* (1930); Oscar Riegel, *Crown of Glory* (1935).

T

TEED, CYRUS READ (b. October 13, 1839 or July 3, 1839, Moravia, New York; d. December 22, 1908, Estero, Florida), founder of the Koreshan Unity (see Appendix A, No. 194). Teed began medical studies at the age of twenty at Utica after working on the Erie Canal for nine years. He married in 1860, and in 1862, he moved to New York City, where he enlisted in the Union Army Medical Corps. After the war, he attended the Eclectic Medical College in New York, graduating in 1868 and opening a practice in Deerfield, New York, that same year.

In the autumn of 1869, Teed had a vision that the universe was all one substance—limited, balanced, integral, and emanating from one source, God. In addition, the vision revealed that the Copernican theory of an illimitable universe was false because the earth had a limited form; it was concave. This theory he called "Cellular Cosmogony."

During the 1870s and 1880s, Teed moved about central New York establishing a small communal household at Moravia in 1880 and publishing a periodical called *Herald of the New Covenant* (1880). In 1888, he moved to Chicago where he established the Koreshan Unity, with "Koresh" (Teed) as its leader. Chicago was his reaping ground, as members joined his church, the Assembly of the Covenant, and he published another journal, the *Guiding Star* (1888). In 1888, a cooperative home for church members, called Beth-Ophra, was established at Washington Heights in Chicago. In addition to Chicago there were groups organized in Denver, Baltimore, Portland, and Lynn and Springfield, Massachusetts. The chief postulates of the society were cellular cosmogony, alchemy, reincarnation, celibacy, communism, and a belief in Teed's inspired leadership. The group at Chicago numbered 300, with 150 living at the cooperative home in Washington Heights.

In 1894, the group moved to Estero, Florida, where they established a successful colony and carried out experiments to prove their theory about the concavity of the earth which they called cellular cosmogony. By 1901, the colony had two thousand acres under cultivation and about fifty members in residence, with that figure rising to two hundred around 1904. Relationships with people in the surrounding area were quite good, but a political dispute in 1906 forced the colony to organize the Progressive Liberty party and to run candidates. During the dispute, they began publishing the *American Eagle,* which is still published at Estero. The colonists believed Teed immortal and were shocked by his death. After his death, dissension split the colony with some members following Teed's co-leader, Victoria Gratia, while others incorporated a new church, the Order of Theocracy, at Fort Myers, Florida. There were few converts to either group and in 1961 only four survived. They donated the colony land to the state of Florida for use as a park.

SELECTED WORKS: Shepherd of Israel (1896); *The Koreshan Unity Cooperative* (1908); *The Law of Optics* (1912).
SOURCES: Howard Fine, "The Koreshan Unity: The Chicago Years of a Utopian Community," *Illinois History* (June 1975); Robert S. Fogarty, "We Live on the Inside," Introduction to Cyrus Teed, *The Cellular Cosmogony or the Earth a Concave Sphere* (1975 reprint); Hedwig Michel, *A Gift to the People* (n.d.).

THOMPSON, ELIZABETH ROWELL (b. February 21, 1821, Lyndon, Vermont; d. July 20, 1899, Littleton, New Hampshire), philanthropist and life-long supporter of cooperative endeavors. Elizabeth Rowell was born into a large New England family. She worked as a housemaid before meeting and marrying Thomas Thompson, a wealthy art collector, in 1843. They lived in Boston until 1860 when they moved to New York City and soon became known for their benevolent work.

With the death of her husband in 1869, Elizabeth was left with an annual income of $50,000. She spent her money on a wide variety of benevolent causes, particularly women's suffrage and temperance. In 1871, she underwrote the establishment of a cooperative workingmen's colony—the Chicago-Colorado Colony* (see Appendix A, No. 151)—at Longmont, Colorado. In 1879 she championed the cause of the English cooperator, George Jacob Holyoake, and in that same year she joined with R. Heber Newton, Felix Adler, and others in establishing the Co-operative Colony Aid Association. Out of this association came the support for the Thompson Colony (see Appendix A, No. 174) at Salina, Kansas in 1880. She also directly supported the writings of both Stephen Pearl Andrews* and John Ballou Newbrough,* who was the founder of the Shalam Colony (see Appendix A, No. 188) in New Mexico. She subsidized the publication costs of Newbrough's mystical work, *The Oashpe,* and published some of her own works under the imprint of the Oashpe Press, most notably her temperance tract, *The Figures of Hell* (1878).

In addition to her interests in cooperative colonization and temperance, Thompson was a strong supporter of scientific research. In fact, she was the first patron of the American Association for the Advancement of Science. Her other major reform interests were directed toward alleviating the conditions of children in urban areas. She found that cooperative colonies complemented that work by relocating families outside of metropolitan areas.

SELECTED WORKS: *Kindergarten Homes* (1873); *The Figures of Hell* (1878); *Heredity* (1882).
SOURCE: *Dictionary of Notable American Women,* 3.

TINGLEY, KATHERINE (b. July 6, 1847, Newburyport, Massachusetts; d. July 11, 1929, Point Loma, California), a leading theosophist and founder of the Point Loma Community* (see Appendix A, No. 217). Little is known about Tingley's early life except that she had three husbands between 1867 and 1880 and that she turned to reform questions in 1887, working with prisons, hospitals, and children's organizations. She was converted to theosophy by William Q. Judge, the leading American theosophist of her day, and she soon became an active leader and publicist for the movement.

After a tour of leading religious and occult centers in 1896, Tingley began to lay plans for a theosophical school and community in California. The Point Loma Community, located just north of San Diego, was founded in 1898 and served as national headquarters for the Universal Brotherhood and Theosophical Society. The community emphasized children's education and cultural enrichment, with the theosophists utilizing the Montessorrian method and the Greek dance as vehicles for expression. The colony at Point Loma was supported by tuition-paying children at the school and by contributions from wealthy patrons, such as Albert G. Spaulding, the sporting goods businessman, and William Chase Temple, the Florida fruit-grower. According to Emmett Greenwalt, Tingley considered Point Loma a "practical illumination of the possibility of developing a higher type of humanity" and stressed its educational rather than cooperative features.

Although the community was the focus of Tingley's later life, she continued her interest in reform work until her death. She organized relief activities during the Spanish-American War, campaigned against vivisection and capital punishment, and staunchly opposed America's entry into World War I.

SELECTED WORKS: *The Gods Await* (1902); *The Mysteries of the Heart Doctrine* (1902); *The Readjustment of the Human Race Through Theosophy* (1924).
SOURCES: Emmett Greenwalt, *The Point Loma Community in California, 1897-1942* (1955); *DAB* 18.

TOWNER, JAMES (b. August 23, 1823, Willsboro, Essex County, New York; d. November 19, 1913, Santa Ana, California), member of the Berlin Heights Community (see Appendix A, No. 126) and the Oneida Community* (see also Appendix A, No. 108). When Towner was twenty-two years of age, he went to Cleveland, Ohio, where he became a Universalist minister. He married in 1851, and for the next three years lived and preached in the area around Westfield, Ohio, before going to Iowa. During 1857, Towner published a series of articles in the *Social Revolutionist,* a magazine of the Berlin Heights Society, a small communal group located east of Sandusky, Ohio. He remained in Iowa reading for the bar, was admitted in 1859, and opened a law practice in West Union, Iowa, that year. In 1861, he enlisted in the Union Army and lost the use of his left eye in the Battle of Pea Ridge. He received a commission in the Invalid Corps and remained with them until July 1866.

Towner took up residence in the Berlin Heights Community in 1867 and simultaneously began corresponding with the Oneida Community. In 1874, he and eleven members of the by then defunct Berlin Heights group came to Oneida, bringing with them $14,000. When the group arrived, the colony was in the midst of internal dissension over the stirpiculture plan and the leadership role of Theodore Noyes, the founder's son. Towner became the center of opposition to the founder of Oneida, John H. Noyes.* The existence of the "Townerites" hastened the demise of the colony. Ironically, as a proponent of free love, Towner presided over the formal marriage ceremonies conducted in 1880.

Towner left central New York in 1882 for California where he helped incorporate the town of Santa Ana and aided in the organization of Orange County in 1885. In 1889, he was made a judge in the newly formed Superior Court of Orange County, holding that position until his retirement in 1897.

SELECTED WORKS: A Genealogy of the Towner Family (1910).
SOURCES: Robert S. Fogarty, "Nineteenth Century Utopian," *The Pacific Historian* (Fall 1972).

TRUTH, SOJOURNER (b. 1797, Ulster County, New York; d. November 26, 1883, Battle Creek, Michigan), social reformer and member of the Matthias sect. Sojourner Truth, born a slave, was active throughout her life in reform causes. Her personal history prior to 1828 is obscure, but it is known that her first language was Dutch and that she served in a New Paltz, New York, household from 1810 to 1827. She had five children in that period and in 1827 she fled her masters and lived with the Van Wagener family whose name she took. In 1829, she worked as a domestic in New York City, became a follower of a religious mystic, Elijah Pierson, and became a street preacher and active worker with prostitutes in New York. During this period, she was known as Isabella Van Wagener, and experienced spiritual visions and heard voices. In 1833, she went to Sing Sing, New York, in order to join the Matthias Colony led by Robert Matthews* and possibly to continue her benevolent work with women prisoners. She placed all of her money in a common fund and contributed her meagre furnishings to the communal household. The colony was rocked by a scandal in 1835 when Matthews was charged with the murder of Pierson and when allegations about free love in the group surfaced. Matthews was acquitted of the charge but jailed shortly thereafter because of an assault charge filed by his daughter. Sojourner Truth defended Matthews against these charges.

In 1843, Isabella changed her name to Sojourner Truth and began a thirty-year career as mystic, preacher, and reformer. After the Civil War, she worked for the National Freedmen's Relief Association in Virginia, and she supported efforts to establish a Negro state west of the Mississippi.

SOURCES: Arthur Fausett, *Sojourner Truth* (1938); Victoria Ortiz, *Sojourner Truth; A Self-Made Woman* (1974); *Dictionary of Notable American Women* 3.

U

UNDERHILL, SAMUEL (b. 1796, New York; d. 1859, Cleveland, Ohio), member of the Forestville Community (see Appendix A, No. 35) and the Kendal Community (see Appendix A, No. 36). Underhill was brought up in the Society of Friends. After an apprenticeship to a blacksmith, he changed vocations, teaching school for a while and then studying medicine. During 1822, he traveled throughout New York State in the guise of a skeptical preacher in order to spread free thought ideas. In 1825, he was director of the Forestville Community, a society which denied the superiority of any religious doctrine and followed Robert Owen's* preachings. The colony, located at Coxsackie, Greene County, New York, lasted until 1827 when its members, including Underhill, joined the Kendal Community in Ohio. In 1829, when this community, or the so-called Friendly Association for Mutual Interests, failed, he moved to Cleveland where he became prominent in local affairs, serving as a justice of the peace. In addition, he was a professor at the Willoughby Medical College but was dismissed because of his religious views.

Underhill edited *The Liberalist* during 1836-1837 and later changed its name to *The Bald Eagle,* a journal noted for "plunging its talons promiscuously into people," according to Elroy Avery. He was president of the Ohio Moral and Philosophical Society in 1837 and began to publish the *Annals of Animal Magnetism,* a mesmerist journal, in 1838. Little is known about Underhill's career after that date, except that he reportedly renounced his atheist beliefs just prior to his death.

SELECTED WORKS: *Underhill on Mesmerism* (1868).

SOURCES: Elroy Avery, *A History of Cleveland and Its Environs* (1918); Wendall Fox, "The Kendall Community," *Ohio Archaelogical and Historical Publications* 20 (1911); Albert Post, *Popular Freethought in America* (1943).

V

VALLET, EMILE (b. April 27, 1834, Orsay, France; d. March 29, 1907, Nauvoo, Illinois), member of the Icaria (Nauvoo) Community* (see Appendix A, No. 111). Vallet's father, a follower of Etienne Cabet,* the French author of *The Voyage to Icaria* (1840), moved his entire family to the United States in late 1849, joining the Icarians at Nauvoo, Illinois. After leaving their Texas settlement, the Icarians had moved into the ruins of the Mormon temple where they hoped to establish a colony. Young Emile Vallet served as Cabet's secretary and was an elected representative to the Icarian General Assembly at Nauvoo. His *Communism: History of the Experiment at Nauvoo of the Icarian Settlement* is a first-hand account of those early years. The Vallet family left the colony in 1856, disillusioned with communal life, but remained at Nauvoo.

SOURCES: Roger Grant (ed.), *An Icarian Communist in Nauvoo: Commentary by Emile Vallet* (1971); Robert Hine, *California's Utopian Colonies* (1966 reprint).

VROOMAN, WALTER. (b. January 8, 1869, Maco City, Missouri; d. December 2, 1909, New York City), wealthy supporter of radical movements. Vrooman came from a remarkable, reform-minded family. His father, Hiram, was active in the Liberal Republican and Greenback-Labor parties in Missouri and reared his five sons in the radical tradition. Walter attended Washburn College Preparatory School in Kansas in 1884-1885, but soon left to embark on a career as a socialist orator. He and his brother Harry published *The Labor Organizer* at Kansas City in 1887 and supported many radical causes, including the Credit Foncier Company at Topolobampo, Mexico. In that same year, Walter joined the Congregational church.

Vrooman moved around quite frequently in the next few years: to Cambridge, Massachusetts, in 1889 to work as a Christian Socialist; to New York City in 1890 to take a job as a reporter for the *New York World;* and to Philadelphia during the early 1890s to work with moral reform associations. In 1895, he published *Government Ownership in Production and Distribution,* where he argued that the state should substitute socialism for competition, and he was active in Populist politics. In 1899, he helped found Ruskin Hall in Oxford, and in 1900, along with his brother Hiram, he supported the Worker's Cooperative Association. In 1901, they became associated with Bradford Peck and his Cooperative Association of America, which had plans to establish a colony modeled on Peck's novel, *The World a Department Store.*

In 1902, Walter organized the Western Cooperative Association and deposited $300,000 in Trenton, Missouri, banks to promote cooperative schemes. An educational corporation, Multitude Incorporated, was formed to complement the business-oriented Western Cooperative Association which purchased five stores in Trenton in 1902. They branched out to Kansas City and hoped to build a model city nearby. The plan to establish a co-operative trust in Missouri was a grand-scale one, but by 1903 it was faltering.

In 1903, Vrooman's wife divorced him on grounds of infidelity; a year later he was committed to a state hospital in New York.

SELECTED WORKS: *Government Ownership in Production and Distribution* (1895); *The New Democracy* (1895); Miss Chunk (1897).
SOURCE: Ross Paulson, *Radicalism and Reform* (1968).

WXYZ

WARREN, JOSIAH (b. 1798, Brookline or Brighton, Massachusetts; d. April 14, 1874, Boston, Massachusetts), writer and community planner. Warren married at age twenty and soon thereafter settled in Cincinnati as an orchestra leader and music teacher. After hearing Robert Owen* lecture in 1825, he developed a keen interest in cooperative societies. In that same year, he sold his lamp factory and moved to the newly established Owenite settlement at New Harmony* (see also Appendix A, No. 30). Two years later, he returned to Cincinnati where he opened an "equity, or time" store. Labor notes, promising a specific number of hours of labor, were exchanged for goods at the store, but the experiment lasted only until 1830. In 1833, he established a journal, *The Peaceful Revolutionist,* to promote his anarchist views and helped plan the Equity Community (see Appendix A, No. 46) at Tuscarawas County, Ohio, but abandoned it in 1835.

For the next fifteen years, Warren worked at the printing trade and perfected a number of inventions regarding printing. He published *Equitable Commerce* (1847) which outlined an individualist stand on the proper reward of labor, the security of personal property, and the freedom of the individual. In 1849, he lived at "Utopia," Ohio near the site of the recently collapsed Clermont Phalanx (see Appendix A, No. 85). Utopia was a modest success, with the total residents in the town approaching one hundred in 1852 and all using the labor exchange system. In March 1851 Warren and Stephen Pearl Andrews* established an anarchist colony at Brentwood, Suffolk County, New York. Modern Times* (see Appendix A, No. 116), as they called the colony, attracted sixty persons by 1853, but allegations that it was a free love colony slowed its growth. Since Warren was no radical on the marriage question, he deplored Thomas Low Nichols'* appearance at the colony. Warren left the colony in 1860-1861 to live in Boston. During his last years he occupied himself with music and the company of friends, Mr. and Mrs. Ezra Heywood, the anarchists.

SELECTED WORKS: *Equitable Commence* (1852); *Written Music Remodeled* (1860); *True Civilization* (1863).
SOURCES: William Bailie, *Josiah Warren: The First American Anarchist* (1906); James Martin, *Men Against the State* (1953); *DAB* 19.

WAYLAND, JULIUS (b. April 26, 1854, Versailles, Indiana; d. November 11, 1912, Girard, Kansas), editor, reformer, and founder of the Ruskin Cooperative Association* (see also Appendix A, No. 204). Wayland was the youngest of seven children. He started in the printing business with the *Versailles Gazette* in 1877 and moved to Harrisonville, Missouri, where he began publishing the Republican paper, the *Cass News*. In 1882, he moved to Pueblo, Colorado, where he made a considerable fortune in real estate, but turned toward socialism after meeting William Bradfield, an English radical and socialist. In February 1893, he moved to Greensburg, Indiana, to start *The Coming Nation* which he continued to edit in irregular fashion until 1913.

Wayland was the major force behind establishing the Ruskin Colony, west of Nashville, in Dickinson County, Tennessee. He hoped to incorporate the aesthetics of John Ruskin with some practical socialism. Wayland had not read Marx before starting the colony and thus represented a native American radical tradition. Wayland used the pages of *The Coming Nation,* which had the largest circulation of any radical periodical, to promote the colony. Most of the colony's early members were drawn from the mills of New England which were hard hit by the 1893 depression. By 1895, the year Wayland left the colony, there were two hundred members on site, and the community buildings, plus other assets, were valued at $100,000. A forced sale of properties liquidated the venture in 1899, by which time Wayland had returned to his paper. He started *The Appeal to Reason* (1895) at Kansas City, Missouri, and moved the publishing to Girard, Kansas, in 1897.

SELECTED WORKS: Julius A. Wayland, *Leaves of Life, A Story of Twenty Years of Socialist Agitation* (1912).
SOURCES: Francelia Butler, "The Ruskin Commonwealth: A Unique Experience in Marxian Socialism," *Tennessee Historical Quarterly* (1964); *Who Was Who* (1897-1942).

WEITLING, WILHELM (b. October 5, 1808, Magdenburg, Prussia; d. January 25, 1871, New York City), founder of the Communia Colony (see Appendix A, No. 107). Weitling had little formal education and was reared in the Catholic tradition. He followed his trade as a tailor throughout Europe while developing his socialist philosophy. As a member of a German socialist organization in Paris, he published his first political treatise, *Die Menscheit,* in 1839. It was followed in 1842 by his major work, published in

Switzerland, *Garantien der Harmonie und Freiheit,* which Heine called the "catechism of German communists."

After his expulsion from Switzerland for political activity in 1846, Weitling came to the United States and organized workers into a Workingmen's League. At a meeting of the Worker's Congress at Philadelphia in 1850, a resolution was adopted urging the promotion of colonies in conjunction with already existing exchange associations in some Eastern cities. Weitling then became an active supporter of Communia, which was founded at Clayton County, Iowa, in 1847 by some German revolutionary refugees on 1,240 acres of land. In 1853, the constitution of the Communia Working Men's League ratified, with Weitling elected administrator. He ruled the colony autocratically and at one point was charged with suppressing the colony newspaper. The colony experienced financial setbacks and internal disputes in 1854, and three years later, a court suit by some dissidents effectively ended the community's life.

After Communia's failure, Weitling returned to his tailoring trade in New York, drifting away from radical politics toward schemes for a universal language (an interest he developed in the 1840s), astronomy, and the development of a buttonhole accessory attachment for the sewing machine.

SELECTED WORKS: Die Menscheit (1839); *Garantien der Harmone und Freiheit* (1842); *Das Evangelium eihes armen Sunders* (1845).
SOURCE: Carl Wittke, *The Utopian Communist* (1950).

WELD, ANGELINA GRIMKE (b. February 20, 1805, Charleston, South Carolina; d. October 26, 1879, Hyde Park, Massachusetts), progressive educator and member of the Raritan Bay Colony* (see also Appendix A, No. 120). Angelina Grimke was born into a distinguished Southern family and was educated at private schools. She turned from Presbyterianism to Quakerism and soon became involved in the antislavery movement. In 1829, she left Charleston for Philadelphia. Her antislavery *Appeal to the Christian Women of the South* (1835) was a major tract. She became an itinerant lecturer and the first woman (in 1835) to testify before a committee of the Massachusetts Legislature. In 1836, she began to press for women's rights and married another abolitionist, Theodore Weld. She was ill during much of the 1840s, and her sister, Sarah, began to live with them during this period.

In 1848, the Welds' straitened economic conditions forced them to start a school, and by 1851, they had twenty children enrolled. Two years later, the Welds joined the Raritan Bay Union at Perth Amboy, New Jersey, where they ran a school in one wing of the main community building. Everyone at the school had to do manual labor and to study bookkeeping, farming, and the domestic arts in addition to the standard subjects. Angelina taught history in what has been described as the most progressive school in antebellum America. It was interracial and coeducational, and one of the most successful features of the colony. In 1863, the Grimke sisters and Weld moved to Massachusetts where they all taught at a progressive school for a while and continued to lecture and write. In 1873, Angelina suffered a paralytic stroke which made her an invalid until her death in 1879.

SELECTED WORKS: *Appeal to the Christian Women of the South* (1835); *Letters to Catherine Beecher* (1838).
SOURCES: Gerda Lerner, *The Grimke Sisters from South Carolina* (1967); *Dictionary of Notable American Women,* 2.

WHITTAKER, JAMES (b. February 28, 1751, Oldham, Manchester, England; d. July 20, 1787, Enfield, Connecticut), major organizer of the Shakers. Whittaker's parents were members of the Shaking Quaker sect led by Jane Wardley, and as a youth he was cared for by Ann Lee,* later Mother Ann Lee of the Shakers. When Ann Lee was imprisoned, according to Shaker legend, it was young James Whittaker who kept her from starving by placing the stem of a pipe through the jail keyhole to feed her wine and milk. He was among the eight Shakers who sailed from Liverpool in May 1774, and was a major speaker and organizer for the group until his death. Imprisoned in 1780 because the Shakers were suspected of being British spies, he was also the object of mob action in New York directed at the Shakers. The first documentary evidence of Shaker interest in community planning is found in a letter Whittaker wrote in 1782 in which he states: "We shall have one meeting together which will never break up."

When Mother Ann Lee died in 1784, Whittaker organized and consolidated the Shaker groups all over the East into a network. During this period, he traveled throughout New England encouraging Shaker believers to gather into covenanted orders. He ordered the construction of the first meeting house at New Lebanon* (see Appendix A, No. 1) and dedicated it. According to the *Shakers Compendium,* his ministry "was short, but very active and laborious." He died while visiting the Shaker community at Enfield, Connecticut* (see Appendix A, No. 5).

SELECTED WORKS: *The Shaker Shaken* (1938 reprint).
SOURCES: Edward D. Andrews, *The People Called Shakers* (1963 reprint); F. W. Evans, *Shakers Compendium* (1972 reprint).

WILKINSON, JEMIMA (b. November 29, 1752, Cumberland, Rhode Island; d. July 1, 1819, Jerusalem, New York), founder of the Jerusalem Colony* (see also Appendix A, No. 3). Wilkinson was born into a prosperous Quaker family which had settled in the state in 1650. At an early age, she became deeply interested in religious ideas and was caught up in George Whitfield's 1776 revival. During that year, she became ill with fever, and during the course of her illness became convinced she had died and had been reborn again to preach a new gospel—this time under the title "The Publick Universal Friend." From 1776 until 1782, she traveled in lower New England, attracting followers to her simple message of repentance and the avoidance of evil. Many of her followers were well-to-do, and they provided her with comfortable homes when she stayed in their area. She was opposed to war and slavery, and urged her followers to be celibate, though married couples did follow her.

In 1788, Wilkinson's supporters, perhaps influenced by the successes of the Shakers and Ephrata* in establishing colonies, established a colony at Seneca Lake, New York, and by 1790 when she joined them, there were 260 members on the land. The settlement was called Jerusalem. Unfortunately, title to the land was soon in dispute, and by 1791 lawsuits between the followers had begun.

From 1790 until her death, Wilkinson lived in a home at Jerusalem preaching and ministering to her celibate congregation, even though she was in poor health during much of the period. She often had visions and dreams which she communicated to her followers. Some people in the area considered her a prophetess; others thought the colony the site of scandalous activity, although there is no evidence of any unusual practices. Her death was noted in the colony Death Book with the notation: "The Friend went from here."

SOURCES: Herbert Wisbey, *Pioneer Prophetess* (1964); *Dictionary of Notable American Women*, 3.

WILLARD, CYRUS FIELD (b. August 17, 1858, Lynn, Massachusetts; d. 1935, Los Angeles, California), organizer and director of socialist and cooperative programs. He was born into a family of six children that moved from Lynn to South Boston in 1866. Willard attended Bigelow Grammar School in Boston, but his unfinished autobiography tells us little more about his early years. While a reporter with the *Boston Globe* in 1888, Willard played a central role in forming the first Nationalist Clubs based on Bellamy's* *Looking Backward*. Willard and Sylvester Baxter organized the Boston Club, and Willard later wrote a regular column for the *Nationalist* (1889-1891). As a life-long theosophist, Willard was a confidant of Annie Besant, the English socialist and theosophist, William Q. Judge, the leader of the American wing of the Theosophical Society, and Katherine Tingley.* His two interests, theosophy and nationalism, complemented each other.

In 1897, Willard became involved with Debs' Social Democracy party, serving as secretary to the colonization committee which sought land for a socialist colony in the West. Willard played a major role in the 1898 Social Democracy convention at Chicago that split over the colonization question. There he argued, unsuccessfully, for the colonization plan, and later joined with Richard Hinton* in purchasing land at what became the Burley Colony (see Appendix A, No. 218) where Willard stayed for two years. After leaving the colony, he actively worked for the Theosophical Society, making it the focus of his activities until his death in 1935.

SOURCES: Charles LeWarne, *Utopias on Puget Sound* (1975), Arthur Morgan, *Edward Bellamy* (1938).

WRIGHT, FRANCES (b. September 6, 1795, Dundee, Scotland; d. December 13, 1852, Cincinnati, Ohio), radical reformer and founder of the Nashoba Community* (see Appendix A, No. 40). Her parents died when she was two and she was raised by relatives in England. She was self-educated and at age 24 published *Altdorf* (1819), a play about Swiss independence, and in 1822 *A Few Days in Athens,* a utopian tract. This ardent and controversial freethinker first came to the United States in 1818 and recorded her travel experiences in a popular memoir, *Views of Society and Manners in America* (1821). In 1824, she followed the Marquis de Lafayette, a close personal friend and confidant, to the United States for his farewell tour. She decided to stay and work for the cause of Negro emancipation, because she had been shocked by slavery during her earlier visit and described it in her *Views of Society* as "odious."

After publishing a pamphlet, *A Plan For the Gradual Abolition of Slavery in the United States Without Danger of Loss to the Citizens of the South* (1825), wherein she urged Congress to set aside large tracts of land for slaves where they could earn money and purchase their own freedom, Wright embarked on a plan to form a communal society as an experiment in racial emancipation and equality. In 1826, at a 640-acre site on the Wolf River near Chickasaw Bluffs, Tennessee, she began her colony, Nashoba (the Chickasaw name for Wolf), with some purchased slaves and a benevolent philosophy. She kept in close contact with the Owenite colony at New Harmony* (see also Appendix A, No. 30). When that experiment failed, she left for England with Robert Dale Owen, the son of New Harmony's founder Robert Owen. At that point her health was not good (she had malaria) and the climate in Tennessee did not agree with her. She left James Richardson, another Scottish-born reformer, in charge.

Nashoba failed essentially because of bad management and inadequate capitalization. What utterly destroyed it, however, was James Richardson's description of sexual relations between the colony's Negroes and whites. The account appeared in Benjamin Lundy's antislavery paper, *Genius of Universal Emancipation.* The colony was left without anyone to defend it since Richardson left abruptly when the furor erupted over the publication of the "Nashoba Books," the official transcripts of the colony affairs, became widespread. Wright returned from Europe where she had been trying to gain support for the colony.

She defended it against its detractors and launched into an attack on religion, segregation and marriage. "Fanny Wrightism" was a term coined by newspapers to describe radical libertarianism. According to Paul Boyer, "Nashoba represented a critical turning point in Frances Wright's life. Once accepted and popular, she was now driven to the fringes of American life, shunned and feared by the conventional and pious majority." She eventually settled the emancipated slaves in Haiti.

Wright's later reform career was distinguished, but involved no other cooperative schemes. She married and later divorced New Harmony member Phiqupal D'Arusmont, and she worked with Robert Dale Owen on projects concerning women's rights and free public schools. She moved to Cincinnati in 1835 and lectured widely in her later years on reform issues. In 1848, she published *England, the Civilizer,* a work urging peace and world federalism.

SELECTED WORKS: Altdorf (1819); *Views of Society and Manners in America* (1821); *A Plan for the Gradual Abolition of Slavery in the United States Without Danger of Loss to the Citizens of the South* (1825); *What is the Matter* (1838); *England the Civilizer* (1848).
SOURCES: William Waterman, *Frances Wright* (1972 reprint); *DAB,* 20; *Dictionary of Notable American Women,* 3.

WRIGHT, LUCY (b. February 5, 1760, Pittsfield, Massachusetts; d. February 7, 1821, New Lebanon, New York), member of the Shaker community at New Lebanon (see Appendix A, No. 1). Wright came from a prominent family, possessed an "exceptional intelligence," and married when she was eighteen. She and her husband joined the Shakers in the 1780s and soon became prominent members. On Mother Ann Lee's death in 1784, Joseph Meachem* appointed her to head the Shaker sisters and to assume an equal symbolic leadership role with him. Wright encouraged the development of Shakerism in the West and took the lead in introducing new elements into Shaker worship, particularly in singing and dancing. However, she opposed the writing down of the so-called millennial laws because she feared they would fall into alien hands and because she believed the laws would have to change with circumstances and the times. After Meachem's death in 1796, Wright led the New Lebanon ministry. She was a vital force in the society during a period when the Shakers experienced their greatest growth.

SOURCES: Edward D. Andrews, *The People Called Shakers* (1962 reprint); F. W. Evans, *Shakers' Compendium* (1972 reprint).

YOUNG, BENJAMIN SETH (b. September 17, 1774; d. 1855, Watervliet, New York), Shaker missionary. Young was a member of a prosperous family. He entered the Watervliet, New York, Shaker community (see Appendix A, No. 2) in 1794. He was one of the three missionaries from New Lebanon sent out in 1805 to convert the West. With John Meachem and Issachar Bates,* he helped win converts and establish new communities in the Ohio Valley. Even though he had only a common school education, he authored *The Testimony of Christ's Second Appearing* (1808), which was a justification for the Shaker position. In 1809, he helped establish the short-lived Busseron, Indiana, community (see Appendix A, No. 22). He was present during the 1810 mob riots at Union Village, Ohio, and helped defend the society against its detractors. In addition, he served as an elder in the South Union community (see Appendix A, No. 20) at South Union, Kentucky, for twenty-five years. His major contribution was in spreading the Shaker message through visits and writing. In October 1836 he left the West for good. He returned to New Lebanon at the age of seventy-two.

SELECTED WORKS: The Testimony of Christ's Second Appearing (1808); *Transactions of the Ohio Mob* (1810?).

SOURCES: Edward D. Andrews, *The People Called Shakers* (1963 reprint); J. P. MacLean, *Shakers of Ohio* (1974 reprint).

COMMUNITIES

A

ALTRURIA (see also Appendix A, No. 203), founded in 1894 by Edward Biron Payne* at Fountain Grove, Sonoma County, California. Inspired by William Dean Howells' novel, *A Traveller from Altruria* (1894), it was organized by a group of Christian Socialists from Berkeley, who met in 1894 to plan a cooperative colony. Most of them were members of Payne's Unitarian church, and they chose a 185-acre site seven miles north of Santa Rosa and near the Thomas Lake Harris* colony, Brotherhood of the New Life* (see Appendix A, No. 163). Their constitution emphasized democratic suffrage, complete equality of community goods, and a labor check system.

In October 1894, six or seven families and six bachelors settled on the site, and by April 1895 they had constructed seven cottages and begun work on a hotel. They published a weekly paper, *The Altrurian,* which outlined their plans and progress. Their $50 initiation fee provided some cash at the outset, but their varied domestic industries were inadequate to provide working capital. By the summer of 1895, their financial problems were apparent, and support from Altruria Clubs throughout California was insufficient to keep the colony going. In June 1895, the original colony closed out its books, and three smaller units emerged from the original settlement: one on an eighty-acre farm at Cloverdale, a second at Santa Rosa, and a third group remaining at Altruria to continue publication of the paper. All three units, however, closed within the year.

SOURCES: Robert Hine, *California's Utopian Colonies* (1953); Morrison Swift, "Altruria," *Overland Monthly* (June 1897).

AMANA SOCIETY, or THE SOCIETY OF TRUE INSPIRATION, located first at Erie County, New York, in 1843 (see also Appendix A, No. 68) and then at Iowa County, Iowa, in 1855 (see also Appendix A, No. 128). The colony originated in the eighteenth-century German pietist movement led by

Eberhard Gruber and Johann Rock. Rock and Gruber were members of the Lutheran church who had become interested in the teachings of the early mystics and sought a new religion based on present-day inspiration. They based their faith on the Bible, but they also believed that God could inspire men in their own day. They felt that God communicated with men through visions and dreams and that divine inspiration did not come to all but only to those who were given the gift of inspiration. The Inspirationists were led in the nineteenth century by Christian Metz* who, in 1826, initiated a common household for the group at Marienborn, Germany, to safeguard their belief in pacifism, pietism, and a separate religious education for their children.

Communism of property was not part of the Inspirationists' original creed and developed only slowly. After one of Metz's visions, the colony purchased a five thousand-acre tract at Ebenezer in Erie County, New York, where they migrated in 1842. The Society of True Inspirationists consisted of eight hundred families, and it was in America that they adopted communism as a means of furthering their religious life. They moved from western New York to Iowa in 1854 because the growth of the city of Buffalo precluded their buying additional land at a reasonable price; they began to fear for the spiritual welfare of their young; and they were raided on occasion by the Seneca Indians. In 1854, they purchased twenty-six thousand acres of land, and over the next ten years they established seven self-sufficient villages at Amana for their twelve hundred members. They took the name Amana from the Song of Solomon, and it signified those who "believe faithfully." In 1859, they were incorporated as the Amana Society.

Each village, while autonomous, was under the nominal control of the board of trustees. The colonists prospered through marketing agricultural and woolen products, and retained their simple Christian beliefs based on divine inspiration through a gifted leader. Each village consisted of a cluster of one hundred homes with their own church, school, bakery, dairy, sawmill, and general store. Several families occupied each home. The economic success of the Amana colonies weakened their religious structures. After the death of Barbara Heinemann, Metz's successor, in 1883, no inspired leader emerged to lead the group. The process of secularization set in and in 1932 the colony was formally dissolved.

SOURCES: W. R. Perkins and Barthinius L. Wick, *History of the Amana Society* (1891); Bertha Shambaugh, *Amana, the Community of True Inspiration* (1908); Barbara S. Yambura and Eunice Bodine, *A Change and a Parting* (1960).

AMITY COLONY (see also Appendix A, No. 221), established by the Salvation Army in 1898 at Holly, Colorado. The genesis of the colony idea was in William Booth's *In Darkest England and the Way Out* (1890), which suggested a plan to alleviate poverty by establishing self-sufficient city and farm colonies. In 1896, when Frederick Booth Tucker became commander of the Salvation Army in America, he proposed what William Booth had suggested in *In Darkest England and The Way Out,* that they "place the waste labor on the wasteland by means of waste capital and thereby convert this trinity of modern waste into a trinity of production." There was widespread support for the idea, with Grover Cleveland, Theodore Roosevelt, Henry Lodge, and Mark Hanna all encouraging the scheme. During 1897, Salvation Army officials traveled throughout the United States looking for sites, and in 1898, three were selected in California, Colorado, and Ohio.

The most successful colony was at Fort Amity in eastern Colorado—the others were at Romie, California, and Fort Herrick, Ohio—where fourteen families from Chicago were settled on 640 acres. Each family was given ten acres, a horse, a small plow, two cultivators, a set of harness, and some basic implements. During the first few years, homes were built and a cantaloupe crop was planted. All of the first settlers had some farming experience, and they were aided by a resident Salvation Army manager. By 1903, the settlement was apparently prosperous, with 450 people in residence. However, excessive alkaline deposits in the soil caused a severe crop failure in 1909, and by 1910, the Salvation Army had closed the program.

None of the farm colonies was communal or cooperative in its economic or social life, but there was an underlying assumption that removing families to a new environment and placing them on the land could improve their material and spiritual welfare. While there was little economic cooperation, there was considerable moral cooperation.

SOURCES: Dorothy Roberts, "Fort Amity, the Salvation Army Colony in Colorado," *Colorado Magazine* (September 1940); Walter Prescott Webb, *The Great Plains* (1931); Herbert Wisbey, Jr., *Soldiers Without Swords* (1955).

ANANDA COOPERATIVE VILLAGE, founded in 1967 by Swami Kriyananda at Nevada City, California. The community was an outgrowth of Kriyananda's teachings and followed the pattern established by Swami Paramahansa Yogananda, author of *Autobiography of a Yogi,* who taught that "self-realization" colonies would form the basis for the future world. From 1948 to 1962, Kriyananda was Yogananda's disciple and lived in monasteries in India and America. In 1962, he was dismissed as vice-president of the Self-Realization Fellowship for advocating decentralization and was forced to leave the society. In 1967, he bought a twenty-four-acre site at Nevada City and came in contact with poets Gary Snyder and Allen Ginsberg. Between 1968 and 1970, he purchased several more parcels of land and established a meditation retreat. Members were required to pay an initial membership fee and to make monthly contributions to the mortgage fund. Several business enterprises were established on the site, including an incense factory and a print shop, and individual craftsmen sold their wares.

In effect there are two Ananda communities, one a farm and the other a meditative retreat house. The seventy-two-acre retreat consists of housing for guests and community members, facilities for meetings and religious worship, and Kriyananda's domed home. The colony farm is six miles distant. The retreat is for monks and single people; the farm, for families with children. Members are expected to lead celibate lives, to cultivate their spiritual awareness by meditation and yoga, and to follow the teachings of Swami Kriyananda. There is some communal labor, but the emphasis is on personal and spiritual growth. The commune has grown in numbers and has constructed several new buildings, while adhering to its original premises. The thirty resident members have a steady stream of visitors for retreats.

SOURCES: Hugh Gardner, *The Children of Prosperity* (1978); Swami Kriyananda, *Cooperative Communities: How to Start Them and Why* (1971).

B

BETHEL-AURORA COLONIES (see also Appendix A, Nos. 90 and 131), founded in 1844 by William Keil* at Shelby County, Missouri. The nucleus of this group came to the society from the Rappite community at Economy, Pennsylvania (see Appendix A, No. 17). Some had settled in Phillipsburg, Pennsylvania, after leaving the Harmony Society* (see also Appendix A, No. 44), and they became members of Keil's Methodist church. In the spring of 1844, the entire congregation—nearly all Germans—moved to a 2,560-acre site in northern Missouri. It was named Bethel after an ancient city near Jerusalem, and by 1847 the colony numbered six hundred. The Bible was their source of inspiration, the Golden Rule their motto, and William Keil their autocratic leader. By 1850, their acreage had increased to four thousand and the colony was prospering. They also constructed a magnificent church which served as Keil's pulpit for his monthly sermons to the colony. The colony observed no distinctive creed except their adherence to simple Christian precepts.

In 1849, a branch colony, Nineveh, was established on the Chariton River in Adair County, Missouri (see Appendix A, No. 112). It eventually consisted of about two thousand acres and supported one hundred and fifty colonists in thirteen buildings. During 1856, another move was made from Bethel, with Keil leading a party to Oregon to establish another group in the Williamette River Valley (see Appendix A, No. 131). He named it Aurora after his daughter; the settlement flourished. It was located about thirty miles from Portland in Marion County and, like Bethel, had few specific guiding principles except a belief in the Bible and Keil's inspired leadership. It was known for its excellent band, its fine hotel, and the general prosperity of its farms. After Keil's death in 1877, no new leader emerged. Bethel was dissolved as a community in 1880 and Aurora in 1881.

SOURCES: R. J. Hendricks, *Bethel and Aurora* (1933); William Hinds, *American Communities* and *Co-operative Colonies,* 327-339 (1908 ed.).

BISHOP HILL COLONY (see also Appendix A, No. 102), founded in 1846 by Erik Jansson* at Henry County, Illinois. The colony's origins were in Sweden where Jansson led a dissident group within the Church of Sweden. He and his followers were charged with spreading heresy, attacking the clergy, and book burning. Jansson had repudiated Luther and relied solely on the Bible for inspiration. Later, his own writings became sacred texts for his followers in their quest for human perfectibility. In 1845, he fled to New York to avoid a jail sentence, and in 1846, twelve hundred of his followers left Sweden to establish a settlement in the New World. Seven hundred of them journeyed to Illinois to join Jansson at Bishop Hill—named after his native parish in Uppland. Their first dwellings were primitive dugouts, and many died during their first hard winter.

By 1855, Bishop Hill was an impressive prairie town laid out around a village square. Several buildings, including the "Big Brick," the largest building west of Chicago in 1851, had been erected. The colonists' original acreage was two hundred, but by 1850 it had grown to fourteen thousand. They produced linen cloth for a commercial market and had large cattle herds and extensive industrial works. After Jansson's death in 1850, Jonas Olsson ruled the colony with the aid of a board of trustees. The economic boom caused by the Crimean War strengthened their economy, but a slump in 1858 made their economic situation precarious. In 1862, they decided to dissolve their common ownership of property agreements and to divide the property between two contending religious factions.

SOURCES: Paul Elmen, *Wheat Flour Messiah* (1976); Olov Issakson, *Bishop Hill, Illinois* (1969); Michael Mikkelsen, *The Bishop Hill Colony* (1973 reprint).

BROOK FARM (see also Appendix A, No. 53), founded by George Ripley* at West Roxbury, Massachusetts, in 1841 as an outgrowth of William Ellery Channing's Transcendental Club of reformers and writers for *The Dial.* An educational association was formed in 1841 wherein all labor, both physical and intellectual, was paid the same rate for work at the Ripley farm. Distinguished intellectuals like Nathaniel Hawthorne, Charles Dana,* and

Isaac Hecker* were among the early members of this joint-stock venture in individual reformation. In 1843, the association was converted to Fourierism and became a phalanx with serial divisions of labor and an emphasis on spreading Fourier's philosophy. *The Harbinger* (1845-1849), an influential reform journal, was published weekly at Brook Farm.

Brook Farm became the center for Fourierist activity in the United States, but was unable to find a steady and stable income to support its philosophical and educational enterprises. A fire in the main building, the phalanstery, in 1846 effectively ended the colony's life since there were insufficient funds to rebuild. Brook Farm's influence was more ideological than practical, with its society attracting major American transcendentalists and reformers to its doors. Yet, it must be seen as a failure of the intellectual idealists to carry through on their plans for societal reformation. In 1847, the society was dissolved.

SOURCES: T. D. Seymour Bassett, "The Secular Utopian Socialists," in *Socialism and American Life,* Donald Egbert and Stow Persons, eds. (1948); Edith R. Curtis, *A Season in Utopia* (1961); Robert S. Fogarty, *American Utopianism* (1974); Marianne Dwight Orvis, *Letters from Brook Farm* (1974 reprint).

BROTHERHOOD OF THE NEW LIFE (see also Appendix A, No. 141), the second of four colonies founded by Thomas Lake Harris,* the spiritualist and mystic. The first of Harris's colonies, Mountain Cove, was established in 1851 in Virginia on the site where he and his followers believed the former Garden of Eden stood (see Appendix A, No. 117). The Virginia colony broke up after two years because of internal disputes. Between 1853 and 1863, Harris developed his curious spiritualist philosophy in several works, including the Swedenborgian journal *The Herald of Light.* Borrowing from Swedenborgianism, Harris developed the notion of the "pivotal man" as the core of his communal plans. He believed himself to have been singled out as the priest and king of a new society. His communities consisted of a group of "regenerate persons breathing in harmony with the 'pivotal man,'" who then became the "vortex of divine power." Colonists developed special breathing techniques in order to inhale a "divine vapor" which aided in repelling "sin-spirits" and "death spirits" which pervade the air. In addition, Harris demanded celibacy from his followers.

In 1861, Harris selected Wassaic, Dutchess County, New York, as the site for his second colony, the Brotherhood of the New Life. During 1863, he sold the original property site and moved four miles to Amenia, where his group (some thirty-five) had a home and a grist mill, and ran a bank. In the autumn of 1867 they moved to yet another site, Brocton (see also Appendix A, No. 143), which he called "Salem-on-Erie." By 1869, there were sixty disciples, including the wealthy Laurence Oliphant and his mother, who had brought some $100,000 into the colony. One unusual feature of the membership at Brocton was the presence of twenty Japanese Christians who had come to study Harris's gospel of the "two-in-one." That doctrine proclaimed a bisexual deity. God was both male and female since mankind had been created in his image. In 1876, Harris moved the colony to its fourth location, Santa Rosa, California, and it was named Fountain Grove (see also Appendix A, No. 163).

What was originally a dairy farm was transformed into a sixteen hundred-acre vineyard within a few years. (There were extensive vineyards at the Brocton Community.) The Fountain Grove Press published tracts and essays by Harris, and openly recruited members. Harris and his followers believed that Fountain Grove was "to be a germ of the Kingdom of Heaven, dropped from upper space and implanted in the bosom of heavenly human-ity," according to Harris. It was a peaceful settlement until rumors about sexual irregularities began to appear in the local press. In 1891, Harris was forced to leave, and in 1892, he married Jane Lee Waring ("Dovie" as she was called) who had brought to the community a fortune estimated at between a quarter and a half million dollars. With Harris's marriage and removal to New York the colony ended. According to Robert Hine, the Santa Rosa properties were worth a quarter of a million dollars in 1900.

SOURCES: William Hinds, *American Communities and Co-operative Colonies* (1908 ed.), 422-434; Herbert W. Schnieder and George Lawton, *A Prophet and a Pilgrim* (1970 reprint).

THE BURNING BUSH (see also Appendix A, No. 262) was founded in 1913 at Bullard, Texas, by a group of Methodists who had become dis-satisfied with their church and formed the holiness-oriented Metropolitan Church Association. This evangelical sect, which had its headquarters in Waukesha, Wisconsin, decided to form religious colonies so that its mem-bers might work and worship together. Colonies were founded in Virginia, West Virginia, Louisiana, and Texas. In 1912, the group purchased a 1,520-acre site in Smith and Cherokee counties and by early spring 1913, 375 members of the Metropolitan Church—commonly called the Burning Bush—had arrived. They first built a tabernacle and several homes. Everyone who joined the colony gave their possessions into a common treasury, drew from a common storehouse, and "ate from a common table," according to Edwin Smyrl. They raised capital for the colony by selling bank notes and receiving financial support from a wealthy Chicago investment banker, Duke Farson.

The colony ran a large farm, a sawmill, and a cannery, and at one point drilled an oil well, unfortunately a dry one. They believed it was possible to gain a "second blessing" (a religious experience after conversion when the

Holy Spirit eradicates natural depravity) and to live a life without sin, to speak in tongues, and to gain the power to cure the sick by faith alone. Liquor and tobacco were forbidden, and the colonists were known to their neighbors as law-abiding citizens. The colony disbanded in 1919 when Farson's bond business began to fail and the association was unable to support itself. Its land was seized for debts and sold at auction on April 15, 1919.

SOURCES: Edwin Smyrl, "The Burning Bush," *Southwestern Historical Quarterly* 3 (1947).

C

CHRISTIAN COMMONWEALTH COLONY (see also Appendix A, No. 214), founded in 1896 at Muskogee County, Georgia, by a group of Christian Socialists. A letter published in 1895 in *The Kingdom,* a socialist magazine, inviting individuals to start a colony, attracted the attention of George Howard Gibson* and Ralph Albertson.* Gibson had organized the Christian Corporation (see Appendix A, No. 212) in Nebraska in 1895, and Albertson was a member of the Willard Colony (see Appendix A, No. 210) at Andrews, North Carolina, at the same time. The two groups merged into the Christian Commonwealth Colony, and in November 1896, John Chipman, an Episcopal rector, purchased a 934-acre cotton plantation in Georgia. The first members were drawn together by a sense of Christian brotherhood, a belief in practical Christianity, and a willingness to try the cooperative life. The doors were open to one and all, and by September 1899, there were ninety-five members. The colonists farmed, published *The Social Gospel,* a periodical devoted to Christian social action, and tried to go into the textile business.

The Commonwealth Cotton Mill was organized and the production of towels begun in 1898. Although this venture failed, the colonists did run a successful printing operation and the circulation of *The Social Gospel* reached two thousand. The journal's name subsequently became the accepted term for Social Christianity. Housing at the colony was always a problem. Some members lived in an old plantation house, while others stayed in makeshift log cabins. In the summer of 1899, several colonists brought suit and requested that a receiver be appointed for the community. They charged that it was mismanaged, that their open door policy was detrimental to the colony's interests, and that it was near bankruptcy. The suit was rejected by the court. An outbreak of typhoid fever suddenly hit the colony in the spring of 1899, killing two members. The final blow came in 1900 when the Right Relationship League, a Chicago corporation organized in

1896 to help support the colony, asked that a mortgage be taken out in order to secure an earlier $2,000 loan. In June 1900, the colony went into voluntary receivership.

SOURCES: Ralph Albertson, "The Christian Commonwealth in Georgia," *Georgia Historical Review* (June 1945); James Dombroski, *The Early Days of Christian Socialism in America* (1936); William Hinds, *American Communities and Co-operative Colonies* (1908 ed.).

COLORADO COOPERATIVE COMPANY (see also Appendix A, No. 205), founded in 1894 at Montrose County, Colorado. The main object of the colony was to build an irrigation ditch, but in its early days the founders hoped for more. The company was incorporated in Denver in 1894 in order to establish a colony which could "reach the highest condition of social and intellectual attainment and material equality," according to their "Declaration of Principles." They purchased twenty-thousand acres of arid land under the Desert Land Act and started to recruit settlers. The colony newspaper, *The Altrurian,* promoted it, and touring speakers proselytized for the colony. Members were required to purchase at least one share of stock ($100 par value), and that allowed them voting rights and water rights when the ditch was completed. Land was to be owned privately. Some ardent socialists opposed private ownership, even though there was a provision that no individual could own more than forty acres.

A central working camp was established at Pinon, and within five years some fifty structures were built to serve a growing population. By 1897, membership had reached two hundred. However, beginning that year, there were increasing signs of discontent among the workers over the policies of the governing board. In 1899, external members—particularly in Denver—complained that they were inadequately consulted about the ditch construction. By 1903, the colony had a population of 232 and the irrigation ditch was half completed. In 1904, water moved onto some land. By 1910, the project was finished and it became a town company called the Nucla Town Improvement Company.

The colony had been communal only in the sense that its settlers worked toward a common goal, had common interests, and subordinated private interests to a corporate end. There were socialists who pressed for greater cooperation, and in the end there was even some cooperative farming, but they were in a minority. In 1908, it was reported that there was pressure to operate the town along single tax lines, but no such system was ever inaugurated.

SOURCES: William Hinds, *American Communities and Co-operative Colonies* (1908 ed.): 500-504; C. E. Julihu, "Pinon—A New Brook Farm of the West," *National Magazine* (October 1899); Alexander Kent, "Cooperative Communities in the United States," *Bulletin of the Department of Labor,* 35 (July 1901): 293-306; Duane Mercer, "The Colorado Co-operative Company, 1894-1904," *The Colorado Magazine* (1967).

COOPERATIVE BROTHERHOOD (see also Appendix A, No. 218), incorporated in 1898 as an outgrowth of the 1897 colonization commission organized by the Social Democracy of America. A colony at Burley, Washington, grew out of this organization which had been formed to encourage the collective ownership, distribution, and manufacture of goods. It was organized as a corporation, and the members had little say in the actual running of the colony. The business of the colony was managed by twelve directors chosen by legal stockholders. During the fall of 1898, a 294-acre site in Kitsap County, north of Seattle, was settled by sixteen persons. The clearing of the land and the publication of a paper, *The Cooperator,* were the members' chief activities. Later, logging—both on colony lands and at other sites—and a sawmill operation were developed. They used a time-check system for labor and issued their own script currency. Cyrus Willard,* a major figure at Burley, resisted efforts by Colorado miners to make it communistic rather than socialistic. A split developed between the external directors and the colonists who worked at the community.

By the end of 1899, the colony had seventy-six members and by the end of 1901, one hundred and fifteen. Communal living was only for bachelors in dormitories as families had their own homes. However, all meals were taken communally in the Commonwealth Hotel. There were about twelve hundred external members who paid a dollar a month and who could become members after ten years. Some of them could be called into the colony early if there was need for a specific skill. In 1904, the colony reorganized, and the Burley Mercantile Rochdale Association was organized under the guidance of Alonso Wardell. By 1906, the colony ceased to function as a cooperative, and in 1913, it dissolved into receivership.

SOURCES: W. E. Copeland, "The Cooperative Brotherhood," *The Arena* 28 (October, 1902): 403-405; William Hinds, *American Communities and Co-operative Colonies* (1908 ed.): 536-543; Charles LeWarne, *Utopias on Puget Sound* (1975).

D

DOMAIN, HARMONIA, KIANTONE COMMUNITY, or THE ASSOCIA-TION OF BENEFICENTS (see also Appendix A, No. 119), established at Kiantone, Chatauqua County, New York, in 1853 by a group of spiritualists including John Murray Spear.* In 1850, a Kiantone blacksmith, while in a trance, learned that the area around a local spring had once been the site of a perfect society where free love was practiced. Water from the spring was sent to leading spiritualists, and it attracted Spear to the site where he hoped to build a city of universal harmony. Originally, ten tiny (10 ′ × 14 ′) oval and octagonal homes were built on the spring site in 1853. Later, a thirty-five-room hotel was constructed. Most of the members wintered in their own homes away from the colony, so the Domain was, in fact, a summer commune. Between twenty and forty individuals were members, most of them spiritualists. The women members were staunch feminists. A contemporary newspaper account in the *Jamestown Weekly Journal* of a spiritualist convention held there in 1858 stated that the lecturers spoke about "the abolition of the marriage and family relations; the elevation of women to perfect freedom or 'individualism' and the change of society to a visionary state of perfection and order."

In 1859, the colonists began a voyage down the Mississippi to promote a "planetary congress" to bring peace to the world. On the way to New Orleans, they established a colony at Patriot, Indiana, where they settled in July 1860. In 1863, both Kiantone and the Sacred Order of Unionists at Patriot organized in 1859 at the outset of their voyage were dissolved.

SOURCES: Russell Duino, "Utopian Themes with Variations: John Murray Spear and His Kiantone Domain," *Pennsylvania History* (April 1962); John M. Spear, *Twenty Years on the Wing* (1873).

DROP CITY, founded in May 1965 by a group of young artists on a six-acre site near Trinidad, Colorado. Many of the first members were young artists from Colorado and Kansas who wanted to build and live in geodesic domes. Their alternative "drop city" combined Eastern mysticism, avant-garde art, and psychedelic drugs. Members of the commune saw themselves as missionaries for the new emerging culture; they traveled around the country promoting light shows and "Droppings"—their name for a "total media environment mix." They came to national attention in 1966, and in June 1967, when they sponsored the "Drop City Joy Festival," which attracted thousands of hippies to the site. In 1968, many of the original settlers left, and by 1970 another group had formed on the site. At that point there were thirty-nine adult members living in a variety of dome structures. There was no real leadership and no distinctive philosophy except a genial anarchism. It was a temporary colony, and they made no attempt to establish any permanent organization on the site. In March 1973, the property was sold and the residents were all evicted.

SOURCES: Richard Fairchild, *Communes, U.S.A.* (1972); Hugh Gardner, *The Children of Prosperity* (1978); William Hedgepeth, *The Alternative* (1970); Peter Rabbit, *Drop City* (1971).

E

EPHRATA COLONY, or **THE SOLITARY BRETHREN OF THE COMMUNITY OF THE SEVENTH DAY BAPTISTS,** founded by Johann Conrad Beissel* in 1732. During the latter part of the eighteenth century, hundreds of different Christian sects flourished in Germany. Some were pietist groups who believed in mysticism, baptism by immersion and observed the seventh day (the Sabbath) as a day of rest. A few groups returned to the early Christian practice of communal living while others formed hermitages. Beissel had come to America in 1720 to join the mystical group "Woman in the Wilderness" led by Johann Kelpius,* but he found only scattered remnants of the sect when he arrived. Toward the end of 1721, he and other pietists formed an "angelic" brotherhood in the Conestoga district of western Pennsylvania. Goods were held in common, and they fasted, prayed, observed Saturday as the Sabbath and abstained from meat and other unclean food according to the Mosaic law.

In 1723, a spiritual revival took place among several German congregations in the area. Many settlers had come from the Palatine region of Germany and had come in contact with separatist and pietist groups before coming to the United States. By 1725, Beissel was the acknowledged leader of the growing sect and he began to give forth what he considered divine utterances received under inspiration. This celibate and hermetic group held love feasts where they broke bread, gave one another the kiss of peace and had a foot-washing ritual. Their church was divided into three orders at this time: married householders, an angelic brotherhood of men and a sisterhood of women called spiritual virgins. All practiced continence.

In 1732, Beissel moved to a site near the Coaclico Creek, Antietam County and his scattered flock moved to this single site over the next few years. Previous to this they had lived in several different places and had come together for religious worship; in 1732 Beissel called them together to form "Ephrata, the Camp of the Solitary." A common house, called the Kedar, was built in 1735. In the Kedar they held their nightly services called the "Night Watch" where men and women dressed in pilgrim's garb consisting of a shirt, trousers, vest and broad-rimmed hats. They worshipped in silence. Ephrata became a center for Dunker (now called the Church of the Brethren) activity in the area. A large house of prayer (bethaus) was erected along with a common granary and bakery. The group became, under Beissel's leadership, more mystical in its teachings and they were led by the Zionitic Brotherhood, a group of well educated young men who practiced mystical rites and set a high spiritual standard for others. By 1740, there were thirty-four men living in the Zionitic Brotherhood and thirty-five women in the Spiritual Virgins class. In that year the solitary brethren were ordered to leave their hermit cabins and move into a communal dwelling.

In 1740, the Eckerlin brothers, with Beissel's blessing, began to organize the society along more practical lines. A split developed in 1742 between the commercial-minded Israel Eckerlin* and the mystic Beissel in what became a public feud in 1745. Beissel attacked Eckerlin as a materialist and all of Eckerlin's writings were put to the torch. The commercial enterprises were reduced, the Zionitic Brotherhood dissolved, and the remnants of Eckerlin's rule destroyed. From 1748 to 1752, the colony was in chaos as Beissel reasserted his rule. After 1757, Beissel was denied control over the colony's finances with Peter Muller taking the lead. During the 1760s, there were continuing disputes and Beissel's senility and drunkenness were causes for concern at Ephrata. After Beissel's death in 1768, Peter Muller continued to lead. In 1770, the land was conveyed to five trustees with each member receiving a quarter acre for gardening and an equal share in the colony profits from agriculture and printing. By that date the colony had effectively ended.

SOURCES: James E. Ernst, *Ephrata: A History* (1963); Julius F. Sachse, *The German Pietists of Provincial Pennsylvania* (1970 reprint).

F

FAIRHOPE (see also Appendix A, No. 211), founded in 1895 by supporters of Henry George at Fairhope, Alabama. Five Iowa Populists met in Des Moines in 1893 to form the Des Moines Single Tax Club. Out of their common interests there developed a plan to start a cooperative colony. In January 1894, the Fairhope Industrial Association was formed in Des Moines, and individuals were invited to apply for stock in the colony ($200 par value). Land was to be owned by the association, and the colony was to serve as a working model of the single tax plan. All business enterprises and homes would remain in private hands, but the public utilities would be owned by the association. It was not solely a socialist colony, and the initial appeal for colonists was broad based. Potential sites were examined in Louisiana and Tennessee, but an area "somewhere in Baldwin County, Alabama" was picked.

An initial land purchase of 132 acres acres on Mobile Bay started the settlement. By 1906, there were sixteen hundred acres under single tax control and between five hundred and six hundred settlers in the town. Several problems beset the early settlers: their land was submarginal; the acreage of contiguous land controlled by the association was too small; those with adequate land acreage were too few; and the socialistic politics of many community members repelled the strict single taxers. Colonists were expected to build their own houses, clear and fence their own land, and find their own employment. Since most of those who came were intellectually curious, the town (incorporated in 1908) got a reputation as an intellectual center. Marietta Johnson's School of Organic Education, a progressive school started in 1907, attracted national attention.

Today, the Fairhope Single Tax Corporation retains extensive holdings within the town of Fairhope, just as it did in 1908. It stands as one of the few practical attempts to apply Georgeist principles to a single muncipality, even though the colonists failed to gain ownership of all the land.

SOURCES: Paul and Blanche Alyea, *Fairhope, 1894-1954* (1956); H. C. Bennett, "Fairhope: A Single Tax Colony," *Colliers* (September 14, 1912); E. B. Gaston, "Fairhope, The Home of the Single Tax and the Referendum," *Independent* (July 16, 1903); Marietta Johnson, *30 Years with an Idea* (1956).

FERRER COLONY (see also Appendix A, No. 267), organized in August 1914 in New York City and established at Stelton, New Jersey, in May 1915. It was an anarchist community led by Harry Kelly,* Joseph Cohen,* and Leonard Abbott.* The Ferrer movement, named after the Spanish freethinker and anarchist Francisco Ferrer, established a cultural center, an evening school, and an experimental day school in New York City. Its Modern School, which was first located in the Lower East Side and then in Harlem, recruited its students from the families of politically radical workers in the garment industry; they joined hands with native-born intellectuals to start a progressive school.

From 1912 to 1916, the school struggled to maintain itself amidst political disputes, erratic leadership, and a growing belief that a libertarian school and colony located outside of New York City could be a more effective force for social change. In 1915, the group moved across the Hudson River to Stelton, New Jersey, where eventually ninety homes were built and one hundred and twenty children enrolled in the school. After 1920, the school came under the supervision of Elizabeth Ferm* and Alexis Ferm; the curriculum centered on manual crafts, nature study, and free expression. Emphasis on inner and individual development brought the Ferms in conflict with the political radicals whose vision was social and outward. This early conflict within the anarchist ranks later spread and ended in a split between the anarchists who preached individualism and practiced community, and the communists who preached solidarity while dividing the colony. By 1918, the colonists had constructed fifty-one dwellings and about twenty families lived on the 143-acre site. Consistent with anarchist beliefs, land was owned by individuals. About three-fourths of the colonists were Russian Jews. At the colony's peak, over one hundred families lived at Stelton on a permanent basis, with double that number in residence during the summer months.

The colony had vigorous social life, including evening lectures, communal dinners, and folk dancing. It ran a cooperative store in conjunction with its neighboring communal settlement, Fellowship Farm. The Ferrer Colony was an odd mixture of anarchists, socialists, and communists who inhabited the same ground for more than twenty years. The Modern School was the colony's center and was run by the Ferms with a firm hand. By the 1940s and after two decades of community and conflict, many of the colonists began to sell their homes and move to warmer sites in the Los Angeles and Miami areas. By 1946, it ceased to exist as a distinct entity in the area.

SOURCE: Lawrence Veysey, *The Communal Experience* (1973).

FRUITLANDS (see also Appendix A, No. 71), founded in 1843 by Bronson Alcott,* Charles Lane,* and Henry Wright on ninety acres near Harvard, Massachusetts. The colony developed after Alcott made a trip to England in 1842 to visit Alcott House, a community and boarding school run by his English followers Lane and Wright. After considerable discussion in London, the three reformers decided to establish an association in New England. Lane purchased a farm, paid Alcott's debts, and on June 14, 1843, Fruitlands began. It was a primitive homestead where simplicity in dress, diet, and lodgings were its hallmark and where the agricultural life reigned. Lane and Alcott were the chief figures, with several others participating, including Isaac Hecker,* a refugee from Brook Farm* (see Appendix A, No. 53).

Abigail Alcott resented Lane, the overcrowded house they all lived in, and the arduous work that fell to her and her two daughters, Anna and Louisa. In a letter to an English friend, Charles Oldhorm, Lane wrote that "Mrs. Alcott has no spontaneous inclination toward a larger family than her own natural one, of spiritual ties she knows nothing. . . ." The colonists cultivated the soil with spades, wore linen garments in protest against slave-produced cotton, and followed both the hydropathic system of cold baths and the Graham system of eating only fruits and grains. They refused to use hired labor or beasts of burden and they plowed crops under to enrich the soil. By mid-winter they were facing poverty and had to be rescued by friends in Concord.

The small community faltered when Lane tried to wean Alcott away from his family and urged him to adopt the celibate life. Alcott resisted the idea. In January 1845, Lane, with his son, left the "consociate family" as they called it to live briefly at a Shaker Community in Harvard (see also Appendix A, No. 6). The Alcotts left the same month to live at a home in a nearby village. Although Fruitlands had a short history, it became a symbol of New England transcendentalism's efforts (in the form of Alcott) to live a higher and purer life.

SOURCES: F. B. Sanborn and William T. Harris, *A. Bronson Alcott's Life and Work* (1893); Clara Endicott Sears, *Bronson Alcott's Fruitlands* (1915); Odell Shepard, *Pedlars Progress* (1937).

G

GERMAN COLONIZATION COMPANY (see also Appendix A, No. 147), founded in 1869 by Carl Wulsten, a Chicagoan and editor of the *Staats Zeitung,* a German language paper in Chicago. The Company was organized in Chicago to help poor German artisans in that city. There was a membership fee of $250. Wulsten believed that economic cooperation would enable colonists to settle and conquer the West. In November 1869, a committee formed to locate land for the colony chose a site at Wet Mountain Valley, near Silver Cliff, Colorado. In February 1870, a special train carried three hundred Germans from Chicago to their new town of Colfax. Temporary cabins were erected, a colony garden planted, and one-acre lots distributed to the settlers. However, their petition to Congress for a joint land grant of forty thousand acres was not supported in Washington, and the colonists lacked clear title to the land. In September, Wulsten resigned as colony president and it began to disintegrate. Members began to leave before the winter set in, and in December the colony store burned down. The majority of the settlers were inexperienced farmers and Wulsten was a temperamental leader. As a reason for the colony's collapse, one member stated: "There was too much Kommunimus."

SOURCES: James Field Willard (ed.), *Experiments in Colorado Colonization* (1926).

H

HARMONY SOCIETY (see also Appendix A, No. 17), founded in 1805 at Butler County, Pennsylvania, by George Rapp,* a prophetic leader who emigrated to the United States in 1803 from Wurttemberg, Germany. When the community was organized in 1805, the colonists pledged their obedience and cooperation in promoting the group's interests and they gave their support to Rapp. Their faith was based on a literal reading of the Bible, their opposition to the established Lutheran church, and their acceptance of George Rapp as an inspired leader and teacher. The original group consisted of over three hundred families.

Their first few years in Pennsylvania were hard ones. They held their goods in common, and, according to a visitor, they "all seem contented and happy." Celibacy was the preferred state, and marriages, though discouraged, were tolerated. In 1814, they sold six thousand acres of land in Butler County and purchased a thirty thousand-acre tract on the Wabash River in southwestern Indiana. They called the town Harmony and developed substantial businesses in agriculture and woolen and cotton goods. One hundred and thirty new immigrants joined them in 1817, by which date there were one thousand members in residence.

In 1825, the Harmonists sold their land and buildings to Robert Owen* for his New Harmony* (see also Appendix A, No. 30) venture. The Harmonists then moved back to Pennsylvania, this time to a site on the Ohio River twenty miles north of Pittsburgh to a town they called Economy (see Appendix A, No. 28). Under Rapp's leadership, they prospered once again. In 1832, a large group left the colony to follow the imposter Count Leon (Bernard Muller*) first to the New Philadelphia Society at Phillipsburg, Pennsylvania (see Appendix A, No. 44) and then to Grand Ecore, Louisiana (see Appendix A, No. 48). Upon Rapp's death in 1847, the affairs of the society fell to Romelius Baker* and Jacob Henrici.*

During the post-Civil War period, the Harmonists continued to expand their financial base and employed a large labor force. They enjoyed a distinguished reputation as bridge builders. However, they made some bad investments, and under the leadership of John Duss* they squandered their fortune. As a result of lawsuits and internal disputes, the colony was dissolved in 1898.

SOURCES: Karl Arndt, *George Rapp's Harmony Society, 1785-1847* (1965) and *George Rapp's Successors and Material Heirs, 1847-1916* (1972); John Duss, *The Harmonists* (1973 reprint).

HEAVEN CITY, founded by Albert J. Moore near Harvard, Illinois, in 1923. Moore predicted world catastrophe which would start in 1923 and end in 1927 with a "new dawn." Specifically, he prophesied a money panic in 1923, universal labor strikes in 1924, a reactionary worldwide revolution in 1925, and a world war which would destroy three-fourths of the world's population in 1926. He therefore organized a religious colony to create a heaven on earth under the aegis of the Humanity Trust Estate. The colony began with a membership of thirty-six on 130 acres. Prior to joining, members turned over their property, and all were expected to labor on their farm. Each family was to have a home of its own, though cooking and laundry facilities were common. Moore's philosophy was a simple one: "Help yourself by doing: then help everyone else by coordinating and cooperating." His was a positive religion which emphasized good works and a belief in reincarnation. According to a local paper, *The Harvard Herald,* the colonists maintained their own school based on the Froebel and Montessori methods. The colony appears to have ended in 1927.

SOURCES: *The Harvard Herald* (May 3, 1923; May 10, 1923); Ernest Wooster, *Communities of the Past and Present* (1971 reprint).

HELICON HALL COLONY (see also Appendix A, No. 246), founded in 1906 at Englewood, New Jersey, by Upton Sinclair.* In June 1906, Sinclair published an article in the *New York Independent* outlining his plan for a colony which would solve the pressing "servant problem," establish a cooperative home, and "realize the Cooperative Commonwealth." A former boys' school situated on nine and one-half acres was purchased, and in October 1906, fifteen members came to a site near the Palisades to live. They came to a palatial setting and a set of buildings which housed an indoor swimming pool, a bowling alley, a theatre, and a billiard room. Sinclair purchased the school and the land for $36,000 from the sale of *The Jungle* (1904).

The colony had a very short history. A fire broke out in 1907, destroying the main building and killing one member. But in those six short months, it had a distinguished roster of colonists, including Edwin Bjorkman, the critic and translator of Strindberg, Michael Williams, later editor of *Commonweal,* and Sinclair Lewis, the novelist who eventually married Edith Summers, Sinclair's secretary at the colony. Although the colony had been organized as a joint-stock company, Sinclair provided nearly all the funds. During 1906-1907, he wrote *The Industrial Republic* while in residence there. After the fire, Sinclair envisioned taking the colony on the road to visit noted socialist authors and writers, including George Bernard Shaw, but "Helicon Hall on the Hoof," as he called it, never materialized.

SOURCES: William Hinds, *American Communities and Co-operative Colonies* (1908 ed.): 581-587; Upton Sinclair, *Autobiography of Upton Sinclair* (1962).

HOME COLONY, or **MUTUAL HOME ASSOCIATION** (see also Appendix A, No. 222), founded in 1898 on Puget Sound by a group of anarchists. The colony developed from the failure of an earlier Bellamy* colony, the Glennis Cooperative Industrial Company (see Appendix A, No. 208), organized in 1894. Three former members of that colony—Oliver Verity, George H. Allen, and B. F. Odell—sought a new location and found twenty-six acres on Joe's Bay. It was a community of individuals rather than a cooperative colony. The founders did not have a formal organization until January 1898, when the Mutual Home Association was formed. Members could secure one or two acres from the association, and all monies would go toward the purchase of additional land.

There were forty members originally, ninety-one by 1900, and 155 by 1906. The colony published a weekly anarchist paper, *Discontent: Mother of Progress,* and maintained a lively social and political life, with numerous outside speakers, such as Emma Goldman, visiting. Local groups attacked the anarchists for their political views. The *Discontent* editors were once fined for obscenity, but they simply replaced it with another journal, *The Demonstrator.* This colony of individualists had few cooperative institutions. A cooperative store was organized in 1902, and some community construction projects were done cooperatively. It was an exciting and colorful community where a high degree of individualism was tolerated and where free speech, free love, and free ideas were encouraged.

In 1909, the articles of incorporation of the Mutual Home Association were changed to allow property to be held privately. Before that time all land was held in trust and could never be sold or disposed of. This change in the articles signalled the end of Home as a cooperative colony, but it continued as a center for anarchist agitation.

SOURCE: Charles LeWarne, *Utopias on Puget Sound* (1975).

HOPEDALE COMMUNITY (see also Appendix A, No. 56), founded by Adin Ballou* in 1842 at Milford, Massachusetts. The community developed out of the reform interest of the members of a Universalist church at Mendon, Massachusetts, who wished to put their Christianity to a practical test. In 1840, they began publishing a semimonthly reform sheet, *The Practical Christian,* which ran articles about Christian communities. After the meeting of their quarterly conference in January 1841, they held discussions about forming a colony. In April 1842, they established a "fraternal community" wherein the twenty-eight members pledged to abstain from murder, hatred, "unchastity," and liquor. They all lived in a unitary house, sent their children to a common school, and farmed 50 of the 258 acres they owned. Early in their history, they modified their constitution to allow for individual ownership of land and the establishment of separate households.

Most of the association members were active in reform activities—particularly the peace and antislavery movements—and often attended reform conventions. By 1845, the colony owned four hundred acres and the membership continued to grow. By 1852, it had one hundred and ten residents and two hundred associated members who supported the colony. They tried an experiment in industrial democracy in 1847 whereby labor decisions were made by small groups, but they quickly returned to a hierarchical labor system with centralized decision-making. Economically, Hopedale was quite prosperous, but it had to abandon the joint-stock partnership arrangement because of a dispute with George Draper, one of the first members. In 1860, they abandoned the publication of *The Practical Christian,* and in 1887, the Hopedale Community merged with the Hopedale Parish.

SOURCES: Adin Ballou, *History of the Hopedale Community* (1973 reprint).

THE HUTTERITES originated in the sixteenth-century German Anabaptist movement. Dissatisfied with the Protestant churches of their day, the

Hutterites advocated adult baptism, pacifism, the separation of church and state, and the supremacy of the individual conscience. From 1528 to the present, the Hutterites have adhered to the practice of holding all things in common. Their communalism is rooted in their desire to emulate the primitive Christian church. They were persecuted throughout Western Europe. In 1770, they received a promise from the Russian government that they could settle in the Ukraine and practice their religion. But in 1870, the Tsarist government withdrew its guarantee of religious toleration, placed the Hutterite schools under government control, and tried to conscript them into the army.

In 1873, two Hutterite men journeyed to North America in search of a new homeland. At that time, about half of the Hutterites lived communally and the others with individual family units. Between 1874 and 1877, eight hundred Hutterites—the entire population—moved to the United States. Four hundred settled in South Dakota in three different colonies at Bon Homme, Wolf Creek and Elmspring (see Appendix A, Nos. 156, 160, 167); the others settled on individual homesteads in South Dakota. Between the time of their settlement at Bon Homme in 1874 and World War I, their numbers grew to seventeen hundred and the number of colonies, or *Bruderhof* (a dwelling place of brothers), to seventeen.

Each *bruderhof* manages itself under the leadership of a five-man council, plus the minister. Families are housed together in apartment dwellings and all take their meals in communal dining halls. The Hutterites are a conservative group intent on maintaining their separation from the world, but unlike the Old Order Amish, they utilize modern labor-saving devices such as tractors and electric mixers. However, movies, television, and other outside recreations are considered too worldly.

The Hutterites' economic system is designed to provide self-sufficiency: they raise most of their own food, make their own clothing, and are careful about purchases made outside the colony. Men and women have clearly defined duties, with the women doing domestic labor and the men tending the farms. They are a close-knit society held together by their religious tenets, their use of the German language, and their maintenance of their own schools. Conflicts with the outside world have been sporadic. Some young men fled to Canada to escape conscription in World War I, and the colonies have been attacked by their neighbors because of the Hutterites' expansionist tendencies. They need more land as their population grows, and they usually have the economic resources to purchase available tracts of land. At present, their population stands at twenty-five thousand in over one hundred colonies in the High Plains states and Canada.

SOURCES: Paul Conkin, *Two Paths to Utopia* (1964); Emerson Deets, *The Hutterites* (1975 reprint); John Hostetler, *Hutterite Society* (1974); Jacob Waldner, "Diary of a Conscientious Objector in World War I," *Mennonite Quarterly Review* (January 1974).

I

ICARIA (see also Appendix A, Nos. 110, 111, 133, 137, 169, 170, 177), founded in 1848 by Etienne Cabet* at Fanin County, Texas. Cabet began a political career as a radical in 1825 when he became a member of a secret political society, the Carbonari. In 1831, he was elected to the French Assembly, but because of his attacks on the king in 1834 he was exiled to England. When in exile, he wrote several historical works, among them *Le Voyage en Icarie* (1840), a utopian tract which gained him wide attention. In 1841, Cabet founded a journal called *Le Populaire,* and between 1843 and 1847, he printed numerous pamphlets. His blueprint for a new social order emphasized a gradual transformation of the society towards socialism, with education providing the means to that end. A central feature of his plan was the immediate establishment of workshops for laborers and the enfranchisement of labor.

In May 1847, Cabet issued a proclamation urging all Icarians to emigrate: "Let us go to Icaria." On Robert Owen's* advice, he went to Denton County, Texas, where his group obtained a million acres along the Red River. The French government's persecution of the Icarians hastened their departure. In February 1848, an advance guard of sixty-nine headed for America, only to find when they arrived in New Orleans that Louis Philippe had fallen and the Second Republic had been established. As a result, the second group that left France consisted of only nineteen members instead of the fifteen hundred who had planned to go before the revolution. Furthermore, the original party found that they owned only 10,240 acres, not a million, and that their thirty-two half-sections were not contiguous but scattered throughout two townships.

By 1849, the Icarian membership had increased to 480, with the bulk of them living in New Orleans because life was too harsh in Texas. In the next year, over two hundred traveled up the Mississippi to Nauvoo, Illinois, to occupy the land and properties vacated by the westward-moving Mormons (see Appendix A, No. 111). The Icarians prospered at Nauvoo. Cabet was president until 1856 when a split in the society resulted in his expulsion. He then led a loyal group of 180 supporters to Cheltenham, near St. Louis, Missouri, to found another colony (see Appendix A, No. 133). Cabet died in 1856, and his colony increased its membership over the years.

In 1857, the group at Nauvoo that had ousted Cabet moved to Corning in Adams County, Iowa, (see Appendix A, No. 137) where they suffered economic reversals until the boom Civil War years. By 1868, their membership reached sixty, and they had seventeen hundred acres under cultivation. Internal disputes over land ownership shook the colony in the 1870s, and in 1878, an Iowa court appointed three trustees to distribute the property. New Icaria and Jeune Icarie (see Appendix A, Nos. 169, 170) grew out of this dispute, with the conservative faction moving eight miles south of the original settlement and sustaining some common life until 1898. In 1881, another group settled in California under the leadership of Armand Dehay. The Speranza Colony at Cloverdale (see Appendix A, No. 177) lasted until 1886.

SOURCES: Robert Hine, *California's Utopian Colonies* (1966 reprint); Christopher Johnson, *Utopian Communities in France, 1839-1851* (1974).

J

JERUSALEM, or **THE SOCIETY OF UNIVERSAL FRIENDS** (see also Appendix A, No. 3), founded in 1788 by Jemima Wilkinson* at Seneca Lake, New York. The colony developed out of the preaching and personal revelations of its founder and prophetess. She may have been influenced by the Shakers or the communists at Ephrata, but it was primarily the "Publick Universal Friend," as Wilkinson was called, who shaped the society. The community had no written covenants, no stated creed or confession of faith, but based its religious beliefs on a literal interpretation of the Bible. Although celibacy was preferred, marriage was allowed in the colony. Each member of the society owned and worked his own land, and donated labor and monies to support Wilkinson and her household.

By 1790, nearly three hundred followers were settled on the lands near Wilkinson's house. They all hoped to escape the corrupting influences of the world and lead pure lives. The distinctive features of the colony were its pacifism, celibacy, and the plain style of its meetings which were modeled after those of the Quakers. During the 1790s, the community began to lose members and there were numerous lawsuits over property. Wilkinson was ill during much of the community history, and her leadership role is little understood. She preached a simple gospel of Christian love and, by some accounts, had an engaging manner and saintly presence. With her death in 1819 the society disintegrated.

SOURCE: Herbert Wisbey, *Pioneer Prophetess* (1964).

K

KAWEAH CO-OPERATIVE COMMONWEALTH (see also Appendix A, No. 189), founded in 1885 by James J. Martin and Burnette Haskell* at Tulare, California. The impetus behind the venture was the publication of

Laurence Gronlund's* *Cooperative Commonwealth* (1884) which was read by some San Francisco labor leaders and socialists. After a November 1884 meeting, sixty-eight individuals formed the Cooperative Land Purchase and Colonization Association of California. In October 1885, fifty-three men in the association went from San Francisco to the Visalia land office and laid claim to lands in the newly opened Sequoia Forest area. They named their colony Kaweah after the river that ran through the property. Most of the men were skilled laborers from the trade unions, but the Nationalist movement also produced some members. Between one hundred and fifty and four hundred colonists were in residence between 1885 and 1891. A cumbersome organizational structure was originally established, with numerous departments, superintendents, and trustees all responsive to the all-powerful general meeting. Membership in the colony cost $500, and a time-check system was used to pay for work done.

There was a large group of nonresident supporters who paid a membership fee and who could vote, but who never actually lived at the colony. Socialists across the country supported the project in this fashion. Most of the resident families lived in tents, but there was an active effort to create a cooperative socialist life. Classes were organized and social gatherings encouraged. The colonists named the larger sequoias after famous socialists (the tree named after Karl Marx is now known as the General Sherman). Much of their time was spent constructing a road to the rich timber forests. In 1890, the government challenged the colonists' right to the land, and in that same year the Sequoia National park was established. In addition to its problems with the government, the colony was plagued by internal disputes stemming from Haskell's erratic leadership and arguments over the voting rights of nonresident members. In 1891, about half of the residents revolted against the time-check system and took possession of the land. During April 1892, amid legal squabbles over ownership, and just prior to a trial arising from charges by the federal government that the trustees had used the mails illegally, the colony ended. By that time, most of the colonists had moved off the colony lands.

SOURCES: Robert Hine, *California's Utopian Colonies* (1966 reprint); James Martin, *Men Against the State* (1953).

KIRTLAND COMMUNITY (see also Appendix A, No. 42), founded by Sidney Rigdon* in February 1830 in Lake County, Ohio. Rigdon convinced a portion of his Baptist congregation at Mentor, Ohio, to accept the idea of a common stock community based on a literal restoration of the primitive Christian church. By February 1830, about one hundred individuals came together on Isaac Morley's farm, and in the fall, they were visited by four young men who represented a new religious sect, the Mormons. Though

Rigdon was the driving force behind establishing the community, he never lived in it; during its formative months, he lived at Independence, Missouri. After reading the Book of Mormon, Rigdon claimed that Mormonism was the true Apostolic church. At that point, both the congregation at Mentor and the community at Kirtland followed Rigdon into Mormonism.

In 1831, Joseph Smith moved to Kirtland and it became the church's headquarters. The members of the "family" at Kirtland had argued about the pattern of community life (how much cooperation, how much individualism), and its future was precarious from the start. However, the communal phase ended on February 9, 1831, after Joseph Smith had a revelation which stated: "Thou shalt not take thy brother's garment; thou shalt pay for that which thou shalt receive of thy brother." Although the Mormons remained at Kirtland until 1835, the holding of goods in common ended with Smith's arrival.

SOURCES: F. Mark McKiernan, *The Voice of One Crying in the Wilderness: Sidney Rigdon, Religious Reformer* (1971).

L

LAMA FOUNDATION, founded in 1967 by Steve Durkee and a group of New York artists who wanted to establish a community based on spiritual and environmental values. Late in 1966, Durkee began to look for land near Taos for the colony, and in June 1967, he purchased 115 acres of mountainside twenty miles from Taos. In February 1968, the Lama Foundation was incorporated, and the group received $7,500 from the Pastorale Foundation to begin constructing their facilities. Since 1968, this spiritual community has grown steadily and has expanded its operations to include a school, regular seminars for visitors, and a publishing house. In 1969, Richard Alpert (a former Harvard professor who later took the name Baba Ram Dass) came to Lama and started a meditative ashram for thirteen monks, seven yogis, and one teacher. His influence on the colony since then has been considerable. Many of the members in residence have independent incomes and are able to spend their time exploring inner space rather than being forced to lay an economic foundation for the colony.

There are three categories of membership: "permanents" who constitute the foundation's core; "actives" who work for six months and then leave; and "students" who come for briefer periods and attend workshops. Initially, new members had to pay an entry fee and then construct their own shelters, but now there is a set monthly fee and the members live in dormitories and domed communal structures. Thirty hours of labor are required each week from members, but the main community focus is on achieving a higher spiritual state through meditation, Sufi dance, and yoga. By 1973, the community was entirely self-supporting and maintained a vigorous educational program for visitors.

SOURCES: Baba Ram Dass, *Be Here Now* (1971); Richard Fairfield, *Communes, U.S.A.* (1972); Hugh Gardner, *The Children of Prosperity* (1978); Robert Houriet, *Getting Back Together* (1971).

LITTLE LANDERS COLONY (see also Appendix A, No. 249), established in 1909 by William E. Smythe* at San Ysidro in the Tiajuana Valley, fourteen miles south of San Diego. Smythe believed that large tracts of land could be purchased cooperatively, irrigated, and subdivided into small plots, "little lands," and made productive. After an initial $300 payment, a colonist would receive a small town lot, an acre of land, and interest in all public utilities. For example, about a dozen families settled on 120 acres at San Ysidro. By 1913, the number had grown to three hundred settlers, with each family working its plot and selling its produce through a marketing cooperative. Many of the first colonists were middle-aged or older, and they hoped to become self-sufficient through the scheme. Between 1909 and 1916, four other colonies were organized—at Cupertino, Runnymede, Hayward Heath, and in the San Fernando Valley—but little is known about them. Smythe believed that in such colonies the values of town and country could be merged and a vigorous social life developed for each participant. But the land holdings were too small for the colonists to make a profit; a flood in 1915 destroyed the first and major settlement.

SOURCES: Robert Hine, *California's Utopian Colonies* (1966 reprint); William Smythe, *City Homes on Country Lanes* (1921).

M

MEMNONIA INSTITUTE (see also Appendix A, No. 129), founded in 1856 by Thomas Low Nichols* and Mary Gove Nichols* at Yellow Springs, Ohio. The Nicholses were universal reformers and participated in all the social movements of the 1840s, including women's rights and free love. In 1851, they opened the American Hydropathic Institute in New York, the first academy for teaching the water cure. Unfavorable publicity, centering on the Nicholses' free love views, forced them to move to Cincinnati in 1855 where they published *Nichols Monthly* and promoted hydropathy. In 1856, they were offered a lease on the Yellow Springs Water Cure, and early that year they founded the Memnonia Institute named after the goddess of waters. Horace Mann, the new president of Antioch College, opposed the colony, but by September 1856, their School of Life, as they called the central and communal part of their enterprise, was ready to open.

It is unclear whether or not other individuals came with the Nicholses, but it is certain that they had colony aspirations in mind. Their social philosophy was derived from Fourier, their search for harmony rooted in perfectionist notions, and their earlier careers spotted with reform ventures. This colony, however, was a short-lived one since the Nicholses dramatically converted to Catholicism in 1857 after both Ignatius Loyola and Francis Xavier visited them during seances. The Memnonia Institute ended on March 29, 1857, when the pair was baptized into the Roman Catholic church. Three other Memnonians had been baptized a month earlier.

SOURCES: Philip Gleason, "From Free Love to Catholicism: Dr. and Mrs. Thomas L. Nichols at Yellow Springs," *Ohio Historical Quarterly* (October 1961).

MORNING STAR, founded by Lou Gottlieb in 1966 on a thirty-two-acre farm at Occidental, Sonoma County, California. Gottlieb, a musician in a folk group, developed an interest in "LSD, Indian mysticism, and cooperative living" in the early 1960s, according to Hugh Gardner. He attempted to turn his vacation home into a free community of hippies and to open the land to all comers. When hundreds of hippies descended on the site, in July 1967, Gottlieb was arrested for being in violation of local health codes. Between July and October, he was taken before the courts on several occasions and fined $15,000. By that time, his land had been overrun by squatters who engaged in public nudity and were deemed a public nuisance by local authorities.

In October 1969, the police and FBI agents raided the "open land" commune in an effort to close this anarchist colony. Despite police action, the colony showed signs of stabilizing itself and had a population of two hundred spread over the thirty-two acres. A dam, a windmill, and a buying cooperative were formed, but by 1972, it was apparent that the inheritance of Bill Wheeler (their major financial backer) had run out and that the land would have to be sold. By then, many settlers had left the area, with some going to other communes in the area and others to Morning Star East in Taos, New Mexico.

SOURCES: Hugh Gardner, *The Children of Prosperity* (1978).

N

NASHOBA COMMUNITY (see also Appendix A, No. 40), founded in 1826 by Frances Wright,* the Scottish reformer and feminist. After leaving New Harmony* (see also Appendix A, No. 30) in 1826, Wright began an interracial colony on the Wolf River at Shelby County, Tennessee. Convinced that sexual and religious emancipation was as important as emancipation from slavery, she allowed the colonists, both black and white, full social and sexual equality. There were never more than fifteen slaves on the 640-acre site and an even smaller number of whites. Wright was at the colony for only brief periods and left its running to James Richardson, an ex-medical student and storekeeper. Although Wright had hoped to make the farm a model plantation where slaves could buy their freedom through cooperative labor, it never functioned as such, for whites led the way in every area.

In May 1827, Wright left for Europe to recover from malaria, and in her absence she turned the colony over to the trustees. During that time, Richardson's sexual relationships with the slaves were made public. Not only had miscegenation occurred at Nashoba, but also Richardson had prepared an article for Benjamin Lundy's antislavery journal, *Genius of Universal Emancipation* which gave explicit details about the free love and interracial colony. The ensuing public outcry against the colony doomed it, and when Wright returned from Europe in early 1827, she found a diminished society and Richardson gone. By June 1827, she too had abandoned the colony. In 1830, part of her colonization ideal was transplanted to Haiti where she was able to place a small group of slaves.

SOURCES: William Waterman, *Frances Wright* (1972).

NEW HARMONY (see also Appendix A, No. 30), founded in 1825 by the Welsh-born industrialist and reformer Robert Owen.* The colony's philosophy was based on Owen's belief in man's rational capacity to construct a new moral order grounded in economic cooperation and education. His visit to the United States in 1824 stimulated interest in his benevolent scheme to organize a colony in America. His writings had attracted attention as early as 1820 when the New York Society for Promoting Communities disseminated his ideas. During 1824-1825, Owen negotiated with George Rapp* for the purchase of Rapp's colony lands on the Wabash River in southwestern Indiana.

Owenism has been called by Arthur Bestor, Jr., more gospel than theory "because Robert Owen had faith in human progress rather than any plan for social amelioration." He believed that the environment shaped individuals; yet he failed to convey, in any specific or concrete fashion, the details that made up that environment. He followed the Swiss educators, Philip Fellenberg and Johann Peslatozzi, in their insistence on combining education with manual labor and their insistence on developing the social as well as the intellectual capacities of their students. Owen had a paternalistic philosophy toward the poor and he believed that they could be led into a better life. He was vague about how that would happen except that colony members had to work for the common good and be supplied with the "necessaries and comforts of life," as one of the rules at New Harmony stated. Owen's speeches in the fall of 1825 attracted many enthusiasts to New Harmony.

New Harmony's membership was drawn from the ranks of working men rather than from the privileged class to whom Owen had appealed. Many joined the colony to improve their own economic condition, while others were attracted by Owen's educational and philanthropic ideas. By October 1825, there were nearly nine hundred settlers on the site. Confusion soon set in inasmuch as Owen, who was rarely at New Harmony, failed to provide the colony with any effective leadership. In addition, there were disputes over the society's constitution, the role of religion in the settlement, and the procedure for selecting new members. Little detailed planning had been done to help bridge the gap between theory and practice. Owen was unclear whether the colonists were employees, almsmen, partners, or tenants.

By February 1826, a second colony had formed, called Macluria after William Maclure,* and it was opposed to Owen's deistic beliefs; however, this religious group did not know that Maclure was himself opposed to organized religion. A second spinoff group consisting of some English farmers formed Feiba-Peveli, a name deriving from the latitude and longitude of the site transformed into letters. By January 1827, Owen was selling property to individuals, and the greater part of the town was in individual lots. On June 18, 1827, he left New Harmony permanently.

SOURCES: Arthur E. Bestor, Jr., *Backwoods Utopias* (1950); John F. C. Harrison, *Quest for the New Moral World* (1969).

NEW ODESSA COMMUNITY (see also Appendix A, No. 184), founded at Glendale, Douglas County, Oregon, in 1883 by William Frey.* After the assassination of Alexander II of Russia in 1881, a series of persecutions and pogroms swept that country and led to the May Laws of 1882 directed against Jews. Two emigration movements developed during this perod: the Bilu, which encouraged flight to Palestine, and the Am Olam, which was directed toward settlement in the United States. Members of the Am Olam ("the eternal people") group from Odessa set out in 1882 to establish a model colony based on socialistic principles. When they arrived in the United States, they were aided by Michael Heilprin,* who raised funds for the purchase of land and for transportation westward. A 760-acre site in Oregon was chosen, and in July 1882, the first party left the East for the Northwest. There were fifty members. The land was held in common, and the constitution reflected their socialist beliefs.

Frey, a non-Jew, had come to the United States in 1869. He was leader of the colony and went to Oregon with them. In the beginning, all resources and earnings were pooled, but the group was unable to sustain an economic life and was soon beset by conflicts. Frey, a positivist, gave lectures to the colonists on the "religion of humanity" and vegetarianism, and often urged them to be "pioneers in a new social experiment." His constant proselytizing for positivism, together with the group's hard life in Oregon, caused the colony to fail. In addition, a fire destroyed many of their buildings. By 1887, the community had broken up. Part of the original contingent returned to New York where they established a cooperative laundry on Henry Street.

SOURCES: Gabriel Davidson, *Our Jewish Farmers* (1943); Leo Shpall, "Jewish Agricultural Colonies in the United States," *Agricultural History* (July 1950); Avrahm Yarmolinsky, *A Russian's American Dream: A Memoir on William Frey* (1965).

NORTH AMERICAN PHALANX (see also Appendix A, No. 66), founded in 1843 by a group of Albany, New York, area residents at Monmouth County, New Jersey, about forty miles south of New York City. The group was brought together by its enthusiasm for Fourierism and through correspondence with some prominent Fourierists, among them Albert Brisbane* and Horace Greeley.* Greeley agreed to become a stockholder and vice-president of the association which issued stock in August 1843. After looking at several sites in New Jersey and Pennsylvania, the group purchased a 673-acre farm near Red Bank, New Jersey, and in September 1843, several families took possession of two farmhouses on the land. While farming was their chief occupation, few of the first settlers had practical agricultural experience.

During 1844, the colony's ninety members attempted to use Fourier's theories about labor. Workers were divided into "labor series" with a chief at the head, and each series was divided into groups with a head—all under an industrial council. In 1847, they built a dwelling house, a phalanstery, for their growing numbers. The phalanx was an economic and social success until 1854 when a fire completely destroyed the flour mill, several shops, and some valuable machinery. The colony had been weakened in 1853 when several members had withdrawn to form the Raritan Bay Union* (see also Appendix A, No. 120) at Perth Amboy, New Jersey. These two events signaled the end of the colony. In the winter of 1855-1856, the land was sold for two-thirds its value, with the nonresident stockholders getting their full investment back. During its history, the North American Phalanx had several significant achievements: profit-sharing, the thirty-hour week, planned recreation for workers, religious toleration, and profitable industries.

SOURCES: N. L. Swan, "The North American Phalanx," *An Expose of the Condition and Progress of the North American Phalanx* (1970 reprint).

O

ONEIDA COMMUNITY (see also Appendix A, No. 108), founded in 1848 by John Humphrey Noyes* at Oneida Creek, New York, twenty miles east of Syracuse. The community was based on a theology of Bible Communism, or a return to the practices of the early Christian church, and on the messianic belief that Noyes was a prophetic leader in the Pauline tradition. Beginning with a membership of fifty-one, the community grew both in numbers and wealth over the years. By 1880 (the date of its dissolution), its membership had reached three hundred. The characteristic features of its theology were security from sin, biblical literalism, intermillennialism, and Christian perfectionism, which they believed was possible in this life. Oneida's social philosophy was rooted both in Christian communism which emphasized the sharing of goods and in a sexual philosophy which some termed free love.

The community was organized around a "complex marriage" theory whereby individuals could choose sexual partners based on love and attraction rather than on marriage terms. A remarkable feature of the complex marriage regimen was the practice of male continence, or coitus reservatus, in which the male enjoyed the early stages of intercourse—the "amative"— but never went on to the "propagative," or orgasm stage. This self-control technique resulted in a low birth rate and in 1868 led the community into another unique sexual program called stirpiculture, a eugenics plan based on the union of scientifically selected parents. In 1868, the plan resulted in the birth of fifty-one children.

The community sustained itself by the sale of traps, silk goods, and horticultural products. The society came to an end in 1880 as the result of aging leadership, sexual tensions, and outside pressure. A spoon industry begun in the 1870s became the basis for the successful Oneida Company, Ltd., makers of quality flatware, and absorbed much of the community leadership and work ethos.

SOURCES: Maren L. Carden, *Oneida: Utopian Community to Modern Corporation* (1969); Robert Fogarty, "Oneida: A Utopian Search for Religious Security," *Labor History* (Fall 1973); Robert A. Parker, *A Yankee Saint* (1937).

P

PEOPLE'S TEMPLE, founded in Guyana in 1977. The group had its origins in James "Jim" Jones'* Christian Assembly of God Church founded in Indianapolis in 1953. That church became the People's Temple in 1963 and maintained that name when seventy families resettled at Ukiah, California, in 1966 after Jones had announced to his Indianapolis congregation that a nuclear holocaust would take place in 1967. In 1970, they purchased churches in Los Angeles and San Francisco where Jones gained a following among inner-city blacks and radical whites, who were drawn to the Temple and its program of social reform. By 1977, there were an estimated 5,000 members, and the church had a mission (established in 1973) in Guyana, South America.

In 1977, over 900 congregants moved to a rural area of Guyana to start a commune. Members turned over their property on entry into the colony, accepted Jones' preachments as gospel, and submitted themselves to his will. "Jonestown" was an interracial colony and attracted the poor and elderly of different races by offering them a safe haven in a hostile world. About 80 percent of the membership was black, but the leadership was predominantly white and radical. According to Charles Krause, a reporter who covered the massacre story, "To the religious, Jones offered religion; to the ideological, he offered politics; to the ignorant and gullible, he offered miracles."

The People's Temple had leased 27,000 acres of land from the Guyanese government in 1973 in an area of northern Guyana that the government wished colonized. The commune, cut out of the jungle, consisted of a farm, some overcrowded cottages for families, a primitive dispensary, a sawmill, and a meeting house. Charges of coercion, brutality, and sexual sadism led to an investigatory visit to Jonestown by Congressman Leo Ryan and several media representatives in November, 1978. Although Jones was an ordained Christian minister in a mainline Christian denomination (Disciples of Christ), his message became increasing secular and paranoid. In his speeches he denounced the Bible and praised Lenin, and at the same time he incorporated conspiracy theories into his sermons. He told his followers, for example, that the United States government was preparing a crematorium for blacks and the visit of the congressional delegation fed those paranoid fantasies.

Just prior to Ryan's departure from Guyana he was murdered, and within hours over 900 colony members, Jones included, had committed mass suicide. The group had been preparing for this act and had mock suicide drills over the years under Jones' direction. Since the colony had grown out of Jones' messianic pretensions and charismatic leadership his message of love and reform was particularly appealing to those needing strong direction. In the end, Jones directed them to commit suicide and they did—by voluntarily drinking a poisoned drink. At the time of the colony's demise there were charges that Jones had diverted millions of dollars into Swiss banks, that he had forced his members to commit deviant sex acts, and that he had gone insane. It seems clear that he lost sight of his original mission. The mass suicides shocked Americans; the event was without parallel in American history.

SOURCES: Chicago Tribune (November 21, 1978); Charles Krause, *Guyana Massacre* (1978); *The New York Times* (November 26, 1978); *Newsweek* (December 4, 1978); *New West* (August, 1977).

POINT LOMA or **THE UNIVERSAL BROTHERHOOD AND THEO-SOPHICAL SOCIETY** (see also Appendix A, No. 219), founded by Katherine Tingley* in 1898 at Point Loma, California. At a theosophical convention in 1898, Tingley invited members of the sect to join her in building a community on 330 acres. There were three hundred members by 1903, and nearly five hundred by 1910. Most were well-educated and committed theosophists and about a third were children attending a rather unique school, the Raja-Yoga school, where children developed their physical, mental and spiritual facilities. Brotherhood and cooperation were stressed, and the children received instruction in the fine arts and music at an early age. Members paid an admission fee of $500 and received no wages for their labor. They could live either in individual bungalows or in a large communal house, the "Homestead." There was a communal nursery and the school had theosophist children from all over the world, with a large contingent coming from Cuba. Education in the arts was stressed, with the colony children putting on excellent theatrical and musical productions. Local hostility toward the colony was intense, but a steady supply of monies from sympathetic theosophists supported the growing enterprise.

Tingley ran the colony with a firm hand. She wrote in the Los Angeles *Saturday Post* in 1902 that "there is a top rung to every ladder," and there was little doubt who stood on that rung at Point Loma. Over the years, the colony lands appreciated in value, and by 1927, their 330 acres were worth more than $1.3 million. After her death in 1929, the colony chose Gottfried de Prucker as leader but by that time it had contracted too many debts to survive the Depression years. By 1940, only the acreage surrounding the central buildings remained in their hands as the 1930s forced physical retrenchment. In 1942 the society moved to Covina, California, and the land was sold.

SOURCES: Robert Hine, *California's Utopian Colonies* (1966 reprint); Emmett Greenwalt, *The Point Loma Community in California, 1897-1942* (1978 revised edition).

QR

RARITAN BAY UNION (see also Appendix A, No. 120), founded in 1853 near Perth Amboy, New Jersey, by thirty dissident members of the North American Phalanx* (see also Appendix A, No. 66). Marcus Spring,* a Quaker and a New York merchant, was a leading figure. The colonists hoped to provide a higher form of industry, education, and religious life than was found at the North American Phalanx. It was a joint-stock company, with education playing a central role. In 1852, 268 acres were purchased, and by the summer of 1853, a unitary building had been constructed. A school occupied one wing, private apartments the other, with a common dining room in the center of the building. Among the early subscribers were Sarah Grimke, and Theodore and Angelina Grimke Weld*; the Welds headed a progressive school run on coeducational principles.

The colony had a vigorous cultural life and attracted a wide range of reformers as lecturers, including Henry David Thoreau, Horace Greeley,* and A. Bronson Alcott.* Among the most distinugished members of the society were the painters George Inness, the chemist Edward Livingston Youmans, and the Shakespearean actor Steele MacKaye. The Welds' school, with its emphasis on practical learning, was the colony's most notable achievement. Raritan Bay succeeded where Brook Farm* (see also Appendix A, No. 53) had failed. However, it was inefficiently run, despite the success enjoyed by the school and the restaurant, both of which attracted visitors from New York.

Although the colony had never required communal living and, in fact, had tried to safeguard family life, it moved away from its own conservative cooperative ideal in 1856 when Spring bought back most of the property from the stockholders and operated the community—including the school—as a private venture. While certain cooperative features, such as the community meal, continued past that date, colony life effectively ended in that year. With the beginning of the Civil War, the Welds gave up the school.

SOURCES: Moncure D. Conway, *Autobiography* (1894); Gerda Lerner, *The Grimke Sisters from South Carolina* (1973); Jayme Sokolow, "Culture and Utopia; The Raritan Bay Union," *New Jersey History* (Summer-Fall 1976).

REUNION COLONY (see also Appendix A, No. 127), founded in 1855 by Victor Considerant* on the Trinity River just outside the then small town of Dallas, Texas. These one hundred and fifty French followers of Charles Fourier left Antwerp in 1855 intent on establishing a phalanx. They came to the United States under the auspices of the European Society for the Colonization of Texas organized by Considerant. By 1856, they had constructed a two-storied main building, a community kitchen, and a dining hall, and had planted a crop. They maintained the nuclear family structure and quickly abandoned communal dining in favor of family dining. By 1857, economic problems emerged because there were too few members skilled in agronomy and the land was unproductive. By that time, the colony membership had grown to three hundred and the colonists could not pay the interest due on the land held by the company. There was a partial liquidation in 1857, and it was clear by 1859 that they were a financial failure.

The colony failed for several reasons: it was unable to attract sufficient capital investment to insure financial stability; it lacked consistent leadership since Considerant spent much time traveling to gain support; and it faced hostile local sentiment and two hard Texas winters. When Considerant returned to France in 1859, it was no longer a viable colony, even though some members remained on the site until 1875 when the final liquidation took place. Over five hundred individuals had participated in the experiment. Many of them became prominent first families in Dallas following the colony's disintegration in 1859-1860.

SOURCES: Rondel Davidson, Introduction to Victor Considerant, *Au Texas* (1975 reprint); William J. and Margaret Hammond, *A French Settlement in Texas* (1958); Ernestine P. Jewell, "La Reunion," *The Folkore of Texas Cultures,* ed. Francis Abernethy (1974).

RUGBY COLONY (see also Appendix A, No. 173), founded in 1880 by Thomas Hughes* at Morgan County, Tennessee. Hughes, who had a long history of involvement with the English cooperative movement, sought to establish a settlement on the American frontier for the second and third sons of English gentry in order to give them an opportunity to gain some skills and to develop their productive abilities. He convinced some American and English entrepreneurs that such a colony was feasible. In 1879, the Board of Aid to Land Ownership, which included Hughes, Sir Henry Kimber, and the Earl of Airlie, bought seven thousand acres for town development and an additional thirty-three thousand for farms. The colony was officially opened on October 5, 1880, with Hughes in attendance. When he arrived, he found the Tabard Inn (named for the Southwark Tabard in Chaucer's *Canterbury Tales*) nearly completed, and a church, a school, and residences under construction. Eventually, forty-five buildings were put up. An ample library was put in place with seven thousand volumes since Hughes hoped that a great Anglo-American university would develop in the Tennessee hills. *The Rugbeian,* a monthly, was begun, and young Englishmen began to arrive.

In 1881, this transplanted English village had four hundred residents (only about 40 percent were English), as well as active social clubs, literary and dramatic societies, and even tennis tournaments. The only cooperative feature was the commissary, which supplied the colonists with everything from pianos to dresses. As a cooperative, it was a success, and Hughes hoped that the system could be extended to production with cooperative herds and gardens.

Hughes wrote of the colony that it was "our aim and hope to create on these highlands a community of gentlemen and ladies; not that artificial class which goes by those grand names in Europe and here, the joint product of feudalism and wealth, but a society in which the humblest will be of strain and culture. . . ."

Hughes hoped to produce an Eden in the New World and to have the participants shaped by two environments—one the hard American countryside and the other the genteel pattern of English village life.

In August 1881, a typhoid infection killed seven colonists and the infection frightened off prospective members, and from that point the colony had difficulties. In 1886, the Tabard Inn burned down, and in 1887 Hughes made his last visit to the site.

SOURCES: W. H. G. Armytage, "Rugby, Tennessee: The Link," Introduction to Thomas Hughes, *Rugby, Tennessee* (1975 reprint); Harriet C. Owsley, "The Rugby Papers: A Bibliographic Note," *Tennessee Historical Quarterly* 17 (1968); Brian Stagg, "Tennessee's Rugby Colony," *Tennessee Historical Quarterly* 17 (1968).

RUSKIN COOPERATIVE ASSOCIATION (see also Appendix A, No. 204), founded in 1894 by Julius Wayland* at Cave Mills, Dickinson County, Tennessee, about fifty miles west of Nashville. In 1893, Wayland published a notice in his journal *The Coming Nation* asking for support for his magazine and promising that if his subscriptions went above one hundred thousand, he would donate the profits toward a colony venture. Members were asked to contribute $500 per family on joining; many came from the mill towns of New England hard hit by the 1893 depression. The initial colony site was on unproductive land; the second site, at Cave Mills, consisted of eight hundred acres. The colony's chief industry was publishing *The Coming Nation,* a radical paper, with a large national circulation. Wayland severed his connection with the colony in 1895, but it continued to function until 1899.

Disputes arose between the anarchists and socialists, and the dream of establishing a national college on the site never materialized. In their best year, there were about two hundred colonists who succeeded in constructing thirty-two homes, a hotel, a communal dining room, a nursery, and a theatre. The Ruskin Theatre occupied all of the third floor of their main building, the Commonwealth Center, and seated seven hundred people. The Ruskin Band played in the theatre when it was not on the road. In 1896, Ruskin became a member of the Brotherhood of the Cooperative Commonwealth (see Appendix A, No. 216), and *The Coming Nation* promoted their activities. Disputes within the colony, rumors of free love, and inadequate leadership forced the colony to sell its property. At that point, it consisted of seventeen hundred acres of land, two hundred acres of growing crops, and two hundred head of cattle.

Some of the colonists then went to Waycross, Georgia, to establish another Ruskin (see Appendix A, Nos. 217 and 223), and to continue publishing *The Coming Nation.* A special train of eleven cars was chartered to cart the press and household goods. The new settlement was on eight hundred acres. The colonists resumed many of their old businesses, including their famed cereal coffee and suspenders. Yet, the same problems emerged in the new location, and the colony closed in 1901.

SOURCES: Francelia Butler, "The Ruskin Commonwealth: A Unique Experience in Marxian Socialism," *Tennessee Historical Quarterly* (1964); Isaac Broome, *The Last Days of the Ruskin Cooperative Association* (1899); William Hinds, *America Communities and Co-operative Colonies* (1908 ed.): 488-489; Julius Wayland, *Leaves of Life: A Story of Twenty Years of Socialist Agitation* (1912); Howard Quint, *The Forging of American Socialism* (1955), 175-209.

S

ST. NAZIANZ COMMUNITY (see also Appendix A, No. 125), founded in 1854 by Father Ambrose Oschwald* in Manitowoc County, Wisconsin. As a result of population pressures which made it difficult for workers in Baden, Germany, to find jobs and the Revolution of 1848 which created social discontent, a group consisting of 113 persons emigrated to the United States. They sold all their property in order to finance their move. Ambrose Ochswald was the colony leader and the impetus behind their starting co-operative life. On their arrival in Milwaukee, they purchased 3,840 acres in Manitowoc County and then sent an advance party to settle the land. During their first summer on the site, the colonists (all of them Roman Catholics) were able to clear seventy acres, plant a crop, and erect a church. The first years were difficult. The winter of 1855-1856 was harsh and a fire in 1857 almost destroyed the settlement, but a philanthropist from Sheboygan gave them funds.

During the first twenty years of colony life, all property was owned in common and meals were served from community kitchens. There were cottages for the married and dormitories for the unmarried men and women. After 1859, the colony prospered and added a tannery in 1864 to supplement their agricultural production.

When Ochswald died in 1873, there was a shift toward private ownership of land; his successor, the Reverend Peter Metz, conveyed land titles to families. In 1898, after many of the original settlers had died or their descendants had moved away, the remaining colony property was taken over by a Roman Catholic order, the Society of Our Divine Saviour.

SOURCES: W. A. Titus, "Historic Spots in Wisconsin: St. Nazianz, A Unique Religious Colony," *Wisconsin Magazine of History* 5 (December 1921).

SHAKER COMMUNITIES (see Appendix A, Nos. 1, 2, 4, 5, 6, 7, 8, 9, 10, 11, 12, 13, 18, 19, 20, 21, 22, 24, 27, 29, 202, 220). The Shakers were founded by Mother Ann Lee* at Bolton, England, in 1774. This English sect drew its inspiration from the French Camisard prophets who came to England in 1705 and from the Quaker tradition. From 1847 until 1874, the Shakers held meetings and gained converts from the area around Manchester. In 1774, Lee and eight others came to the United States settling first in New York City, then in the area near Albany, New York. From 1781 to 1783, Lee traveled throughout New England converting individuals to her beliefs. In 1787, three years after her death, the first American Shaker group was "gathered in" at New Lebanon, New York.

The distinctive characteristic of all the Shaker societies was their belief that Ann Lee had ushered in a period of spiritual regeneration, that she was the manifestation of Jesus Christ in female form, that salvation came through the Shaker family, and that sexual intercourse was a covenant with the devil and the cause of human suffering. There were five distinct periods of Shaker development in America: 1774-1783; 1783-1803; 1803-1837; 1837-1847, and 1847-1875. The first period was dominated by Ann Lee and her vision of Shaker life. This was the period when a handful of believers established themselves in the area of Albany, New York, and spread the word of Shakerism into New England. The second phase saw the founding of distinct Shaker communities under the direction of Joseph Meachem* and Lucy Wright.* Colonies were organized, formal covenants signed and a society took shape.

The third phase saw the Shakers expand their influence into the West. Colonies were established in Ohio, Indiana and Kentucky. By 1826, nineteen permanent communities had been founded. Missionaries moved about the Middle West, and the Shakers grew prosperous through agriculture and commercial trades. The fourth period, 1837-1847, was one of intense spiritual and religious revivalism, called Mother Ann's Work, which swept the colonies. This revitalization movement was marked by the emergence of mediums and seers and by the appearance of inspirational drawings, songs, and poems produced by the membership. This period of excitation ended in 1847 when the Shakers returned to their prosaic round of religious life. On the eve of the Civil War, the total Shaker population stood at six thousand, and the individual societies carried on a variety of agricultural and commercial trades. The Shakers were noted for the simplicity of their buildings, the utility and beauty of their products, particularly their furniture, and their capacity to sustain a common life and successful industries. The last period of Shaker life was from 1847 to 1875. It was period of declining numbers, declining religiosity and declining mission and purpose. In 1875, the first of the Shaker communities begun in the earlier period was closed.

From 1875 to 1947, the decline was precipitous with society property sold off to meet debts and colonies consolidated because there were too few members at a particular site and those members too old to care for themselves and their property.

Only two Shaker colonies remain today, at Sabbathday Lake, Maine (see Appendix A, No. 12), and the other at Canterbury, New Hampshire (see Appendix A, No. 8). The Shaker rolls have been closed and there are no new members admitted.

SOURCES: Edward D. Andrews, *The People Called Shakers* (1953); Henri Desroche, *The American Shakers* (1971); Mary L. Richmond, *Shaker Literature: A Bibliography,* 2 vols. (1977); June Sprigg, *By Shaker Hands* (1975).

SICILY ISLAND COLONY (see also Appendix A, No. 176), founded by Herman Rosenthal* on Sicily Island, Catahoula Parish, Louisiana, in 1881. Aided by the Alliance Israelite Universelle and a committee of New York Jews, about thirty-five families from Kiev and twenty-five from Yelisanetgrad settled in this remote island ninety miles from New Orleans. Among them were young idealists who were enamored of the colonization idea, practical farmers who wanted to till the land, and those who simply wished to leave Russia and escape the pogroms. Each family was offered 160 acres. The Jewish community in New Orleans was eager to help, and there was a genuine cooperative spirit among the settlers.

In addition to farming, the colonists hoped to establish factories and industries and to reinvest their earnings in cooperative ventures. They arrived in the winter of 1882 and began to farm the land. As spring came, however, a series of events wrecked the colony: the heat disturbed some colonists, others came down with malaria, others were lonesome for their wives, and finally, the Mississippi River rose and destroyed their holdings. Some of the colonists joined another agricultural cooperative, the Cremieux Colony in South Dakota (see Appendix A, No. 179), but the majority took up other trades in Louisiana. The secretary of the colony later wrote: "The aim of the first colonists was to do pioneering work. We wanted to pave the way for those who would join us or establish agricultural colonies elsewhere. We wanted to show them what we have accomplished, so as to make it easier for others. We wanted to show them how to become successful farmers. This, however, we could not do under existing conditions."

SOURCES: Gabriel Davidson, *Our Jewish Farmers* (1943); Leo Shpall, "Jewish Agricultural Colonies in the United States," *Agricultural History* (July 1950).

SILKVILLE COLONY, or **PRAIRIE HOME** (see Appendix A, No. 148), founded in 1870 by Ernest de Boissiere* near Williamsburg, Kansas.

De Boissiere, a member of a French aristocratic family, visited the United States during the 1850s and 1860s. In 1868, he met with Albert Brisbane,* Elijah Grant,* and Charles Sears to plan a Fourierist colony. With the purchase of thirty-five hundred acres that year from the Kansas Educational Association, a colony devoted to Fourierism and the production of silk was established. De Boissiere, Brisbane, and Grant subscribed $29,000 to the venture, and forty French immigrants arrived in 1869 to provide the necessary labor.

By 1870, a three-story frame dwelling had been erected and 150 acres were under cultivation, with thousands of mulberry trees planted. While Grant and Sears remained in the East, de Boissiere came to Kansas to oversee the operation. Even though the French workers drifted away from the project and the Panic of 1873 severely disturbed the colony's growth, it continued to market silk. It exhibited its silk products at the Centennial Exposition of 1876 in Philadelphia. By 1882, however, de Boissiere curtailed silk production because of its unprofitability, and in 1884 he returned to France. In 1892, he visited Silkville for the last time before bequeathing the property to the Odd Fellows for use as an orphanage. The property was then worth $125,000.

SOURCES: Garrett R. Carpenter, *Silkville* (1952); William Hinds, *American Communities and Co-operative Colonies* (1908 ed.); William Zornow, *Kansas, The Jayhawk State* (1957).

SKANEATELES COMMUNITY (see also Appendix A, No. 72), founded in 1843 by John Collins* at Mottville, Onandaga County, New York. It was a Fourierist phalanx that grew out of several reform meetings held in the Syracuse area in 1843. The proposed constitution of this joint-stock association was published in April 1843, and by November, a three hundred-acre site had been secured for $15,000, with thirty-six individuals committed to the project. At the same time, Collins issued a statement of principles for the community which emphasized anarchist political views, stressed community of ownership, prohibited the use of meat, narcotics, and alcohol, and suggested a free love philosophy. By early 1844, the colony had started on the site, with agriculture its main industry and Fourierism its guiding philosophy.

The community members worked hard and steadily at their farm, which by 1846 had doubled in value. A dispute between Quincy Johnson, a Syracuse lawyer and one of the original settlers, and John Collins festered for several years, with Johnson withdrawing in 1845. Johnson had joined with Collins to purchase the original land, but Johnson disapproved of Collins' radical social beliefs and this dispute between two major figures weakened the colony. In November 1845, the community sought incorporation from the state in a move which would have allowed the members to hold their property as a group. A bill allowing them to incorporate was defeated in the state legislature. Shortly thereafter, Collins tired of the colony and withdrew. Like most phalanxes, it was short-lived and was unable to resolve disputes among major leaders; it achieved some distinction among the phalanxes for its financial success. Several members later joined the Oneida Community* (see Appendix A, No. 108) at Kenwood, Madison County, New York.

SOURCES: Lester G. Wells, "The Skaneatles Communal Experiment, 1843-1846," Onandaga Historical Association, Syracuse, New York, 1953.

SNOW HILL NUNNERY (see Appendix A, No. 15), also called the Seventh Day Baptist Church at Snow Hill, founded in 1798 as an offshoot of the Ephrata Colony.* The colony was begun around 1800 by a group of Sabbatarians from congregations in the area of Antietam Creek who sought to perpetuate the mysticism taught and practiced at Ephrata. In addition, they wanted to preserve the ornamental writing style, and the printing and the unique system of music and harmony started at Ephrata by Johann Conrad Beissel.* The community was located in Franklin County, Pennsylvania, on the property of Andreas Schneeberger (or Snowberger), where a large stone house had been built in 1793 to accommodate the congregation. Eventually, Schneeberger deeded the property to the five-member board of trustees and a community was organized.

Members were required to be baptized and single and to belong to Seventh Day German Baptist church. In addition to those who took the monastic orders, there were other members called "outdoor members," who lived in the surrounding area, but who did not wish the regime of community life. The first community house was built in 1814 and another meeting house was erected in 1829. The cloister was modeled after Ephrata, and its leaders were Peter Lehman* and Barbara Karper Snowberger. There were separate orders for men and women, and a monastic regime was followed, with members rising at dawn for hymns and prayer. It was a small community: at its peak in the 1820-1840 period the membership never exceeded forty members. During the 1830s, several new buildings were erected. In 1838, a convent for the brothers was added and in 1843 one for the sisters. They operated a school where history, music, and theology were taught to children in the area. By the end of the nineteenth century, only a single brother and single sister remained on the site. Snow Hill was the subject of a romantic novel, *Katy of Catictin* (1886) by George Alfred Townsend. In 1900, the monastic order was dissolved and became a church society.

SOURCES: Eugene Doll, *Ephrata Cloister* (1944); Eugene Doll and Felix Reichmann, *Ephrata As Seen by Contemporaries* (1953); Julius Frederich Sachse, *The*

German Sectarians of Pennsylvania (1971); Charles M. Treher, "Snow Hill Cloister," *Publications of the Pennsylvania German Society* 2 (1968).

STRAIGHT EDGE INDUSTRIAL SETTLEMENT (see also Appendix A, No. 224), founded in 1899 by Wilbur F. Copeland* at New York City as a cooperative business venture, but later established as a workers' residence at Alpine, New Jersey. The group took its name from the fact that Jesus as a carpenter used the carpenter's straight-edge rule. The members described themselves as a "School of Methods for the Application of the Teaching of Jesus to Business and Society" which promoted community industries including a bakery, a printing establishment, and a periodical called *The Straight Edge*. In 1906, they purchased a four-acre site and a house in New Jersey for their Straight Edge Industrial Settlement and their play-work school for the children of the workers.

In its first seven years, two hundred workers passed through the society and the association broke even. The settlement at Alpine was both a day-care center and an experiment in self-reliance for the children, while the enterprise in New York tried to instill good work habits and cooperative values in the workers. In 1918, the society was forced to curtail its operations when it began to experience some economic difficulties. The Copelands tried to reopen their school in 1924, and in 1934 still had dreams of a co-operative colony at the Alpine site.

SELECTED WORKS: The Straight Edge, 1899-1921.

SOURCES: William Hinds, *American Communities and Co-operative Colonies* (1908 ed.): 548-555; Alexander Kent, 'Cooperative Communities in the United States," *Bulletin of the Department of Labor,* 35 (July 1901): 626-628.

SUNRISE COMMUNITY, founded by Joseph Cohen* at Saginaw, Michigan, in 1932. The original settlers of the community were Jewish anarchists from New York City. Earlier, in 1915, Cohen had helped organize the Ferrer Colony* (see also Appendix A, No. 267) at Stelton, New Jersey. He had a long career as a publicist, and in 1932, he was editor of the anarchist journal *Freie Arbeiter Stimme*. He saw cooperative living as a solution to the Great Depression conditions, and in January 1933, he published a prospectus for a colony, *A Project for a Collectivist Cooperative Colony,* which he hoped would attract participants from all over the United States. Interested families were expected to contribute $1,000. In June 1933, Cohen purchased a ten thousand-acre working farm for $33,000 cash and a $125,000 mortgage. Requirements for membership were stringent: individuals over forty-five years of age were discouraged from joining, as were large families and professed communists. Eventually, one hundred families joined.

In accommodating the first settlers and meeting the payroll for the hired hands needed to run a large commercial farm problems soon developed. Most of the colonists had little experience in farm management, and they suffered considerable losses in their first year. There were disputes between the anarchists and the Yiddishists, and by early 1934 there were splits in the colony's board of directors. In addition, disputes arose over Cohen's leadership, and in 1935 (after his reelection as president), a dozen families withdrew. But the basic problem was meeting the large mortgage payments.

Loans from various federal agencies, especially the Rural Rehabilitation Corporation (RRR), kept the colony on its feet; but it was never able to make a profit with its beef, produce, or poultry operations, even though income reached about $50,000 one year. During 1936, the land was sold to the RRA for over $277,000, a sum which merely went to pay bank obligations. Those remaining on the site rented their land from the governmental agency.

SOURCE: Joseph Cohen, *In Quest of Heaven* (1975 reprint).

SUNRISE HILL, founded in 1966 at Greenfield, Massachusetts, after a conference at the School of Living, Heathcote, Maryland. The conference had brought together individuals interested in forming communes or in developing self-sufficient decentralist homesteads like those advocated by Ralph Borsodi.* One participant volunteered a forty-acre homestead for a commune, and after several meetings a decision was reached by about twenty individuals to start a colony. The site was in the Deerfield River Valley, near Greenfield; on it were a single nine-room house and some agricultural buildings.

During the summer of 1966, the first members came—a "collection of beautiful people," as one participant described them—and community life began. The group advocated sexual freedom, group meditation, and collective decision making though no-clear cut ideology shaped the commune. By September 1966, the group had dwindled to twelve as a result of internal disputes. The Sunrise Hill Community was legally incorporated in 1967. When an individual joined, he or she had the option of either keeping or turning in private wealth. There were no collective religious rituals, though an evening mealtime blessing was conducted. Nor was there a coherent organizational structure in the community; work was done as needed.

SOURCE: Rosabeth Kanter, *Commitment and Community* (1972).

T

TOPOLOBAMPO BAY COLONY, founded in 1884 by Albert Kimsey Owen* at Topolobampo Bay on the west coast of Mexico. After promoting the establishment of a railroad line from Texas to the coast for over twenty years, in 1884, Owen finally hit upon the idea of establishing colony sites along the route. At the terminus of the line, he planned to develop a planned city—Pacific City—based on the principles of integral cooperation outlined in his *Integral Cooperation* (1885). For Owen integral cooperation meant that the processes of production and distribution would be located at one place and that ownership of those processes would reside with the colonists. In 1885, he organized the Credit Foncier Company and tried to attract colonists. The colony had a credit exchange economy based on labor and production units; a residential hotel based on Godin's Familisterie at Guise, France; cooperative enterprise to aid individual initiative; community parks, newspapers, libraries, restaurants; and a ban on lawyers, advertising, prostitution, taverns, and taxes.

With the aid of Marie Howland,* John Lovell, and Christian B. Hoffman,* Owen was able to attract settlers in 1886, particularly from Colorado and Kansas. Hoffman had organized the Kansas-Sinoloa Company in 1886 to purchase land for the Credit Foncier colonization group and led a contingent of settlers from Kansas to Pacific City in 1891. However, when the first group arrived, instead of a planned city they found a tropical harbor where no provision had been made for them. They worked on an irrigation ditch in order to develop an agricultural base since life at the harbor site was impossible. Owen paid little attention to daily affairs, and the colonists lived in makeshift shacks, were often starving, and quickly split into warring factions.

During mid-1892, there were nearly five hundred settlers, but the project always lacked adequate capital. A dispute over reorganization broke out in 1894 among Owens, Lovell, Hoffman, and Michael Flurscheim, the German Georgeist; the argument wrecked the venture. At this juncture, some colonists tried to organize a settlement along the lines proposed by Theodor Hertzka, an Austrian economist, in his utopian novel, *Freeland.* Hertzka and Owen had had some correspondence about a cooperative venture at an earlier date. After May 1893, Owen never returned to Topolobampo Bay. Late in 1893, Owen wrote the remaining colonists—some four hundred— that he did not have the funds to reincorporate. The colonists began to leave in great numbers during 1894, and for the next several years. Owen attempted to sell the site or to interest new investors. He even approached Thomas Lake Harris* of the Fountain Grove Community (see Appendix A, No. 163) with a proposal, but the Harris colony had just broken up and Owen still owed him $1,000 from an earlier loan. By 1899, there were only a few colonists left in the area, and the both the railroad and irrigation schemes had been abandoned.

SOURCES: Albert K. Owen, *Integral Cooperation* (1975 reprint); Ray Reynolds, *Cat's Paw Utopia* (1974).

TWIN OAKS, founded in 1967 on a 123-acre farm near Louisa, Virginia, by eight individuals who wished to put the theories of the behavioral psychologist B. F. Skinner into practice. Although influenced by Skinner's novel *Walden Two* (1961), the group never intended to use it as a working model for their community. Rather, they place their emphasis on Skinner's general theories of behavior modification through positive reinforcement. They hope to phase out the biological family and substitute a new system wherein the whole community would have parental responsibility, with "child managers" taking the lead in that area. Members are called by their first name only; family names are never used.

The economic base of the community was originally agricultural, but their hammock-making industry now produces up to a quarter of their income. Another quarter comes from visitors' fees, and the balance from jobs the members take in the outside world. Most members work six or seven hours a day, and a labor credit system is used to determine wages. More desirable jobs pay less, and members can, in effect, buy leisure time by taking on some of the onerous tasks of community labor. By 1973, the group had grown to thirty-six, though only two of the eight founding members remain. The members, self-conscious about their utopian heritage, hold weekly meetings to discuss utopian history and to explore colony problems. Twin Oaks is one of the most visible and more enduring of the contemporary communities.

SELECTED WORKS: Journal of a Walden Two Commune: The Collected Leaves of Twin Oaks (1972); Kathleen Kinkade, *A Walden Two Experiment* (1973). *SOURCE:* Robert Houriet, *Getting Back Together* (1971).

U

UNION COLONY (see also Appendix A, No. 146), founded in 1869 by Nathaniel Meeker* on the site of what is now Greeley, Colorado. Meeker organized the colony as a cooperative land venture but allowed individual ownership of residential, business, and farmland. After the publication of the proposed scheme for the colony in the *New York Tribune* in late 1869, 442 members joined and paid a $155 membership fee. It was a Christian but nonsectarian town, which prohibited the sale of liquor. Although the colony was designed to have extensive cooperative features, including collective housekeeping, in actuality its collectivity was limited to land purchase, irrigation, and fencing. Inadequate funds, insufficient understanding of farming and cattle-raising practices, and a pastoral vision hampered the settlement.

Over three hundred "model" single-family homes were constructed in the first year, as a result of which the possibility of any sustained colony life faded. By 1871, the colonists had voted to replace the community officers with an elected town government. Shortly thereafter, the land was made available to the general public. During 1871-1872, an effort was made to establish a cooperative stock and dairy association, but it failed for lack of funds. By 1872, the Union Colony had merged into the town of Greeley, and its meagre cooperative base had disappeared.

SOURCES: Dolores Hayden, *Seven American Utopias* (1976); James F. Willard (ed.), *The Union Colony at Greeley, Colorado, 1869-1871* (1926).

VW

WOMEN'S COMMONWEALTH, or **THE SANCTIFICATIONISTS** (see also Appendix A, No. 157), organized in the late 1860s by Martha McWhirter* at Belton, Texas. Women's Commonwealth was a celibate, religious society that came together out of the religious and social needs of its members and their faith in Martha McWhirter's leadership. This cooperative society originated in meetings held by Methodist women in Belton between 1866 and 1869, who had gathered to pray for patience with their husbands who kept them deprived of money and in constant need. Martha McWhirter preached Wesley's doctrine of sanctification and the necessity of the regenerate to separate from the sinful. The women believed themselves sanctified and began to leave their unregenerate husbands. Their actions provoked considerable dissension and discord in the town. Some of the women were tried for insanity, while others were simply ostracized.

In addition to their perfectionist beliefs, the group practiced dream interpretation. Their cooperative schemes gave them independence and allowed them to live apart from their unsanctified husbands or to lead secure lives after they were widowed.

By 1879, most of the women (about fifty) were able to live independently of their husbands by taking in wash and by selling produce and eggs. The women attained economic security when, in 1886, they opened the Central Hotel in Belton. By 1892, they owned three farms in the area and had thirty-four members, four of them men. The hotel prospered, and in 1899, they sold it and retired as a group to Washington, D.C. With McWhirter's death in 1904, the colony disintegrated, though some members continued to live at a farm in suburban Maryland into the 1930s.

SOURCES: George P. Garrison, "A Women's Community in Texas," *Charities Review* (November 1893); Eleanor P. James, "The Sanctificationists of Belton," *American West* (Summer 1945).

XYZ

YELLOW SPRINGS COMMUNITY (see also Appendix A, No. 31), founded in 1825 by John Roe, a Swedenborgian minister from Cincinnati, at Yellow Springs, Ohio. Beginning in 1822, Roe's Swedenborgian congregation in Cincinnati experienced dissension over religious practices. After Roe met Robert Owen* in New York in 1824, Roe turned from anticlericalism to socialism. Many members of his congregation became interested in starting an Owenite colony, and in 1825 seventy-five came to Greene County, Ohio. Some of the members were wealthy and most were well educated.

Their experiment on the west bank of Yellow Springs Creek lasted just six months, primarily because of disputes over the labor question and because many of them found the work too arduous. By 1826, only nine members were still on the property. Other members had started a hotel at Yellow Springs, but they did not share their profits. In January 1827, the property was deeded back to the original owners. It was the first failure of an Owenite colony in America.

SOURCES: Marguerite Beck Block, *The New Church in the New World* (1968 reprint); William Galloway, *The History of Glen Helen* (1932).

APPENDIX A: Annotated list of communal and utopian societies, 1787-1919

OTOHIKO OKUGAWA

1. Shaker Community at Mount Lebanon or New Lebanon (1787-1947), Mount Lebanon, New Lebanon Township, Columbia County, New York.

   This first Shaker community based on Mother Ann Lee's millennialism was officially called the United Society of Believers in Christ's Second Appearing. As in many other instances, the formation of Shaker communism as an actual institution at Mount Lebanon was derived from revival meetings of 1779. Mount Lebanon, also known as the Holy Mount, served the center of Shakerism. The total membership during its entire existence numbered 3,202.

2. Shaker Community at Niskeyuna or Watervliet (1788-1938), Shakers, Colonie Township, Albany County, New York.

   Niskeyuna, then a desolate wilderness about eight miles northwest of Albany, was where the seven original "Shaking Quakers" settled after arriving in the New World from Manchester, England, in 1774. Niskeyuna possessed 2,580 acres in its home estate, and another 32,000 acres were owned by the community. It also had a branch of black Sisters in Philadelphia. When it was dissolved in 1938, the remaining members moved to Mount Lebanon.

3. Jerusalem,* or the Society of Universal Friends (1788-1820), Jerusalem, Yates County, New York.

   This community was founded by Jemima Wilkinson,* the "Publick Universal Friend." Its members, numbering 260 in 1790, had been either Quakers or

---

1. Okugawa is assistant professor of sociology at the University of Pittsburgh at Bradford. The research was supported in part by the Faculty Development Fund, 1976, University of Pittsburgh at Bradford, and the Provost Research Development Fund, 1978, University of Pittsburgh. The author would like to acknowledge his appreciation to Robert Fogarty, Antioch College; Robert Hine, University of California at Riverside; John Hostetler, Temple University; Janet McCauley, University of Pittsburgh at Bradford; Gilbert Shapiro, University of Pittsburgh; and the many librarians who assisted in locating source materials.

*An asterisk denotes the presence of a main entry in the dictionary.

New Light Baptists. After the founder's death in 1819, the community slowly declined, but some members continued to reside in Jerusalem until 1863.

4. Shaker Community at Hancock or West Pittsfield (1790-1960), Shaker Village, Town of Hancock, Berkshire County, Massachusetts.

Located in the Berkshire Hills, three miles east of the Mount Lebanon community, New York, the Hancock community, at its height, owned about three thousand acres. Although this was one of the smaller Shaker communities in terms of total membership, many of the buildings in Shaker Village have been restored and are open for exhibit during summer months.

5. Shaker Community at Enfield, Connecticut (1790-1917), Shakers, Town of Enfield, Hartford County, Connecticut.

Noted for their garden seeds, these members were among the first in this country to establish this business. Its large-size trade with the South was ruined with the outbreak of the Civil War. The Enfield society recruited a great number of its members from a religious revival among the Baptist "Christians" in Rhode Island during the 1830s.

6. Shaker Community at Harvard (1791-1918), Shaker Village, Town of Harvard, Worcester County, Massachusetts.

Harvard was one of Ann Lee's centers of New England mission in the early 1770s. The transcendentalists at Fruitlands* (No. 71) often visited the Harvard community. While there were usually more women than men in a Shaker community, the disproportion of the sexes was uncommonly great at Harvard. The average longevity of the Harvard believers increased by twenty years; namely, 51.1 during 1791-1800 to 71.3 during 1881-1889.

7. Shaker Community at Tyringham (1792-1875), Town of Tyringham, Berkshire County, Massachusetts.

Tyringham was another area which Ann Lee covered in her ecclesiastic labors. When it was dissolved in 1875, the remaining members moved to the Hancock (No. 4) and Enfield (No. 5) communities.

8. Shaker Community at Canterbury (1792-Present), Shaker Village, Town of Canterbury, Merrimack County, New Hampshire.

The founders and early members of this community were Free Will Baptists in the Canterbury-Loudon district before conversion to Shakerism. This community was governed less strictly than most Shaker communities. Members were allowed to eat meat, drink tea, and read newspapers; girls had gymnastic exercise; boys played ball and marbles and went fishing. Three sisters were still residing at Canterbury in 1978.

9. Shaker Community at Shirley (1793-1908), Shaker Village, Town of Shirley, Middlesex County, Massachusetts.

Eleven years after the conversion of four prosperous farmers in Shirley, the Shirley society was gathered in 1793 with seventy believers. The membership grew to one hundred and fifty in the 1820s, but it gradually declined: seventy-five in 1850, sixty in 1855, and forty-eight in 1875. Their main business was apple sauce, of which they sold five to six tons every year. Physiology was taught in the Shaker school at Shirley.

10. Shaker Community at Enfield, New Hampshire (1793-1923), Upper and Lower Shaker Villages (twelve miles southeast of Dartmouth College), Town of Enfield, Grafton County, New Hampshire.

Of the New England Shaker communities, this was the first that arose indirectly through Ann Lee's personal influence. President James Monroe visited the Enfield community in 1817. The expansion of the community continued until the 1840s, with 330 members in 1845. Seven remaining members moved to Canterbury (no. 8) in 1923 upon its dissolution.

11. Shaker Community at Alfred (1793-1932), Shaker Hill, Town of Alfred, York County, Maine.

This community and one at Sabbathday Lake (No. 12) were founded after a revival among a radical branch of the New Lights called Come-Outers. When the Shakers considered moving to a milder climate in the early 1870s, they offered their entire property, including an estate of 1,100 acres, for $100,000. They found no buyer. Some remaining members moved to Sabbathday Lake.

12. Shaker Community at Sabbathday Lake, or New Gloucester, or Poland Hill (1794-Present), Sabbathday Lake, Town of Gloucester, Cumberland County, Maine.

As late as the 1870s, this community was said to be less prosperous than most other Shaker communities because of a severe financial loss which had to be paid off by other societies. But today it is one of the two remaining Shaker communities and has six sisters.

13. Shaker Community at Gorham (1794-1819), Town of Gorham, Cumberland County, Maine.

The community at Gorham did not prosper. In 1819, members sold their land, with some going to the Alfred community (No. 11) and others to the Sabbathday Lake community in New Gloucester (No. 12).

14. Dorrilites (1798-1799), Leydon, Franklin County, Massachusetts, and Guilford, Windham County, Vermont.

A former English army officer named Dorril brought together a circle of about forty followers in adjoining neighborhoods on either side of the Massachusetts-

Vermont line. He enforced a strict vegetarianism on his followers. The Dorrilites apparently dispersed after a year or two.

15. Snow Hill Nunnery,* or Seventh Day Baptist Church at Snow Hill (1798-1870), Snow Hill, Quincy Township, Franklin County, Pennsylvania.

This was a group of German Seventh Day Baptists who, in every respect, modeled themselves after the cloister at Ephrata,* Lancaster County, Pennsylvania. No vows of celibacy were taken, but those who married had to seek homes outside the cloister, as did the secularist members who resided in the surrounding farming country. The community never exceeded forty members.

16. The Union (1804-1810), Clark's Crossing, between Potsdam and Norwood, St. Lawrence County, New York.

The Union was probably the first American cooperative experiment—in the Owenite and Fourierist sense of the term—ever put into practice whose community theory was not based on religious doctrine. Three years after a constitution was adopted in 1807, it was dissolved because of the "virus of self-interest." After dissolution, the land (2,427 acres) was divided; most of the members, a dozen families or so, continued to reside on the tract.

17. Harmony Society* (1805-1814), Harmony, Jackson Township, Butler County, Pennsylvania.

Formed by Separatist immigrants from Wurttemburg, Germany, under the leadership of George Rapp,* the Harmony Society was established at their first settlement in Harmony, twenty-five miles northwest of Pittsburgh. Because of an unsatisfactory location for viniculture, the Rappites (approximately a total of eight hundred) moved to a larger site in southeastern Indiana on the Wabash River in 1815 (No. 23). They sold about nine thousand acres of land with 130 buildings for $100,000.

18. Shaker Community at Union Village (1805-1912), Union Village (commonly known as Shakertown, three miles west of Lebanon), Turtle Creek Township, Warren County, Ohio.

This first Shaker community west of the Allegheny Mountains "gathered" as a result of the missionary sent from Mount Lebanon (No. 1). The converts were recruited from the Presbyterian Schismatics in extraordinary revivals of Kentucky and neighboring states after 1800. It served as the center of Shakerism in the West. The total membership during its entire existence was the greatest (3,873) of all the Shaker societies.

19. Shaker Community at Watervliet, Ohio (1806-1910), Shakertown (on Little Beaver Creek, six miles southeast of Dayton), Van Buren Township, Montgomery County, Ohio.

From the time of its establishment, this society, named after the original settlement in the East (No. 2), was under the direct supervision of the Union Village ministry (No. 18). The most amiable relations existed between the people of Dayton and the Watervliet believers. There were fifty-five members (nineteen males and thirty-six females, seven under twenty-one) in 1875, compared with one hundred in 1825. Much of the community's 1,350 acres was leased to tenants.

20. Shaker Community at South Union or Gasper Springs (1809-1922), South Union, Logan County, Kentucky.

The society at South Union was founded on the scene of the Kentucky revival of 1807 by the converts from the New Light Presbyterians. As early as 1813, there existed a group of former black slaves, with its own elder, living on the same terms as the white members at South Union. They also hired blacks as outside laborers. One of the New Harmony* (No. 30) families joined South Union in 1827 after the former disbanded.

21. Shaker Community at Pleasant Hill (1806-1910), Shakertown (nine miles northwest of Harrodsburg), Mercer County, Kentucky.

For about two decades since its inception, novitiate residents at Pleasant Hill lived on three outlying farms while maintaining conjugal families—a very unusual arrangement for a Shaker family. During the Civil War, Pleasant Hill of Zion was in the path of the Confederate troops; they served eight thousand to nine thousand meals free of charge.

22. Shaker Community at West Union or Busro (1810-1827), Busseron Township (two miles east of the Wabash River on Busseron Creek), Knox-Sullivan County border, Indiana.

This was the only Shaker society gathered in Indiana. A year after its settlement, they were joined by a substantial influx of the Shakers from Eagle Creek, Adams County, Ohio. During the War of 1812, they moved to Union Village (No. 18) for two years. After suffering several bad epidemics, they left Busro forever. Some who stayed on with the order went to South Union (No. 20); others went to Pleasant Hill (No. 21).

23. Harmonie (1814-1825), Harmonie (now New Harmony), Harmony Township, Posey County, Indiana.

This is the second settlement of the Rappites (No. 17) which proved to be continually infected with malaria. As they turned more and more to manufacturing, it became apparent that this site was too far from the markets for their goods. The whole town of Harmonie (with twenty thousand acres of land) was sold to Robert Owen's* New Harmony* (No. 30), and the community moved back to Pennsylvania (No. 28).

24. Shaker Community at Savoy (1817-1825), Town of Savoy, Berkshire County, Massachusetts.

This community was abandoned after a short period of existence because of a severe drought. The members moved to Mount Lebanon (No. 1) and Niskeyuna (No. 2).

25. Society of Separatists of Zoar (1817-1898), Zoar, Lawrence Township, Tuscarawas County, Ohio.

Suffering religious persecutions in southern Germany, some of the Separatists migrated to America in 1817 with financial aid given by English Quakers. Because of the hard pioneering life and poverty, they (about one hundred and fifty in total) established the communal ownership of property two years later under the leadership of Joseph Bimeler* (formerly, Baumeler), who at first rejected communism. Unlike the Shakers and the Rappites, the Zoarites did not require celibacy except for the first ten years or so.the Zoarites, the Rappites, and the Shakers gave some consideration to the proposal for a union of all three societies in the 1850s, but because of religious differences nothing materialized.

26. Pilgrims (1817-1818), South Woodstock, Windsor County, Vermont.

Originating in lower Canada near the forks of the St. Francis River, the Pilgrims, in their search for salvation through a return to a biblical way of life, settled in the Woodstock district. Their stay there was brief, and they continued their search for their Promised Land as far west as New Madrid, Missouri.

27. Shaker Community at North Union (1822-1889), Warrensville Township (now Shaker Heights suburb of Cleveland), Cuyahogo County, Ohio.

Known as the Valley of God's Pleasure in Shaker tradition, North Union was organized into church orders with the help of the visiting elders from Union Village (No. 18). Joseph Smith is said to have been influenced by the North Union Believers in his schemes for a religious community while the Mormons still lived in Kirtland,* Lake County, Ohio (No. 42), some thirty miles northeast of Cleveland.

28. Economy (1824-1905), Harmony Township (now Ambridge), Beaver County, Pennsylvania.

Economy, one of the most prosperous communal enterprises, was the third and final settlement of the Rappite Harmony Society until the last three members dissolved the society in 1905. Its industries, including the Economy Oil Company located near Titusville, were at one time so extensive that the outsiders employed outnumbered members ten to one. During its one hundred years existence in three different locations (see No. 17 and No. 23), the Harmony Society was closely in touch with other communities and served as a model for later communitarian experiments.

29. Shaker Community at Whitewater (1825-1907), Dry Forks Creek of the Whitewater (near Preston), Hamilton County (partly in Butler County), Ohio.

A group of Darby Plains Believers, Union County, Ohio, and those at Whitewater jointly founded the society. A majority of the Shakers from the abandoned project at Busro (No. 22) came in 1827. About thirty-three Believers of Whitewater joined Union Village (No. 18) in 1856 to strengthen the latter. The Mount Lebanon ministry (No. 1) ordered the dissolution of the society in 1907.

30. New Harmony* (including such subdivided units as Macluria, Feiba Peveli, and Community No. 4) (1825-1827), New Harmony (site of the second Rappite community), Harmony Township, Posey County, Indiana.

    Based on Robert Owen's* social theory of the "communities of united interests," the well-celebrated experiment of the new social system was organized at New Harmony. It suffered a heavy turnover in members; many of the first arrivals did not stay long enough to develop a working acquaintance with each other. Six constitutions were amended in two years.

31. Yellow Springs Community*—Owenite (1825-1826), Yellow Springs, Miami Township, Greene County, Ohio (site now occupied by Antioch College).

    Settled largely by Cincinnati Swedenborgians, Yellow Springs was the only Owenite community to receive financial as well as moral support from Robert Owen.* It disintegrated because of factional strife.

32. Coal Creek Community and Church of God (1825-1832), Stonebluff, Fountain County, Indiana.

    William Ludlow, the leader who had previously been a resident at the Shaker community in Mount Lebanon (No. 1) and at New Harmony* (No. 30) later, first tried to organize the group in Warren County, Ohio. They moved to Coal Creek on the Wabash with sixty families. He withdrew in 1827, and internal disagreements led to large-scale withdrawals and eventual dissolution.

33. Goshen Community (1825-1826), Goshen Field (about three miles southwest of New Harmony), Posey County, Indiana.

    A former member of New Harmony* (No. 30) organized a group of Posey County farmers, predominantly Methodists. When a boatload of produce sank en route to New Orleans during their second year of community life, they decided to return to their original farms.

34. Franklin Community, or Haverstraw Community—Owenite (1826), Haverstraw, Rockland County, New York.

    Owen's* gatherings in New York between 1824 and 1825 resulted in the formation of this community. The leaders were drawn from among the militant freethinkers of the city. It lasted only five months. Some quit, and the rest joined the Forestville Community (No. 35) in the upper Hudson Valley.

35. Forestville Community, or Coxsackie Community—Owenite (1826-1827), Lapham's Mills, Coxsackie, Greene County, New York.

    Some sixty colonists engaged in farming and handcrafts. Suggestions were made for a merger with the Kendal Community (No. 36), Ohio. When it came to an end in October 1827, half its members made an arduous winter journey to join the Kendal Community.

36. Kendal Community, or Friendly Association for Mutual Interests at Kendal—Owenite (1826-1829), Kendal (now part of the city of Massillon), Perry Township, Stark County, Ohio.

The seed of the community was planted when two of Owen's* disciples from New Harmony* (No. 30) visited Kendal in 1825. This was the most successful of all the lesser Owenite experiments. Owen himself visited in July 1828.

37. Valley Forge Community, or Friendly Association for Mutual Interests—Owenite (1826-1826), Valley Forge, Chester County, Pennsylvania.

A group of Philadelphians, advocating "villages of self-supporting cooperation," moved into Washington's headquarters on the historic campground in the spring of 1826. But they immediately were met by hostility from local people, and by September the Valley Forge Friendly Association disbanded. About fifty dejected members of the defunct community joined the Mount Lebanon Shaker community (No. 1) in May 1827.

38. Blue Spring Community—Owenite (1826-1827), near Stanford, Van Buren Township (seven miles southwest of Bloomington), Monroe County, Indiana.

Unlike the New Harmony* members, almost all the members of Blue Spring had already been settled in the vicinity and had established themselves as dependable citizens. After a year of operation, dissension became apparent. When the women argued over what color to dye the homespun cloth for their husbands' trousers, it touched off disintegration.

39. Shaker Community at Sodus Bay (1826-1836), on Sodus Bay, in Sodus and Huron Townships, Wayne County, New York.

Those involved in a revival at Sodus Bay in 1826 sent to Mount Lebanon (No. 1) for assistance. A few members remained there to guide the new venture. When a Sodus canal was being proposed, they moved to a site in Livingston County, New York (No. 50).

40. Nashoba Community*—Owenite (1826-1829), on Wolf River (near present-day Germantown), Shelby County, Tennessee.

After a visit to the Rappite community (No. 23) and a series of conferences with the leaders of New Harmony* (No. 30), Frances Wright,* a radical reformer, founded Nashoba to provide slaves a means of earning the price of their freedom. When the colony was abandoned, she took thirty-one black residents to Haiti.

41. Teutonia or Society of United Germans (1827-1831), Columbiana County, Springfield Township, Ohio (exact location unknown).

After a year's residence at Economy (No. 28) as a language teacher in 1826, Peter Kaufman founded Teutonia, which inherited both members and financial support from the aborted Concordia group in Tuscarawas County. The reason for its dissolution is not clear, but it seems that the members simply became bored with community life.

42. Kirtland Community* (1830-1838), Kirtland, Lake County, Ohio.

Sidney Rigdon,* the founder of Kirtland, earlier became acquainted with the Rappites at Economy (No. 28) while preaching in Pittsburgh. After moving to Mentor, Ohio, he organized a group of Campbellites in the neighboring town of Kirtland into a communal arrangement. Rigdon and most of his group subsequently converted to Mormonism.

43. United Order of Enoch at Independence (1831-1834), Independence, Jackson County, Missouri.

This unfinished experiment of the Mormon United Order, as given by Joseph Smith, was communism in a Shaker sense but was designed to effect a redistribution of property such that a measurable degree of economic equality among the Mormons could be achieved. They were expelled from Independence by the old settlers after two years of trial.

44. New Philadelphia Society (1832-1833), Philipsburg (now Monaca), Beaver County, Pennsylvania.

Count Leon (formerly, Bernard Muller*), with his fifty followers from Germany, arrived in Economy (No. 28) in 1831 as a self-proclaimed "Lion of Judah." Discontent among some of the Rappites with celibacy and rallied by Count Leon, about 250 people seceded from the Harmony Society* and formed the New Philadelphia Society about ten miles northwest of Economy.

45. Oberlin Colony (1833-1841), Russia Township, Lorain County, Ohio.

Eight families, all recent emigrants from New England and New York, agreed to establish "as perfect a community of interests as though we held a community of property" under the leadership of John Shipherd. One of the goals of the colony was to establish a school where students might receive a Christian education. The Oberlin Colony eventually faded away as it became subjected to Oberlin College by 1841.

46. Equity (1833-1835), in the Tuscarawas River Valley (exact location unknown), Tuscarawas County, Ohio.

Josiah Warren,* one of the earlier members at New Harmony* (No. 30), whose career as a community planner stretched over two decades, inaugurated Equity Village based on his time-labor system. The village was abandoned because of epidemics that struck the population.

47. The First Community of Man's Free Brotherhood (1833-1835), near Covington, Fountain County, Indiana.

Isaac Romine, who was instrumental in founding Coal Creek and Church of God (No. 32), immediately founded the First Community in the same neighborhood after the former was dissolved. Later, the nucleus of its members moved to Warren County, Indiana (No. 97).

48. Grand Ecore (1834-1836), Natchitoches Parish, Louisiana.

After the New Philadelphia Society (No. 44) failed in the legal suit against the Rappites (No. 28), Count Leon (Bernard Muller*) and a group comprised chiefly of those who had come with him from Germany sailed down the Ohio to Grand Ecore, Louisiana. Their new locality was to be on the same latitude as Jerusalem.

49. Germantown (1836-1871), eight miles north of Minden, Webster Parish, Louisiana.

After Count Leon's (Bernard Muller's*) death at Grand Ecore (No. 48), his followers, including those who had recently arrived from Germany, moved to higher and healthier land in the upper Red River Valley. They continued to live on a communal basis until the society broke up peacefully after the Civil War.

50. Shaker Community at Groveland, or Sonyea (1836-1895), near Sonyea, Groveland Township, Livingston County, New York.

Speculating promoters induced the Believers of Sodus Bay (No. 39) to sell their 1,450 acres of land. The Believers moved to a new site at Groveland, some sixty miles away. With the establishment of Groveland, there was no more expansion of major Shaker settlements except for much smaller branches in Florida (No. 202) and Georgia (No. 220) in the 1890s. When the society was dissolved in 1895, the remaining members moved to Watervliet (No. 2).

51. Community of United Christians (1836-1837), Berea, Middleburgh Township, Cuyahoga County, Ohio.

The Berea community was organized by the advocates of abolition and temperance movements after several years of careful planning, including visits to North Union (No. 27) and Union Village (No. 18) Shaker societies, as well as others in Ohio. It lasted only a little over a year because of disagreements between leaders.

52. Sholem or Sholom (1837-1842), Sholem, Wawarsing Township, Ulster County, New York.

A small group of New York Jews of German and Dutch descent established a colony in virtually inaccessible mountainous land. Finding it impossible to support themselves (twelve families), many sold their holdings and moved back to the city.

53. Brook Farm* (originally called the Brook Farm Institute of Agriculture and Education, then renamed the Brook Farm Association for Industry and Education, and finally reorganized as the Brook Farm Phalanx) (1841-1847), West Roxbury (now within the city limits of Boston), Norfolk (now Suffolk) County, Massachusetts.

By far the most well-known of all the "utopian" societies, Brook Farm was started by George Ripley,* a Unitarian minister of Boston. The Transcendental Club formed in Boston in 1836 made up a nucleus of the initial membership. It had such prominent literary people as Nathaniel Hawthorne and Charles A. Dana.* *The Harbinger,* a weekly publication of Brook Farm, not only served as the official organ of the Fourierist movement, but it also reported a wide range of communal activities across the nation.

54. Marlborough Association or Marlboro Community† (1841-1845), Marlboro Township (6 miles northwest of Alliance), Stark County, Ohio.

Marlborough occupied farm land of some 500 acres, located about forty-five miles southeast of Cleveland. At first, it consisted of two separate farms, donated by Edward Brooke and his brother Abram Brooke, which were a mile apart. Eventually they purchased the middle land as the number increased to upwards of fifty. A community mansion was erected, where each family lived in a separate apartment. Many of the members were Freethinkers, who did not practice religion. After the death of one of the leaders, Joseph Lukens, the members adopted a constitution. For the first time, they realized that they differed radically on the basic questions of communal property and the principles of government. Torn by internal dissension, the group dissolved in the latter part of 1845. Abram Brooke participated only in the initial phase of the planning, though he left the community in possession of his property in Marlboro. He later tried a small experiment of his own in Clinton County (see No. 73).

†In transcribing A. J. MacDonald's manuscript, an unpublished account of communal societies written between 1842 and 1854, John Humphrey Noyes spelled the name "Marlboro" despite the fact that it is consistently spelled "Marlborough" in the original text. All the subsequent works that used Noyes' as a reference, therefore, repeated the abbreviated spelling.

55. Social Reform Unity—Fourierist (1842-1843), in the Pocono Mountains, Pike (now Monroe) County, Pennsylvania.

This first Fourierist phalanx was organized by a group of mechanics in Brooklyn, New York. They obtained land at the foot of the Pocono Mountains, a couple of miles northwest of Skytop. It lasted only ten months without a trace of Fourierism except for its original impulse from Albert Brisbane* and Horace Greeley.*

56. Hopedale Community,* or Fraternal Community No. 1 (1842-1867), Hopedale, Town of Milford, Worcester County, Massachusetts.

Adin Ballou,* previously a Universalist minister in Milford, organized a Fourierist-like joint-stock community of Practical Christians. Pleasant excursions were enjoyed mutually between Hopedale and Brook Farm* (No. 53). The membership, consisting of both factory workers and farmers, numbered about 175. Upon its dissolution it merged with the Hopedale Parish.

57. Northampton Association of Education and Industry (1842-1846), Broughton's Meadows (now Florence), Town of Northampton, Hampshire County, Massachusetts.

Northampton, perhaps the most thoroughly industrial secular communal enterprise, originated in a silk company as early as 1835 and was gradually transformed into a communal organization. It had strong ties with Garrisonism, with several former black slaves living in the community.

58. Teutonia, or McKean County Association, or Society of Industry (1842-1844), Ginalsburg (five miles southwest of present-day Smethport), McKean County, Pennsylvania.

Under the leadership of Henry Ginal, a Lutheran minister from Philadelphia, a radical element among the German immigrants founded Teutonia in a northern county which was almost unbroken wilderness. At its peak, the colony numbered four hundred. Because of huge financial losses, the settlers left after two years.

59. Society of One-Mentians, or Promisewell Community—Owenite (1843-1844), in the Pocono Mountains, Monroe County, Pennsylvania.

The Society of One-Mentians, with its branches in New York, Newark, and Philadelphia, founded the Promisewell Community. Before it had existed for more than a few months, disagreements with the branches caused friction. The members returned to New York after its dissolution.

60. Goose Pond Community—Owenite (1843-1844), near Goose Pond (in the Pocono Mountains), Barrett Township, Pike (now Monroe) County, Pennsylvania.

One of the leaders of the Promisewell Community (No. 59) seceded to form another community on the site of an earlier Fourierist phalanx, Social Reform Unity (No. 55). Some sixty people were engaged in the community, which lasted scarcely a year.

61. Colony of Equality, or Hunt's Colony—Owenite (1843-1846), North Prairie, Mukwonago Township, Waukesha County, Wisconsin.

Thomas Hunt, a prominent Owenite in London, came to America to found a cooperative colony with a party of twenty-one persons. Difficulties of pioneer farming in Wisconsin ended the project in three years. Some members later became active in Wisconsin local politics.

62. Jefferson County Industrial Association—Fourierist (1843-1844), Cold Creek (two miles east of Watertown), Jefferson County, New York.

This association was organized in Watertown, one of the two Fourierist societies that was developed there (see also the Iowa Pioneer Phalanx, No. 88), by Alonzo M. Watson, a Watertown lawyer who had written articles on the association for local papers. He served as the vice-president of the American Industrial Union, a confederation of phalanxes. The community lasted only a year.

63. Sylvania Association—Fourierist (1843-1845), Darlingville, or Darlingsville (now Greeley), Lackawaxen Township, Pike County, Pennsylvania.

This association was started in New York City and Albany by working people in the winter of 1842-1843. Horace Greeley* was listed as a treasurer in 1843. It lasted about a year and a half.

64. Morehouse Union—Fourierist (1843-1844), Piseco, Arietta Township, Hamilton County, New York.

Andrew K. Morehouse, who owned sixty thousand acres of land in the northeastern counties of New York, offered to any association land up to ten thousand acres. Moorehouse Union, organized in New York City, chose the village of Piseco, five miles north of Lake Pleasant. Despite this free land offer, it seems the experiment died out in less than a year.

65. Bureau County Phalanx, or Lamoille Agriculture and Mechanical Association—Fourierist (1843-1844), La Moille, La Moille Township, Bureau County, Illinois.

This community is mentioned only briefly in MacDonald's unpublished manuscript and *The Phalanx;* there is little information on it.

66. North American Phalanx*—Fourierist (1843-1856), Phalanx, Atlantic Township, Monmouth County, New Jersey.

This was the longest-lived of all the Fourierist experiments. It originated in Albany, New York, and was located at a place still called Phalanx, about five miles southwest of Red Bank. Resident members varied between one hundred and one hundred and twenty. Both Albert Brisbane,* who drew up its constitution, and Horace Greeley,* who held a large number of stocks, though not residents, took active roles in its organization.

67. Peace Union, or Friedens-Verein (1843-1845), Limestone Township, Warren County, Pennsylvania.

The Peace Union Settlement was the dreamchild of Andreas Bernardus Smolnikar,* who, by his own statement, was a Benedictine monk in Austria. His handful of followers were German immigrants in Pennsylvania. He or some of his followers either purchased or agreed to purchase ten thousand acres, but there appears to be no local record. Another Peace Union was attempted by Smolnikar later in 1859 at Spring Hill, Perry County, Pennsylvania, but there is no record to evidence its establishment.

68. Ebenezer Society, or the Society of True Inspiration (1843-1855), Ebenezer (former Seneca Indian reservation), Erie County, New York.

The Society of True Inspiration, which had experienced a communal life in Germany prior to coming to America in 1842, established Ebenezer about ten miles southeast of Buffalo. They also set up two Canadian Ebenezer villages, twelve and forty-five miles north of Buffalo, respectively, with land donated by people who joined the society. Because more land was needed for expansion and they were too close to the rapidly growing city of Buffalo, they later moved to Iowa (No. 128).

69. Putney Society, or Putney Community (1843-1848), Putney, Windham County, Vermont.

This was the first community of the perfectionists founded by John Humphrey Noyes,* which they called a "sociology." The membership consisted of seven to eight families that lived in several houses in different parts of the village. Because of the persecutions deriving from the adultery charge against Noyes, all the perfectionists started moving to a new site at Oneida* (No. 108) in 1848; the rear-guard left in 1849.

70. Congregation of Saints (1843), Lexington, Lagrange County, Indiana.

The Saints were hardly organized before disorganization began, and the society was disbanded before the new mode of living was tested. It is not clear to which Christian principle they aspired. Little is known about this short-lived group.

71. Fruitlands* (1843-1844), Harvard, Worcester County, Massachusetts.

Organized by such notable New England transcendentalists as A. Bronson Alcott* and Charles Lane,* Fruitlands was, though much smaller in its membership, similar to Brook Farm* (No. 53). After its short life, Lane and his son joined the Shaker Community at Harvard (No. 6).

72. Skaneateles Community* (1843-1846), Community Place, Mottville, Onandaga County, New York.

This communal experiment originated in Syracuse, New York, when John Collins,* a salaried abolition agent from Massachusetts, visited there with Frederick Douglass to promote the abolition cause. He instead organized a socialist community and forbade the practice of all organized religion. It published a paper called *The Communitist.* After several members were dismissed because of religious quarrels, they joined the Oneida Community* (No. 108).

73. Abram Brooke's Experiment (1843-1845), Oakland, Chester Township, Clinton County, Ohio.

It appears that Abram Brooke, who was an ascetic physician, tried his own experiment in the community of ownership after he withdrew from the Marlborough Association (No. 54). He never attracted enough members, as is indicated in his letter to *The Harbinger* in which he said that only his own and his mother's family lived on sixty acres of land in 1846.

74. Prairie Home Community (1844-1844), near West Liberty, Logan County, Ohio.

After attending a socialist convention in New York in 1843, John O. Wattles and Valentine Nicholson launched this loosely structured community. The original membership of 130 was composed of farmers, most of whom had been Hicksite Quakers. The community had no ruling government and no constitution; the only principle they had was: "Do as you would be done by." It lasted less than a year.

75. Highland Home (1844-1844), Zanesfield, Logan County, Ohio.

This was a small branch community of the Prairie Home (No. 74), located about nine miles north of West Liberty. Life in this small settlement was much like that of the parent group.

76. LaGrange Phalanx—Fourierist (1844-1846), near Mongoquinong (now Mongo), Springfield Township, LaGrange County, Indiana.

The settlement originated by a group of prominent citizens of Springfield Township. All of the families, totaling about 120 people, lived in the large phalanx building. While the system had many advantages for the early pioneers, those who came only for want of a home or for the winter were a hindrance to the community. Some members later came from the Alphadelphia Phalanx (No. 81), Michigan.

77. Sodus Bay Phalanx (later reorganized as the Sodus Phalanx)—Fourierist (1844-1846), Shaker Tract on Sodus Bay, Sodus and Huron Townships, Wayne County, New York.

This was one of the two Fourierist organizations formed in Rochester, New York. Another, Ontario Phalanx, was only projected. Under the leadership of Benjamin Fish, who was one of Rochester's wealthiest citizens, they purchased a tract formerly occupied by the Shakers (No. 39). Because of a sharp disagreement between the religious group and the liberal portion of the society, dissolution eventually became inevitable. A. M. Watson, previously with the Jefferson County Industrial Association (No. 62), became president of the phalanx after the religious group withdrew.

78. Bloomfield Union Association, or North Bloomfield Association (1844-1846),

Honeoye Creek, North Bloomfield, at the juncture of Monroe, Livingston, and Ontario Counties, New York.

Under the leadership of Edwin A. Stillman of Rochester, a Fourierist convention was held at North Bloomfield on February 27-28, 1844; community life began on March 15 with 148 resident members. Honeoye Creek then provided for several industrial enterprises, some of whose mills were taken over by the Fourierists.

79. Leraysville Phalanx—Fourierist (1844-1844†), Le Raysville, Pike township, Bradford County, Pennsylvania.

The leading spirit of this Fourierist community was Lemuel C. Belding, a preacher of the Swedenborgian Church of New Jerusalem. The majority of the forty original members were Swedenborgians in Le Raysville, whose farms formed a community. Some members came from Maine and New York. Conflict between the original forty members and those who came from outside the area led to the dissolution in 1844.

†According to MacDonald's manuscript, it lasted only eight months. Some later writers gave the duration as eighteen months, or even four years.

80. Ohio Phalanx (originally named the American Phalanx before its inception)—Fourierist (1844-1845), Bell Air (now Bellaire), Pultney Township, Belmont County, Ohio.

The principal leadership came from the Associationists of Pittsburgh, Pennsylvania, and Canton, Ohio. They purchased a domain known as the Pultney Farm (two thousand acres) on the western bank of the Ohio River some seven or eight miles south of Wheeling, West Virginia. After a couple of reorganizations with three constitutions, they finally dissolved their sixteen-month-old enterprise. A few members moved to the Trumbull Phalanx (see No. 86).

81. Alphadelphia Phalanx—Fourierist (1844-1848), near Galesburg, Comstock Township, Kalamazoo County, Michigan.

In response to a call for a convention by Henry R. Schetterly of Ann Arbor in a Universalist paper, fifty-six interested individuals from southeastern Michigan met in Columbia, Jackson County, in December 1843. About two hundred pioneers (thirteen hundred, including nonresident members) put their plan into practice in the following May. In the meantime, this community apparently absorbed the group at Ann Arbor who had projected the Washtenaw Phalanx. Schetterly attempted a merger with the Integral Phalanx (No. 93), Illinois, before its dissolution.

82. Clarkson Association, or Clarkson Domain (originally called the Western New York Industrial Association, later reorganized as the Port Richmond Phalanx)—Fourierist (1844-1845), one mile from the mouth of Sandy Creek (now the

village of North Hamlin), Clarkson (now Hamlin) Township, Monroe County, New York.

The Western New York Industrial Association was one of the successors to the projected Ontario Phalanx of Rochester. Community life began in February 1844 with 350 members, many of whom were Hicksite Quakers. After the summer was over, half of them left while the other half stayed four months longer. During its brief period of existence, a few perfectionists joined from the Oneida Community* (No. 108).

83. Mixville Association (originally called The Genesee Valley Association)— Fourierist (1844-1845), Mixville (now Wiscoy), Hume Township, Allegany County, New York.

The society seems to have originated in Dansville, Livingston County, where the Genesee Valley Association was organized in 1843 after the Fourierites had fragmented. Most of the members, however, came from the Dansville area. It was reported that the association was in difficulties after a year's existence.

84. Ontario Union, or Manchester Union—Fourierist (1844-1845), Bates' Mills (later Littleville), Manchester and Hopewell Townships, Ontario County, New York.

Theron C. Leland, who was on the board of directors of the Sodus Bay Phalanx (No. 77), was one of the leaders of Ontario Union (which should not be confused with the projected Ontario Phalanx of Rochester). The association, originally the Rochester Industrial Association, with seventy-five original members, was the smallest of the Rochester Fourierist groups that came into existence.

85. Clermont Phalanx (originally called the Cincinnati Phalanx)—Fourierist (1844-1846), Rural and Utopia, Franklin Township, Clermont County, Ohio.

This was originally named the Cincinnati Phalanx from the place of its founding. The group purchased 1,140 acres of land on the lowlands of the Ohio River, thirty-five miles upstream from Cincinnati. Some members of the Ohio Phalanx (No. 80) came after its dissolution. Many returned to Cincinnati when failure to meet the payments on the land forced dissolution, but a few joined Utopia (No. 104). The lower part of the site became the property of the Brotherhood (No. 103).

86. Trumbull Phalanx—Fourierist (1844-1848), Phalanx Station (eight miles west of Warren), Braceville Township, Trumbull County, Ohio.

This was organized by a group of Pittsburgh Associationists with thirty-five families as its original members. Soon the community grew to two hundred members, but disease originating from the low-lying swampy nature of the land took a heavy toll. It was once dissolved during the winter of 1847-1848, but the aid from Pittsburghers (one of them was H. H. Van Amringe, a former member of the Ohio Phalanx, No. 80) prolonged its communal life a few months.

87. Wisconsin Phalanx—Fourierist (1844-1850), Ceresco (now within the city limits of Ripon), Fond du Lac County, Wisconsin.

Next to the North American Phalanx (No. 66), this association was the second longest lived Fourierist experiment. Its original nucleus of the *New York Tribune*-reading Yankees, who had recently migrated from New England, came from Southport (present-day Kenosha). Most of the 180 members were liberals in religion and "Whigs or Nothing" in politics. This communal experiment, it is said by a leading member, was "pecuniarily successful but socially a failure." One of the causes of its dissolution was the get-rich-quick call of the frontier.

88. Iowa Pioneer Phalanx—Fourierist (1844-1845), on the north bank of the Des Moines River (now Scott Township), Mahaska County, Iowa.

This community was organized at Watertown, Jefferson County, New York, for the purpose of emigrating to Iowa Territory. It was located about nine miles west of Oskaloosa, but the river has since changed its course and now cuts across the lands once owned by the phalanx. The community consisted of about fifty persons, mostly from Watertown and a few recruited in Iowa. They gradually left the phalanx to locate land of their own.

89. Union Home (1844†-1846), Cabin Creek (near Unionsport), White River and West River Townships, Randolph County, Indiana.

John O. Wattles of the Prairie Home Community (No. 74) visited Randolph County from Ohio where he persuaded a group of Spiritualists to form the Union Home on seven hundred acres donated by Hiram Mendenhall, an extensive landowner who resided in Unionsport. This brief socialistic experiment greatly weakened Mendenhall's financial ability; shortly after its failure, he went to California.

†Some sources indicate that the community was founded in 1842.

90. Bethel Community* (1844-1880), Bethel (including Elim, Mamura, and Hebron), Shelby County, Missouri.

This religious colony of German-Americans was founded by William Keil,* an independent preacher who was acquainted with the Rappites (No. 28) while he worked as a tailor in Pittsburgh. Among its original members were the Rappite seceders who formed the New Philadelphia Society (No. 44). Membership was about 650 in 1856 when Keil led about half of them west and established Aurora Community (No. 131) in Oregon; the other half remained at Bethel. While they shared property and labor, private earnings were allowed. The Bethel Society never had any written agreement and it remained an unincorporated group throughout its history.

91. Voree (1844†-1849), on the White River prairie (near Burlington), Walworth and Racine Counties, Wisconsin.

James Jesse Strang,* who was converted to Mormonism in Nauvoo, Illinois, in 1844, was sent back to Wisconsin by Joseph Smith. He established a Mormon colony at Voree, while Brigham Young led the rest in the overland trek to Utah after the Prophet was assassinated by a mob in Nauvoo. Realizing that Voree, where 500 families had settled with a communal form of government, was only a temporary location, the Strangites began their exodus to Beaver Island (No. 109), Michigan in the winter of 1847-1848.

†In his checklist Bestor mistakenly identifies the year of establishment as 1848.

92. Philadelphia Industrial Association—Fourierist (1845-1847), Portage (a village since absorbed by the city of South Bend), German (now Portage) Township, St. Joseph County, Indiana.

Some phalanxes, aside from the lofty cause of Associationism, were unable to escape land speculation. The South Bend group, apparently with no relationship to the city of Philadelphia, was established on the farm of William McCartney, who was interested primarily in getting his land cleared up and improved for nothing. The dispute with McCartney forced the association's move to a new site in Greene Township, but they were still unable to survive.

93. Integral Phalanx (later absorbed the Sangamon Association)—Fourierist (1845-1846), Manchester Mills (near Middletown), Butler County, Ohio, and later moved to Lick Creek (now Laomi), Laomi Township, Sangamon County, Illinois.

Under the leadership of John S. Williams of Cincinnati, the Integral Phalanx was first settled in Butler County, Ohio, about twenty-three miles north of Cincinnati. In spite of its initial success, the community moved to a site thirteen miles southwest of Springfield, Illinois, where it absorbed the Sangamon Association and occupied its domain of 555 acres. Some members, unwilling to accompany the main body to Illinois, joined the Columbian Phalanx (No. 95).

94. Canton Phalanx—Fourierist (1845-1845), Section 18, Canton Township, Fulton County, Illinois.

Little is known about this settlement which languished less than one year. John F. Randolph, a native of Indiana who was one of the most extensive farmers and stockraisers in Fulton County, organized the association consisting of fifteen members with their families. It appears that most of them were Swedenborgians.

95. Columbian Phalanx or Columbian Association—Fourierist (1845-1845), on the Muskingum River (seven miles above Zanesville), Muskingum County, Ohio.

This was the last Fourierist community to be established in Ohio. The phalanx, it seems, was at least partly organized by the Pittsburgh Associationists. It absorbed the Beverly Association, projected at Beverly, Washington County, Ohio.

96. Fruit Hills (1845-1852), Foster's Crossing, Deerfield Township, Warren County, Ohio.

Orson S. Murray, a native of Vermont, who was sympathetic to Owenism and Garrisonian anarchism, established a small community on the Miami River twenty-six miles from Cincinnati. The community maintained a close association with Grand Prairie Community (No. 97) and Kristeen Community (No. 98) through its paper, *Regenerator.*

97. Grand Prairie Community, or Grand Prairie Common Stock Company (1845-1847), Rainsville, Warren County, Indiana.

Some former members of the First Community of Man's Free Brotherhood (No. 47) established the Home of Humanity based on the "common stock" doctrine in the adjoining county of northwestern Indiana. These Friends of Humanity, numbering about twenty families on 230 acres of land, began to disband when they tried to decide on a constitution after two years of communal operation. Andreas Smolnikar,* the eccentric reformer, may have been a member of the group.

98. Kristeen Community (1845-1846), on the Tippecanoe River, Marshall County, Indiana.

This community was established by Charles Mowland and others who had previously participated in the Prairie Home Community (No. 74). They purchased 376 acres of land on the Tippecanoe, about thirty to thirty-five miles from Peru on the Wabash and Erie Canal. Orson S. Murray of Fruit Hills (No. 96), John O. Wattles (previously with the Prairie Home Community, No. 74, and later the Brotherhood Community, No. 103), among others, were listed as trustees at the time of its founding. The community subsisted on the timber and lumber trades.

99. Utilitarian Association of United Interests†—Owenite (1845-1848), near Mukwonago, Mukwonago Township, Waukesha County, Wisconsin.

A group of sixteen London mechanics and their families, who were undoubtedly aware of the Hunt's Colony (No. 61) which had settled in Waukesha County three years earlier, purchased a farm of two hundred acres. After three years of struggle to maintain the colony on the cooperative plan, they "finally were starved out" and moved to Milwaukee.

†According to Bestor's checklist, the Utilitarian Association of United Interests is included within the Hunt's Colony. While these appear to be two subgroups of one community unit, they were organizationally two distinct communities: (1) they were approximately thirteen miles apart from each other; (2) the former continued to exist after the latter was disbanded; and (3) each kept its distinct membership.

100. Spring Farm Phalanx—Fourierist (1846-1848), Town of Mitchell, Sheboygan County, Wisconsin.

This settlement had its inception in the quiet little village of Sheboygan Falls, where a Fourierite from Ohio agitated for community reform. Ten families agreed to join in founding a phalanx, but disagreement developed over the choice of location. Unable to reconcile their differences, the families divided, each group starting a colony of its own. (See Pigeon River Fourier Colony, No. 101). Their request for incorporation after a year's communal residence was turned down by the territorial legislature, and consequently the organization disbanded.

101. Pigeon River Fourier Colony—Fourierist (1846-1847), north of Sheboygan, Sheboygan County, Wisconsin.

This was the lake shore group of the original ten families (see Spring Farm Phalanx, No. 100) that chose the site north of Sheboygan (on Lake Michigan) at the mouth of the Pigeon River. One of the families that settled at the Pigeon came from a larger Fourierist community at Ceresco (No. 87). The cause of its termination is unknown.

102. Bishop Hill Colony* (1846-1862), Bishop Hill, Henry County, Illinois.

To escape persecution in their homeland, a group of Swedes called the Readers, or Janssonists, emigrated to America under the leadership of Erik Jansson.* Their communal arrangement developed mostly out of the necessities they faced during their first winter on the pioneer prairie. New members continued to arrive from Sweden until 1855, when the total membership numbered about five hundred. Discontent among younger members of the colony eventually broke up the commune. A few Janssonists left to join the Shakers at Pleasant Hill (No. 21) in 1854.

103. The Brotherhood, or Spiritualist Community (1846-1847), on part of site of Clermont Phalanx (No. 85), Franklin Township, Clermont County, Ohio.

After a brief sojourn with the Prairie Home Community (No. 74), John O. Wattles published a social reform paper called *The Herald of Progression* in Cincinnati. In May 1846, he and other prominent citizens of Cincinnati organized a Spiritualist community of agricultural association. About one hundred members rebuilt the building which the Clermont Phalanx had erected on the Ohio River bank. They also built a large store in Cincinnati to sell their farm produce. The flood of December 1847, which detroyed all the buildings, ended the life of the community.

104. Utopia, or Trialville (1847-1858), Utopia, another part of Clermont Phalanx (No. 85), Franklin Township, Clermont County, Ohio.

The ex-phalansterians who remained at Clermont (No. 85) to perserve hope in the eventual success of some type of communal life were visited by Josiah

Warren,* whose earlier attempt in Tuscarawas (No. 46) was destroyed by disease. Nearly two dozen families occupied the site. Each owned its own lot and house, but the members cooperated with Warren's "equitable commerce" in all areas found mutually advantageous. Warren himself left Utopia after hardly more than a year. The community continued to exist in mutualism until the late 1850s, when cooperative features gradually began to disappear.

105.   Bettina, or Darmstaedter Kolonie (1847-1848), on the Llano River (about one mile south of Castell), Gillespie (now Llano) County, Texas.

A group of thirty-three radical students from Darmstadt, Germany, came to Texas with the aid of the Society for the Protection of German Immigrants to Texas. Their motto "friendship, freedom and equality" soon created an idle atmosphere without governing rules, and the community "went to pieces like a bubble" at the end of the following summer.

106.   Zodiac (1847-1853), four miles southeast of Fredericksburg, Gillespie County, Texas.

Lyman Wight, who had previously been a member of the United Order of Enoch at Independence (No. 43) and who refused to acknowledge the leadership of Brigham Young, founded a Mormon settlement in Texas. About fifteen Mormons engaged in agriculture, producing mostly corn. In 1853, after their mill on the Pedernales was destroyed by flood, the Mormons abandoned the settlement.

107.   Communia (later reorganized as Communia Working Men's League) (1847-1856), Communia (six miles south of Elkader), Clayton County, Iowa.

This community was organized by a circle of German socialists who had recently emigrated to America. Among its original members were the Swiss who had attempted a colony named New Helvetia, in Osage County, Missouri. Communia, situated on 1,240 acres of virgin prairie in northeastern Iowa, later merged with Wilhelm Weitling's* "Arbeiterbund," or Working Men's League, which had twenty chapters in the large eastern cities. The union was not a happy one, for the colonists were soon divided into two factions. When Communia disbanded, a few of the members joined the Icarians at Nauvoo (No. 111).

108.   Oneida Community* (1848-1881), Kenwood, Oneida Township, Madison County, New York.

After the perfectionists were driven out of Putney (No. 69), a group of fifty men, women, and children gathered at Oneida in the "burned-over" district of central New York, where a few converts to perfectionism owned farms. The community, under the persuasive leadership of John Humphrey Noyes,* became quite prosperous, and the membership grew steadily. Totaling 306 in 1878, including those at the Wallingford, Connecticut, Community (No. 115). They developed such uniquely perfectionist communal practices as "mutucal criticism," "complex marriage," and "stirpiculture." As Noyes aged to semi-retirement, the question of complex marriage split the community into two factions in the late 1870s. Coupled with pressures aroused by the clergy of the surrounding country, they transformed their communal enterprise into a joint-stock corporation, Oneida Company, Ltd.

109. Kingdom of St. James (1848-1856), St. James (on Beaver Island in Lake Michigan), Manitou (now part of Charlesvoix) County, Michigan.

Those schismatic Mormons under James J. Strang* from Voree (No. 91), as well as many of the smaller Mormon settlements in the eastern states, moved into the Beaver Colony after 1848. Strang was crowned King James of the "Kingdom of Beaver Island" in 1850. As the Mormons increased their numbers, 2,608 of them living on the island in 1854, their non-Mormon neighbors, who were mostly Irish Catholic, became alarmed. By then, Strang abandoned, for the most part, communal government. In 1856, three members conspired against him and wounded him seriously. After his death, many went to Utah and were received into the Brigham Young church.

110. Icaria*—Texas (1848-1848), Frenchtown prairie at the mouth of Oliver Creek (twenty miles south of Justin), Denton County, Texas.

Etienne Cabet* organized the first vanguard of sixty-nine Icarians in France. They left for Texas three weeks before the outbreak of the 1848 Revolution. The Icarian Colony in America, the first of several that was eventually organized, settled in Denton County on 10,240 acres granted to the Peters Land Company of Cincinnati. Because of sickness and unfavorable circumstances, the colony gave up its cause after only four months. They, together with those from a second party that arrived in 1849, left for Nauvoo, Illinois (No. 111).

111. Icaria*—Nauvoo (1849-1859), Nauvoo, Hancock County, Illinois.

Regrouping in New Orleans, approximately 280 Icarians landed at Nauvoo, which the Mormons† had occupied until 1856 after leaving Independence (No. 43). They prospered reasonably there and opened stores in St. Louis to sell the surplus product of shoemaker and tailor. Membership doubled to upward of five hundred; however, there was great flux in the membership. In 1856, when dissension arose over the division of work and labor, they voted Etienne Cabet* out of the presidency. This was the beginning of successive splits (see Nos. 134 and 137).
†By then, the Mormons no longer practiced communal ownership.

112. Nineveh (1849-1878), Nineveh Township (now Connelsville), Adair County, Missouri.

This colony was a branch of Bethel Community (No. 90), founded four years after the parental colony had been in operation. Most members, 150 at its peak, came from Bethel and continued the same religious community life.

113. Ephraim at Green Bay (1850-1853), Tanktown (now the Eighth Ward of the city of Green Bay), Brown County, Wisconsin.

This Moravian religious commune was organized by Nils Otto Tank, an enormously wealthy Norwegian convert to Moravianism who established a colony along the same lines as Count Zinzendorf's at Herrnhut, Saxony. He recruited twenty-five families of poor Norwegians who were the members of A. M. Iverson's congregation in Milwaukee. After three years of communal life, when Tank refused to grant legal titles to the lots the members occupied, Iverson and his followers withdrew and formed another Ephraim (No. 124).

114. Jaspis Kolonie, or Jasper Colony (1851-1853), Jasper, Lenox Township, Iowa County, Iowa.

After thoroughly studying various communal groups already established, a group of twenty German Swedenborgians of St. Louis, most of whom left Germany after the Revolution of 1848, resolved to organize a colony in Iowa. A total of about one thousand acres of land was purchased during 1851 and 1852, but in the spring of 1853, the colony abandoned communal ownership and returned to private ownership. They continued to be active in the New Church in Iowa.

115. Wallingford Community (1851-1881), Wallingford, New Haven County, Connecticut.

This community was the only branch community to remain in perfectionist possession to the end of the Oneida Community* (No. 108). Other "foreign" branches—located at Brooklyn, New York; Newark, New Jersey; Putney (second, see No. 69) and Cambridge, Vermont; and Manlius, New York—were eliminated during 1854 and 1855 in order to concentrate all interests in the two communities. They kept close communication with those at Oneida through daily journals and reports. The membership of the Wallingford Community varied from twenty-five to eighty-five, according to the demands of its business.

116. Modern Times (1851-1863), Modern Times (now Brentwood), Suffolk County, Long Island, New York.

Leaving the scenes of his labor in Ohio and Indiana, Josiah Warren* set up another community of anarchism on Long Island (26.2 miles from the city line of New York) with the support of Stephen Pearl Andrews,* a veteran reformer. Like his earlier attempt, Utopia (No. 104), the community advocated a cooperative, nonprofit system of labor and commodity exchange while each member owned a house and land. A group of the former members of Brook Farm* (No. 53) joined in 1857; the community numbered two hundred inhabitants in total. Some members, including T. L. Nichols* and his wife Mary,* put into practice their ideas of free love. Although Warren went to Boston in 1863 and never returned to Modern Times, a few community residents were still living in Brentwood after the turn of the century.

117. Mountain Cove Community (1851-1853), Mountain Cove (exact location unknown), Fayette County, Virginia (now West Virginia).

This community was the first of a series of religious communes founded by Thomas Lake Harris,* an English-born Universalist-Swedenborgian minister who was acquainted with Horace Greeley* at the church he organized in New York in 1848. With one hundred members of the "Apostolic Circle" gathered in Auburn, New York, Harris and James L. Scott organized a spiritualist community which they regarded as the Garden of Eden. Though little is known about this venture, it seems that the group expected to witness the second coming of Christ at Mountain Cove. The commune disintegrated as a result of a property quarrel.

118. Ole Bull's Colony, or New Norway, or Oleona (1852-1853), Oleona (now Ole Bull State Park), Potter County, Pennsylvania.

Ole Bull, a gifted Norwegian violinist who had come to America on a concert tour in the 1840s, financed and organized the Norwegian colony of four villages—Oleona, New Norway, New Bergen, and Walhalla—on 11,444 acres. Between three hundred and four hundred settlers came in 1852. Defective land title caused dissolution, with many residents going to Wisconsin and Minnesota.

119. Harmonia, Kiantone Community, the Domain,* or the Association of Beneficents (1853-1863), Kiantone Creek or Spiritualist Springs (one mile south of Kiantone), Chautauqua County, New York, on Pennsylvania border.

This spiritualist colony was organized by John Murray Spear,* an ex-Universalist active in prison reform in Boston. The community site of 123 acres had two springs which the members believed had special magnetic and healing qualities. The membership fluctuated constantly but never exceeded forty. They were staunch feminists, whose theme for the spiritualist convention of 1858 at Harmonia was feminine equality. John Orvis,* formerly of Brook Farm* (No. 53), was one of the leaders.

120. Raritan Bay Union*—Fourierist (1853-1858), Eagleswood (now part of Perth Amboy), Middlesex County, New Jersey.

Thirty to forty families that had withdrawn from the North American Phalanx* (No. 66), partly over religious controversy, organized another community with less emphasis upon Fourierism. Marcus Spring,* one of the leaders, purchased all of the shares of stock in the late 1850s in the midst of dissatisfactions among some members. The semi-capitalistic Union probably disbanded at this time.

121. Rising Star Association (1853-1857), Stelvideo (five miles northeast of Greenville), Darke County, Ohio.

Through correspondence with Albert Brisbane,* Stephen P. Andrews,* Thomas L. Nichols* (see Modern Times, No. 116), and other noted communitarians, John S. Patterson organized a small colony on a large farm which he inherited east of Stelvideo. The dress-reform movement orginated by Amelia Bloomer became so popular among the feminine members that earlier settlers called the village "Bloomertown." Patterson and his confreres moved to Berlin Heights (No. 126) later on when his paper, *The Social Revolutionist,* became an organ of "Free-Loveism."

122. Preparation (1853-1858), Preparation, Monona County, Iowa.

In their westward movement during the 1850s, little Mormon groups broke away from the main body. Such was the case of Preparation led by Charles B. Thompson who organized about thirty families in Iowa. He held the complete ownership of property and imposed tithings on his members. When he refused to divide the property or settle with the members of the society under a court order in 1858, he was compelled to flee.

123. Grand Prairie Harmonial Institute† (1853-1854), Prairie Township, Warren County, Indiana.

John O. Wattles, despite the tragic ending of the Brotherhood (No. 103) in Ohio, again instituted an "association for educational and social reform purposes." Horace Greeley* was one of the trustees to whom Wattles deeded his 350 acres. The experiment, like his two previous ones, lasted little more than a year.

†Not to be confused with Grand Prairie Community, No. 97.

124. Ephraim (1853-1864), Ephraim, Door County, Wisconsin.

Removing themselves from Tank's Colony in Green Bay (No. 113), the Moravians under Pastor Iverson founded another Ephraim on the west shore of Door County peninsula. Without Tank's financial resources, they received a loan from a church leader in Bethlehem, Pennsylvania, to purchase four hundred acres. When Iverson left Ephraim in 1864 to take up a new pastoral assignment in Illinois, its communal features began to disappear. However, Ephraim became the center of extensive Norwegian settlements numbering several thousand people.

125. St. Nazianz Community* (1854-1874), St. Nazianz, Eaton Township, Manitowoc County, Wisconsin.

This community, which, so far as is known, is the only Roman Catholic communal society ever established in America, was founded by a group of 113 German immigrants from Baden. Under their leader Father Ambrose Oschwald,* all property, including 3,840 acres of land, was held in common and all service was rendered without compensation other than food and clothing. At its height membership totaled 450 persons, 180 of whom were married. After Oschwald's death in 1873, the married members were given their share of the property, and its remaining property was subsequently taken over by a Catholic order, the Society of Our Divine Saviour.

126. The Free-Lovers at Davis House (official name is unknown) (1854-1858), Berlin Heights, Erie County, Ohio.

    The group of "long-haired, sleek-looking" free-lovers, most of whom were spiritualists, first appeared in Berlin Heights in 1854 under the leadership of Francis Barry. It soon became the hotbed of their "warfare against marriage." They did not live in one family, but rather were scattered in small fruit farms along one side of the village. Because of their neighbors' hostility, they moved, to a farm one mile out of the village, where they lived together, about thirty in total.

127. Reunion,* or Victor Considerant's* Colony—Fourierist (1855-1859), three or four miles west of Dallas across the Trinity River, Dallas County, Texas.

    This colony was one of two Fourierist enterprises with French rather th .n American leadership and personnel. Victor Considerant, the leading theorist of the Fourier School in France, organized the European Society for the Colonization of Texas in 1854 upon his return from America. Five hundred people participated in the experiment during its five years, but they never numbered more than 350 at any one time.

128. Amana Society,* or the Society of True Inspiration (1855-1932), Amana, West Amana, South Amana, High Amana, East Amana, Middle Amana, and Homestead, Iowa County, Iowa.

    Despite their economic success, the True Inspirationists sold their land near Buffalo (No. 68) and established seven villages within an agricultural and industrial territory of forty square miles. Theirs was probably the largest (twenty-six thousand acres—part of it was previously occupied by Jaspis Kolonie, No. 114) and the most systematically developed communal site. Dissatisfaction among the younger members of the society created an attitude receptive to change, and the financial setbacks beginning in 1921 eventually forced the "great change" of 1932. When it was reorganized into a stock company with private ownership, there were 239 families living in the villages.

129. Memnonia Institute* (1856-1857), Yellow Springs, Greene County, Ohio.

    After leaving Modern Times (No. 116) on Long Island, Thomas L. Nichols* and his wife, Mary Gove Nichols,* established a "School of Life" in Yellow Springs, Ohio. Its establishment was vehemently opposed by Horace Mann, president of Antioch College, who mistook it as a "free love colony." In reality, it followed a rigid rule of asceticism, fasting, and spiritual penance. The group of twenty members grew less and less Fourierist, and more and more religious. After six months, most members joined the Roman Catholic church.

130. Union Grove (1856-1858), Union Grove Township, Meeker County, Minnesota.
    This community was an offshoot of Hopedale Community* (No. 56). Those

who were sent from Massachusetts, together with the Minnesota pioneers, secured eight hundred acres of land under the U.S. Preemption Act as part of the Practical Christians' western movement. Because of Indian troubles and the lack of support from the parent community, they returned to Hopedale after a few years.

131. Aurora Community* (1856-1881), Aurora, Marion County, Oregon.

Unhappy with the location chosen at Willapa on Schoalwater Bay in Washington Territory by the scouts from Bethel (No. 90), William Keil,* the leader, moved his followers to the rich farmland in the Williamette Valley in Oregon. Their migration from Missouri to Oregon continued until 1867, when the settlement numbered about six hundred persons occupying eighteen thousand acres of land. After Keil's death in 1877, the colonists dissolved the communal organization, and all the property and holdings were divided. Although the community never had the semblance of a constitutional agreement, there never was a single lawsuit involving the community and its members during its existence.

132. Germania Company (1856-1879), Germania, Marquette County, Wisconsin.

This Millerite colony of the Second Adventists originated at a camp meeting in Groton, Massachusetts, in 1855. The original membership consisted of six families and five unmarried females, most of whom came from Rochester, New York. The colony became prosperous, but when Benjamin Hall, their leader, died in 1879, the members divided the property.

133. Icaria*—Cheltenham (1856-1864), Cheltenham (six miles west of St. Louis), St. Louis County, Missouri.

The 180 Icarians who were loyal to Etienne Cabet* (d. 1856) when the colony was divided at Nauvoo (No. 111) purchased a twenty-eight acre estate called Cheltenham in the suburbs of St. Louis. The group began to disintegrate rapidly after 1859 when forty-two members withdrew over a constitutional dispute. There were only eight families left in the community when the Cheltenham group finally abandoned their communal efforts.

134. The Fourier Phalanx, An Integral School of Science and Art (1858), Moore's Hill, Sparta Township, Dearborn County, Indiana.

This colony was founded by Alcander Longley,* whose father was a member of the Clermont Phalanx (No. 85). Prior to his own undertaking, he resided at the North American Phalanx (No. 66) from 1852 to 1854. The phalanx, only the first of a series of communities which Longley continued to be involved in until his death in 1918, lasted only a couple of months as he rejected Fourierist socialism in favor of Christian communism.

135. Harmonial Vegetarian Society (1860-1864), near Maysville, Benton County, Arkansas.

About eighteen families from New York, Ohio, and the South formed a commune to pursue a vegetarian way of life and to practice free love. While marriage was not recognized in the society, the members, fifteen males and eleven females, were allowed to choose their "mates" by lot. It was intended that the children born of members were to be considered the offspring of the society rather than of the parents. At the close of the Civil War, the buildings, some of which were used by the armies in the war, were burned.

136. Point Hope Community, or Berlin Heights Community (1860-1861), Berlin Heights, Erie County, Ohio.

This community to be a continuation of the "Free-Lovers at Davis House" (No. 126) after they were communally settled on a farm outside Berlin Heights. After about a year, the community (twenty members with sex equally divided) was reorganized as the Industrial Fraternity. The Free Thinkers at Berlin Heights, some of whom came from Modern Times (No. 116), published several papers (for example, *Age of Freedom, Good Time Coming*). It is not clear if these papers were official organs.

137. Icaria*—Corning (1860-1878), Village of Icaria (four miles west of Corning), Adams County, Iowa.

The anti-Cabet Icarians who remained in Nauvoo (No. 111) moved to the southwestern part of Iowa in 1857. After three years of legal settlement of property questions in Illinois, they purchased 3,115 acres, reduced to 1,000 later, as membership remained small (between thirty-five and eighty-five). As was the case at Nauvoo and Cheltenham (No. 133), factionalism developed and divided the colony between the Progressives who set up Jeune Icarie (No. 169) and the Non-Progressives of New Icaria (No. 170).

138. Adonai Shomo Corporation, or Community of Fullerites (1861-1897), Petersham (the land now owned by Harvard University), Worcester County, Massachusetts.

Like the Germania Company (No. 132), this small commune of Adventists originated at a Groton camp meeting in the aftermath of the Millerite excitement. Under the leadership of Frederick T. Howland, an ex-Quaker, ten or so people, primarily women, settled at Leonard Fuller's home in Athol. When the membership grew to twenty-five to thirty, they moved to a large farm in Petersham in 1864, about eight miles south of Athol. The community dissolved after a number of litigations.

139. Ora Labora Community, or Christian German Agricultural and Benevolent Society of Ora Labora (1862-1868), between Caseville and Wildfowl (now Bay Port), Huron County, Michigan.

About thirty German Methodist families from Ohio and Pennsylvania spent over ten years of preparation with several preliminary constitutions before

Ora Labora came into existence. The community, under Emil Gottlob Baur, was modeled after the Harmony Society* (No. 28) and in fact was partly funded by the Rappites. Civil War conscription and the war's financial burden quickened its dissolution.

140. Celesta (1863-1864), Celesta (two miles west of Laporte), Sullivan County, Pennsylvania.

This small religious commune arose directly out of Millerism. In 1852, Peter Armstrong, a Second Adventist preacher from Philadelphia, set out to develop a grandiose Heavenly Celestial City of 144,000 saints at the top of the Allegheny Mountains in Sullivan County. After eleven years of preparation and clearing the land, he succeeded in recruiting no more than a dozen families through his paper, *The Day Star of Zion,* even though it was widely read among Adventists in the East.

141. Amenia Community, or the Brotherhood of the New Life* (1863-1867), Amenia, Dutchess County, New York.

Ten years after the Mountain Cove (No. 117) experiment failed, Thomas Lake Harris* founded the first home of the Brotherhood of the New Life in Dutchess County, New York. During a preliminary two-year stay in nearby Wassaic, prior to Amenia, communal life was not practiced. The nucleus of the membership consisted of thirty-five faithful Harris followers from his Swedenborgian congregation in New York City.

142. Berlin Community, or Christian Republic (1865-1866), Berlin Heights, Erie County, Ohio.

Little is known about this community. It seems that Berlin Community, with twelve adults and six children, was similar, if not directly related, to the two short-lived colonies established at Berlin Heights by the free lovers (see Nos. 126 and 136).

143. Brocton Community, or Salem-on-Erie (1867-1881), Brocton, Town of Portland, Chautauqua County, New York.

With the resources of well-to-do members from the South and New York and $100,000 donated by Lady Oliphant and her son, Laurence,* whom Thomas Lake Harris* recruited in England, Harris moved his Brotherhood of the New Life from Amenia (No. 141) to sixteen hundred acres of the finest land in northern Chautauqua, near the shore of Lake Erie. The community grew and prospered at Brocton. The membership fluctuated between seventy-five and one hundred, twenty of whom were Japanese of Samurai class. The "Brotherhood wines" from their vineyard came into strong favor throughout a large area. Following a heavenly vision, in 1875 Harris took the elect few to California (No. 163) while the critics remained in Brocton. All remaining members moved to California by 1881.

144. Davisite Kingdom of Heaven (official name is unknown) (1867-1881), near Walla Walla (between Mill Creek and Russel Creek), Walla Walla County, Washington.

Accompanied by forty schismatic Mormons from Utah, William W. Davies,* a Welsh mystic, came to Washington State to found the "Kingdom of Heaven." Through his missionary work, new members came from San Francisco and Portland, numbering about seventy in total. When Davies' two sons (the eldest was regarded as the "Walla Walla Jesus"—the reincarnation of Christ) died of diphtheria, peace in the community was at an end.

145. Reunion Colony,* or the True Family (1868-1870), near Minersville (now Oronogo), Jasper County, Missouri.

After an eight-month stay at the Icarian community in Iowa (No. 137) in 1867, Alcander Longley* (see also No. 133), now under the influence of Icarian communism, established his own commune in Missouri. The membership remained small, twenty-seven adult members, most of whom had responded to Longley's call for a "community convention" in the *The Communist* which he published in St. Louis. After a group of the opposing faction withdrew, Reunion, troubled by mortgage payments for forty acres of land, ended.

146. Union Colony* (1869-1872), Greeley, Weld County, Colorado.

Nathaniel C. Meeker,* formerly a member of Trumbull Phalanx (No. 86), visited the Shakers, Mormons, and Oneida perfectionists before coming to Colorado. The original 442 members, who paid a $150 fee, came primarily from New York and partly from Ohio and Pennsylvania. Though nonsectarian, the colony practiced temperance. Within four years of its founding, the colonists transformed their communal institutions into a town indistinguishable from others in the region. Some years later, a dozen families joined the Puget Sound Co-operative Colony (No. 193) in Washington State.

147. German Colonization Company,* or German Colony of Colfax (1870-1871), Colfax (seven or eight miles south of Silver Cliff), Fremont (now Custer) County, Colorado.

This German colony was never intended to be a scheme for an ideal society; rather, it was a means of migration for Chicago artisans to cooperate and to take advantage of the federal government's liberal land policy in the West. Organized in Chicago by Carl Wulsten, a Prussian, about eighty families settled in Colorado's Wet Mountain Valley. Despite their plan to maintain communal life for five years, the colony lasted less than a year.

148. Kansas Co-operative Farm (later renamed Prairie Home Colony, also called Silkville*)—Fourierist (1870-1884), Silkville, Williamsburg Township, Franklin County, Kansas.

This community was probably the last attempt of a direct Fourierist-line experiment, which was established by Ernest Valeton de Boissiere* of a noble family from Bordeaux, France. Located in the northeastern corner of Kansas, where French immigrants were already well established, the colony had about forty French people, who were the experts in the production of silk. The membership also included several American families, most notably Charles T. Sears, who had previously been president of North American Phalanx (No. 66). He wrote a series of articles about this colony which appeared in the Oneida Community* paper (No. 108).

149. Progressive Community (1871-1878), near Cedar Vale, Howard (now Chautauqua) County, Kansas.

After the dissolution of Longley's* Reunion Colony* (No. 145), William Frey* (formerly Vladimir Konstantinovich Geins) and his two Russian associates, with substantial funding from Russia, moved to Kansas to try their own social experiment. Although membership was initially restricted to Russians, there were also about fifteen American spiritualists in the group.

150. Warm Springs Colony (1871†), on the French Broad River, Madison County, North Carolina.

After an enthusiastic meeting for colonizing the South held at the Cooper Institute, New York City, about fifty colonists purchased fifteen hundred acres of land in the western portion of North Carolina, a well-known summer resort before the Civil War. They had barely organized their communal life when the colony found itself in debt for $88,000. The administrative office was kept in New York. Little else is known about this colony.

†It is not exactly clear when the colony disbanded. According to a visitor's account, it is unlikely that it lasted more than a year.

151. Chicago-Colorado Colony (1871-1873), Longmont, Boulder County, Colorado.

As the *New York Tribune* supported the colonization scheme of Union Colony* (No. 146) at Greeley, preliminary formation of the colony was organized partly by the *Chicago Tribune*. The constitution was modeled after Union Colony's, and it required the same membership fee. The majority of the four hundred members came from Chicago, but some ninety people already living in the vicinity also joined. As in the case of Union Colony, the communal features quickly disappeared when irrigation projects were completed.

152. Western Colony (later renamed St. Louis-Western Colony) (1871-1872), Evans, Weld County, Colorado.

This colony was first organized in Ayres Point (now Oakdale), Washington County, Illinois, by Andrew C. Todd, a Reformed Presbyterian minister, and his parishioners in 1870. The headquarters of the organization was moved to St. Louis before their westward migration. A former member of Union Colony* (No. 146), who was also from Ayres Point, was instrumental in deciding the colony site, only four miles from Greeley. The colony had about five hundred members the first summer. Apparently, Greeley deprived Evans of its potential growth.

153. Friendship Community (1872-1877), near Buffalo, Dallas County, Missouri.

In less than two years after the dissolution of Reunion* (No. 145), Alcander Longley* launched the second Missouri experiment. Although there were only five members at the outset, membership increased in 1873, with the neighboring people joining in the wake of the depression. The community never attained a strong financial footing. Sensing hostility from neighbors who regarded the experiment as something equivalent to disgraceful Mormonism, Longley closed business.

154. Bennett Co-operative Colony (1873-ca. 1877), two miles north of Long Lane, Dallas County, Missouri.

William H. Bennett, dissatisfied with Alcander Longley's* leadership, withdrew from Friendship Community (No. 153), taking with him most of what he had invested, to organize his own cooperative enterprise. Nothing is known of its operation except that it probably ceased to exist in 1877 with the return of prosperity to the area after the Panic of 1873.

155. Social Freedom Community (1874-1880), Chesterfield County (exact location unknown), Virginia.

This community is briefly mentioned in Charles Nordhoff's book, *The Communistic Societies of the United States,* which seems to be the only written document about the community. The commune was so small, consisting only of two women, one man, and three boys, that there appears to be no local record.

156. Bon Homme Colony—Hutterites* (1874-present), Bon Homme, Bon Homme County, South Dakota.

This colony was the first of twenty-one Hutterite colonies founded in America before 1920. The communal religious sect of the Hutterische Bruder originated in the Anabaptist movement in Moravia during the Protestant Reformation. Because of religious persecutions, both colony and noncolony Hutterites kept migrating from Moravia to Hungary, Transylvania, Wallachia, and the Ukraine before settling in the Dakota Territory. Bon Homme, the parent colony of the later *Schmiedeleut* colonies, purchased twenty-five hundred acres of land along the Missouri River. It received a $6,000 loan from the Harmony Society* (No. 28) to construct a mill. When World War I broke out, only Bon Homme remained populated in South Dakota. Between 1918 and 1920, ten out of sixteen Hutterite colonies in South Dakota left for Canada because of local hostility to "Germanism." Bon Homme is today regarded as as the "mother" of all *Schmiedeleut* colonies (or one group led by Michael Waldnew who practiced communal living) in North America.

157. Women's Commonwealth,* or the Sanctificationists (1874-1906), Belton, Bell County, Texas (later moved to Washington, D.C.).

This celibate group of the Sanctified Sisters ("sanctification" was the group's term for a pentecostal vision) originated in prayer meetings under the leadership of Mrs. Martha McWhirter.* Most of the original members were married women of well-to-do families with their young children. Their communal tendencies developed gradually as they rebeled against the authoritarian doctrines of their local churches, and they asserted financial and sexual independence form their husbands. The commonwealth women were successful in the hotel business, which was incorporated as the Central Hotel Company in 1891. Among thirty-two original members in 1874, four were unmarried men. The group retired to Mt. Pleasant, outside Washington, D.C., in 1899. With the death of McWhirter in 1904, the Commonwealth declined within two years.

158. Dawn Valcour (1874-1875), at Colchester, Vermont, and Valcour Island, New York.

This spiritualist colony was started by Oren Shipman and John Wilcox. Wilcox wrote a prospectus for the colony, describing it as "The Head Center of Advanced Spiritualism and Free Love." Shipman offered his eight hundred-acre farm on Valcour Island and a mainland farm for the colony. A small group settled but there were disputes. In March 1875, Shipman was sued by Wilcox. In November 1875, the remaining settlers left Valcour Island for New York City and the free love experiment ended.

159. Orderville United Order (1875-1884), Orderville, Kane County, Utah.

This was the second Mormon experiment of a United Order of Enoch (see No. 43). The Muddy Mission Mormons who had settled in Long Valley in southern Utah since 1870 were instructed by President Brigham Young to organize a communal system. (There were other attempts to put the United Order into practice in the Rocky Mountains, but none lasted longer than a few months.) At one time over six hundred people belonged to the Order, which continued, according to the initial agreement with church elders, until 1884. As soon as the Order disbanded, the land was surveyed and sold to the highest bidder.

160. Wolf Creek Colony—Hutterites* (1875-1930), near Freemen, Hutchinson County, South Dakota (later moved to Stirling, Alberta, Canada).

After a temporary settlement at Silver Lake for the winter of 1874-1875, the *Dariusleut* (the followers of Darius Walter who practiced communal living), who were among the forty families emigrating with the *Schmiedeleut* group, bought a site in the James River Valley, forty miles north of Bon Homme (No. 156). In 1889, the colony had twenty-seven families, with a population of 160. By 1912, they had a dynamo that provided electric lights and power.

161. Investigating Community (1875), near Cedar Vale, Chautauqua County, Kansas.

Because of his opposition to the spiritualist group within the commune, William Frey* withdrew from the Progressive Community (No. 149) in 1875 and relocated nearby. One-third of the Progressive Community's land was ceded to the secessionists, consisting of five adults and two children, all Russians. The commune soon disbanded to join another group of Russians (No. 162).

162. Cedarvale Community, or Cedar Vale Benevolent and Educational Society (1875-1877), Cedar Vale, Chautauqua County, Kansas.

A small following of "God-men" led by Alexander Kapitonovich Malikov arrived in New York in 1874 to form an agricultural commune. These fifteen young Russian revolutionalists, who had knowledge of Frey's* activities, purchased 160 acres on the Caney River about four miles from the Investigating Community (No. 161). The merger with Frey's commune intensified the God-men's distress. After the commune broke up, one faction of the God-men joined the Shaker Society at Groveland (No. 50) and at South Union (No. 20).

163. Fountain Grove (1876-1900), two miles north of Santa Rosa, Sonoma County, California.

An impressive, costly establishment with a dignified Adams-Georgian home was constructed on seventeen hundred acres in the sunny wine country of northern California. This proved to be the last settlement of the Harrisite Brotherhood of the New Life* after it left Brocton (No. 143), New York. The community of theo-socialism, as it was referred to by Harris,* became well known for its "divine liquor," producing seventy thousand gallons of wine a year by 1886. Among the thirty members were a few married couples, including Harris and his wife Emily, but they maintained celibacy in their doctrines. Because of widespread publicity involving an alleged sex scandal that appeared in Santa Rosa and San Francisco newspapers, Harris left for New York in 1892. After his departure, the community became progressively less communal and more commercial.

164. Modjeska Colony (1877-1878), Anaheim, Orange County, California.

A small group of distinguished artists from Cracow, Poland, settled on some one hundred and fifty acres in Santa Ana valley, near the old German settlement of Anaheim. The idyllic life on a cooperative farm which they had dreamed of to escape the political harassment of Poland turned into a disaster after their funds were exhausted in one year. The majority of about thirty colonists returned to Poland, but their actress leader, Helena Modjeska,* remained in California to pursue her theatrical career.

165. Esperanza (1877-ca. 1878), Urbana, Neosho County, Kansas.

After Friendship Community (No. 153) disbanded in 1877, a determined group of a dozen families started their own community in Kansas, where their leader, N. T. Romaine, had been an old resident. The local paper, describing the arrival of the commune, identified Esperanza as "a branch of the Oneida (New York) Communists." In 1878, *The Star of Hope* published by the commune reported receiving sixty-one new applications for membership, but it is not clear if they actually joined. How long it lasted is obscure.

166. Hays City Danish Colony (official name is unknown) (1877), on the Smokey Hill River (five to ten miles south of Hays), Ellis County, Kansas.

A group of eighteen socialists from Denmark (some were Germans) emigrated to Kansas to establish a commune under the leadership of Louis Albert François Pio,* principal leader of the Danish socialist party and a participant in Karl Marx's First International. Their well-planned colonization scheme in the New World was soon victimized by constant arguments of the colonists' wives over domestic task allocations. It lasted less than two months.

167. Elmspring Colony (later called Old Elmspring)—Hutterites* (1878-1929), near Parkson, Hutchinson County, South Dakota (later moved to Warner, Alberta, Canada).

The third group of the Hutterite movement, the *Lehrerleut*, left Russia in 1877 and began to live communally for the first time as they arrived in South Dakota. There were originally thirteen families who settled on 5,440 acres of land about twenty miles west of Wolf Creek Colony (No. 160). The *Lehrerleut* colonies were in general a bit more liberal than the *Schmiedeleut* and the *Dariusleut*.

168. Bible Community (official name is unknown) (? -1879- ?), Plattsburg, Clinton County, Missouri.

When the Progressive Community (No. 149) collapsed sometime between the spring of 1878 and 1879, its 320 acres of land were offered to the Bible Community in Missouri. John C. Priegal, representing the Bible Community, rejected the offer because its location was not near commerical and manufacturing centers. Thus, the community seemed to be in operation in 1879 when Priegal wrote the letter. Nothing else is known of the community. There are no local documents, nor does the Clinton County Recorders Office contain any record of the community.

169. Icaria*—Jeune Icarie (1879-1887), on part of site of Icaria—Corning (No. 137), Adams County, Iowa.

After the bitter split of 1878 (see Icaria—Corning, No. 137) that involved a settlement by the civil court, the young party of about thirty-five, largely women and children, took possession of the old village. The new constitution abolished the presidency to promote a more democratic participation, and it extended the right of suffrage to women. While the membership rose to seventy-five by the fall of 1880 and new industries were established, the commune slowly started to decline through frequent withdrawals of members. Some of those who departed set up a new Icarian commune (No. 177) in 1881 in California. Those remaining decided to join the California group, but because of the dispute over the sale of land, the union of these two bodies never materialized.

170. Icaria*—New Icarian Community (1879-1895†), near a site of Icaria—Jeune Icarie (No 168), Adams County, Iowa.

The conservative group of thirty Icarians occupied the eastern portion (about eleven hundred acres) of the domain a mile southeast of the old village, where they started anew after a split from the young party (No. 169). Their leader was one of the advance-guard that settled in Texas (No. 110) in 1848. Eight of the thirty-four members in 1883 were over sixty years of age, and twelve were children under the age of thirteen years. While their communal life was modest compared with that of other Icarian settlements of the past and two of their contemporaries in Iowa and California, this group happened to be the last remaining Icarians until its dissolution in 1895 because of the old age of the members.

†It was not legally dissolved until 1898.

171. Societas Fraternia (1879-?), four miles northeast of Anaheim, Los Angeles County, California.

This small colony came to the public's attention when a Dr. Schlesinger, the leader, was convicted (though later acquitted) of letting a colonist's small child die of starvation. He imposed a strict vegetarian diet on his followers, comprising three adults and four children. The colony, situated on a small farm of twenty-five acres near Anaheim, lived in a building of circular rooms, which were intended to promote the circulation of air.

172. Tripp Colony—Hutterites* (1879-1884), Tripp, Hutchinson County, South Dakota.

As Bon Homme (No. 156) became crowded in a few years with new arrivals, the *Schmiedeleut* organized a second colony thirty-six miles to the northwest. The Hutterites' policy was to establish daughter colonies whenever the mother colony's population grew to about one hundred and fifty. Facing financial problems, the Tripp Colony borrowed money from the Amana Society* (No. 128). Based on an agreement with the Rappites (No. 28), who were facing problems caused by aging and celibacy, all nineteen families moved to the land owned by the Rappites in Pennsylvania (No. 187), near the Titusville oil fields.

173. Rugby Colony* (1880-1887), Rugby, Morgan County, Tennessee.

Thomas Hughes,* an English reformer and writer, was the central figure in the establishment of this Anglo-American cooperative venture. The colony, located on the Cumberland Plateau in eastern Tennessee, at its height in 1884 had over four hundred residents and forty-two buildings, including a church, school, library, and hotel. After 1887, most of the cooperative aspects of the colony slowly disappeared, and its principal body, the Board of Aid to Land

Ownership which funded the project, was reorganized in 1892 into a land-holding company.

174. Thompson Colony* (1880-?), near Salina, Saline County, Kansas.

This communal farming settlement was organized by the Co-operative Colony Aid Association of New York City. The fund was subsidized by Elizabeth Rowell Thompson,* a philanthropist who also aided the establishment of the Chicago-Colorado Colony (No. 151). The colonists were allocated separate lands and homes, but the large fields were worked jointly, with a certain portion of time devoted to colony works. The profits were divided *pro rata* among them.

175. Washington Colony (1881-1884), Town of Whatcom (now part of the city of Bellingham), Whatcom County, Washington.

Organized in Kansas for the purpose of locating on Puget Sound, Washington, the colony of twenty-five families agreed with local promoters that the townsite owners of Whatcom were to give the colony a millsite and a half-interest in the land. In return, the settlers would build a sawmill, a wharf, and fifty dwellings. The work progressed smoothly, and the colony quickly brought prosperity to Bellingham Bay with its lumber business. However, the land title dispute between the colonists, creditors, and landowners eventually led to its breakup.

176. Sicily Island Colony* (1881-1882), Sicily Island, Catahoula Parish, Louisiana.

This was the first agricultural colony of Russian Jews in America. Under the leadership of Herman Rosenthal,* it was comprised of twenty-five families and some single men, mostly from Kiev—in all about one hundred twenty-five persons. The twenty-eight hundred-acre colony site chosen by the New York branch of the Alliance Israelite Universelle, which provided part of the funds, did not please the colonists because of its seclusion. A flood of the Mississippi in the spring of 1882 washed away practically everything. Most members scattered, but a determined group under Rosenthal left for South Dakota to try anew (Cremieux, No. 179).

177. Icaria*—Speranza (1881-1886), three miles south of Cloverdale, Sonoma County, California.

The Icaria Speranza Commune, originally called Speranza, was formed by a family that seceded from Jeune Icarie (No. 169), together with several French socialists who resided in the San Francisco area. Some families, numbering fifty-five, joined from the Iowa group in 1884. Their settlement was on nine hundred acres of land located seventy-five miles north of San Francisco. This last splinter group of Icarians for the most part followed the traditional Icarian practice, but, unlike earlier cases, their constitution permitted some private ownership. Realizing that neither funds nor members were likely to be transferred from Jeune Icarie, the commune was dissolved and property divided among the members.

178. Beersheba Colony (1882-1885), on Pawnee Creek (near present-day Kalvesta), Hodgeman County, Kansas.†

   Through the efforts of the Cincinnati Hebrew Union Agricultural Society, a group of twenty-four Russian Jewish families was brought to Kansas. The colony showed marked progress for the first two years, but then disputes between the settlement manager and the colonists emerged; the manager confiscated some cattle and farm implements. Without other funds available, the colony soon disintegrated.

   †There were several other attempts to establish Jewish agricultural colonies in southern Kansas; for example, Lasker, Gilead, Touro, Leeser, and Hebron. Because of a paucity of information, however, it is not clear to what extent their organizations were based on cooperative principles. Therefore, they are not included in this list.

179. Cremieux (1882-1889), on the division line between Davison and Aurora counties, South Dakota.

   After liquidation of the Louisiana colony (No. 176), young Jews of the Am Olam movement settled on a deserted Indian reservation in the Dakota Territory, where the climate resembled that of Russia. Each colonist lived on his own farm, comprising a 160-acre quarter section, while agricultural implements, housing lumber, and livestock were bought with the common fund. The colony numbered about two hundred at one time, but most of them had to move by 1889, after a series of natural disasters and because of a lack of financial resources.

180. Painted Woods (1882-1887), Painted Woods (near Bismarck), Burleigh County, North Dakota.

   This community was organized by a St. Paul, Minnesota, rabbi for Jewish refugees from Russia. In the course of a year, the colony increased from the original twenty families to fifty-four, representing about two hundred individuals. At first, things seemed to go rather well, but before the township to be called Nudelman materialized, crop failures, a prairie fire that destroyed almost all dwellings, and the destructive drought of 1886 ended all hopes.

181. Alliance, or Vineland Colony (1882-1908), Alliance, Salem County, New Jersey.

   The Alliance Colony, organized under the combined auspices of the Hebrew Emigrant Aid Society and the Alliance Israelite Universelle, was the most successful of the Russian Jewish agricultural colonies that were established in the 1880s as a solution to the mass migrations to the United States. Situated on 1,150 acres of rich farmland in south Jersey, the colony comprised forty families from southern Russia, mostly from Odessa, Kiev, and Elizabetgrad. By grouping the farms in units of four, each set of four families worked cooperatively and shared horses and farm implements. In addition, some of the land remained as common property of the colony. Although the Alliance colony as such ended in about 1908, many settlers remained in various parts of New Jersey.

182. Rosenhayn (1882-1889), Rosenhayn, Deerfield Township, Cumberland County, New Jersey.†

As was the case with Alliance (No. 181), six families were initially settled by the Hebrew Emigrant Aid Society. The population grew gradually to sixty-seven families, numbering about 250 individuals by 1889. Many of the latecomers joined upon hearing of the success of the neighboring Alliance colony. They built a clothing factory, operated by contractors. While some communal institutions were maintained, it appears that the colony ceased to be a cooperative farm sometime after 1889.

†Other attempts to establish Jewish agricultural colonies in New Jersey, such as Carmel, Woodbine, Montefiore, Figa, and Ziontown, are not included in the list because of paucity of information.

183. Bethlehem Yehudah (also spelled Jehudah) (1882-1885), South Dakota (exact location unknown).

Of the Russian Jewish immigrant colonies, this colony was the most highly communal in its organization. Established by the Kremenchung party of Am Olam known as the Sons of Freedom, thirty-two members, all unmarried men, settled on government land near Cremieux (No. 179). Unlike other Jewish colonies, they refused outside support from American Jewish philanthropists because of their desire to stay away from traditional Jewish petty trades. When conditions began to improve, each colonist wanted to become independent. The colony was liquidated in three years, with most colonists going to New York.

184. New Odessa Community* (1883-1887), Cow Creek (near Glendale), Douglas County, Oregon.

After a brief stay in the New York area for fund-raising activities, another group of Am Olam established a commune on a wooded tract of 780 acres in southwestern Oregon. What was unique about this Jewish colony was that the leading spirit of the colonists (about sixty young members between the ages of twenty-one and thirty from Odessa) was William Frey,* a non-Jewish Russian who had previously established several communes in the Midwest (see Cedarvale Community, No. 161, for his last involvement). Religion, while not tabooed, was virtually nonexistent. In a year or so after its foundation, an ideological split occurred between Frey's group which emphasized positivism and another group which opposed it. Frey and a few of his followers left before the colony dissolved. Some returned to New York to launch a common household with a cooperative laundry which lasted another five years.

185. Mutual Aid Community (1883-1887), near Glen Allen (now Glenallen), Bollinger County, Missouri.

Between the dissolution of Friendship (No. 153) in 1877 and the establishment of the Mutual Aid Community in 1883, Alcander Longley* twice tried unsuccessfully to establish a "Liberal Community" (St. Louis) and "Principia" (Polk County, Missouri). The 120-acre colony of twenty to thirty members had the same constitution that governed Friendship. The community disbanded in a few years for lack of members and financial support. Mutual Aid Community was probably the last "legitimate" commune established by Longley. It seems doubtful that his later attempts at Higby (1895-1897) in Randolph County and Altruist (1907-1911) in Jefferson County had any resident members other than Longley himself and his family.

186. Joyful, or Association of Brotherly Co-operators (1884), near Bakersfield, Kern County, California.

Following a two-year vegetarian experiment called the Edenic Diet, Isaac B. Rumford and his wife Sara, both active reformers for temperance and women's rights, founded a small commune of six members based on rudimentary Christianity. The colony's paper *Joyful News Co-operator* (twelve issues in 1884) is said to be the first vegetarianist newspaper in California.

187. Tidioute Colony—Hutterites* (1884-1886), four miles south of Tidioute, Warren County, Pennsylvania.

This colony was a continuation of the *Schmiedeleut* colony at Tripp (No. 172) in South Dakota. Despite a generous arrangement of the Rappites (No. 28), who were apparently interested in making the Hutterites their heirs, the terrain and wooded area were too unfamiliar for the Hutterite plains farmers. Constantly borrowing more money from the Rappites and probably feeling isolated from their brethren, they returned to Milltown, South Dakota (No. 191).

188. Shalam* (1884-1901), near Dona Ana, Dona Ana County, New Mexico.

Following the 1883 convention of leading spiritualists in New York City, John Ballou Newbrough,* formerly a member of the Domain* (No. 119) near Jamestown, New York, together with twenty disciples, founded a commune for the care of foundlings and orphaned children, as directed in Oahspe's Book of Shalam. On 1,490 acres in Mesilla Valley, on the east bank of the Rio Grande, the Children's Land of Shalam adopted fifty small children, from African to Chinese, between 1887 and 1900. After the leader's death in 1891, Mrs. Newbrough and Andrew M. Howland, who provided most of the funds, continued the mission until its dissolution in 1901. The children were sent to individual homes and orphanages in the Southwest.

189. Kaweah Co-operative Commonwealth (later reorganized as Industrial Co-operative Union of Kaweah),* (1885-1892), near Visalia (now part of Sequoia National Park), Tulare County, California.

Organized by James J. Martin and Burnette Haskell,* the two labor leaders of the International Workingmen's Association in San Francisco, this socialist colony sprang up from Laurence Gronlund's* *Cooperative Commonwealth,* a book that attempted to translate Marx into practical American terms. Taking advantage of the Timber Act of 1878 and the Homestead Act of 1862, over forty men, mostly skilled laborers from trade unions, filed claims on six hundred acres of the great timber belt of Sierra Nevada in northeastern Tulare County. In the course of its seven years' existence, there were altogether about four hundred members, most of whom were affiliated with the Bellamy* movement. The colony survived the mass withdrawals of fifty members and an internal split until the U.S. government evicted the colonists to found Sequoia Park.

190. Columbia Co-operative Colony (later renamed Nehalem Valley Co-operative Colony) (1886-ca. 1892), Mist, Columbia County, Oregon.

Although the Nehalem Valley Co-operative Colony and the Columbia Co-operative Colony are separately listed by Julia E. Williams, the former was actually the name of the latter when it was incorporated in September 1889. Judging from its constitution, the colony was communal, but the source of its fifty members is unknown. As late as 1892, the Nehalem Valley Co-operative Colony was listed in the directory as owner of a sawmill.

191. Jamesville Colony—Hutterites* (1886-1918), near Utica, Yankton County, South Dakota (later moved to Rockyford, Alberta, Canada).

This is the second *Dariusleut* colony that branched off the Wolf Creek Colony (No. 160). After refusing to buy Liberty Bonds, the colony was raided by local citizens in 1918. The increasing hostility of their neighbors and their inability to obtain conscientious objector status for their members caused Jamesville to be moved to Alberta, Canada. (In 1898, when the Spanish-American War broke out, the *Dariusleut* established a colony near Dominion City, Manitoba, with the intention, in the event of military conscription, of moving to Canada.)

192. Milltown Colony—Hutterites* (1886-1907), Milltown, Hutchinson County, South Dakota.

Returning to South Dakota from an ill-fated trial in Pennsylvania (No. 187), the original *Schmiedeleut* group of Tripp (No. 172) founded the Milltown Colony on the James River. The colony moved again ten years later to a new site in Beadle County.

193. Puget Sound Cooperative Colony (1887-1890), Port Angeles, Clallam County, Washington.

The nucleus of the anti-Chinese movement among the working class in Seattle established a model city based on cooperation. The colony published a newspaper called the *Model Commonwealth*. The four hundred members in 1887 were mainly from Washington and the Midwest, including a dozen or so families from Union Colony* (No. 146). Disputes over management of properties caused constant turnover of leadership. By 1890, many members were drifting away, some to a recently opened reservation.

194. Koreshan Unity—Chicago (1888-1903), Chicago, Cook County, Illinois.

This was the first of the Koreshan Unity settlements founded by Cyrus R. Teed,* a physician who had earlier tried a small colony in Moravia, New York, where he practiced. In 1878, he visited Economy (No. 28) to study the organization of the successful commune. In 1886, he and his disciples moved to Chicago where they established a church initially named the Assembly of the Covenant and an educational institution called the World's College of Life; the two were combined in 1888 into a cooperative home for his seventy-some followers. He also established a cooperative business organization, the Bureau of Equitable Commerce, to encourage laborers to join the Unity. A union of the Koreshans and the then declining Shakers was proposed in 1892 but came to nothing. The Chicago home remained active until its one hundred members relocated to Florida (No. 206) in 1903.

195. Lord's Farm, or Woodcliff Community* (1889†-ca. 1907), Woodcliff Lake, Bergen County, New Jersey.

This loosely organized commune of vegetarian celibates lived on twenty-three acres under the leadership of Paul Blandin Mnason (formerly Mason T. Huntsman*). Although the regular membership remained small, numbering twenty-seven men, eight women, and five children in 1906, there were numerous others, mostly socialists and anarchists from all over the country, who paid extended visits to the farm. At various times, Brother Paul was arrested for violations such as Sabbath-breaking and blasphemy, conspiracy to defraud and running a disorderly house, kidnapping, and rape. The leader was evicted by his brother, and soon the farm disbanded.

†It appears that a precursor of the community started sometime earlier than 1889.

196. Koreshan Unity—San Francisco (1890-1891), San Francisco, San Francisco County, California.

Another community of the Koreshans was organized in San Francisco by the Chicago group called the Golden Gate Assembly of the Koreshan Unity. This colony included branches of the College of Life, the Bureau of Equitable Commerce, and the Guiding Star Publishing House. The Guiding Star issued its newspaper, first called the *Pruning Hook,* later the *Plowshare and Pruning Hook.* Upon the colony's dissolution late in 1891, the remaining members joined the Unity group in Chicago (No. 194).

197. Kutter Colony—Hutterites* (1890-1918), near Mitchell, Hanson County, South Dakota (later moved to Redlands, Alberta, Canada).

This is the third colony of the *Dariusleut* which branched off from the Wolf Creek Colony (No. 160).

198. Rockport Colony—Hutterites* (1891-1934), near Alexandria, Hanson County, South Dakota (later moved to Magrath, Alberta, Canada).

The *Lehrerleut,* generally wanting larger colonies than the two other groups, established a first daughter colony, Rockport, about six miles north of the parent colony of Old Elmspring (No. 167). Part of the colony moved to Alberta in 1918. When the remaining members left for Alberta, the *Schmiedeleut* of Bon Homme (No. 156) purchased its facilities for a daughter colony in 1934.

199. Union Mill Company (1891-1897), Nehalem, Tillamook County, Oregon.

In 1891, Daniel Cornen and his wife Catherine filed the deed to the Union Mill Company. According to Alexander Kent's brief description (which seems to be the only second-hand information on this commune), all property was held in common and lumbering was carried on cooperatively with equal pay among all members. The sheriff's deed of 1897 attests to the seizure of all the right to the company's property. While this community appears to resemble the Nehalem Valley Co-operative Colony (No. 192) established earlier in the adjacent county, it is not clear if they were connected.

200. Co-operative Brotherhood of Winters Island (1893-ca. 1898), upper portion of Suisun Bay (two miles west of Antioch), Contra Costa County, California.

Erastus Kelsey, a leader of the Oakland Nationalist Club during the early 1890s and owner of Winters Island (640 acres), founded a colony along the pattern of Kaweah* (No. 189). The Articles of Incorporation of 1893 stipulated the maximum number of the members at one hundred, with a monthly membership fee of $5 for one hundred months. However, only eighty-six signed the Articles and twenty-two members resided in 1896. The *Winters Island Co-operator,* published monthly by the colony, reported news about the Ruskin Co-operative Colony (No. 204) with close affinity. Due to inability to pay monthly dues in the depression following the Panic of 1893, few members remained by 1898.

201. Hiawatha Village Association (1893-1896), Hiawatha, Schoolcraft County, Michigan.

The Hiawatha colony grew directly out of *The Product Sharing Village,* written by Walter T. Mills, a peripatetic socialist educator. Upon reading Mills' work, several pioneering families who had already settled in upper Michigan invited him to be president of a communal experiment in which all were to work together and everything was to be divided evenly. Some later came from Chicago after hearing Mills' lectures. The colony had 1,080 acres of hardwood land and over two hundred people, who paid $100 in cash, land, or personal property. Mills withdrew in late 1895; dissension among the members who did not want equalization led to abandonment.

202. Shaker Community at Narcoossee (1894-1912), Narcoossee, Runnymede Township, Osceola County, Florida.

Established by a small delegation from the Watervliet community (No. 2) near Albany, New York, the "Olive Branch," as it was referred to by the Shakers, occupied a total of 7,046 acres in Osceola County. The group of about 24 believers mainly relied on the production of pineapples, citrus fruits, fish, and cattle. There was a great deal of interest among the Koreshans (No. 206) in Shakerism, and there was much visiting between these two celibate communes. One of the Koreshan adherents joined the Narcoossee community in 1906. When the original members began to grow old, they dissolved the communal arrangement, as was the fate for other Shaker colonies.

203. Altruria* (1894-1895), Mark West Creek (six miles north of Santa Rosa), Sonoma County, California.

Settled just a few miles from Fountain Grove (No. 163) was a group of Christian Socialists led by Edward Biron Payne,* a Unitarian minister from Berkeley. It was a small group, some six or seven families and a half dozen bachelors, mostly middle-class artisans; there was a network of local clubs linked by its communal organ, *The Altrurian.* After seven months, the colony was divided into three smaller groups. A band of sixteen settled on an eighty-acre farm west of Cloverdale, another section moved to Santa Rosa, and fourteen members remained at Altruria on 185 acres of wooded land. All three groups were discontinued within a year as they failed to turn a profit.

204. Ruskin Cooperative Association* (1894-1899), Tennessee City and Ruskin, Dickinson County, Tennessee.

The first Ruskin colony was formed largely through the efforts of Julius A. Wayland,* publisher of *The Coming Nation* (circulation over fifty thousand in 1894), a socialist weekly which provided the main income for the colony. The first site of the colony was on two adjoining five hundred-acre tracts near Tennessee City about fifty miles west of Nashville. Late in 1895, the colony bought additional property of eight hundred acres in the Yellow Creek Valley, five miles north of the original site. The move was completed by the beginning of 1897. The population of the colony had increased to over two hundred, with the majority of adults between thirty and forty years of age. Members came from at least thirty-two states, with Ohio and Pennsylvania most heavily represented. During its five years of existence, there was a constant turnover of membership. Of thirty-three who joined in 1895, only four were members in 1899. A few families who withdrew in the fall of 1897 and early 1898 formed a new colony at Dixie on the Tennessee River, which lasted only until the end of the year. Conflict between original members, who were middle-class urbanites with an intellectual interest in socialism, and the latecomers, predominantly from rural areas or the depressed working class, gradually split the colony into three factions. (Wayland, the founder, departed bitterly disillusioned after a year, though the newspaper remained in the colony.) The majority group voted to abolish the Ruskin Cooperative Association and to create a new colony, the Ruskin Commonwealth (No. 223). About a dozen families joined a single tax colony at Fairhope* (No. 211), one or two moved to another socialist colony at Burley (No. 218) in Washington, while others gave up a communal life.

205. Colorado Cooperative Company* (1894-1910), Nucla, Montrose County, Colorado.

The colony aimed at reclaiming by irrigation some twenty thousand acres of desert in Tabegauche Park in southwestern Colorado. It was based on Henry George's single tax system of land tenure (see the Fairhope Industrial Association,* No. 211). Cash received from membership, a fee of $100 per share per person, was used to purchase tools and supplies. There were about four hundred stockholders, only one-fourth of whom actually engaged in the irrigation project. When it was completed in 1910, the cooperative features were replaced by a town company under the title of the Nucla Town Improvement Company. Several members still interested in the communal experiment joined the Newllano Cooperative Colony (No. 269) in Louisiana. Although a weekly newspaper published by the Colorado Cooperative Company was called *The Altrurian,* it is doubtful that it was connected with a California commune whose paper had the same title (see Altruria,* No. 203).

206. Koreshan Unity—Estero (1894-present), Estero, Lee County, Florida.

Estero, the third and final† settlement of the Koreshan Unity, was first organized as a branch colony of the Chicago community (No. 194). The original 320 acres (later increased to two thousand acres), sixteen miles south of Fort Myers, was donated by an earlier settler who subsequently became a member. By 1904, the entire Chicago group relocated to Florida to make Estero the site of its New Jerusalem, comprising about two hundred members. Active in local politics, in 1906 the Unity established the Progressive Liberty party, with its organ called the *American Eagle.* After Cyrus Teed's* death in late 1908, the Koreshans, who were "so united in spirit and so confident of the fulfillment of all their hopes," split into warring factions. Mrs. Annie G. Ordway, perhaps Teed's most trusted disciple from the early days in Chicago, led a band of her followers to establish a Koreshan community in Hilsborough County, Florida, but it quickly dissolved. Another group of dissidents formed a new colony in Fort Myers (No. 252). Although about 130 remaining members stayed at Estero to continue communal life, the Unity never prospered again. The membership declined to sixty in 1928 and a dozen in 1948. The Unity donated the major portion of the land to the state, which, in 1967, became Koreshan State Park.

†Immediately before the death of Cyrus Teed, a new Koreshan colony was established in Washington, D.C., in 1908. Whether it had regular residents is not clear.

207. Home Employment Co-operative Company (1894-ca. 1906), Long Lane, Dallas County, Missouri.

After the collapse of the Bennett Co-operative Colony (No. 154) around 1877, William H. Bennett rekindled his communitarian zeal along the lines of the Ruskin colony (No. 204). The colony remained small but increased from the original three members to about twenty. It is not known whether the 180-acre tract which the colony owned was situated on the previous colony site. Bennett and his wife liquidated their holdings sometime between 1904 and 1906 and moved to Arkansas. Little else is known about this colony.

208. Glennis Cooperative Industrial Company† (1894-1896), Eatonville, Pierce County, Washington.

Inspired by the Bellamy* Nationalist movement, the colony was founded on 166 homestead acres about seventeen miles south of Tacoma and at one time had some thirty members. Because of all kinds of bylaws restricting the communal life that were in reality "private matters," the colony quickly disbanded. Many left. A few tried another experiment based on their experience at Glennis and founded the Home Colony* (No. 222) on the other side of Tacoma.

†This colony is mentioned only briefly in reference to the Home Colony, and there appears to be no record or study devoted fully to Glennis.

209. Israelites, or New House of Israel (1895-ca. 1920), between the towns of Livingston and Leggett, Polk County, Texas.

In search of a Promised Land, the Canadian sect known as the Flying Roll, or Israelites, settled on a 144-acre tract donated by a local family in east Texas. The vegetarian group that followed the Mosaic law recruited seventy-five local families around 1900. They built a church which they named the New House of Israel. The male members had long hair and beards. After the death of the "high priest," no one took the leadership role and families began moving away. Israel became a ghost town in the early 1920s.

210. Willard Co-operative Colony (1895-1896), Andrews, Cherokee County, North Carolina.

Organized in Harriman, Roane County, Tennessee, about fifty prohibitionists sought a better environment than a capitalist society in which to educate their children. The colony was named after Frances Willard, the founder of the Women's Christian Temperance Union in Harriman, which still enforces prohibition today. William C. Damon and Ralph Albertson,* the leaders, worked out plans for "The People's University" there. After two years of struggle, the colony disbanded. Many of the members, under the leadership of Albertson, joined the Christian Commonwealth* (No. 214).

211. Fairhope Industrial Association (later renamed the Fairhope Single Tax Corporation)* (1895-present†), Fairhope, Baldwin County, Alabama.

A group of four families met in Des Moines, Iowa, in 1893 to establish a colony on the eastern shore of Mobile Bay. Their goal was to apply Henry George's single tax principles, as far as possible under existing laws. Under the system, land and ground rent are treated as common property and used for the common good. All public utilities are owned and operated by the colony. Other cooperative features in the early days included a cooperative store, a steamer, a wharf, and the Fairhope Exchange, organized to facilitate the exchange of products and services. Most of these had a relatively brief existence. The municipality of Fairhope was incorporated in 1908, covering eleven thousand acres, 40 percent of which belonged to the enclave, the rest privately owned. Funds for initial expenses and the purchase of land were raised by a membership fee of $200 (reduced to $100 after the colony located), and were paid mostly in monthly installments of $5. In 1915, there were about 130 leaseholders averaging about a half acre each, and about 100 dwellings on 120 plots. Today the corporation's land constitutes about 15 percent of the total lands of Fairhope.

†It is evident that since the early days of the settlement many cooperative features have disappeared from the Fairhope Single Tax Colony. The colony is cooperative today only in terms of its landholding, not in terms of the social life. Therefore, it is debatable whether the Fairhope Single Tax Colony as it exists today can still be considered a "legitimate" communal organization.

212. Christian Corporation (1896†-1897), Lincoln, Lancaster County, Nebraska.

This colony was founded by George Howard Gibson,* an advocate of Christian Socialism. In *The Kingdom,* a small socialist magazine, he wrote in 1896: "Earlier American colonies had failed, for example, the Brook Farm, because they were imperfectly Christian." Gibson and his group of twenty-six persons joined the Christian Commonwealth* (No. 214) in the summer of 1897 after a difficult three-month journey in prairie schooners.

†This small Christian commune was probably founded a few years earlier. There is no record of its beginning.

213. Magnolia at Shepherd, Texas (1896).

This short-lived colony was also known as the East Texas Cooperative Association. Scattered references indicate that it started with 479 acres and that it began "practical operations" on April 1, 1896. One reason given for its failure was a low membership fee of $300, according to the *Coming Nation.*

214. Christian Commonwealth Colony* (1896-1900), Commonwealth (twelve miles east of Columbus), Muskogee County, Georgia.

About twenty-five families responded to Ralph Albertson's* series of articles in *The Kingdom* (1895-1896) on socialism, property, and the relation of Christianity to social problems. They settled on the 934 acres of an old plantation in west-central Georgia. The membership included those who had come from the Willard Co-operative Colony (No. 210) and the Christian Corporation (No. 212). Among sixty-four adult members were twenty-three unmarried men and ten unmarried women. The Commonwealth lasted four years and had the usual problems with membership (most came emptyhanded and few added much to the financial strength of the colony), economics, and eventually the courts. Their noteworthy success was its periodical, *The Social Gospel,* with a circulation of two thousand and so widely known that it became the accepted name for Social Christianity. About seventeen members joined the Southern Co-operative Association (No. 234) in Florida after the Commonwealth disbanded.

215. Freedom Colony (1897-1905), six miles northwest of Fulton, Bourbon County, Kansas.

Organized as Branch 199 of the General Labor Exchange Organization with headquarters in Independence, Missouri, fourteen families purchased 160 acres on the Osage River bottom, a short distance from the Missouri state line. Only members of the General Labor Exchange organization were admitted to membership. To avoid conflicting with laws, the exchange script issued by the colony was printed in denominations of "one-half," "one-quarter," "one-tenth," and so forth, without the mention of dollars. The colony was important enough to warrant a visit by Eugene Debs, the perennial Socialist presidential candidate and labor leader. One member, Carl Browne, ran unsuccessfully for the U.S. Congress while at the colony. A fire in 1905 ended the colony.

216. Equality, or Brotherhood of the Cooperative Commonwealth (later reorganized as Freeland) (1897-1907), Equality (two miles southwest of Edison), Skagit County, Washington.

The precursor of the colony was organized by Eastern reformers in 1895 as the Brotherhood of the Cooperative Commonwealth with a plan for a socialized state. The Equality Colony, named after Edward Bellamy's* novel of that name, was the first of numerous colonies which the Brotherhood was to establish in Washington. For a short period the Brotherhood of Cooperative Commonwealth No. 2 colony existed at Edison. Another planned colony by a small group of Populists in Lewis County, called Harmony Colony, failed to develop. The membership increased rapidly during 1897, from 115 in March to 300 in November, and came from the Midwest, South, Pacific Coast, and nearby Northwestern states. At its peak there were over three thousand nonresident members who paid dues to the Brotherhood. Prior to the colony's publishing *Industrial Freedom,* the Ruskin colony's *The Coming Nation* (No. 204) was used as the colony's mouthpiece. Frequent contacts were maintained with nearby colonies, especially with Burley* (No. 218), the socialist colony on Puget Sound. When the membership declined to thirty-eight in 1904, the colony came under the influence of a small band of newly arrived anarchists from New York. Revising the constitution along the lines of Theodor Hertzka's Freeland movement, the colony quickly divided into two factions. After two years of bitter legal fights, the colony was dissolved by court order.

217. American Settlers Association, or Duke Colony (1898-1899), Duke (now Ruskin), Ware County, Georgia.

This community was organized in Dayton, Ohio, by a group of poor farmers and originally consisted of nine families who moved to Okefenokee land in southeastern Georgia. At first there was no communal aspect in its organization, but when it became necessary to clear 760 acres of timber land, the work became cooperative. "Each for all and all for each" was the colony's motto. It was later joined by several families from Indiana. In 1899, Duke Colony merged with the Ruskin Commonwealth (No. 223), following the latter's re-

organization from the Ruskin Cooperative Association* (No. 204) and reloca-
tion from Tennessee.

218. Cooperative Brotherhood,* or Burley Colony (1898-1908), Burley, Kitsap
County, Washington.

A year after a founding convention in June 1897 organized by the colonization
commission of the Social Democracy of America, along with Populists in the
East, the socialist colony at Burley was started immediately after the leaders'
visit to the Ruskin colony (No. 204) in Tennessee. The population of the colony
reached one hundred fifteen in 1901, forty-five of them men, twenty-five
women, and forty-five children; these figures remained fairly stable for several
years. There were also nonresident members, numbering over one thousand at
one time. In early 1904, the colony was reorganized, and much of the original
communal concept disappeared, though the newly organized Burley Mercantile
Rochdale Association continued to exist until 1908. Cyrus F. Willard,* one of
the founders, and some of those who belonged to the Theosophist Club at the
colony, later joined the theosophists at Point Loma* (No. 219). Throughout its
existence, the Burley Colony maintained frequent contacts with the Equality
(No. 216) and the Home* (No. 222) colonies.

219. Point Loma,* or the Universal Brotherhood and Theosophical Society (1898-
1942), Point Loma (site now occupied by Point Loma College), San Diego
County, California.

The Point Loma community, the first of three splinter theosophical groups
founded in southern California, originated in Helena Petrovna Blavatsky's
theosophy, a mix of New England transcendentalism and Eastern mysticism.
Organized in New York in 1875, the Theosophical Society supported, for a
brief period during the 1880s, Bellamy's* Nationalism in the reform movements.
Katherine Tingley,* who took control of the society after the death of Blavatsky's successor, established Point Loma on 330 acres of peninsula protecting
San Diego Bay. By 1910, membership reached about five hundred, nearly
three hundred of whom were children in the Raja-Yoga School, an important
experiment which Point Loma started in 1900. Over seventy-five small children
were recruited from Cuba during 1901-1902. The colony prospered for many
years, but its fortunes began to decline in the mid-1920s. All holdings, including
a huge domed temple and the first Greek amphitheater in California, were
sold in 1942. Many left Point Loma; the remaining theosophists moved to
Covina, east of Los Angeles.

220. Shaker Community at White Oak (1898-1902), White Oak, Camden County,
Georgia.

A small colony of Believers, mostly from the Union Village Community
(No. 18) in Ohio, was established on four thousand acres in southeastern
Georgia in 1898. This was probably the last Shaker colony established, though
it was much smaller than any other Shaker group. The group had attempted to

settle in 1897 near Bruswick, Glynn County, Georgia, on some seven thousand acres. In 1902, the Georgia Shakers sold out and went back to Ohio.

221. Salvation Army Colonies* (1898-1910), Fort Amity, Colorado; Romie, California; Fort Herrick, Ohio.

These colonies were designed to help the urban unemployed get a new start by placing them on the land. Even though the colonies stressed the family unit and cooperated only minimally on economic matters, they were clearly utopian in character.

222. Mutual Home Association,* or the Home Colony (1898-1921), Carr Inlet (four miles southwest of Gig Harbor), Pierce County, Washington.

The Home, or an "anarchist colony" as contemporaries more commonly referred to it, was founded by the three who had participated in the Glennis Colony (No. 208). Except that land was held in common, the organizational structure was not highly communal. In fact, it was incorporated as a landholding company in 1898, and houses were considered private property. Despite the founders' denial that it was a cooperative colony, it had communal features, especially in its ideology. Reconverted socialists arrived from the defunct Ruskin Colony (No. 204) in Tennessee, the Cooperative Brotherhood (No. 218), the Puget Sound Cooperative Colony (No. 193), and the Equality Colony (No. 216). Visitors from other communes included the Koreshans in Chicago (No. 194) and Elbert Hubbard of the Roycrofters (No. 235) near Buffalo. Because of its anarchist leanings, the colony, which published a succession of anarchistic periodicals *(New Era, Discontent: Mother of Progress, Demonstrator,* and *Agitator),* was in constant trouble with local officials. Most notably, the Home became the target of public and press attacks following the assassination of President McKinley in 1901. Although the Mutual Home Association continued to be a community organization until its dissolution by court order, long before it had lost its singleness of community spirit.

223. Ruskin Commonwealth (1899-1901), Ruskin, Ware County, Georgia.

The majority group of the Ruskin Cooperative Association* (No. 204), having lost the land in Tennessee, joined the Duke colonists (No. 217) who had settled a year earlier in Georgia. Upon dissolving their organization, the Duke colonists became members of the Ruskin Commonwealth. The new Ruskin colony, with over one thousand acres and a membership of three hundred, resumed publication of *The Coming Nation.* However, before they were able to organize community life completely, fire, malaria, and suspicious neighbors brought their colony to an end.

224. Straight Edge Industrial Settlement* (1899-1918), New York City, New York.

This settlement was for the most part an experiment in cooperative enterprise. In the beginning, for economic reasons only a small group of a dozen or so Straight-Edgers participated in communal living. Wilbur F. Copeland,* who, though not a resident, had been associated with the Christian Commonwealth* (No. 214), started "A School of Methods for the Application of the Teachings of Jesus to Business and Society." It was a school of cooperative industry in various fields of trade. The settlement also ran cooperative farms on Staten Island and later in Alpine, Bergen County, New Jersey. It appears that communal life disappeared around 1906, although the industrial organization continued to exist until 1918.

225. Friedheim (1899-1900), Virginia (exact location unknown).

This religious community is listed in Frederick A. Bushee's list of communistic societies in the United States with a note that Friedheim failed because of "Human weakness, lack of intelligence." Bushee fails to give his source for that information. The author's search for local records turned up nothing.

226. Lystra (1899-1902), Virginia (exact location unknown).

Another religious community appears in Bushee's list with no further information. As in the case of Freidheim (No. 225), the author's search of local records was fruitless.

227. Commonwealth of Israel† (1899-ca. 1900), Mason County (exact location unknown), Texas.

The Baptist commune was situated on nine hundred acres in central Texas, with a membership of 150 in 1901. The colony's post office, named Adullam, lasted until 1902; thus, the Commonwealth appears to have ended then. Little else is known about this religious community.

†The group called the Israelites, No. 209, in Polk County may have been part of the same movement, but they appear to be two separate settlements.

228. Christian Social Association (1899-1904), Wisconsin (exact location unknown).

This community is listed in Bushee's article with a note that it had forty-eight members, and disbanded due to the defection of members. The author has been unable to confirm its existence through any written documents of the State Historical Society of Wisconsin.

229. Spirit Fruit Society (1899-1908), Lisbon, Elkrun Township, Columbiana County, Ohio (later moved to Ingleside, Lake County, Illinois).

Jacob Beilhart,* a Second Adventist who turned faith healer, organized a small gathering of thirteen followers into a spiritualist-theosophist colony. The Home, as it was referred to by neighbors, was often the target of criticism by the press because of its renunciation of the conventional marriage. In 1905, Beilhart and his following, some of whom were recruited locally in Lisbon, were forced to leave the farm and relocated on a ninety-acre farm near Chicago. Beilhart had lectured at the Roycrofters (No. 235). After his death in 1908, the Spirit Fruit Society lasted for a few years, but by 1920 most of the group had moved elsewhere.

230. Niksur Co-operative Association (1899), Lawrence (now Wahkon), Mille Lacs County, Minnesota.

A group of fifteen Minnesota socialists established a colony patterned after the Ruskin Cooperative Association (No. 204) in Tennessee and the Equality Colony (No. 216) in Washington. Two tailors, who were the first to settle on a site on the southwestern shore of Lake Mille Lacs, were to start a tailor shop for the benefit of the community. It appears that the colony lasted less than a few months. The failure of the Ruskin socialists discouraged the Niksurs from continuing.

231. Kinder Lou (1900-1901), Kinderlou (four miles west of Valdosta), Lowndes County, Georgia.

Realizing that the new Ruskin colony (No. 223) in Georgia was not located on a healthy site, a few families moved to Kinderlou, about sixty miles southwest of Ruskin, to organize their own Ruskin. This group of Ruskinites informally established a communal life. As they found employment in a local lumber company the idea of formalizing the colony disappeared.

232. Freeland Association (1900-ca. 1906), Freeland, Whidby Island, Island County, Washington.

Disenchanted members of Equality (No. 216) started a less formally organized experiment on the eastern shore of Whidby Island. Some came from another socialist colony at Burley* (No. 218). Freeland was a gathering of like-minded radicals to retain a socialist entity outside the confines of a regimented communal existence. Although there seems no clearcut date for its termination, some documents suggest that it ended in 1906. Some members who turned spiritualists joined the theosophists at Halcyon (No. 241) in California.

233. Arden (1900-present), Arden, New Castle County, Delaware.

The second single tax colony was formed by the Philadelphia Georgeists in Delaware, six miles north of Wilmington. Although the colony did little more than hold its own for the first few years, by 1915 there were 130 leaseholders averaging about a half acre each and about one hundred dwellings on 120 plots. Today seventy-two acres of residential land is owned by the trustees; the remaining ninety acres is owned communally through the incorporated village of Arden. The idea of an experimental community based on the single tax was extended in 1922, with the creation of Ardentown (one hundred and ten acres) and later, in 1950, Ardencroft (sixty-three acres). Ardencroft was established to integrate the community with blacks.

234. Southern Co-operative Association of Apalachicola, or Co-operative Association of America (1900-ca. 1904), Apalachicola, East Point, Franklin County, Florida.

Originally called the Brotherhood of the New Age, a Swedenborgian association, this experiment in cooperative living was part of a grandiose scheme of the National Production Company to change the basis of society. Under the leadership of Harry C. Vrooman, the colony secured seventeen hundred acres on Apalachicola Bay. The seventeen members were mainly refugees from the defunct Christian Commonwealth* (No. 214) in Georgia. The Co-operative Association of America, the parent organization, was involved in a variety of cooperative ventures in Missouri, Maine, Illinois, and Massachusetts. Apparently, the colony in Florida came to an end when Vrooman left for Indianapolis in 1904.

235. The Roycrofters (1900-1915†), East Aurora, Erie County, New York.

This was a unique case of a profit-sharing "semi-communistic corporation," as it was described by its founder Elbert Hubbard. Between three hundred and five hundred people worked on a farm, in a bank, printing plant, bookbindery, furniture factory, and blacksmith shop. Some lived in the quarters called the Roycroft Phalanstery. All of the company's proceeds, including a considerable profit from the multimillion sales of the inspirational and patriotic pamphlet published after the Spanish-American War, "A Message to Garcia," went, according to Hubbard, "into the common fund of The Roycrofters—the benefit is for all." During one of his lecture tours around the country, Hubbard visited the Home* (No. 222) in Washington, and one of the Roycroft families joined the Home.
  †With the death of Hubbard aboard the "Lusitania" in 1915, colony features disappeared, and the community became a purely commercial enterprise.

236. Maxwell Colony—Hutterites* (1900-1918), Hutchinson County, South Dakota (later moved to Headingly, Manitoba, Canada).

The second daughter colony of Bon Homme (No. 156) and the fifth *Schmiedeleut* was established on the James River. Although the colony moved to Manitoba during World War I, part of the original Maxwell Hutterites returned to South Dakota in 1936.

237. New Elmspring Colony—Hutterites* (1900-1918), near Ethan, Hutchinson-Hanson County line, South Dakota (later moved to Magrath, Alberta, Canada).

The third *Lehrerleut* colony branched off from Old Elmspring (No. 167).

238. Zion City, or Christian Catholic Apostolic Church in Zion (1901-1906), Zion, Benton Township, Lake County, Illinois.

Following a successful career in faith-healing, John Alexander Dowie,† a Scot from Edinburgh, organized Zion City on Lake Michigan, forty-two miles north of Chicago, to isolate his followers from the world. It was not, however, a simple withdrawal from the outside world, for Zion's political wing, the Theocratic party (formed in 1902), was intended to reform American politics. Under Dowie's autocratic rule, Zion, with its peak population of eight thousand, grew rapidly. Such businesses as the Zion City bank, general stores, planing mill, brickyards, fresh fruit supply, laundry, and lace industries, were all under Dowie's absolute ownership. While Zion City was a self-contained colony, the Dowieites did not maintain such communal features as communal housing and dining, which are so often associated with utopian life. As Dowie's finances became shaky, his kingdom revolted against and deposed him in 1906.

†After the fall of the prophet, the name of Dowie was scratched from the Zion literature, and "apostolic" was dropped from the title of the organization.)

239. Rosedale Colony—Hutterites* (1901-1918), Hanson County, South Dakota (later moved to Elie, Manitoba, Canada).

This was the first *Schmiedeleut* granddaughter colony from the Milltown Colony (No. 192).

240. House of David (1903-1928), Benton Harbor, Berrien County, Michigan.

The Israelite House of David, founded by "Queen Mary and King Benjamin" Purnell,* derived from the Hebrew Scriptures. Their followers numbered about five hundred in 1907 and close to one thousand at its peak. Some members came from branches in Australia and England. With growing prosperity, a thousand-acre tract they owned included several large buildings, an auditorium, cannery and drying house, steam laundry, carpenter shop, tailor shop, coach factory, automobile house, and power house. The expected arrival of Jesus, King Benjamin's older brother, did not come as predicted in 1916 to begin the millennium at the commune. A rift developed between the "king's" adherents and his detractors, which eventually led to a lawsuit in 1920. After Benjamin's death in 1927, the commune was divided between Mary's group, which set up the City of David, and another faction, which continued as the House of David.

241. Temple Home Association, or Halcyon Theosophists (1903-1913), Halcyon, San Luis Obispo County, California.

William H. Dower's group of theosophists, rejecting Katherine Tingley* as successor of the Theosophical Society (No. 217), formed the Temple Home Association in southwestern Arroyo Grande Valley, relocating from Syracuse, New York. About forty-four original members settled on three hundred acres north of Santa Barbara. The Home had about 140 residents in 1906 and owned the Halcyon sanatorium and hotel. Each member received half an acre to farm on his own, but all land and means of production were owned by the colony. Financial difficulties eventually forced the end of the cooperative venture, but the temple of the theosophist organization still exists.

242. Spink Colony—Hutterites* (1905-1918), Spink County, South Dakota (later moved to Fort MacLeod, Alberta, Canada).

The fourth *Dariusleut* colony was established from the Wolf Creek Colony (No. 160) in Spink County, where hostility to the Hutterites proved to be most severe.

243. Beadle Colony—Hutterites (1905-1918), Beadle County, South Dakota (later moved to West Raley, Alberta, Canada).

The Dominion City group (see Jamesville Colony, No. 191) in Manitoba moved back to South Dakota because of poor land, floods, and distance from other Hutterite colonies. It was situated south of Spink Colony (No. 242) in Beadle County, another area hostile to the Hutterites. They were joined by a few families from Wolf Creek (No. 160).

244. Huron Colony—Hutterites (1906-1918), Huron, Beadle County, South Dakota (later moved to Elie, Manitoba, Canada).

This was the third daughter colony of Bon Homme (No. 156). After World War I, the Huron Colony site was sold to a small *Dariusleut* group that came from Spring Creek, Montana (No. 258) via Canada to settle once again in South Dakota in 1920.

245. Richards Colony—Hutterites* (1906-1918), Sanborn County, South Dakota (later moved to Lethbridge, Alberta, Canada).

This was the fifth *Dariusleut* colony to emerge from the Wolf Creek Colony (No. 160).

246. Helicon Hall Colony* (1906-1907), near Englewood, Bergen County, New Jersey.

Five months after a plan announced in the *New York Independent* in June 1906, Upton Sinclair* organized a group of young literary couples into co-operative life. The colony was situated on a nine-acre former boys' school on the western brow of the Palisades. Among forty-six adults and fifteen children were Sinclair Lewis and others who became well-known writers. In March 1907, fire abruptly ended the dream-like socialist colony only six months after it began.

247. Buffalo Colony—Hutterites* (1907-1913), Beadle County, South Dakota.

The second *Schmiedeleut* granddaughter colony from Milltown (No. 192) was founded in Beadle County. It was moved to James Valley (No. 261) in 1913.

248. Fellowship Farm Association (1907-1918), Westwood, Norfolk County, Massachusetts.

Settled on a seventy-acre tract, about twelve miles southwest of Boston, the farm was organized by George E. Littlefield, a Unitarian minister. Each of the forty members was assigned an acre; the rest was common land. Most members were skilled tradesmen who cooperated in house building. A simple one-room house cost only $16.

249. Little Landers Colony No. 1*† (1909-1916), San Ysidro (site now partly occupied by the United States Naturalization and Immigration Office), San Diego County, California.

With support from the California Promotion Committee, William E. Smythe,* renowned leader of the national reclamation movement, organized a settlement of the Little Landers. The colony's land, originally 120 and later 500 acres, was in the Tiajuana Valley, fourteen miles south of San Diego, facing the hills of Mexico. Each settler held his own land, usually an acre, but the community living was carried on cooperatively as much as the members were willing, without any formal structure. Membership expanded, and by the fourth year there were 116 families, three hundred people in all, largely middle-aged and elderly. The cooperative store was established in the heart of San Diego to sell produce. The Little Landers were confident that their social ideal and settlements were becoming permanent in the San Diego area. But the 1916 flood caused the loss of all the houses at the colony.

†Besides San Ysidro, there were at least four other Little Landers colonies: (1) Runnymede near Palo Alto, (2) Hayward Heath in Alameda County, (3) San Fernando Valley, and (4) Cupertino near San Jose.

250. Tahanto (1909-1934), Harvard, Worcester County, Massachusetts.

First of a series of single tax colonies established by Fiske Warren, a wealthy paper manufacturer, the enclave was about thirty-two miles west of Boston. The single tax landholding of Tahanto increased from 116 acres in 1912 to 611 in 1921. The Rochdale Society of Tahanto was organized in 1915.

251. Milford Colony—Hutterites* (1910-1918), Beadle County, South Dakota (later moved to Raymond, Alberta, Canada).

This was the fourth *Lehrerleut* colony to branch off from Old Elmspring (No. 167). The *Lehrerleut* group experienced no further expansion before their migration to Canada during World War I.

252. Order of Theocracy (1910-1931), Fort Myers, Lee County, Florida.

Seceders from the Koreshan Unity (No. 206), who lost the struggle for leadership in the post-Teed* era, established their own commune. Although their organizational structure and religious principles were quite similar to those of the Unity, the Order was bitter about the Estero group.

253. Free Acres Association (1910-1950), New Providence (now Berkeley Heights) Township, Union County, New Jersey.

The fourth single tax community was established on sixty acres of land donated by Bolton Hall, a Georgeist from New York. It was originally begun as a summer colony, but by the mid-1930s more than one hundred persons resided year-round. For their homesites, the residents paid a yearly tax, or rent, to the association. The association, in turn, paid taxes to the Township of New Providence. Social life developed around various community activities, such as the Folk's Guild, Dramatic Guild, and Arts and Crafts Guild.

254. Fruit Crest (1911-1912), Independence, Missouri.

This cooperative colony was planned by several socialists including C. B. Hoffman* and George Littlefield. A thirty-five-acre site was purchased in 1911. It was modeled after the Fellowship Farm (No. 248) colony at Westwood, Massachusetts. Another colony was planned at Everglades, Florida, but never materialized.

255. Halidon (1911-1938), Westbrook, Cumberland County, Maine.

This was another single tax colony organized by Fiske Warren (see Tahanto, No. 250). The enclave was on 172 acres of low plateau on the north bank of the Presumscot River, six miles west of Portland. One of the three trustees, or "representers," was an Arden Georgeist (No. 233). About half of forty members worked at Warren's paper mill. With Warren's death in 1938, the enclave seems to have disbanded.

256. Lopez Community (official name is unknown) (1912-ca. 1920), Lopez, Lopez Island, San Juan County, Washington.

This community comprised 175 "Come-Outers" settled on Lopez Island on Puget Sound. The fundamentalist colony lasted several years.

257. Krotona Community of Adyar Theosophists (1912-1924), Hollywood, Los Angeles County, California (later moved to Ojai, Ventura County, California).

The Adyar theosophical group originated in the Adyar branch of the Theosophical Society, India, led by Annie Besant after Madame Blavatsky's death (see Point Loma,* No. 217). Of three theosophical groups that practiced communal life in California, the Krotona Community was the last organized by Albert Powell Warrington, a close friend of Besant. In 1924, the colony moved to the Ojai Valley, where it operates a school of theosophy with branches in more than fifty countries.

258. Spring Creek Colony—Hutterites* (1912-1920), near Lewiston, Fergus County, Montana (later moved to Rockyford, Alberta, Canada).

The *Dariusleut* of the Wolf Creek Colony (No. 160), in an unprecedented move, established a colony of sixty people in central Montana, the first outside of South Dakota. Part of the Spring Creek colony moved to Alberta in 1919; others returned to Beadle County, South Dakota, in 1920.

259. Los Angeles Fellowship Farm (1912-1927), northeast of Puente, Los Angeles County, California.

Patterned after Littlefield's Fellowship Farm (No. 248) in Massachusetts, a group of twelve families settled on seventy-five acres in the La Puente Valley, about twenty miles east of Los Angeles. Each family had an acre for farming, and six central plots were used for communal activities. The colonists, finding cooperative farming unprofitable, dissolved the colony in 1927 and reorganized into the Maple Water Company.

260. Warren Range Colony—Hutterites* (1913-1918), Fergus County, Montana (later moved to Cardston, Alberta, Canada).

This was the second *Dariusleut* colony established in Montana by some colonists from Wolf Creek (No. 160) and some from Richards (No. 245).

261. James Valley Colony—Hutterites* (1913-1918), James Valley Junction, Beadle County, South Dakota (later moved to Elie, Manitoba, Canada).

This colony was the continuation of the Buffalo Colony (No. 247) of the *Schmiedeleut*.

262. Metropolitan Institute of Texas, or The Burning Bush* (1913-1919), one mile southeast of Bullard, Smith County, Texas.

A group of dissatisfied Methodists in Chicago, who founded the Metropolitan Church Association,† with headquarters in Waukesha, Wisconsin, purchased 1,520 acres in east Texas. The Burning Bush community had 375 members, whose occupational background varied widely, from farm laborers to professionals. "All wealth was held in common, and everyone who lived on the land ate from the common table," according to historian Edwin Smyrl. While the "Holy Jumpers," as neighbors called them because of their religious rituals, prospered for several years, the end came abruptly after World War I when the colony's financial backer lost his bond business in Chicago.

†Smyrl states that the association founded several other colonies in Virginia, West Virginia, and New Orleans.

263. Bohemian Co-operative Farming Company (1913-1916), one mile west of Mayland, Cumberland County, Tennessee.

A group of economically depressed Bohemian immigrants residing in urban centers of the North during the difficult years following the Panic of 1907 settled on a wooded tract of 5,300 acres of the Cumberland plateau in Tennessee. The settlement attempted to set up the village life they had known in their homeland. Instead of scattering houses on individual tracts, according to the prevailing American pattern, they grouped them in one spot. All land was held in common, and a common treasury and a common storehouse were maintained. With dissension between Camp 1 and Camp 2 and the return of prosperity in northern industrial areas, the settlement was abandoned.

264. Llano del Rio Company (1914-1918), Llano, Los Angeles County, California.

Job Harriman,* active in socialist politics in California since the early 1890s and a charter member of Altruria* (No. 203), established a cooperative colony for socialists and labor union members. Harriman and five other families settled on about two thousand acres of desert land in the Antelope Valley, about forty-five miles northeast of Los Angeles. By the end of the first year, an additional one hundred families came, most of whom originated from west of the Rocky Mountains. By 1917, the membership reached a phenomenal nine hundred, of whom 175 were enrolled in Llano schools. The recruitment of new members was mostly through the Llano promotional magazine *The Western Comrade*. While the colony's industries proliferated in much the same way as its social life, many members were hired as day laborers by neighboring farms because the colony's operations were small and unprofitable. Financial difficulties, conflict between nonresident directors and the resident members, and lawsuits against the colony ended the California site. In 1917, forty remaining members moved to a new location in Louisiana (No. 269).

265. Pisgah Grande (1914-1921), near Santa Susana, Ventura-Los Angeles County line, California.

Following the charitable activities for the downtrodden on the back streets of Los Angeles and various Pisgah institutions elsewhere, Finis E. Yoakum, a physician, established a Pentecostal Christian commune on a 3,200-acre cattle ranch in the Santa Susana Mountains. Among the three hundred residents were those recruited from the mission in Los Angeles, plus farmers, teachers, nurses, and artists. After Yoakum's death in 1920, the colony slowly crumbled. The Pisgah movement remained in Los Angeles for several years, and later the headquarters were moved to Pikeville, Tennessee.

266. Army of Industry (1914-1918), near Auburn, Placer County, California.

The precursor of this small socialist colony was the local Socialist Club at Auburn. As some members joined the Llano colony (No. 259) in southern California, Gerald Geraldson, a subscriber to the Kaweah colony* (No. 189) from 1890 to 1892, established a colony of about thirty members on a one hundred-acre fruit ranch in the orchard districts west of Auburn. As described by a participant, the colony comprised those " 'broke' people working together as one family, each one doing his or her share of the work according to ability in return for food, clothing, shelter, education, recreation, and other human rights according to available resources.'' Hampered by financial hardships from the beginning, the colony ceased its battle for the cooperative commonwealth in 1918. Geraldson later moved to New York City, where he opened a settlement house on the East Side.

267. Ferrer Colony* (1915-1946), Stelton (now Edison), Middlesex County, New Jersey.

This colony of anarchists originated in the Francisco Ferrer Association organized in New York in 1910. Nine of 143 acres situated near New Brunswick were used for the Modern School; other land was shared communally. By 1920, the membership totalled over one hundred families, many of whom were Russian Jews. One of the founders of the colony was Joseph Cohen,* who later established the Sunrise Colony* in Michigan. Other colony leaders included Harry Kelly* and Leonard Abbott.*

268. Llano del Rio Company of Nevada, or Nevada City (later renamed Nevada

Colony Corporation) (1916-1918), four miles east of Fallon, Churchill County, Nevada.

Although Nevada City was founded by C. V. Eggleston,* formerly a fiscal agent of the Llano colony in California (No. 264), and it had some former Llano members, the two were in many ways competitors. In fact, the Llano colony repeatedly repudiated its connection with the Nevada colony. The colony's 1,640 acres were not contiguous, being scattered twelve miles east, twelve miles west, and thirty-five miles north of the colony headquarters. The membership reached near two hundred at its peak in 1918. At least one of the Home Colony* (No. 222) families joined Nevada City. Financial mismanagement sent the colony into receivership in May 1919.

269. Newllano Co-operative Colony (1917-1938), Newllano, Vernon Parish, Louisiana.

Relocating from California (No. 264), about one hundred Llanoites, with twenty-five families from Texas, occupied an abandoned mill town of twenty thousand acres of cutover timber land owned by Gulf Lumber Company. Membership was small in the beginning, but with new members who came during the financial depression of 1920-1921 the colony expanded gradually, reaching a maximum of about five hundred in 1930. The financial status was never bright because of debts of about $145,000 from the California venture. To gain members who paid the admission fee of $2,000, Newllano became less selective in admission standards and thus became a producer's cooperative. Unlike the earlier cooperative structure in California, all household goods, houses, automobiles, and the like remained private property. The colony went bankrupt in 1936, and two years later was dissolved.

270. Holy City (1919-ca. 1958), Holy City, Santa Clara County, California.

With a proposal to rid California of "negroes and orientals," William E. Riker* established a colony with thirty followers of the Perfect Christian Divine Way. The new Zion was situated on two hundred acres in the Santa Cruz Mountains in central California. The community provided housing, clothing, meals, and the means of production. At its peak there were over two hundred converts. Riker's notoriety in court and the press, however, eventually caused a decline in the membership. Only twelve remained in 1952 after he was charged with sedition.

APPENDIX B: *Communal History in America: A Bibliographical Essay*

In 1973, the editors of *Choice,* a publication of the American Library Association, asked me to write an essay on utopian and communal history. At that time, there were few general essays that one could turn to for an overview of the literature. In fact, there was too little recognition at that time that such a literature existed.

The situation today is not the same as it was in 1973. The subject, whether called utopian studies, communal history, or future studies, has gained academic respectability. At least two professional organizations sponsor annual meetings, and papers on such subjects are given regularly at academic meetings. There is a journal, appropriately named *Alternative Futures,* which promotes interdisciplinary inquiry in this area and serves as an intellectual focus for utopian scholarship. That scholarship has proceeded along several fronts, and the study of communal history, theory, practice, and futures research constitutes a genuine interdisciplinary effort.

During the past fifteen years, collective schemes and societies have surfaced once again to suggest an alternative to our individual quests for health and happiness. Communes have been founded with such exotic names as Lama, Sons of Levi, Magic Mountain, Children of Light, Atlantis I, Walden Two, and the House of the Seventh Angel. During this period, northern New Mexico became dotted with communes as formerly placid villages from Truchas to Placitas found strange and wonderful visitors descending on them in search of "community." Some of the communards had clear notions about what that meant, while others believed it could be found by settling within fifty miles of the Sangre de Cristos and the Taos Pueblo. The tragedies associated with the followers of Charles Manson and Jim Jones reflect the darker side of communal life and alert the public to the potential dangers of collective life. A line from Jean Cocteau's *Beauty and the Beast* is an appropriate warning for those contemplating utopian projects: "My heart is good. But I am a monster." During this same fifteen-year period, other groups—most notably Synanon and the Unification church—have achieved a certain degree of economic security, despite the fact that some believe their philosophies are as immoral as that practiced at Jonestown. During the 1970s, there was a resurgence of interest among Christian and charismatic communities in the primitive gospel. Groups such as Panandaram in southern Indiana, Reba Place Fellowship in South Evanston, Illinois, and Eskdale in Utah all attracted earnest Christian believers who believed that community of property was the Christian way.

While many of these communal ventures failed, several were able to sustain a common life and to suggest that "community" was possible. However, any reader of American social history knows that communes or the communitarian movement was not an invention of the 1960s, but a vibrant and enduring part of both Western and Eastern tradition. What flourished in the mountains of New Mexico and the heart of New York and Boston had been there before—and in the same varied and colorful fashion.

Communities had existed in seventeenth- and eighteenth-century America with such names as Plockhoy's Commonwealth, Society of the Woman in the Wilderness of the Contented of the God-Loving Soul, and Jerusalem, while the nineteenth century saw such efforts as Feiba-Peveli, Society of One-Mentians, Memnonia Institute, Shalam, and the Straight-Edgers. And, of course, before them there were the Levellers of seventeenth-century England, the Adamites of twelfth-century Bohemia, the Essenes of first-century Christianity, and the Taoists of fifth-century B.C. China. There is a substantial history of communal activity which predates the current efforts and, in fact, an enormous body of literature about that history.

The present interest in new communities has generated both scholarly and popular interest in the subject of the communes (throughout this essay I'll use the terms *communes* and *communal* in place of the ponderous *communitarian*). Scholarly interest has in turn generated a growing reprint business with all the promise and problems of these ventures. Some valuable material has been put back into print, while some discredited tales about communal life are being freely circulated without the benefit of scholarly commentary or editing. While the reprint houses are putting material back into print, some university presses are letting valuable works on communal life go out of print.

We are at a fortunate crossroads. An increasing interest in communal history has coincided with a growing body of both primary and secondary material, particularly on the sociology of the family, small group theory, and the possibility of a viable counterculture. In addition, there is an emerging literature about the communes of the 1960s and 1970s which lack a history as such but have a place in a larger historical narrative.

Before discussing the communal tradition or the histories of individual communities in America, it is essential to place such material within the large perspective of world history. Norman Cohn's *The Pursuit of the Millennium* is a good place to begin since he outlines the development of revolutionary messianism in medieval and Reformation Europe, and probes what he considers "subterranean fanaticism" as the source of modern totalitarianism. Ernest Tuveson's *Millennium and Utopia* complements Cohn's history since it carries the pursuit of the millennium into the modern, progressive world of the seventeenth-century English Platonists. Notions about religious perfectibility and secular progress were often wedded in communal theory and practice, and Tuveson's work is a fine guide to the source of that marriage.

German sociologist Karl Mannheim tried to understand the tension between current needs and future expectations in *Ideology and Utopia* wherein he offered a major theoretical, though occasionally misleading, historical view of communal history. Two other works which attempt to comprehend the sweep of utopian thought are Joyce Oramel Hertzler's *The History of Utopian Thought* and *Utopias and Utopian Thought,* edited by Frank Manuel and originally published as a *Daedalus* volume. The Manuel collection contains a number of excellent essays by Lewis

Mumford, Northrop Frye, Crane Brinton, and twelve other contributors. In general, the essays are scholarly, literate, and provocative pieces intended to stimulate some dialogue about the significance of ideal and real communal projects.

Another suggestive collection of essays is Sylvia Thrupp's *Millennial Dreams in Action* which probes the possibilities of using messianic and communal movements as vehicles for social analyses. Essays by Aberle, "A Note on Relative Deprivation Theory . . ."; Cohn, "Medieval Millenarianism"; Kaminsky, "The Free Spirit in the Hussite Revolution"; and Shepperson, "Nyasaland and the Millennium," suggest the range of the collection. A detailed study of millennialist sects born in the wake of disasters is David Barkun's *Disaster and the Millennium.*

Frank Manuel's work is particularly valuable since his writings are suggestive for a number of fields. His *The New World of Henri Saint-Simon* and *The Prophets of Paris* are both sturdy intellectual guides to the rationalist utopian thinkers of eighteenth-century France. And the collection *French Utopias,* edited with Fritzie Manuel, outlines French idealism from Sir John Mandeville to Pierre Teilhard de Chardin. Their masterful *Utopian Thought in the Western World* is without equal. Christopher Johnson's award-winning *Utopian Communities in France: Cabet and the Icarians, 1839-1851* throws fresh light on this working-class movement that produced American colonies in Texas, Illinois, Missouri, and California. The English tradition is the subject of W. H. G. Armytage's thorough *Heaven's Below: Utopian Experiments in England, 1560-1960,* and George Jacob Holyoake's two-volume *The History of Co-operation in England.* J. F. C. Harrison's comparative study of Anglo-American religious enthusiasm *The Second Coming: Popular Millenarianism, 1780-1850* should broaden our understanding of Mormonism, Shakerism, and Southcottianism. The growing tendency of researchers on American colonies is to look at the European tradition and to move away from simple analyses that treat colonies as frontier settlements created by unique American conditions.

There is no single compendium of communal societies in America, but an indispensable guide to the field is the two-volume *Socialism and American Life,* edited by Donald Egbert and Stow Persons in 1952 and in need of updating. Volume one contains a number of significant essays ("Terminology and Types of Socialism," "Christian Communitarianism in America," "The Secular Utopian Socialists"), while the second volume has a detailed critical bibliography without equal in the field. Although it does not have information about every known communal venture, it does provide a massive array of bibliographic references about the history of socialist activity and its relationship to the arts, psychology, and social history.

Another central critical and bibliographic source is Arthur E. Bestor's *Backwoods Utopias: The Sectarian and Owenite Phases of Communitarian Socialism in America, 1663-1829.* It outlines with admirable scholarship the movement of "communitarian" thought from the early pietist settlements in the East through the frontier experiments led by Robert Owen at New Harmony. Bestor's books and articles have established the notions that communal societies have been "patent-office models" for social improvement and that such societies serve the cause of social reform by being test tubes for the future.

Within a larger context, there is a body of literature which suggests that the whole of American life has been utopian and experimental. H. Richard Niebuhr's *The Kingdom of God in America,* Charles L. Sanford's *The Quest for Paradise,* and Ernest Tuveson's *Redeemer Nation* all examine facets of utopian thought. In the same vein, Michael Fellman has written *The Unbounded Frame*. Fellman argues that utopians sought to control the chaotic American environment and their own conflicted lives by resorting to planned and perfected settlements.

Although the early nineteenth-century Continental thinkers like Fourier and Owen spurred the development of societies in America, there were a significant number of religiously motivated colonies which brought their pietist zeal with them either in flight from European persecution or in pursuit of the New Jerusalem. A good account of an early group, the Labadists, can be found in Bartlett James, *The Labadist Colony in Maryland,* originally published in 1899 as part of the Johns Hopkins University Studies in Historical and Political Science.

What has been called the first significant communal settlement in America—Ephrata—was founded in 1732 by the German mystic, Johann Conrad Beissel. There is a competent biography of Beissel by W. C. Klein, *Johann Conrad Beissel, Mystic and Martinet, 1690-1768;* an early history of Ephrata, *Chronicon Ephratense,* was written by two brothers of that celibate colony, Brother Lamech and Brother Agrippa. The colony was noted for its music, and a short volume, *The Music of the Ephrata Cloister* by Julius Friedrich Sachse, reproduces some of the scores and illustrations. Sachse's two-volume *The German Sectarians of Pennsylvania, 1708-1800* and *The German Pietists of Provincial Pennsylvania* are valuable accounts of early mystical groups whose leaders led them into solitary contemplation and communal celibacy. There is a brief biography of another Ephrata leader, Israel Eckerlin, by Klaus Wust, *The Saint-Adventurers of the Virginia Frontier.*

The most significant Moravian settlement in America was founded at Bethlehem in 1741. The religious roots of that collective enterprise are outlined in Joseph Mortimer Levering's *A History of Bethlehem, Pennsylvania, 1741-1892.* An intelligent and scholarly study of the Moravian settlements at Bethlehem, Pennsylvania, and Herrnhut, Saxony, is Gillian Lindt Gollin's prize-winning *Moravians in Two Worlds.*

Just as the German pietist groups were experiencing some difficulties, the most enduring of all communal projects landed in New York. With the arrival of Ann Lee in 1774 the long history of Shakerism begins. No other set of colonies has received so much attention, adulation, and loving restoration. At first, however, the Shakers were vilified and treated as English spies transplanted in New York to undercut revolutionary activity.

Edward Deming Andrews catches every detail of Shaker life from the curve of their furniture to the decline of their numbers. His *The People Called Shakers* remains the standard work; a number of other works by Andrews emphasize particular facets of Shaker life. For their furniture, see *Shaker Furniture,* and for music and dance, his *The Gift to Be Simple.* June Sprigg's magnificent account of Shaker crafts, *By Shaker Hands,* helps us understand the practical side of colony life. For some, the Shakers were either peaceful saints or "females in meal bags," as one observer characterized the Shaker sisters. Sprigg's illustrated work brings out the beauty and the practicality of this celibate groups. *The American Shakers,* a recently translated work by a French sociologist at the Sorbonne, Henri Desroche, places them within a larger structure of European religious and social radicalism which Andrews ignores, but Desroche reads too much radicalism into their religious history. There is an excellent study of a single Shaker community by Thomas Clark and F. Gerald Ham, *Pleasant Hill and the Shakers.* John Patterson MacLean's *Shakers of Ohio* is another valuable local source complementing Julia Neal's study of the South Union Shakers in *By Their Fruits.*

An old but still valuable account of Shaker history written by two members of the Mount Lebanon family is Anna White and Leila S. Taylor, *Shakerism; Its Meaning and Message.* There are a number of "inside" accounts by former members, and they exhibit varying degrees of hostility toward their former celibate life. Thomas Brown's *An Account of the People Called Shakers* was published in 1812 from a friendly, though apostate, perspective. A hostile view is presented in David Lamson's 1848 account, *Two Years' Experience Among the Shakers.* However, the Lamson book does contain some interesting detail about their spiritualist phase.

The Shakers' own formal history was published in 1858 by Elder Frederick Evans as *Shakers; Compendium of the Origin, History, Principles, Rules and Regulations, Government and Doctrine of the United Society of Believers in Christ's Second Appearing.* It contains simple biographies of the early leaders and a simple exposition of their faith. How one arrived at the Shaker faith can be gleaned from George Frederick Evans' *Autobiography of a Shaker,* which is a fine introduction to the thought of their most learned and vigorous spokesman for the post-Civil War period. Mary L. Richmond's massive two-volume bibliographic work, *Shaker Literature: A Bibliography,* now enables scholars to find a wide range of Shaker publications. The Richmond volumes supplant the older MacLean bibliography.

While the Shakers were establishing their colonies on the frontier, other groups were forming. One of the most unusual was the New Jerusalem Colony of Jemima Wilkinson, "The Publick Universal Friend." Her colony has been well treated in Herbert Wisbey's *Pioneer Prophetess,* but the recently reprinted 1821 Hudson study on Wilkinson contains too many factual errors to be of any value.

Numerous colonies were set up on the frontier, and some prospered in incredible fashion. The Harmony Society under the leadership of George Rapp grew from a rural settlement in western Pennsylvania to a large and wealthy community which at one point could afford to underwrite a traveling company of the Metropolitan Opera House Orchestra.

The Harmony Society's original inspiration came from the Book of Revelation, and its history has been chronicled in excellent detail by Karl J. R. Arndt. His first volume, *George Rapp's Harmony Society, 1785-1847,* records the period of Rapp's direction and the three colony locations on the Connoquenessing, Wabash, and Ohio rivers. The second volume, *George Rapp's Successors and Material Heirs, 1847-1916,* examines the colony's growing financial prosperity and declining spiritual fortunes through the legal dissolution in 1916.

There are two other sources for the Harmonist history, both written by contemporaries of participants in this century-long communal enterprise. John Duss's *The Harmonists, A Personal History* and Aaron Williams' *The Harmony Society at Economy, Pennsylvania* are good accounts, with the Duss volume particularly helpful for the latter part of their history—though marred by his own need to protect his place in Harmonist history.

Although some communal efforts sought separation from the world and hoped to found "little commonwealths," they were often linked to the world or each other by historical accident or common impulse. The Shaker, Harmonist, and Oneida communities are important not only because they lasted, but also because of their inspiration and guidance to new groups. When Robert Owen decided to found his community in America, it was from the Rappites that he purchased his Indiana land. Oneida saw itself as following in the footsteps of Brook Farm, and the Silkville Colony in Kansas sought advice from Oneida. The continuum between old and new communities is striking in the communal history of America.

The literature about Robert Owen and his colony is extensive. Two scholarly works provide the bedrock upon which a collection might be built: Bestor's *Backwoods Utopias,* and J. F. C. Harrison's *Quest for the New Moral World.* Bestor's work is concerned with the Owenite phase in America, while Harrison's book deals with the Owenite influence on the English reform tradition. Frank Podmore's biography, *Robert Owen,* remains the standard work, and Owen's autobiography, *The Life of Robert Owen,* supplements the critical work.

Owen's writings were extensive. His *A New View of Society* and *The Book of the New Moral World* provide his basic views, while the appendix to his autobiography and issues of the periodical *The Millennial Gazette* give depth to these sources. Other biographies and accounts of life at New Harmony are available, including Paul Brown's account of his time in the colony, *Twelve Months in New Harmony,* but the works cited at the end of this essay should provide an adequate list for a general library.

At the same time as Owen was floundering in Indiana, another English-born reformer, Frances Wright, was beginning her interracial experiment in communal living at Nashoba in Tennessee. She was the leading woman in the communal movement of her day; William Waterman's biography, *Frances Wright,* is a sound and factual study.

After the disintegration of the New Harmony Colony in 1828, there were a few scattered efforts at communities including the Mormon attempts. It was not until the 1840s, however, that the writings of the French eccentric, Charles Fourier, took hold in America and produced a flurry of communal activity. Nicholas M. Riasanovsky's *The Teaching of Charles Fourier* presents an excellent guide to his complicated system; Riasanovsky's book should be a standard source in any library. For those who want Fourier untouched by rational mind, Hugh Doherty's two-volume translation of *The Passions of the Human Soul* should be sufficient. However, his collected works are available in French *(Les Oeuvres de Fourier)* in twelve volumes. A new biography of Fourier by Richard Bienvenu is expected soon.

Fourier's ideas were translated for an American audience by Albert Brisbane in *The Social Destiny of Man* and in the journal *The Phalanx,* both of which have been reprinted recently. Another reprint, Redelia Brisbane's *Albert Brisbane: A Mental Biography,* tells us less about the Fourierist movement than about the personal hegira of Fourier's chief American disciple.

For information about the varied colonies which were started under Fourierist inspiration, there are some excellent collections of primary materials in John H. Noyes, *History of American Socialisms,* and in my own *American Utopianism.* The most famous Fourierist colony was Brook Farm; there is a disproportionate amount of detail on that literary and educational group. The social and intellectual ferment which led to the creation of the colony can be traced in *The Dial* and in their weekly newspaper, *The Harbinger,* while more personal statements are available in Lindsay Swift's *Brook Farm, Its Members, Scholars, and Visitors* and Marianne

Orvis' *Letters from Brook Farm, 1844-1847.* Unfortunately, we still do not have an adequate history of the North American Phalanx or any other of the Fourierist efforts. Observations about certain aspects of life at the North American Phalanx can be found in the recent reprint *Expose of the Condition and Progress of the North American.*

Although the philosophies of Owen and Fourier dominate the intellectual temper of the period, in the mid-1840s other communities came into existence under the leadership of charismatic figures or collective philosophy. The Methodist pietist Dr. William Keil led colonies in Missouri and Oregon during the 1840s and 1850s, and that history can be found in Robert Hendricks' *Bethel and Aurora.*

During the antebellum period, varied forces were at work supporting the notion of a new commonwealth. For general background data, readers would do well to consult Alice Felt Tyler's *Freedom's Ferment* and Whitney Cross's *The Burned-Over District.* A specialized work, Taylor Stoehr's *Hawthorne's Mad Scientists,* shows the interplay between reform and pseudoscience in the transcendental period.

Both Mormonism and Swedenborgianism were integral philosophies of the period, yet their literature more properly belongs in a discussion of religions rather than communal history. However, Marguerite Beck Block's *The New Church in the New World,* on Swedenborgianism, and Leonard Arrington's *The Great Basin Kingdom* can suggest leads on collective settlements generated by both churches.

The community way offered a solution to numerous social problems which pressed in on the reformers of the day. Some Negro leaders saw colonies as halfway stations to the white world and established settlements to aid recently freed Negroes. Jane and William Pease's *Black Utopia* looks at a number of such colonies established in Canada. Wilhelm Weitling, the German socialist, saw cooperative settlements as a solution to immigrant problems, and Carl Wittke devotes considerable space to the Communia Colony in his biography *The Utopian Communist.*

Other reformers like Adin Ballou saw collective efforts bringing together the forces of reform into a unitary household. His "Practical Christianity" is outlined in his marvelous *Autobiography of Adin Ballou, 1803-1890,* and the history of the successful Hopedale Community at Northampton, Massachusetts, in his *History of the Hopedale Community.*

Some continued to flee European persecution and colonize in America on the older pattern, and we find a Swedish colony established in Illinois at Bishop Hill by Erik Jansson in 1846. M. A. Mikkelsen's *The Bishop Hill Colony* is an old monograph on the group. Paul Elmen's biographical study of Jansson, *Wheat Flour Messiah,* emphasizes the Swedish evangelical and pietist tradition and the colony's roots in the old country.

The most interesting of all the nineteenth-century groups was the perfectionist commune of Oneida started by John Humphrey Noyes. There is a considerable literature about these Victorian sensualists viewed by the outside world as free lovers and by the modern world as the flying wedge of progressive thought. They were neither. While in the past they were at the mercy of newspapermen looking for juicy material, they are currently at the mercy of sociologists looking for modern morals.

Robert Allerton Parker's *A Yankee Saint* is still a good source as long as it is balanced by Maren Lockwood Carden's *Oneida: Utopian Community to Modern*

Corporation, which is quite good on the community period and weak on the company history. Constance Noyes Robertson's *The Oneida Community: The Breakup, 1876-1881* uses private sources and is important for examining the colony's sexual tensions, though it remains a "family" account.

There are a number of good sources about Noyes' personal development and his theology. One should begin with his partial autobiography, *The Confessions of John H. Noyes,* and then proceed to George Wallingford Noyes' benevolently edited two volumes, *The Religious Experiences of John Humphrey Noyes* and *The Putney Experience.* Robert D. Thomas' *The Man Who Would Be Perfect* examines young Noyes from a psychoanalytical point of view. Noyes' theology can be found in the community "bible," *The Berean,* and *Bible Communism,* and his sexual theory in his *Essay on Scientific Propagation.* An excellent inside view of the daily life at Oneida can be found in the *Daily Journal,* now in print.

Because of the controversial nature of Oneida, a number of accounts were published to discredit the enterprise. Some have been reprinted recently and have little historical value except to indicate that such communities have sometimes raised hostility wherever they landed.

Another charismatic contemporary of Noyes was Thomas Lake Harris, who combined Swedenborgianism, Christianity, spiritualism, and Oriental mysticism into successful community structures in New York and California. There is an excellent biography of Harris and his circle by Herbert W. Schneider and George Lawton, *A Prophet and a Pilgrim.* An interesting sidelight to the Harris community is explored in *The Unknown Edwin Markham* by Louis Filler.

Whereas Harris was exotic in both his philosophy and social relations, the German colony of Amana was steady and prosaic in its success. Bertha Shambaugh's *Amana, The Community of True Inspiration* is the standard work, and a good account of Amana in 1874 can be found in Charles Nordhoff's *The Communistic Societies of the United States.* Nordhoff visited a number of colonies in his travels and viewed them with sympathy since he saw them as an alternative to the growing labor movement which he feared.

The followers of Etienne Cabet journeyed to America in 1848 in order to put into practice the cooperative socialist schemes outlined in Cabet's *Voyage en Icarie.* In Texas, they found harsh weather, sickness, and bad luck, and moved temporarily to Nauvoo, Illinois—in fact to the site of the recently abandoned Mormon community. In 1857, a third community was set up at Corning, Iowa, and a splinter group established a site at Cheltenham, Missouri, at the same time. Their sturdy history is told by Albert Shaw in *Icaria, A Chapter in the History of Communism.*

There is little material in print about the communities begun after the Civil War, though my own research indicates that they were as significant and as varied as those started during the height of the Fourierist and millennialist activity.

An excellent source for communities started in the industrial period is William Hinds, *American Communities and Co-operative Colonies,* the 1908 edition. The earlier 1878 edition and even the 1903 edition simply cannot compare with the last Hinds compilation. The 1908 edition is now back in print. Hinds was a member of the Oneida Community for all of his adult life and is particularly helpful in ferreting out information about little known groups like the Straight-Edgers and the Spirit Fruit Society.

The only other general compilation of sources for the post-Civil War period is Ernest Wooster's *Communities of the Past and Present.* His data are not always accurate, but his material suggests the range of community available to researchers.

Alexander Kent, a minister active in the reforms of the 1890s, put together a compilation for the Department of Labor, and his listing is helpful to researchers. See Alexander Kent, "Cooperative Communities in the United States," *Bulletin of the Department of Labor* 35:563-646 (July 1901). Ralph Albertson's *A Survey of Mutualistic Communistic Communities in America* could be used in conjunction with Kent's listing.

Two other works, Mark Holloway's *Heavens on Earth* and Everett Webber's *Escape to Utopia,* touch on colonies of the period, but their sources are too limited to be of significant value. Oto Okugawa's annotated checklist published in this volume is the most comprehensive listing available for the period 1776 to 1919, and it includes many new listings for the antebellum period. For the period, we must rely on separate studies of individuals and communities, and there is no better personality to begin with than Alcander Longley, who was involved with at least six groups during his commune career. His *What Is Communism?* is a good statement of his socialist beliefs.

Another active community organizer was the Russian emigrant William Frey, who has received a good biography at the hands of the Slavic scholar Avrahm Yarmolinsky in *A Russian's American Dream.* Warren Chase, the American anarchist, speaks of his communal experiences in *The Life-Line of the Lone One,* and James Martin's *Men Against the State* examines the earlier anarchist involvement with communities, as does Madeleine Stern's biography of Stephen Pearl Andrews, *The Pantarch.*

Studies of individual communities are in short supply, and histories of Shalam, Koreshan Unity, Ruskin, Rugby, and others are needed. Thomas Hughes' *Rugby, Tennessee* is a first-hand account of that heroic English colony in Tennessee, while John Ballou Newbrough's *Oahspe* provided the inspiration and guidance for the New Mexico colony of Shalam.

The Topolobampo Colony started by the American railroad builder A. K. Owen is sketchily treated in Thomas A. Robertson's *A Southwestern Utopia,* but it is the only substantial source outside of periodical literature, though Ray Reynold's *Cat's Paw Utopia* fills in many gaps. Owen's views can be found in his *Integral Cooperation.* An account of the remarkable Koreshan Unity group can be found in my introduction to the reprinted Cyrus Teed's *The Cellular Cosmogony.*

Colonies of the Pacific Northwest have been treated by Charles LeWarne in his *Utopias on Puget Sound.* LeWarne's treatment is thorough and is informed by a close reading of the sources. Robert Hine has surveyed the California colonies in his thorough and insightful *California's Utopian Colonies.* A study of a single California colony, the theosophical settlement of Katherine Tingley at Point Loma, has been written by Emmett Greenwalt in *The Point Loma Community,* just reissued.

The publication of Edward Bellamy's *Looking Backward* stimulated communal thinking, and there are a number of valuable sources available about the Nationalist movement. Hine looks at the Kaweah community in his *California's Utopian Colonies,* and there are varied references to projects scattered throughout the Nationalist periodicals *The Nationalist* and *The New Nation.* Arthur Morgan's biography, *Edward Bellamy,* together with Sylvia Bowman's *The Year 2000,* remain the standard sources about Bellamy's thought. Morgan's own writings stand examination on their own utopian terms; his *Nowhere Was Somewhere* and *The Community of the Future and The Future of Community* outline a personal perspective which has shaped the intentional community movement of this century.

In connection with the general reform spirit of the 1890s, one should look at Paul and Blanche Alyea's *Fairhope, 1894-1954,* a study of the colony devoted to Henry George's single tax philosophy.

The history of the Ruskin colony led by Julius Wayland is covered in Howard Quint's *The Forging of American Socialism;* the Christian Commonwealth in James Dombrowski, *The Early Days of Christian Socialism in America;* and the activities of the Vrooman brothers with varied communities in Ross Paulson's *Radicalism and Reform.* Elbert Hubbard and the Roycrofter group are the subjects of Freeman Champney's study *Art and Glory.*

The Hutterite colonies deserve special notice since they have been studied so well and have been such a successful cooperative society. With the aid of the wealthy Rappite Harmony Society of Pennsylvania, they established a colony in South Dakota where they grew and prospered. One standard historical account is Victor Peters, *All Things Common,* and there are a number of excellent psychological studies. Joseph W. Eaton and Robert J. Weil's *Culture and Mental Disorders: A Comparative Study of the Hutterites and Other Populations* was a National Institute of Mental Health study, while Lee Emerson Deets' *The Hutterites* is a sociological account by a researcher who lived with the Hutterites. John Hostetler's *Hutterite Society* is the definitive study by a scholar whose field work complements his acute historical understanding of close-knit social units.

The contrast between the secular and the religious utopians is deftly handled by Wisconsin professor Paul Conkin in his *Two Paths to Utopia.* By comparing the Hutterites with the socialist colony of Llano, Conkin brings into sharp focus the comparative values of the collectives. Llano was founded by the socialist leader Job Harriman after his defeat in the Los Angeles mayoralty election of 1911. There is a full account of its California and Louisiana history in Conkin, Hine, and Wooster. An offshoot of the Llano Colony was another socialist colony located in Nevada. Wilbur Shepperson's *Retreat to Nevada* is an exemplary short history of a single colony led by C. V. Eggleston.

After 1900, for glimpses of communities we must rely almost exclusively on periodical literature and newspapers. Even the famous Helicon Hall Colony of Upton Sinclair is without a history. Founded on the proceeds of the sales from *The Jungle,* the colony had a brief life but attracted such figures as Sinclair Lewis, Allen Updegraff, Michael Williams, Edwin Bjorkman, and Frances Maule. The colony is discussed in one chapter of Sinclair's *The Autobiography of Upton Sinclair.* Another scattered set of colonies is mentioned briefly in an appendix to Gabriel Davidson's *Our Jewish Farmers and the Story of the Jewish Agricultural Society.*

During the 1920s, there was a gradual growth of agrarian and decentralist notions which form much of the philosophical basis for today's communes. The work of Ralph Borsodi is slowly coming into vogue with his *This Ugly Civilization* (the primary work) and his *Flight from the City,* a personal account of his subsistence homestead in Rockland County, New York.

During the 1930s, a number of large and small communities based on communal models and assumptions were planned. Paul Conkin's *Tomorrow a New World* is an excellent survey of New Deal programs in new town and subsistence farming operations. As the Depression became a fact and as towns became cities, there was a slow movement toward a redefinition of community in relation to urban life. The establishment of a colony in rural Michigan is but one facet of that drive, and Joseph Cohen's *The Sunrise Community* examines the difficulties which New York labor leaders had on the Michigan frontier.

An experiment on the Georgia frontier begun in 1942 still exists today after two decades of local opposition. Clarence Jordan's interracial Christian community of Koinonia at Americus, Georgia, is the subject of Dallas Lee's *The Cotton Patch Evidence.*

During the 1940s and 1950s, the commune movement was aided and sustained by the Fellowship of Intentional Communities, a loose affiliation of communal societies which met yearly to share ideas and projects. Its constitution, along with other supporting statements, can be found in my *American Utopianism.* Literature about the intentional community approach is available through Community Service, Inc., and a few of its publications are worth noting. Its *Handbook on Intentional Communities* and *The Community Land Trust* are basic statements of principle.

The literature about current communal groups is still too unformed to be of significant value, but a periodical literature, some self-conscious history, and a few good overviews are available. Many of the current accounts are by free-lance journalists and sociologists on the run, and we can only hope there is a Nordhoff and a Weber among them.

There is an emerging periodical literature by and about the communal life-style and, in fact, *Lifestyle* is devoted to looking at the general communal thrust. Recently, three groups which had been publishing separate magazines *(Alternatives,* formerly *The Modern Utopian; Communitarian; Communitas)* have combined to put out *Communities,* which ranges widely over communal literature and philosophy.

Richard Fairfield and Consuelo Sandoval have been active in the hip communal movement, and their impressions are recorded in *Communes, U.S.A.* One community, Twin Oaks, has pieced together a history of its first four years in a *Journal of a Walden Two Commune* which it is hoped other current communities will emulate. It is the first effort of the Community Publishing Cooperative, and other volumes are expected to follow. A steadier view of the range of community settlements of the 1960s can be found in Ron Roberts, *The New Communes.* A "how to" guide to communal living can be found in Swami Kriyananda's *Cooperative Communities: How To Start Them and Why.*

Of a number of "personal trip" accounts by commune joiners and followers, Robert Houriet's *Getting Back Together* is the most readable and perceptive. *Families of Eden* by Judson Jerome, a personal and positive account of decentralist experiments, is based, in part, on his own experiences at Downhill Farm in Maryland. Elaine Sundancer's *Celery Wine* chronicles, in an open manner, her move from Berkeley to a commune in the Pacific Northwest.

It is hoped that future researchers will take Benjamin Zablocki's *The Joyful Community* as a model for their work. His study of the *Bruderhof* is thorough, sympathetic, without condescension, and well written. Less satisfying is Rosabeth Kanter's recent effort at comparative judgments in her *Commitment and Community.* Her generalizations appear to be based on sketchy evidence, and her generalizations about community life ought to be regarded with some caution, although her theoretical framework is a striking one. Finally there is Laurence Veysey's outstanding comparative study, *The Communal Experience,* which fuses past history with current experiences by focusing on the mystical and anarchist traditions in communal societies.

Other comparative works will surely be published. There is also some evidence that geographers, architects, and psychologists will bring new understanding of the plans and programs set forward by self-conscious community builders and wreckers. A striking example of this new scholarship is Dolores Hayden's *Seven American Utopias,* which examines the design process and the community-building process in seven representative colonies. Hayden's work has opened up a whole new area for scholarship and analysis. Communal history abounds in excellent anecdotal material as stories about intrigue, fakery, seduction, and megalomania are mixed with tales of high purpose, social resourcefulness, and exemplary altruism. One of my favorites concerns the Llano colony. The members celebrated their May Day by dressing up in their best clothes and marching through the streets of the colony bearing a red flag and a banner with the inscription "If you have two loaves of bread, sell one and buy a hyacinth to feed your soul." The mass suicides at Jonestown, the current revelations about Synanon, and the questions raised about the Unification church ought not to turn us toward simple morals or even simpler conclusions about communal groups. There has been and there continues to be an astounding range of social philosophies, settlement patterns, and leadership forms, and, as this bibliographic survey indicates, an ever-growing literature that seeks to take us beyond simple facts and simple models.

Selected Bibliography

Albertson, Ralph. *A Survey of Mutualistic Communistic Communities in America.* AMS, 1973 (orig. pub. in 1936).

Alternative Futures. V. 1, 1978.

Alyea, Paul and Blanche. *Fairhope, 1894-1954: The Story of a Single Tax Colony.* Alabama, 1956.

Andrews, Edward D. *The Gift to Be Simple: Songs, Dances and Rituals of the American Shakers.* Dover, 1963 (orig. pub. by J. J. Augustin, 1940).

_____. *The People Called Shakers: A Search for the Perfect Society.* Dover, 1963 (orig. pub. by Oxford, 1953).

Andrews, Edward D. and Faith. *Shaker Furniture, The Craftsmanship of an American Communal Sect.* Dover, 1964 (orig. pub. by Oxford, 1937).

Armytage, W. H. G. *Heaven's Below: Utopian Experiments in England, 1560-1960.* University of Toronto, 1961.

Arndt, Karl J. R. *George Rapp's Harmony Society, 1785-1847.* Pennsylvania, 1965.

_____. *George Rapp's Successors and Material Heirs, 1847-1916.* Fairleigh Dickinson, 1972.

Arrington, Leonard. *The Great Basin Kingdom: An Economic History of the Latter-Day Saints, 1830-1900.* Harvard, 1958.

Ballou, Adin. *Autobiography of Adin Ballou, 1803-1890,* ed. by William S. Heywood. Vox Populi Press, 1896.

_____. *History of the Hopedale Community: From Its Inception to Its Virtual Submergence in the Hopedale Parish.* Porcupine Press, 1973 (orig. pub. by Thompson and Hill, 1897).

Barkun, David. *Disaster and the Millennium.* Yale University Press, 1974.

Bestor, Arthur E. *Backwoods Utopias: The Sectarian and Owenite Phases of Communitarian Socialism in America, 1663-1829.* Pennsylvania, 1950.

Block, Marguerite Beck. *The New Church in the New World: A Study of Swedenborgianism in America.* Octagon, 1969 (orig. pub. by Holt, 1932).

Borsodi, Ralph. *Flight from the City: An Experiment in Creative Living on the Land.* 3d ed. Harper & Row, 1972 (orig. pub. by School of Living, 1947).

_____. *This Ugly Civilization.* Simon and Schuster, 1929.

Bowman, Sylvia. *The Year 2000: A Critical Biography of Edward Bellamy.* Bookman Associates, 1958.

Brisbane, Albert. *The Social Destiny of Man; or, Association and Reorganization of Industry.* B. Franklin, 1968 (orig. pub. by C. F. Stollmeyer, 1840).

Brisbane, Redelia (Bates). *Albert Brisbane: A Mental Biography, with a Character Study.* B. Franklin, 1969 (orig. pub. by Arena Publishing Co., 1893).

Brown, Paul. *Twelve Months in New Harmony.* Porcupine Press, 1973 (orig. pub. by W. H. Woodward, 1827).

Brown, Thomas. *An Account of the People Called Shakers.* AMS, 1972 (orig. pub. by Parker & Bliss, 1812).

Carden, Maren Lockwood. *Oneida: Utopian Community to Modern Corporation.* Johns Hopkins, 1969.

Champney, Freeman. *Art and Glory: The Story of Elbert Hubbard.* Crown, 1968.

Chase, Warren. *The Life-Line of the Lone One; or, Autobiography of the World's Child.* B. Marsh, 1857.

Clark, Thomas, and F. Gerald Ham. *Pleasant Hill and the Shakers.* Shakertown Press, 1968.

Codman, John Thomas. *Brook Farm: Historic and Personal Memoirs.* AMS, 1971 (orig. pub. by Arena Publishing Co., 1894).

Cohen, Joseph. *The Sunrise Community.* Porcupine Press, 1973 reprint.

Cohn, Norman. *The Pursuit of the Millennium: Revolutionary Millenarians and Mystical Anarchism of the Middle Ages.* Oxford, 1970.

Communities. v. 1—; 1971—. Communities Publications Cooperative.

Community Service, Inc. *The Community Land Trust.* Community Service, Inc., 1972.

_____. *A Handbook on Intentional Communities.* Community Service, Inc., 1973.

Conkin, Paul K. *Tomorrow a New World: The New Deal Community Program.* Cornell, 1959.

_____. *Two Paths to Utopia: The Hutterites and the Llano Colony.* Nebraska, 1964.

Cross, Whitney. *The Burned-Over District: The Social and Intellectual History of Enthusiastic Religion in Western New York, 1800-1850.* Harper, 1965 (orig. pub. by Cornell, 1950).

Davidson, Gabriel. *Our Jewish Farmers and the Story of the Jewish Agricultural Society.* L. B. Fischer, 1943.

Deets, Lee Emerson. *The Hutterites: A Study in Social Cohesion.* Porcupine Press, 1973 reprint.

Desroche, Henri. *The American Shakers: From Neo-Christianity to Pre-Socialism,* trans. and ed. by John K. Savacoal. Massachusetts, 1971.

The Dial, v. 1-4, 1840-1846. Russell and Russell, 1961.

Dombrowski, James. *The Early Days of Christian Socialism in America.* Octagon Books, 1966 (reprint of a thesis, Columbia University, 1937).

Duss, John. *The Harmonists, A Personal History.* Porcupine Press, 1973 (orig. pub. by the Pennsylvania Book Service, 1943).

Eaton, Joseph W., and Robert J. Weil. *Culture and Mental Disorders: A Comparative Study of the Hutterites and Other Populations.* Free Press, 1955.

Egbert, Donald, and Stow Persons, eds. *Socialism and American Life.* 2 vols. Princeton, 1952.

Elmen, Paul. *Wheat Flour Messiah.* Southern Illinois Press, 1976.

Evans, Frederick W. *Shakers: Compendium of the Origin, History, Principles, Rules and Regulations, Government and Doctrine of the United Society of Believers in Christ's Second Appearing.* B. Franklin, 1972 (orig. pub. in 1859).

Evans, George Frederick. *Autobiography of a Shaker and Revelation of the Apocalypse.* Porcupine Press, 1973 (orig. pub. in 1888).

_____. *Expose of the Condition and Progress of the North American Phalanx.* Porcupine Press, 1974.

Fairfield, Richard, and Consuelo Sandoval. *Communes U.S.A.: A Personal Tour.* Penguin, 1972.

Fellman, Michael. *The Unbounded Frame.* Greenwood, 1973.

Filler, Louis. *The Unknown Edwin Markham: His Mystery and Its Significance.* Antioch, 1966.

Fogarty, Robert S. *American Utopianism.* F. E. Peacock, 1977, 2 ed.

Fourier, François Marie Charles. *The Passions of the Human Soul and Their Influence on Society and Civilization,* trans. by Hugh Doherty. 2 vols. A. M. Kelley, 1968 (orig. pub. by H. Baillière, 1851).

Gollin, Gillian Lindt. *Moravians in Two Worlds: A Study of Changing Communities.* Columbia University Press, 1967.

Goodman, Paul and Percival. *Communitas: Means of Livelihood and Ways of Life.* 3d ed. Vintage, 1960.

Greenwalt, Emmett. *The Point Loma Community in California, 1897-1942: A Theosophical Experiment.* Point Loma Publications, 1978.

The Harbinger. v. 1-8, 1845-1849. AMS, 1971.

Harrison, John Fletcher Clews. *Quest for the New Moral World: Robert Owen and the Owenites in Britain and America.* Scribner, 1969.

Hayden, Dolores. *Seven American Utopias.* MIT Press, 1976.

_____. *The Second Coming: Popular Millennarianism, 1780-1850.* Rutgers University Press, 1979.

Hendricks, Robert J. *Bethel and Aurora, An Experiment in Communism as Practical Christianity: With Some Account of Past and Present Ventures in Collective Living.* AMS, 1971 (orig. pub. by the Press of the Pioneers, 1933).

Hertzler, Joyce Oramel. *The History of Utopian Thought.* Cooper Square, 1965 (orig. pub. by Macmillan, 1923).

Hinds, William. *American Communities and Co-operative Colonies.* Porcupine Press, 1974 (reprint of 1908 ed.).

Hine, Robert. *California's Utopian Colonies.* Yale, 1966 (orig. pub. by Huntington Library, 1953).

Holloway, Mark. *Heavens on Earth: Utopian Communities in America, 1680-1880.* Dover, 1966 (orig. pub. by Turnstile Press, 1951).

Holyoake, George Jacob. *The History of Co-operation in England: Its Literature and Its Advocates.* 2 vols. AMS, 1971 (orig. pub. by Trübner, 1875-1879).

Hostetler, John. *Hutterite Society.* Johns Hopkins, 1974.

Houriet, Robert. *Getting Back Together.* Coward, McCann & Georghegan, 1971.

Hughes, Thomas. *Rugby, Tennessee.* Macmillan, 1891.

James, Bartlett B. *The Labadist Colony in Maryland.* Johns Hopkins, 1899.

Jerome, Judson. *Families of Eden.* Seabury, 1974.

Johnson, Christopher. *Utopian Communities in France: Cabet and the Icarians, 1839-1851.* Cornell, 1974.

Kanter, Rosabeth. *Commitment and Community: Communes and Utopias in Sociological Perspective.* Harvard, 1972.

Kent, Alexander. "Cooperative Communities in the United States." *Bulletin of the Department of Labor* 35:563-646, July 1901.

Klein, Walter Conrad. *Johann Conrad Beissel, Mystic and Martinet, 1690-1768.* Pennsylvania, 1942.

Kriyananda, Swami. *Cooperative Communities: How to Start Them and Why.* Ananda Publications, 1974.

Lamech, Brother, and Agrippa, Brother. *Chronicon Ephratense: A History of the Community of Seventh Day Baptists at Ephrata, Lancaster County, Penna.* B. Franklin, 1972 (orig. pub. by S. H. Zahm, 1889).

Lamson, David R. *Two Years' Experience Among the Shakers.* AMS, 1971 (orig. pub. by the author, 1848).

Lee, Dallas. *The Cotton Patch Evidence.* Harper & Row, 1971.

Levering, Joseph Mortimer. *A History of Bethlehem, Pennsylvania, 1741-1892, with Some Account of Its Founders and Their Early Activity in America,* AMS, 1971 (orig. pub. by Times Publishing Company, 1903).

LeWarne, Charles. *Utopias on Puget Sound.* Washington, 1975.

Lifestyle. v. 1—1971—Madison (Ohio), *Mother Earth News.*

Longley, Alcander. *What Is Communism?* 2d ed. AMS, 1971 (orig. pub. by the Altruist Community, 1890).

MacLean, John Patterson. *Shakers of Ohio.* Porcupine Press, 1974 (reprint of 1907 ed.).

Mannheim, Karl. *Ideology and Utopia: An Introduction to the Sociology of Knowledge.* Harcourt, Brace, 1936.

Manuel, Frank. *The New World of Henri Saint-Simon.* Harvard, 1956.

_____. *The Prophets of Paris.* Harvard, 1962.

_____. ed. *Utopias and Utopian Thought.* Houghton, Mifflin, 1966.

Manuel, Frank and P. Fritzie. *French Utopias: An Anthology of Ideal Societies.* Free Press, 1966.

_____. *Utopian Thought in the Western World.* Harvard, 1979.

Martin, James J. *Men Against the State: The Expositors of Individualist Anarchism in America,* 1827-1908. Adrian Allen Associates, 1953.

Mikkelsen, Michael Andrew. *The Bishop Hill Colony, a Religious Communistic Settlement in Henry County, Illinois.* Porcupine Press, 1973 (orig. pub. by Johns Hopkins, 1892).

Morgan, Arthur. *The Community of the Future and the Future of Community.* Community Service (Ohio), 1957.

_____. *Edward Bellamy.* Columbia, 1944.

_____. *Nowhere Was Somewhere: How History Makes Utopias and How Utopias Make History.* North Carolina, 1946.

The Nationalist. v. 1-3, 1889-1891. Greenwood, 1968.

Neal, Julia. *By Their Fruits: The Story of Shakerism in South Union, Kentucky.* Porcupine Press, 1974 (reprint of 1947 ed.).

The New Nation. v. 1-4/no. 5, 1891-1894. Greenwood, 1968.

Newbrough, John Ballou. *Oahspe, the Kosmon Revelations in the Words of Jehovah and His Angel Ambassadors.* Kosmon Press, 1935.

Niebuhr, Helmut Richard. *The Kingdom of God in America.* Willett, Clark and Company, 1937.

Nordhoff, Charles. *The Communistic Societies of the United States.* Schocken, 1965 (orig. pub. by Harper, 1875).

Noyes, George Wallingford, ed. *The Putney Experience.* Syracuse, 1973.

_____. *The Religious Experiences of John Henry Noyes.* Syracuse, 1973 (orig. pub. in 1923).

Noyes, John H. *The Berean: A Manual for the Help of Those Who Seek the Faith of the Primitive Church.* University Microfilms, 1957 (orig. pub. by office of the Spiritual Magazine, 1847).

_____. *Bible Communism.* Porcupine Press, 1973 (orig. pub. in 1853).

_____. *The Confessions of John H. Noyes.* University Microfilms, 1947.

_____. *Essay on Scientific Propagation.* University Microfilms, 1957 (orig. pub. by Oneida Community, 1875?).

_____. *History of American Socialisms.* Dover, 1966 (orig. pub. by Lippincott, 1870).

Oneida Community. *Daily Journal.* 1866-1868. Porcupine Press, 1973.

Orvis, Marianne. *Letters from Brook Farm, 1844-1847.* Porcupine Press, 1973 (orig. pub. by Vassar College, 1928).

Owen, A. K. *Integral Cooperation: Its Practical Application.* Porcupine Press, 1974 (reprint of 1885 ed.).

Owen, Robert. *The Life of Robert Owen.* Augustus Kelley, 1967 (orig. pub. by E. Wilson, 1857-1858).

_____. *Millennial Gazette,* Nos. 1-16, March 22, 1856-July 1, 1858. AMS, 1973.

_____. *A New View of Society: or, Essays on the Principle of the Formation of the Human Character, and the Application of the Principle to Practice.* Augustus Kelley, 1972 (orig. pub. by R. Taylor & Co., 1813).

_____. *A Supplementary Appendix to the First Volume of the Life of Robert Owen.* Augustus Kelley, 1967 (orig. pub. by E. Wilson, 1857-1858).

Parker, Robert Allerton. *A Yankee Saint: John Humphrey Noyes and the Oneida Community.* Porcupine Press, 1973 (orig. pub. by G. P. Putnam's Sons, 1935).

Paulson, Ross. *Radicalism and Reform: The Vrooman Family and American Social Thought, 1837-1937.* Kentucky, 1968.

Pease, William and Jane. *Black Utopia: Negro Communal Experiments in America.* State Historical Society of Wisconsin, 1963.

Peters, Victor. *All Things Common: The Hutterian Way of Life.* Minnesota, 1966, ca. 1965.

The Phalanx, Nos. 1-23, 1843-1845. AMS, 1971.

Podmore, Frank. *Robert Owen: A Biography.* 2 vols. in 1. Augustus Kelley, 1968 (orig. pub. in 1906).

Quint, Howard. *The Forging of American Socialism: Origins of the Modern Movement.* South Carolina, 1953.

Reynolds, Ray. *Cat's Paw Utopia.* Printed by the author, 1973.

Riasanovsky, Nicholas M. *The Teaching of Charles Fourier.* California, 1969.

Richmond, Mary L. *Shaker Literature: A Bibliography.* 2 vols. Shaker Community Inc., 1977.

Roberts, Ron. *The New Communes: Coming Together in America.* Prentice-Hall, 1971.

Robertson, Constance Noyes. *The Oneida Community: The Break-up, 1876-1881.* Syracuse, 1972.

Robertson, Thomas A. *A Southwestern Utopia.* Ward Ritchie, 1964.

Sachse, Julius Friedrich. *The German Pietists of Provincial Pennsylvania.* AMS, 1970 (orig. pub. by the author, 1895).

_____. *The German Sectarians of Pennsylvania, 1708-1800: A Critical and Legendary History of the Ephrata Cloister and Dunkers.* 2 vols. AMS, 1971 (orig. pub. by the author, 1899-1900).

_____. *The Music of the Ephrata Cloister.* AMS, 1971 (orig. pub. by The Society, 1903).

Sanford, Charles L. *The Quest for Paradise: Europe and the American Moral Imagination.* Illinois, 1961.

Schneider, Herbert W., and George Lawton. *A Prophet and a Pilgrim.* AMS, 1970 (orig. pub. by Columbia, 1942).

Shambaugh, Bertha M. *Amana, the Community of True Inspiration.* The State Historical Society of Iowa, 1908.

Shaw, Albert. *Icaria, A Chapter in the History of Communism.* Porcupine Press, 1973 (orig. pub. by G. P. Putnam's Sons, 1884).

Shepperson, Wilbur. *Retreat to Nevada: A Socialist Colony of World War I.* Nevada, 1966.

Sinclair, Upton. *The Autobiography of Upton Sinclair.* Harcourt Brace, 1962.

Sprigg, June. *By Shaker Hands.* Knopf, 1975.

Stern, Madeleine. *The Pantarch: A Biography of Stephen Pearl Andrews.* Texas, 1968.

Stoehr, Taylor. *Hawthorne's Mad Scientists.* Archon, 1978.

Sundancer, Elaine. *Celery Wine.* Community Publications, 1973.

Swift, Lindsay. *Brook Farm, Its Members, Scholars, and Visitors.* Corinth Books, 1961.

Teed, Cyrus. *The Cellular Cosmogony; or, the Earth a Concave Sphere.* Porcupine Press, 1974 (reprint of 1905 ed.).

Thomas, Robert, *The Man Who Would Be Perfect.* Pennsylvania, 1977.

Thrupp, Sylvia Lettice, ed. *Millennial Dreams in Action: Studies in Revolutionary Religious Movements.* Schocken, 1970.

Tuveson, Ernest. *Millennium and Utopia: A Study in the Background of the Idea of Progress.* California, 1949.

_____. *Redeemer Nation: The Idea of America's Millennial Role.* Chicago, 1968.

Twin Oaks Community. *Journal of a Walden Two Commune: The Collected Leaves of Twin Oaks.* Dist. by Community Pub. Cooperative, 1972.

Tyler, Alice Felt. *Freedom's Ferment: Phases of American Social History to 1860.* Minnesota, 1944.

Veysey, Laurence. *The Communal Experience: Anarchist and Mystical Counter-Cultures in America.* Chicago, reprint of 1973 ed.

Waterman, William. *Frances Wright.* AMS Press, 1972 (orig. pub. as Columbia University Studies in history, economics and public law, CXV, 1, 1924).

Webber, Everett. *Escape to Utopia: The Communal Movement in America.* Hastings House, 1959.

White, Anna, and Leila S. Taylor. *Shakerism: Its Meaning and Message.* AMS, 1971 (orig. pub. in 1904).

Williams, Aaron. *The Harmony Society at Economy, Pennsylvania, Founded by George Rapp, A.D. 1805.* Augustus Kelley, 1970 (orig. pub. in 1866).

Wisbey, Herbert A., Jr. *Pioneer Prophetess: Jemima Wilkinson, the Publick Universal Friend.* Cornell, 1964.

Wittke, Carl. *The Utopian Communist: A Biography of Wilhelm Weitling, Nineteenth-Century Reformer.* Louisiana, 1950.

Wooster, Ernest. *Communities of the Past and Present.* AMS, 1971 (orig. pub. by Llano Colonist, ca. 1924).

Wust, Klaus. *The Saint Adventurers of the Virginia Frontier.* Shenandoah History, 1977.

Yarmolinsky, Avrahm. *A Russian's American Dream: A Memoir on William Frey.* Kansas, 1965.

Zablocki, Benjamin. *The Joyful Community: An Account of the Bruderhof, a Communal Movement Now in Its Third Generation.* Penguin, 1971.

An earlier version of this essay was published by the author in *Choice,* Volume 10, NO. 4, June 1973.

Index

ABOUT THE AUTHOR

Robert S. Fogarty is Associate Professor of History at Antioch College, and editor of *The Antioch Review.* A specialist in communal history of the United States, he has published articles in *New England Quarterly, Journal of American Studies,* and *Labor History.* He edited *American Utopianism* and *Letters from a Self-Made Merchant to His Son,* and was consulting editor for the seventeen-volume series, *The American Utopian Adventure.*